THE WEB
OF PROGRESS

THE WEB OF PROGRESS

Private Values and Public Styles in Boston and Charleston, 1828–1843

William H. Pease

Jane H. Pease

The University of Georgia Press

Athens and London

Published in 1991 by the University of Georgia Press
Athens, Georgia 30602
© 1985 by William H. Pease and Jane H. Pease
All rights reserved
The paper in this book meets the guidelines for
permanence and durability of the Committee on
Production Guidelines for Book Longevity of the
Council on Library Resources

Printed in the United States of America
95 94 93 92 91   P   5 4 3 2 1

Library of Congress Cataloging in Publication Data
Pease, William Henry, 1924–
The web of progress : private values and public styles
in Boston and Charleston, 1828–1843
/ William H. Pease, Jane H. Pease.
p.   cm.
Reprint. Originally published: New York :
Oxford University Press, 1985.
Includes bibliographical references (p.   ) and index.
ISBN 0-8203-1390-4 (pbk. : alk. paper)
1. Boston (Mass.)—Social conditions—Case studies.
2. Charleston (S.C.)—Social conditions—Case studies.
3. City and town life—United States—History
—19th century—Case studies. I. Pease, Jane H. II. Title.
HN80.B7P43   1991
306'.09744'6109757915—dc20   91-4003
                                     CIP

British Library Cataloging in Publication Data available

*For the friends and family, colleagues and students
who have endured our preoccupations
and encouraged our work.*

Preface

When, in 1971, we began this comparison of Boston and Charleston, we embarked not only on the study of two specific cities but also on an exploration of those ways of proceeding peculiarly appropriate to urban history. To the materials associated with the new social history and the framework of a comparative perspective we soon added some minimal techniques of quantification and, eventually, the computer's ability to digest and aggregate large bodies of data. Our central purpose, however, was to reconstruct, as well as we could, the experience of two cities at a particular time in an attempt to understand how cities function in their complex entirety—private and public; economic, social, and political; institutional and unorganized. Beyond that, we sought to put those cities in the national context of antebellum America and to use them as a prism through which to assess an old regionalism rapidly turning into a new sectionalism.

There seemed no better time for all this than the 1830s. On the one hand it was the Age of Jackson and the nullification crisis, the bank war, the panic of 1837, the second party system, the early transportation revolution, emerging industrialism, and a new rhetoric of egalitarianism. On the other, it was the Age of Reform, the Second Great Awakening, the Benevolent Empire, free public schooling, immigration and nativism, as well as abolitionism and a new defense of slavery.

Ideally the cities we would study should be established centers of their regional cultures, important enough to reflect the economic issues perplexing the Jacksonian decade, focal in the political life of their respective areas, and both sufficiently coherent and diverse to illuminate patterns of urban development. Established and major port cities, one at the North, one at the South, seemed best suited to fulfill these criteria. But which ones?

We rejected the biggest cities—New York and New Orleans—not only for their unmanageable size but because they were too cosmopolitan to represent characteristically sectional differences. We rejected Philadelphia and Baltimore because their physical proximity clouded sectional issues; and we discarded Portland and Savannah for their relative national obscurity. Thus Boston, the heartland of high tariff, free labor, and social reform, and Charleston, spokesman for free trade, states' rights, and patriarchal values, seemed the best exponents of their particular cultures. Old cities with established ways and wealth, they were challenged by the times—the steam-powered transportation revolution, industrialism, migrating populations, and a politics avowedly for the common man.

During the 1820s Bostonians and Charlestonians were anxious lest their cities (respectively the fourth and sixth largest in the country in 1830) be overwhelmed by New York, a city whose growing links with the West fed its dominance in European trade so as clearly to threaten the prosperity of all other Atlantic coast ports. How both cities responded—with projected railroads, the extension of banking and commercial facilities, and cultural inducements to entrepreneurial venture—and how the interests and aspirations of their hinterlands shaped those responses constitute a major portion of antebellum economic history. Similarly, the ways their responses shaped and were shaped by the growing sectionalism of the 1830s, focused in debates over slavery and tariffs, illuminate the interaction between national and urban politics. In addition, both cities reveal underlying social similarities in the importance they attached to kinship bonds, religious affiliation, and associational life. So, too, anxiety and social unrest, and how they manifested themselves in crime, riotous behaviour, and reactions to major crises of depression, fire, and epidemic, not only demonstrate the dynamics of urban life but provide insight into the rationale for coincident urban efforts to improve life for the disadvantaged and to repress challenges to the status quo.

There they were, Boston and Charleston, with all their apparent similarities and with many glaring differences. What did the comparison amount to? How were they to be judged? Aware that every generation's present shapes its understanding of the past, we nonetheless listened to what Bostonians and Charlestonians thought their own times were all about, to learn from them not only what they did, but what their goals were. And in attempting to assess their pasts according to how they fulfilled, modified, or failed to reach goals they themselves set, we have not always heard what we anticipated. Sometimes the perceived wisdom of our own times comes a cropper. We have been forced to give economics a role so central that our decade has been stretched to accommodate an economic cycle from 1828 to 1843: from hard times, to boom, to bust, to new recovery. We have been startled by clashing definitions of public authority and private responsibility. And we have come to understand how deeply conservative values and social institutions both blocked modernization, predisposed to change, and created new radicalisms.

We have also fallen back on old truths. It is as impossible to understand the urban as to understand the rural South without giving slavery and agrarian values a major role. Nor could we assess Boston without addressing the work ethic—be it the fruit of Puritanism or secular shrewdness or an amalgam of both. And having addressed those central themes of sectional history, we were led inexorably to the ways in which southern preoccupations with planting and Yankee educational enthusiasms molded their respective societies.

But it is the cities themselves—not theories of hegemonic ideology or modernization—which have held our attention. It is not alone their rich individual histories nor even the handsome severity of the one and the lush beauty of the other which has held us hostage for fifteen years. There was also the promise that in knowing and comparing them we would finally understand the relationship between the common bonds of urbanity and the shifting rifts of section in antebellum America.

February 1984   W. H. P.
                                                                                                J. H. P.

Acknowledgments

Little did we know when first we undertook to compare Charleston and Boston how much help we would ultimately need and receive. Nor can we here acknowledge individually all those thoughtful people who have brought sources to our attention, shared their own insights with us, worked with us, and provided us the diverse facilities we needed to complete this study. Whatever the merits of this book, they would have been fewer without such help.

From the outset, the University of Maine at Orono has generously granted us leaves and sabbaticals and through its Faculty Research Fund financed long months of research and a sizeable part of the computer analysis. The American Philosophical Society awarded us a grant-in-aid to start this project; the National Endowment for the Humanities, a general research grant (RS-1454-80) to complete it. And, when funds for computerization ran short, a National Science Foundation grant (SES-8023796) came to the rescue.

Equally important, the University of Maine Social Science Research Institute, especially its director, David Kovenock, and its assistant director for computing, Garrett Bozylinsky, provided the professional expertise that enabled us to organize and assess the extensive data about individual Bostonians and Charlestonians, unmanageable except by quantification. Many students helped us record data from newspapers and manuscript census rolls—Rita Bouchard, Patricia Kelly, Paul Dube, and Robin Astbury among them. Sharon White of SSRI did the key punching with a keen eye for rooting out error. Sharon Stover of the Word Shop typed a marvelously accurate final manuscript in record time. And Tessa DeCarlo of Oxford

Acknowledgments

University Press demonstrated how much excellent copy editing can improve a manuscript.

But before any of that happened, we had increased the collective debt historians owe librarians and archivists for the expertise and dogged perseverance with which they make research collections maximally available to scholars. While we spent only days in many libraries, in others we stayed for weeks and in some for months. Almost without exception their staffs helped us examine all the relevant material in their repositories. And where we stayed longest, we accumulated the greatest debts to directors, curators, and archivists. Carolyn Wallace of the Southern Historical Collection at the University of North Carolina at Chapel Hill, Mary Elizabeth Prior and later Gene Waddell and David Moltke-Hansen of the South Carolina Historical Society, Virginia Rugheimer of the Charleston Library Society, Kathleen Pilcher and Ralph Melnick of the College of Charleston, Wylma Wates of the South Carolina Archives, and Allen Stokes and E. L. Inabinett of the South Caroliniana Library of the University of South Carolina stand out among those who made our work on Charleston better and easier. Robert Lovett at Baker Library of Harvard University, Ellen Oldham at the Boston Public Library, Martha Clark of the Massachusetts Archives, and, most extensively, Winifred Collins and Louis L. Tucker of the Massachusetts Historical Society made our research on Boston more convenient and efficient.

Fellow historians have been helpful critics. Among those who went well beyond the call of duty was Michael O'Brien, who read a draft of the book in its entirety. Ronald Formisano, who encouraged our first venture into Charleston's politics, also read and commented on the political chapters. And Stanley Engerman has helped in many ways, not least by reading and commenting extensively on the chapters which are especially rooted in economics. We benefited from their suggestions and, as is customary, hereby absolve them from any responsibility for the final product.

The following institutions have given us generous permission to quote from manuscripts in their collections: The Massachusetts Historical Society, the Baker and Houghton Libraries of Harvard University, the Trustees of the Boston Public Library, the William R. Perkins Library of Duke University, the Historical Society of Pennsylvania, the South Carolina Historical Society, the Southern Historical Collection of the Library of the University of North Carolina at Chapel Hill, the South Caroliniana Library of the University of South Carolina, the Waring Historical Library of the Medical University of South Carolina. The *Journal of Urban History* granted us contractual permission to reproduce several paragraphs from our "Social Structure and the Potential for Urban Change: Boston and Charleston in the 1830s," VIII (February 1982).

More personally, the late Misses Edith and Charlotte Smith not only welcomed two Yankees into their home but, during our first long stay in Charleston, introduced us to the warm hospitality and traditions of their city. Since 1973 Elias Bull has been a valued friend and advisor on all things Carolinian, leading us to sources, regaling us with stories, setting our mispronunciations straight, and helping us locate obscure geographical references.

We thank them all.

J. H. P.
W. H. P.

Contents

I. INTRODUCTION
    1. The Places and Their People   1

II. NURTURING ECONOMIC GROWTH
    2. The Economic Heritage   13
    3. Boston's Boom Years   23
    4. Charleston's Dream of Prosperity   40
    5. Hub and Hinge   54

III. STRUCTURING PUBLIC RESPONSIBILITIES
    6. Pragmatic Politics and the Politics of Passion   71
    7. Policing the City and Providing Welfare   90
    8. Education, Work, and Cultural Values   108

IV. BALANCING SOCIAL INTERESTS
    9. Class, Family, and Church   121
    10. Play and Philanthropy   138
    11. Disorder, Violence, and Community Control   153

V. RESPONDING TO REVERSES
    12. Charleston in Panic and Depression   171
    13. Meeting Catastrophe   189
    14. The Uses of Adversity   200

VI. CONCLUSION

15. The Web Spun   215
Appendix A. The Quantification of Biographical Data   225
Appendix B. Property and Changes in Property Ownership   238
Note on Sources   259
Abbreviations   261
Notes   266
Index   325

THE WEB
OF PROGRESS

PART I · INTRODUCTION

1

The Places and Their People

Boston faced north; Charleston, south. Atlantic ports ripe in years, their common past endowed them with similar institutions, parallel economic expectations, common republican beliefs, and dreams not dissimilar. American they both were. Yet the geographic fact stood symbol for many things, and visitors were quick to mark the difference.

The "handsome" sight of Charleston harbor in 1830 charmed Anne Royall, whose journalist's pen lauded that "most happy and triumphant specimen of beauty on the Atlantic shore." Yet to Bostonian Samuel Jackson the surrounding view was pleasant enough but offered "nothing striking" to the eye.[1] Accustomed to his native city's harbor, approached through hazardous passages running between craggy islands and submerged ledges, Jackson neither saw nor imagined the hidden hazard of Charleston's bar, which even at high tide snared vessels drawing more than sixteen feet. Similarly, the low-country capital, so different from Boston's hilly crest, seemed flat, deriving what vertical profile it had from church steeples and spreading live oaks.

Still, had these travelers, like aeronauts, viewed both cities from the air, they would have seen peninsulas so similar as to seem the mirror image of each other. Both were shaped by rivers. Charleston had the Ashley on its west and the Cooper to its east. Boston's western flank was similarly defined, bounded by the Charles River until it met the open harbor, which swerved around the city's North End and easterly wharves until navigable waters bottomed out in the shallows of South Cove.

Slightly bulbous as they jutted out into their respective harbors, both small peninsulas narrowed where they joined the mainland. Boston's area, less than two square miles, was widest where Beacon, Copps, and Fort hills delineated its northern prominence. To the south it threaded an ever narrowing way until a single street, running between marshes neither firm enough for horses nor deep enough for boats, linked the city with the village of Roxbury. Less clearly etched even at its southern end, Charleston's marshy perimeter often blurred the distinction between land and water. Nonetheless its battery, built to protect the city's outermost tip from high tides and hurricane floods, was a distinguishing landmark for ships headed up toward the wharves which lined the Cooper or, more sporadically, extended from its southern and western shores. From the battery's palmetto cribbing, the city's one and a half square miles of dry land fanned out to the north only to be choked by swampland where organized municipality gave way to suburban neck. Lacking Boston's hills, which during the 1830s furnished fill for the northern city's swamps, Charleston could extend her land area only with the refuse of city life, old bricks, "oyster shells, rubbish and other offals," or with sand and clay from excavations.[2]

From their colonial origins as villages and then towns, these cities had enjoyed peninsular perspectives, looking out beyond surrounding islands to the Atlantic Ocean and toward Europe, but also linked to the land—to the colonies, states, regions, and ultimately the nation of which they were part. Each welcomed the visitors—whether country cousins or foreign sophisticates—who regularly chronicled their impressions. Two centuries after Boston's founding, when British visitor G. T. Fox climbed Beacon Hill to view the city from Bulfinch's gold-domed State House, he saw a place adorned with handsome buildings, a spacious harbor filled with ships, and a meadowed Common in the city's very center. American Enoch Wines, who believed Boston's vista from the sea quite equaled those of Naples and Genoa, found in the view from the State House the full equivalent of the ones he had enjoyed from Pisa's leaning tower and Florence's Duomo.[3]

But its own citizens knew Boston best. Take Harrison Gray Otis, whose deep roots and ample fortune made him one of Boston's most respected gentlemen, one who had served it in Congress and who, in December 1828, had been elected its mayor. Looking out from his Beacon Street drawing room, Otis introduced many a guest to his Boston. Sure of himself as he was of his class, he would start where he lived, on Beacon Hill across the street from the Common. Behind him, at the top of the hill, was Mt. Vernon Street, where he had once lived in the second of the three houses which Charles Bulfinch had built for him. Before him, all around and beyond the Common, as behind him up to the top of the hill, were the mansions of lawyers and merchants, physicians and bankers—the most wealthy, the most powerful, the most prestigious Bostonians, who all knew each other well.[4]

The Places and Their People

They lived in the heart of the city in old mansions between the harbor and the Common and in new ones north of the Common on Beacon Hill. In either case they were only blocks from the wharves and warehouses, the banks and stores where breathed the city's commercial life. If their businesses and their homes were clustered close to the docks, they were also near Washington Street, which, running from the Old State House at the meeting of State and Court streets out through the South End and over the neck, linked city to country.

With a smile almost of possession, Otis could point from his windows to the old Burying Ground and the new Tremont House Hotel; to Park Street Church, where old-fashioned fire and brimstone was still preached, and to King's Chapel, whose merged Anglicanism and Unitarianism tolerated no such fervor. Off to the left—one could not quite see it without stepping out into the street—was the new State House, up whose steps and through whose porticoes passed Massachusetts's governors and legislators doing the Commonwealth's business. And at the foot of Beacon Hill, before one reached the State Street offices and Kilby Street stores, was the colonial State House where, above the first floor post office, Mayor Otis and the city council met to transact Boston's official business. Still farther off, at the very end of State Street, lay Long Wharf and the heart of foreign trade.

To the north of State Street, hidden by buildings many of which were four-storied, was the old red brick Faneuil Hall, and next to it the new granite central market which Mayor Josiah Quincy had pressed the city to build in 1824. In the new market and at the stalls which surrounded both buildings, Bostonians shopped for food. North of the markets were shipyards, mechanics' shops, and retail businesses of all sorts. South of them were insurance offices, wholesale dealers, and still more retailers. And all along Boston's eastern edge, wharves and docks were laden with incoming and outgoing cargoes. Across the street were the businesses which traded them. Indeed, arcing from the North End was a crude crescent of trade and commerce that followed along Boston's eastern edge, engulfing the old residential area of Fort Hill before it bowed westward to curve around the Common's southern side. In this area most Bostonians worked—whether Otis's associates or shopkeepers and clerks or artisans and unskilled laborers. To it they walked from homes which, if they were not one and the same as their workplaces, were generally nearby.

Otis's city was a bustling place. Ships crowded the harbor, arriving from and sailing to ports in Asia, Europe, and up and down the American coast from Halifax to Rio de Janeiro. Vessels bringing firewood and produce from nearby towns passed under bridges whose draws were frequently raised to disrupt the heavy traffic crossing the river to and from Cambridge and Charlestown. Pedestrians scurried along streets through which horse-drawn carts and carriages rumbled. The din was sometimes unbearable when ox-drawn wagons lumbered over the main streets' cobblestone centers, competing for space with well-mounted young sports intent on bowing to stylish ladies picking their way along irregular brick sidewalks.

Stable and somber amid the bustle were the massive buildings of gray Quincy granite dragged into town by oxen to furnish foundations for warehouses, lintels for brick mansions, and whole walls for hotels and banks. Surrounded by small wooden houses and shops, these stone structures were already proclaimed the "Boston style" in architecture and were the physical tokens of Boston's strength.[5]

As a man of keen sensibilities and an old Federalist given to lamenting Boston's lost past and changing present, Otis would doubtless reflect on the changes this urban growth had created. What troubled him was not so much the "general noise of the City," which drove wealthy Peter Brooks and his family to live half the year in Medford in a spacious quiet farmhouse far less cramped than their prestigious Summer Street mansion.[6] Nor was it the North End's small, nondescript, and still more crowded dwellings in which lived the artisans, storekeepers, and clerks who peopled main arteries like Commercial Street and short back streets like Snow Hill. Rather his unease stemmed from the troublesome dives and densely packed rooming houses which were crowded into alleys and cul-de-sacs leading off Hanover and Ann Streets. It was exacerbated by the reeking slums along Broad Street, in which recent arrivals, the unskilled, and the impoverished lived with one or more families jammed into a single room in small houses with little air, few sanitary facilities, and no water. It was intensified by the shanties near the Mill Pond, on the marshes of Back Bay, and on swampland south of the Common. Scenes of dire poverty and roisterous riot, these enclaves throbbed with those whose race, religion, or ethnicity isolated them in a Boston still overwhelmingly Protestant and of English extraction. The Irish—most of them Catholic and constituting perhaps a twelfth of the city's population in 1830—clustered in Broad Street or in the back courts of the North End. Blacks, two thousand strong, lived either in the North End or pressed against the back side of Beacon Hill, where the variety of cheap entertainment outweighed the influence of the single African Baptist church in Belknap Street.[7]

Physically distinct though they largely were, these slums and their inhabitants challenged Boston's leaders, who, though well aware of their existence, were unclear about how they should be treated. Retired paper merchant Moses Grant, self-appointed guardian of the city's moral life, could only condemn the slum dwellers' viciousness, while Unitarian city missionary Joseph Tuckerman attempted understanding and reform. Both

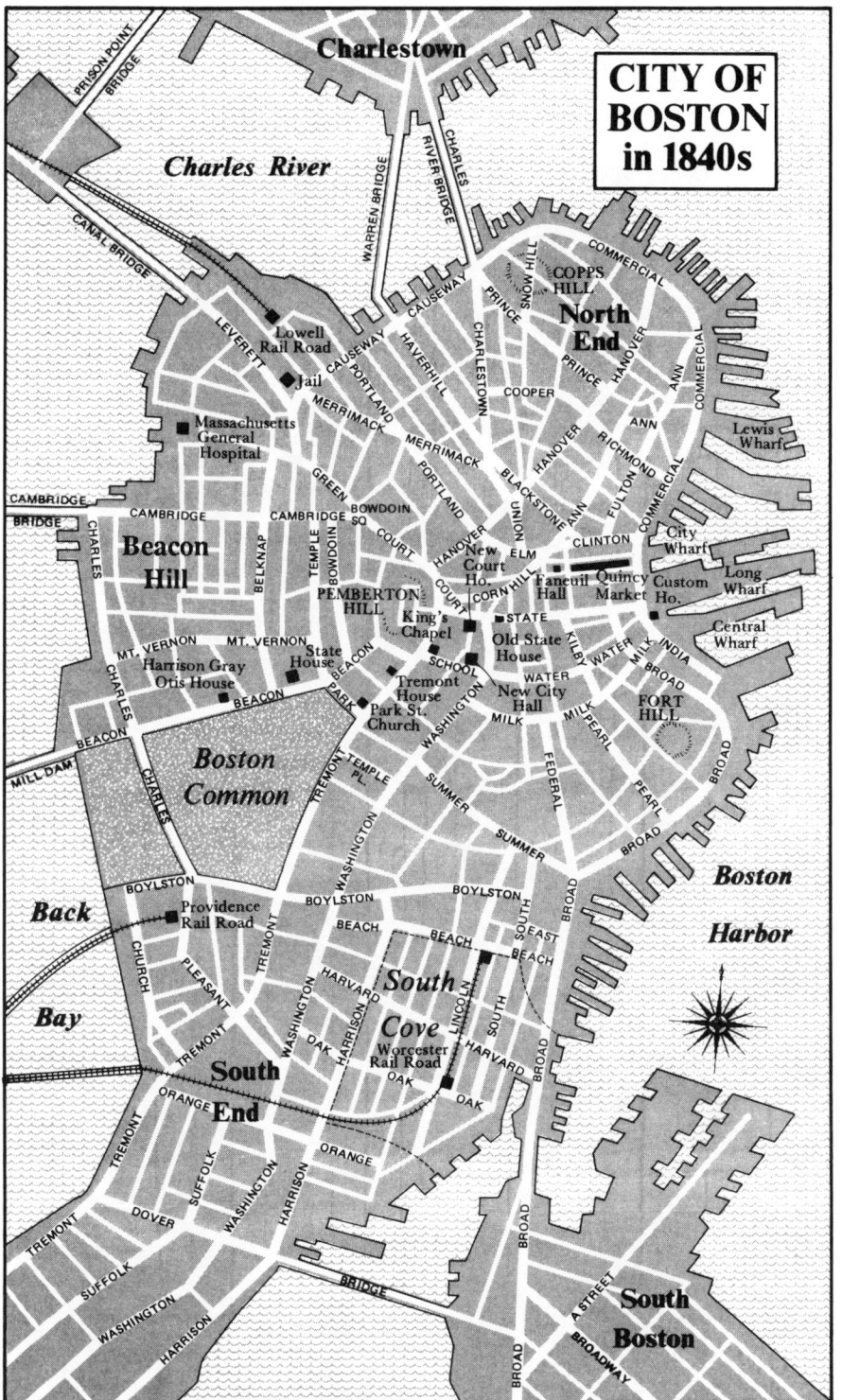

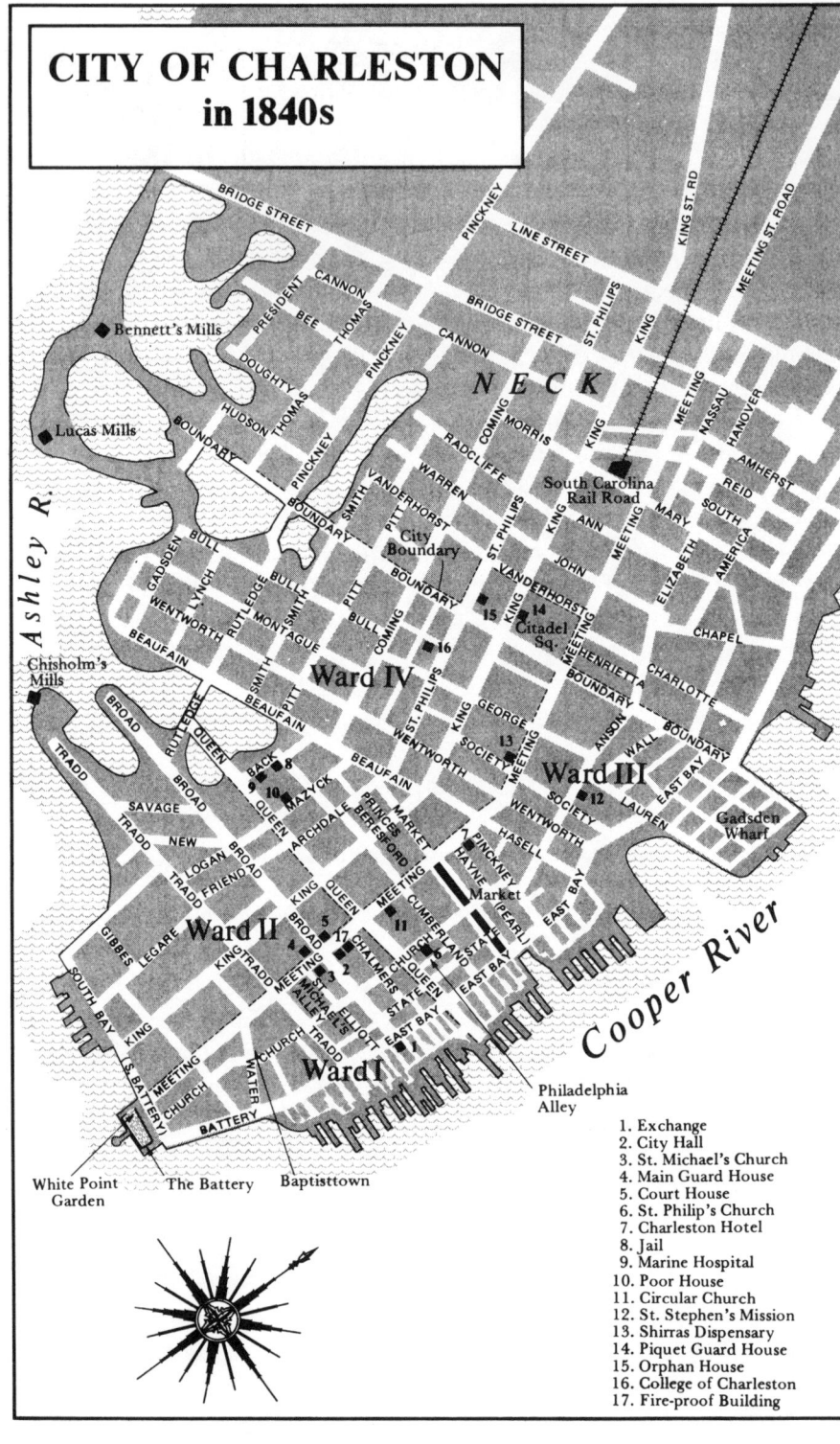

The Places and Their People

agreed, however, that intemperance stalked Broad Street, that Buttolph Street—mere blocks from the State House—was a center of "prostitution and crime . . . dance halls, and grog shops, and gaming houses, and brothels, and all [the] multiplied engines of Satan," and that the Mill Dam settlement threatened the city with "moral contagion."[8]

Despite these unsightly and sinful slums, Boston's spokesmen were proud of the city whose fate rested very largely in their hands. Otis might confess that, compared to Philadelphia with its 170,000 people or New York with its 200,000, Boston was "a small establishment" of only 60,000 inhabitants. Nonetheless he was satisfied that it was "well conditioned." Quite consistently, visitors remarked on its quiet, peaceful, clean, and neat atmosphere, its respectful and dignified people. To artist John Audubon, it was simply a "beautiful City."[9]

• • •

Regularly, whether they came to Charleston from Carolina's up-country or from Europe, visitors climbed the steps of St. Michael's church tower from which they scanned the city's panorama. From here, as far as vision permitted, they could see its whole and plot its landmarks on streets which, unlike Boston's meandering throughways and involuted byways, formed a flat if somewhat irregular grid. Standing above the intersection of two major streets—Meeting and Broad—the stranger looked east down Broad, past banks, offices, and stores to the balconied brick Exchange at its end. In and out of the 1762 building, merchants strode to settle their customs bonds and collect their mail before they threaded their way back to their stores through the outdoor auctions which, in midday, crowded the surrounding open spaces. As the spectator's eyes ranged up and down East Bay Street along the Cooper River, he saw wharves piled high with cotton bales and rice barrels in transit from local boats to the coastal schooners and foreign-bound ships which sometimes lay two and three deep at dockside. Lining the land side of East Bay were mansions, hotels, warehouses, coffee houses, countinghouses, and shops which sold rope, tar, and seamen's clothing. Within the right angle described as the viewer turned his eyes southward were sailors' dives along Elliott Street; Baptisttown's crowded houses, where white pilots and black fishermen lived close to their trade; South Battery's noisy impromptu markets; and, finally, lower Meeting Street, shaded by Pride of India trees and studded with great houses.

Alive with language—French and Spanish almost as common as English and Gullah—Charleston's first ward was also redolent with the smells of dried fish from New England, coffee from Brazil, tobacco from Cuba, and ripe fruit from the Caribbean. Dark African faces mingled with pale Scots-

Irish ones to mark an ethnic spectrum which embraced French Huguenots, North and South Germans, Sephardic Jews, and Creole émigrés from San Domingo. No part of the city was more cosmopolitan.

The western side of the city lacked the southeastern side's economic if not its ethnic diversity. Yet an eye moving west from Meeting Street, at whose intersection with Broad stood not just St. Michael's but City Hall, the Court House, and the Guard House, saw the Ashley River marshes and the rice and lumber mills, in which steam engines already supplemented tidal power. But the shoreline was only punctuated by the sawing and threshing establishments which marked the western ends of Tradd, Broad, and Boundary streets. It embraced primarily the wooden shops and houses in which more than half of the city's people worked and lived.[10] Over these low buildings hovered the domes and spires of the churches in which many of the inhabitants worshipped as Catholics, Lutherans, Presbyterians, Methodists, and Unitarians. Also between the Ashley and Meeting Street ran King Street, which, north of Broad, was the city's major commercial thoroughfare, serving both city shoppers and country buyers as characteristically as East Bay accommodated the waterborne staples trade. King Street, down whose often muddy ruts cotton-bearing wagons lurched, was by 1828 primarily the scene of dry goods emporia, hardware stores, farmers' hotels, and the shops in which crockery, glass, fancy goods, and shoes were sold. Like Meeting, it extended northward across the Neck and out into the country, whence came so much of its trade.

But all that lay well beyond the landmarks which inspired local pride, and any Charlestonian would call back the tourist's eye to the buildings more immediately visible. Only a block to the north of St. Michael's stood the recently completed fireproof building whose sturdy arches, designed by Robert Mills, stood guard over the public records. Beyond it was the squat Circular Church of the Congregationalists and, to the right, the massive square tower of St. Philip's, which, with St. Michael's, named the governmental as well as the Episcopal parishes of which the city was part.

It was, however, only at ground level that one grasped the city's pulse. Its long summers and humid sultriness constantly eroded its buildings, giving them a "hue of age" and, to some observers, a look of untidiness. Walking between them one discovered the passageways which led to interior courts where the separate kitchens, the resplendent gardens, the slave quarters, and the surrounding walls alerted Yankee visitors to an unfamiliar dynamic. Breathing in the aroma of spring flowers or early summer decay, the stranger's nose also detected the public market even before he arrived at its semi-open buildings, which stretched for three blocks between Meeting and East Bay. There fish, meat, fruit, and vegetables, each in a special section, were hawked by black women resplendent in "gay turbans of Madras" and black men in blood-stained butchers' aprons. If the bazaar atmosphere was exotic, the turkey buzzards which scavenged it were startling. Huge, ugly, and efficient, they snapped up discarded provender as rapidly as, elsewhere in the city, they might descend on an animal carcass "and in a few minutes" strip it clean til "not a vestige of flesh or sinew [was] left."[11]

For visitors the city was a medley of beauty and unease. The nightly curfew with its tolling of bells and rolling of drums reminded them that within municipal boundaries fewer than 13,000 whites coexisted with more than 15,000 black slaves and 2,000 free people of color. Six thousand of the adjoining Neck's 10,000 population were black. And in the entire Charleston District, blacks outnumbered whites three to one.[12] If the omnipresent anxiety this racial imbalance generated was seldom discussed with strangers, they nonetheless were attuned to it—perhaps even looked for it—and surely found it. But it was the recurrent threat of yellow fever which drove nonnatives from the city each summer. If Charleston was heaven in the spring, it was frequently hell in summer, and a hospital in the fall. Only after the first autumn frost did curious tourists and ailing strangers seek its mild winters and its radiant springs. And those who came for cure or amusement frequently found there a Charleston they romanticized. Enveloped in its hospitality, they often wrote home about an urban society which was dominated by planters whose style of life and city homes in the most healthful northern reaches of town and on the Neck intrigued the uninitiated. On the whole, they had far less to say about the merchants and professionals who lived intermixed with the planters, albeit more merchants than planters populated the east side nearest East Bay's commercial area. Charlestonians did not cluster either by class or by function as much as Bostonians did. Even so, a goodly number of merchants and professionals, like their northern equivalents, lived close to downtown stores and offices in residences which lined Broad Street and fanned out into the southwestern quarter of the city. Storekeepers lived in or near their shops on King Street; mechanics and most of Charleston's humbler white workers lived and worked in the northern wards bordering and above Queen Street.[13] Yet none of this blurred the startling variety which visitors constantly encountered.

• • •

However much her citizens praised their city, many in 1828 feared for her future. In the days of her colonial greatness, Charleston had traded rice, indigo, and lumber and naval stores for the goods which prosperous planters bought generously from the rest of the British empire. The city had grown rich to the rhythms of shipping and commerce and had been, on the eve of the Revolution, the third busiest port on the Atlantic coast—more substantial even than New York. The capital of a province whose politics were dominated by planters and the factors who served them, South Carolina's colonial legislature had also quite appropriately served as the city's legislative council. At this level there was no apparent conflict between town and country, for planters often maintained second residences in town to which they came to enjoy the winter social season and to escape the summer fevers of the country. Agrarian-based yet urbane, Charleston's Revolutionary generation and their immediate successors enjoyed an economy and shaped a culture as varied as her population was diverse.

But the postwar shift of plantations up-country to grow the short-staple cotton which Eli Whitney's gin made profitable, the accompanying westward population movement, the postrevolutionary creation of a new state capital at Columbia, the stultifying impact of the War of 1812 and the depression which followed, all undermined Charleston's power and prosperity. Her shipping, which had lagged from the Revolution onward, was killed by the second war with Britain; her cotton trade, which had revived only slowly thereafter, was wrenched by the 1825 boom and bust in world markets. And however appropriate textile manufacturing might appear in a state rich with raw cotton and water power, it never attracted sufficient capital or support to thrive. In 1808 John L. E. W. Shecut and fifteen or twenty other Charleston businesmen had chartered the South Carolina Homespun Company, only to see it fail by 1815. Perceiving in that a lesson well learned, city investors left textiles to the up-country, where a series of small mills languished in subsequent years.[14] Charleston remained in the 1820s, as she had always been, the region's major commercial city exporting only agricultural goods—rice and cotton—in significant quantities.

Even though in 1828 she shipped out her greatest rice crop and her second greatest cotton export ever (some 214,000 bales), it was not in Charleston bottoms. All around this single token of economic growth were other signs of relative declension. The Charleston District population had grown less than 7 percent during the 1820s, a decade in which up-country growth overshadowed that of the low country and Georgia's and Alabama's overshadowed South Carolina's.[15] By 1830 New Orleans replaced Charleston as the South's major port while, almost unnoticed, raw young Mobile grew rich shipping Gulf state cotton.

Charleston's political strength, like her economic, was threatened by the population surge westward. Merchant failures following the 1825 crash had accentuated the mercantile decline which had begun by 1810 and which had given the city's political power increasingly to resident planters, who frequently sacrificed urban commercial interests to agriculture.[16]

By 1828 economic stalemate seemed the city's lot. Business had not revived after 1825—indeed, the market was so glutted with every "article of Northern produce or Manufacture" that even sharply reduced prices could not attract buyers. And while New York, whose trade had thrived since the Erie Canal's opening in 1825, was also in the doldrums, New York's impasse was an interruption of a decade's growth, while Charleston's was a continuation of decay. There were many tenantless houses and grass grew "uninterrupted in some of her chief business streets." The chamber of commerce lamented that real estate prices had fallen by half and, even more, that "[i]ndustry and business talent, driven by necessity, [had] sought employment elsewhere." It was not, however, an organ of business but the *Southern Agriculturist* which laid bare the mood these changes fed. "These 'terrible Yankees,' . . . are too deep for us, they '*undermine* us' as the cant term in Charleston is. Why will the Charleston people not '*countermine?*' " Yankees knew the ways of trade and practiced them to "get rich," while Southerners refused to learn—and starved.[17]

• • •

When Boston celebrated her bicentennial on September 17, 1830, her most ardent supporters called her the Athens of America. Yet however much she had been shaped by her founders' Puritan faith to be a city upon a hill, her citizens' quest for economic gain and a thriving commerce had always been central to her regional role. As the principal port and capital city of Massachusetts, she had long dominated New England's economy northward through Maine, westward to the Connecticut River if not to the Berkshires, and southward into northern Connecticut and Rhode Island. After the Revolution, Boston had cultivated a national role as well; and if she was brought to her knees by the War of 1812, she soon profited from the adversity of New England's smaller and harder-hit ports to make them her tributaries, as she had earlier made its inland towns her clients. By 1830 she held three-quarters of eastern Massachusetts's bank capital in her twenty-one banks. In addition, though still overwhelmingly a commercial city—in 1827 over seven hundred vessels brought imports into her harbor from European and Caribbean ports—Boston also cultivated manufacture. Within the city was a diversity of small shops each producing a specialty, hats, earthenware, linens, cable, cordage, candles, shoes, soap, rum, mustard, and type among them.[18] But equally important, Boston cultivated the textile industry which took advantage of country labor and fall-line power in interior Massachusetts to make New England the major American textile producer. By furnishing its capital, importing its raw materials, and selling its produce, Bostonians made their city its center.

The demands of both commerce and manufacture engendered the transportation which connected Boston's diverse economy to the rest of the world. An extensive steamboat and stage network tied the city to her coastal neighbors, her hinterland, and the major cities of the North. Her brigs and schooners plied from Maine to New Orleans. Her ships sailed to Liverpool, Le Havre, Leghorn, St. Petersburg, Manila, Canton, Calcutta, Montevideo, and Buenos Aires. Her population, which had grown 40 percent during the 1820s,[19] had triggered major land and building developments for private homes, commercial facilities, and that solidly stylish granite hotel, the Tremont House. Her merchants and entrepreneurs solidified their control of the city's power—Searses, Thorndikes, Jacksons, Lawrences, Lymans, Appletons, Lowells, and Otises among them. Not necessarily from families long prominent or even resident in the city, many of them had been lured from barren farms and dying coastal towns to make their fortunes in Boston.

All was not well, however. Boston's foreign shipping had declined throughout the decade until, in 1828, 680 arrivals and 527 departures marked its lowest point since the decade began. While New York's several regular packet lines to Liverpool flourished, Boston's efforts to establish even one such service failed twice between 1822 and 1827. Moreover, her old fur trade in the American Northwest had fallen steadily as, less visibly, her China trade had begun to slip.[20]

Had there not been a panic in 1825 and a recession in 1828, the jeremiads would surely have been fewer. But the long-range threats to Boston's continued economic viability were harshly pressed home by textile firms which missed dividends, business failures so frequent that the mercantile community demanded uniform bankruptcy legislation, and a real estate slump so severe that "gentlemen [who] wish to sell . . . can get no purchasers."[21]

More critical than any of these, however, were Bostonians' perceptions that their city was falling ever farther behind New York, her principal commercial rival. That city's new access to the western grain trade through the Erie Canal and Great Lakes, her highly efficient auction system for foreign imports, her aggressive growth in coastal shipping all threatened that Yankee success in trade which Charlestonians envied. Boston's major asset, entrepreneur Samuel Appleton was sure, lay in her manufacturing hinterland, on which he believed half of Boston's commerce depended in 1828. If the merchants of Boston were to "consult their own interest . . . ," he said, "they [must] encourage the Manufacturers of Massachusetts & New hampshire." But old Peter Brooks doubted even that salvation. Noting recent fires in Lowell, he lamented, "Our *good* factories are burnt down and our *poor* ones ruin their owners."[22] Nonetheless, when each city set out to stage an economic comeback in the 1830s, Boston was notably richer in resources than was Charleston.

PART II · NURTURING ECONOMIC GROWTH

2

The Economic Heritage

The views from Beacon Hill and St. Michael's tower told much about each city. Yet the sights, sounds, and smells the visitor experienced were only surface impressions. It was the interaction of people which most fully displayed the underlying difference between the cities and manifested their distinctive values and styles.

Intangible attributes as much as tangible assets differentiated the two cities' economies, and not least among them were the attitudes of that third of each city's work force engaged in commercial activity. It was a variegated group in each city, ranging from wealthy merchants to inconsequential corner grocers—some with less than $50 invested in their stock in trade. China trader Thomas Handasyd Perkins or textile wholesalers Abbott and Amos Lawrence in Boston stood on a par with Charleston factors Samuel Wragg, Arthur Middleton, and James Rose—who all had planting interests as well—in their unchallenged prestige and power. Less visible but no less necessary to trade were the commission merchants, the brokers and auctioneers, the generalized and specialized traders who merged wholesale and retail operations, and the small shopkeepers selling hardware, dry goods, or some trifling combination of necessities and amenities.

But once their similar structures are delineated, the cities' commercial communities diverged to reflect their different pasts and the values shaped by them. While Carolina expectations linked family continuity and kin networks primarily to land and planting, Massachusetts's port towns had, in the eighteenth century, excelled in pooling family resources for concentrated commercial efforts in which joint trading ventures were funded and staffed by trusted relatives. However much, by the the nineteenth century, sons of merchant families gravitated to the professions, there were still other sons and nephews and cousins who continued the old way, operating the branch houses in Europe, South America, and China which bought and sold for Boston's profit.

Rather than honoring the agrarian values which drew native talent away from Charleston, Boston utilized family ties and individual aspirations to lure city sons and country cousins into city trade by touting its personal rewards and civic importance. As Amos Lawrence told his son, his prospects were "made easier from the circumstance of so many of [his] connexions having been successful before [him]."[1] Those connections multiplied as the children of merchant families intermarried, but never so much as to exclude outsiders. Able sea captains, whose ability to make commercial decisions on the spot in distant ports was often as critical as their navigational skill in getting there, were frequently welcomed as partners by their previous employers. The mercantile training process was a carefully monitored recruiting ground where clerks, whether family members or not, were promoted when they showed ability to carry on business successfully. As sweeping the office and building fires gave way to copying letters, running errands, and keeping accounts, so office work might be set aside altogether for an assignment as supercargo on a trading vessel. If the novice learned quickly, if he made profitable decisions, whether in counting room or officers' cabin, he could fairly anticipate a junior partnership, where his willingness to exert himself proved as good as capital. Nonetheless, kinsmen retained their traditional advantage.[2]

There is little question that in Charleston, too, kin and commercial ties overlapped; but there successful careers in the mercantile world were often only stepping-stones to a planter's life. The successful merchant frequently used his profits to buy plantation land and slaves—if not for himself, for his children. In the process, both capital and the real and potential entrepreneurial talent of those born to business-minded families were lost to the city's commerce. Of more than three hundred factors and merchants who, in 1830, traded either along East Bay and Broad or on King Street, almost a fifth of them owned plantation land at some time during the 1820s and 1830s. This was no aberration, for of the 210 whose occupations were still known five years later, one in twenty had, by then, given up trade to become a full-time planter.[3] Clearly, being and remaining a merchant was less attractive in the southern than in the northern city.

It was not necessarily because commercial profits were smaller in Charleston that those who had the choice opted for planting, for such noneconomic values as social prestige and political power were vested in the conduct of large-scale agricultural pursuits. In turn, such values and the economic decisions they shaped created a commercial dynamic which

The Economic Heritage 15

appealed to strangers more than to natives. Thus citizens lamented that too much of the city's mercantile activity was controlled by Northerners and Europeans who, more often than not, left town once they had gained their competencies. Although they seldom accumulated assets exceeding $100,000 or $200,000 and usually far less, like native sons turned planters they made a constant drain on the city's potential capital when they returned to their native places.[4] Yet as agents of distant houses they provided much of the city's mercantile strength, although they thereby made Charleston not the center of overlapping family and business networks, but only the outpost of webs whose centers were in Baltimore, New York, and Boston—or even London and Paris. Thus Irish-born James Adger, who atypically stayed on in Charleston, brought to it the resources of Baltimore's international bankers, Alexander Brown & Sons; James Gibbes was agent for the British Baring Brothers; Pitray and Viel bought cotton for the House of Quesnell in Rouen; Lewis Trapmann represented the trading interests of several German firms; and James Lamb as well as Doddridge Crocker handled local commercial matters for Thomas Lamb of Boston.[5]

• • •

That the style and practice of business in each city differed as much as did business structures was nowhere clearer than in their merchant associations. Although in America private arbitration of business differences had largely given way by 1830 to civil litigation, the older method still flourished in Charleston. The chamber of commerce, founded in the eighteenth century and, after a period of inactivity, revived in 1823, had codified the rules and regulations guiding local business conduct and continued to adjudicate commercial disputes. Led by the city's most prominent merchants, with members elected by formal vote, its powerful position made it a respected judicial board whose binding arbitration resolved differences over contracts, prices, damages, insurance claims, and the like. Serving nonmembers, who paid a special service fee, as well as members, its nonconfrontational style kept commercial questions almost entirely out of the courts.[6]

The Charleston practice had no counterpart in Boston. There the briefs of litigants' lawyers rather than the judgment of their commercial peers decided mercantile disputes, And while businessmen did organize their own libraries and associations to press political causes of special interest, their efforts to create a viable chamber of commerce were unsuccessful. The chamber called into being in 1836 to replace its long-defunct predecessor as a mediator when "vexed questions . . . arise between individuals" and an agency for the "general advancement of the mercantile interests" was only minimally active until, in the 1840s, it died altogether.[7]

The effectiveness of Boston's familial and collegial business network did, however, provide an informal mechanism for resolving disputes. That Charleston had no similar web may well account for its reliance on the more formal chamber of commerce structure and procedure, just as its preference for arbitration surely reflected the desire to avoid courtroom confrontations which might offend gentlemen's honor and produce violent conflict. By contrast, Bostonians' swift turn from friendly give-and-take to litigation in the courts marked their willingness to contest business issues publicly, a willingness which contributed to their reputation in the South as sharp dealers. Yet the cities were not polar opposites. Charleston too had aggressive and sometimes exceedingly unpopular businessmen, despite its social commitment to rounded edges, just as Boston's great merchants cultivated a smooth business and social style equally well suited to the southern city.

Nonetheless, the fact remained that in Boston profit was the measure of economic activity. Local folk sometimes chastised businessmen for being too cautious, for calculating so closely that they passed up promising future returns because, while expecting long-term credit for themselves, they seldom extended it to others. Yet it was their pursuit of sure, steady profit which made others believe that nowhere were merchants "more correct or intelligent or respectable" than in Boston.[8]

The cities' differing business styles were well illustrated by the men chosen to press the corporate development and construction of railroads. Both Elias Horry and Patrick Tracy Jackson were men of estimable character, highly respected in their communities. But the other attributes which led fellow investors to elect each of them president of their respective companies set them apart. Horry, who, following William Aiken, a retired merchant long since turned rice planter, became the second president of the South Carolina Canal and Rail Road Company, had been trained in the law. His sole business experience was in operating his eleven plantations. But he had served twelve years in the South Carolina House of Representatives, had been appointed to several city commissions, had been chosen intendent (mayor) in 1815, and was active in church and educational societies.[9] To him was entrusted construction of the railroad on which many believed the city's future economic prosperity depended.

When Boston investors sought a man to develop a railroad connection to Lowell, already a major textile center in which Boston capital was heavily invested and on whose operations much of her trade hung, they turned to Patrick Tracy Jackson. Member of a trading family originally from Salem and with strong ties to the Lowells, Jackson had been an original member of the Boston Associates, which had first developed the Massachusetts textile industry, and had himself gone on to organize other textile ventures. His public service was limited to a brief term as trustee of the Massachusetts General Hospital.[10]

Jackson was chosen because he was an experienced businessman whose dedication to entrepreneurship had reaped profits for himself and his associates. Horry, a man heavily in debt and unfamiliar with corporate operations, was experienced in persuading people and qualified for business leadership primarily by his political skills and personal grace. Jackson was direct; Horry moved without roiling the waters.

• • •

Indeed, that rapidly emerging business form, the corporation, seemed made to order for Yankee business ways. Massachusetts had early encouraged corporations as agencies whose principal purpose was fostering the enterprises needed for community well-being by enticing private investors to undertake them in exchange for state guarantees of limited monopoly. By 1820, however, it was evident that a shift in both intent and purpose had already occurred. The corporate form was rapidly becoming a simple device for drawing together the capital requisite to prosecute almost any sort of business.[11]

Boston merchants, who had long used corporate charters to form bridge companies, banks, and insurance companies, increasingly sought them for manufacturing establishments. In 1830 the steady flow of petitions to the legislature for such charters led Massachusetts to adopt a general incorporation statute and, even more important to would-be investors, to provide limited liability for all corporate stockholders except bank directors.[12] Despite limitations on the amount of real and personal property an organization might hold, and stipulations setting the number of directors it must have and the types of business in which it might engage, the corporation provided a business structure responsive to innovation.

While Boston took up incorporation with unfeigned enthusiasm, Charleston lagged in its use. Boston-educated Silas Holbrook, visiting Charleston in 1830, was struck by the paucity of corporations in all of South Carolina. Although they increased in number in the 1830s, they remained relatively sparse. The state incorporated only fifteen businesses other than banks between 1830 and 1835—eighty-five fewer than Massachusetts incorporated in the same time. Furthermore, the Carolina charters reflected the still prevailing belief that a corporation should serve the public interest and dominant social values. To insure open sales of corporate stock the charters always required that commissioners offer the stock in publicly announced subscriptions. Frequently they required that stock be sold at several locations in the state other than Charleston. There was thus little opportunity for the common Boston practice of a small group of incorporators' subscribing the entire stock issue before it was offered to the public at large.[13] In addition, South Carolina charters often established weighted voting of stocks so that large shareholders could not vote all their stock and small shareholders had a voice disproportionately greater than their investment.[14] However much South Carolina cultivated a patrician social outlook, its quasi-public corporate ventures were subject to democratic economic tenets more generally associated with populist politics.

Equally important in shaping business investment was Charlestonians' proclivity to vest noneconomic as well as economic value in certain kinds of property. Plantation land was a source, and often a rich one, of income. But because it qualified its owner for political power and social prestige, it also had extrinsic value as well. So too slaves, whether they worked in fields, shops, homes, or elsewhere, provided not only income but the means to display their owners' leisure and symbolize their community loyalty. These perceptions of property as more than a variant form of investment complicated what in Boston were simple economic decisions. Bostonians were freer to respond to shifts in economic opportunity, to invest time, labor, and resources in those enterprises which promised economic growth to their city as well as profits to individuals. Charlestonians, no less concerned for their own and their city's prosperity, were, however, encumbered by wide-ranging value judgments shaping those decisions which Yankees made solely on the basis of a property's security and productivity. They were circumscribed in their responses to new opportunities because civic and social values seemed more often to be in conflict with individual profit.

That is not to say that available options and potential returns were not central to their investment strategies. Simply on those grounds, cotton planting was attractive during most of the 1830s. High prices and growing demand lured city dwellers' capital to the country. While some became full-time planters, others only supplemented their professions and businesses in Charleston, spending the spring planting season and the fall harvest season in the country and almost always celebrating the Christmas holidays there. For the fifth of Charleston merchants and factors who were probably also planters this meant a convenient schedule, for busy seasons on the plantation coincided with slack seasons in trade. And for the fourth of the physicians and lawyers who were also planters, the situation was little different.[15] The convenient schedule, the promise of increased income from dual occupations, the pleasant seasonal migrations only added to the other social and economic attractions of investing in rural land and slaves. Thus bank president and physician Joseph Johnson enjoyed entertaining city friends at his country seat in Goose Creek. Factor

Daniel Webb's generally unprofitable Chatworth provided his family with a vacation home from which he could commute to the city. Merchant Anthony Barbot, judge Charles Colcock, lawyer James Petigru, and port collector James Pringle all planted with no apparent interruption to their urban vocations.[16]

Yet this investment pattern told against the city, in part because it was not a reciprocal activity. Full-time planters seldom invested much in the city—even in secure bank stock. Of all known investors in Charleston banks, only 30 percent had also invested in rural land, and no more than a tenth planted as their major occupation. Rejecting its most conservative stock, perhaps because planting seemed just as safe and more profitable, they rejected as well more speculative investments in transportation. Few planters who had no alternative occupation chose to subscribe for South Carolina Canal and Rail Road stock when it first went on the market in 1830, and the profile of all known railroad investors almost mirrors that of Charleston bank stock holders.[17]

In Charleston as in Boston, it was the merchants and factors who bought bank stock, with half of each city's bank investors coming from their ranks. Indeed, those engaged in any sort of commerce comprised as many as three-quarters of all stockholders in each city.[18] Yet even that similarity is limited, for Bostonians were twice as likely as Charlestonians to own stock in different corporations and different kinds of corporations.[19]

Since four out of ten stockholders in each city were persons of at least modest wealth, total resources seem less critical in explaining their distinctive investment strategies than dissimilar goals and options. Boston folk could invest heavily in their city and yet protect their interests by diversifying. When they bought corporate stock, they could choose not just among the bank, insurance, and transportation company stock available in the southern city, but also among wharf, aqueduct, and power companies as well as manufacturers of textiles, glass, rubber, and metal products. Thus it was that when Adam Tunno, one of Charleston's great merchants, died in 1832 he left, in addition to his slaves, his plantation, and his mansion, only $81,000 worth of stock, which was invested in five banks, two insurance companies, a bridge company, and the local theater. When the next year Boston's Israel Thorndike died, he left half the $1 million he had gained from trade and investment in the city in the stocks of twenty-seven diverse companies.[20] Hedging for security, Boston merchants were satisfied with a sure 6 percent return if they could thus shelter the gains they had made in high-risk commercial ventures. Southerners, however, judged corporate returns against the 7 to 9 percent they expected from planting. And when they sought security above all else, they looked either to government bonds or to the Philadelphia-based Bank of the United States, in which Carolinians had invested over $5 million to control 20 percent of its entire stock in 1829.[21] In either case, funds which might have been invested in Charleston enterprises of immediate benefit to its commercial economy were siphoned off.

Those with only a small capital also chose among different options in the two cities. It may have been, as Mayor Otis insisted, that Massachusetts textile firms' decision to issue stock in $100 rather than $1,000 denominations was a move enabling those of only modest means to share in economic modernization. Nonetheless, choosing among corporate investments remained both hard and hazardous for those with little business experience. Easier to understand and manage for Charleston's novices was the slave labor with which all were to some degree familiar. Thus it was that in the southern city those with limited means more frequently owned slaves than any other kind of income-producing property, with the possible exception of city land. And, as their modest wills attest, their slaves—ranging in value from $100 for female servants to $1,000 for skilled male artisans—were frequently their only significant property. Catherine LaCroix, who signed her will with a mark, left two slaves and nothing else. Louisa Cabeuil, in addition to five pieces of table silver, some bedding, and a few pieces of furniture, also bequeathed two slaves. And Sarah Wing, who was prosperous by comparison, left, in addition to her seventeen bank shares, six slaves—a valuable cooper among them.[22]

Thus while investment choices in both cities were made by individuals and oriented to community values, they were also shaped by the options available. It was Boston which most effectively developed the institutions to channel the funds of small and inexpert investors into the city's business and thus to serve her broader economic priorities. The trust had evolved gradually over time to serve both the safety of individual property owners and the community's broader economic needs. Then, in 1829, Massachusetts courts clarified the traditionally conservative but largely undefined responsibilities of trustees by ruling that they met their fiduciary obligations if their practices were "prudent" and conformed to established business procedures of the day. Freed thus from restraints which had, in the past, restricted their investment choices, trusts were at liberty to lend their funds to a variety of business ventures. And after 1839, when legislation removed the remaining limitations on the kinds of stock which trusts might hold, they expanded their corporate holdings to include not only bank shares but insurance, manufacturing, and railroad stock as well.[23]

Well before then, however, the Massachusetts Hospital Life Insurance

Company, chartered in 1811, had emerged as Boston's major trust institution. Established initially to benefit the newly founded Massachusetts General Hospital with the proceeds of its insurance business, in 1823 the firm began a trust business under policies established by its mathematician actuary, Nathaniel Bowditch. In the following years, most of the major eleemosynary institutions entrusted their funds to Bowditch's management, as did those leaving bequests to "society's dependents or those inexperienced in business—widows, orphans, children, single women, the aged, teachers, ministers, and naval officers." With $5 million already held in trust by 1830, the Massachusetts Hospital Life prudently extended its investments during the following decade. Thus it not only provided a safe haven for the assets of individual Bostonians and of the city's public service institutions, but also funneled millions of dollars back into the local economy.[24]

John Lowell once described Boston's first modern trust company as *"eminently the Savings bank of the wealthy."* The Provident Institution for Savings was, in turn, the Massachusetts Hospital Life for those possessing little property. Founded in 1816, the Provident was designed to encourage even the poorest citizens to save against the future. An institution managed by prestigious and astute businessmen, who gave their advice and service free, it promised safety for the hard-earned resources of artisans, clerks, seamstresses, servants, and laborers. Indeed, while the institution accepted larger deposits, it paid interest only on sums of $500 or less, believing that possessors of greater riches should manage them personally or move them to the Massachusetts Hospital Life. Clearly meeting a need, the Provident was a magnet for small depositors. By 1829 it had almost $1 million in its savings accounts, a quarter of which was invested in the stock of Boston's commercial banks, a third lent out on security, and all its reserves serving, in one way or another, the capital needs of Boston and her hinterland. Five years later, with almost twice as much on deposit, it increased its financial commitment to surrounding cities and towns.[25]

Charleston could not equal these Boston institutions. While individuals there also established trusts to administer testamentary bequests, marriage settlements, and other property arrangements for their kin, no institutionalized trust system developed. Moreover, although the state chartered a savings bank in 1833, the institution was not organized for another decade. Small savers, like the financially inexperienced, could only rely on well-disposed individuals to act as trustees, or else themselves seek the familiar investments with which they were most comfortable—slaves, loans to friends, perhaps bank stock. They lacked the protection which the diversified investments of a large institution promised. And local business enterprises in need of capital had no access to the collectivity of small savers' resources.

Nor could Charleston's insurance companies make available the ample funds which the capital and reserves accumulated by Boston's seventeen companies in 1830 (twenty-five, six years later) funneled into other Boston businesses. With but three insurance companies in 1830—two of which failed when claims from disastrous fires in 1835 and 1838 ate up their reserves—Charleston benefited little from premiums drawn to or kept in the city for insurance. Thus she lacked as well the potential for commercial loans with which the insurance companies' customary purchase of bank stock provided the northern city.[26] Indeed, even the endowments of clubs, churches, and philanthropies, which indirectly served Boston's economic growth through the trusts in which so many were deposited, seeped less fully into Charleston's economy. There they were routinely invested in bank stock—much of it in the Bank of the United States as well as in local banks—and in government securities. How limited their alternatives were was suggested by planter John Grimball's annoyance that the South Carolina Society, which had lent him $5,000, preferred that he delay repaying the loan. "They found it difficult," he observed, "to invest and when they got possession of a safe bond they preferred much to let the bond remain unpaid. . . ."[27]

• • •

The values, the property preferences, the ways of doing business, and the commercial institutions of each city had been shaped by their experiences and pasts. They did not, however, provide either city the stamina to keep up with New York, whose rapid growth in the 1820s Charleston as well as Boston eyed with trepidation. Both, on the eve of the 1830s, believed that they were slipping ever farther behind. Each was sure her future depended on reviving commerce and increasing trade with hinterland and overseas markets alike. But how well had their heritages equipped them to reach their goals? And where past directly ill-served future, what potential resources were there for effective change?

3

Boston's Boom Years

The capital resources, the financial and commercial organizations, and the mercantile skills with which Boston faced the 1830s stoked an entrepreneurial enthusiasm which drove the city through a decade of boom and bust. Her citizens' intense preoccupation with economic success was clearly charted in their preoccupation with time. Unlike the South, where agricultural rhythms framed time, the passage of Boston time was chimed in economic gains and losses. Traders responded to fluctuations in credit; capitalists reacted to shifting dividends; artisans set their prices as demand rose and fell; and laborers sweated out the push and pull of the job market. In Boston, time implied progress; for Charleston, it did not.

From 1830 to 1837, Bostonians' dominant expectation was growth and prosperity. Yet as individuals they experienced temporal disjunctions as the economic pendulum swung unevenly between dull doldrum and wild activity in unpredictable patterns which alternately threatened their security and promised still greater prosperity. Anticipating growth through most of the 1830s, they also remembered the late 1820s when, wherever one looked, to whomever one spoke, times were bad, money was tight, interest rates high, dividends low, businesses failing, and unemployment pressing hard on the poor. To Gardiner Greene, president of the local branch of the Bank of the United States, the "Press on [the] Mercantile community" was almost unbearable by late 1828. Hard-nosed Frederic Tudor, who had made his fortune shipping ice cut from Boston ponds to Charleston, New Orleans, and even Calcutta, recorded in June that interest rates were even then up to "9 pr. ct. pr. ann. for the best security." The lucky survived long months when "the various branches of mans activity" were extraordinarily dull and gloomy; the unlucky suffered "the losses of whole fortunes."[1]

Textile manufacturing, which had overexpanded in the 1820s, furnished little hope for economic recovery. Merrimack Company stock had fallen from a high of $1,600 in 1825 to a low of $900 in 1829, while Boston Company stock had slid from $1,000 to $600. Shipowners complained that even Boston ships preferred to dock in New York. Nor did things look better among landlords and shopkeepers, whose prosperity was tied to the retail stores and modest dwellings which lined Washington and Tremont streets. There "hundreds of houses and stores [were] without occupants," and even those which were rented brought their owners but a paltry "2 or 3 per cent. per annum."[2] In the homes and shops of North End craftsmen and in laborers' tenements south of the Common, hard times were yet more directly felt. City missionary Joseph Tuckerman, whose social work brought him into daily contact with real want, wrote in 1829, "There is scarcely a mechanic occupation pursued among us, in which large numbers, through the summer and autumn, have not found it very difficult, and often impracticable, to obtain work enough to enable them to pay their rent, and to purchase absolutely necessary food and clothing. . . ." And for those women dependent on their earnings as seamstresses, the situation was desperate. With unemployment rampant, even those who did find work seldom earned more in a week than a male laborer earned in a day. So it was that "many who would have done any thing and suffered every thing sooner than appeal to charity, have been compelled to become applicants for its bounty."[3]

Amid these reports Joseph T. Buckingham, who edited the Boston *Courier,* struck a rare note of optimism in July 1830. He admitted he would "probably be laughed at for an ignoramus, or hissed and hooted down as a fool" for saying it, but say it he would: the city was not in decline. Within six months what had seemed ridiculous proved prophetic. In January 1831, textile merchant and capitalist Amos Lawrence fairly chortled that "in our city . . . the people have not had greater prosperity for twenty years." Sound observation and promising prospects vindicated his enthusiasm. In 1831 imports rose 60 percent over the previous year; the following year exports soared 70 percent over the levels of 1831. While this sharp improvement did reflect a national trend, Boston's recovery ran somewhat ahead of the country's. By mid-decade her imports had tripled from 1830 levels, while the nation's fell somewhat short of that mark.[4]

Whatever caused the shift, Bostonians associated it with their efforts to improve their commercial facilities. Spurred by an association of merchants who contracted to operate and rent space on it, the city had built a new wharf. Upon it between 1831 and 1833 its private managers built ten stores, rented out warehousing space, and collected wharfage fees to turn an annual profit of $5,000. Owners of private wharves improved their properties, repairing sagging structures and extending their dockage ever farther into the stream to accommodate the largest vessels. Around the North End and at Mill Pond new wharves were built and operated aggressively. Typical of such entrepreneurial activity was the Lewis Wharf Company, incorporated in 1834. Its facilities, jutting out from the intersection of two major North End streets, Ann and Commercial, had attracted a capital of some $500,000 to build and then improve and extend Lewis Wharf. By 1836 the company had both deepened the docks and constructed seawalls, ferry slips, and eight four-storied warehouses, each providing 8,000 square feet of storage space. Such accommodations attracted the sizable ships of foreign trade, whose arrivals more than doubled during the 1830s.[5]

If the public eye lingered on the romantic but lagging China trade it was gazing at Boston's past, for by 1830 the city's growing international trade was with Europe. But as always the challenge was in finding the export cargoes needed to balance imports. Put simply, from 1828 to 1836 Boston imported $138 million worth and exported only $66 million worth of goods. To meet the imperative for balanced trade the city drew on her past, mimicking her colonial triangular carrying trade by intergrating coastal and foreign shipping. Thus her vessels carried northern goods south (generally the least profitable leg of the journey), then loaded cotton, delivered it abroad, and thence returned to Boston—or New York if the market was better there—with assorted goods from Baltic, Atlantic, and Mediterranean ports.[6]

Nor could coastal shipping be understood merely as a supplement to foreign trade. In 1830 Mayor Otis celebrated the centrality of domestic trade to manufacturing. To insure its regularity, Boston cultivated the packet lines which linked it to other coastal ports—Portsmouth and Portland to the north, New York and Baltimore to the south. In the year ending in September 1831 the three packet lines linking Boston to New York handled cargoes worth more than $6 million. Not surprisingly, Central Wharf, where these scheduled vessels docked, guaranteed them conveniently situated regular berths.[7] Equally if not more important, however, were the schooners and brigs which plied the coast irregularly, their courses charted only by the bulky freights awaiting shipment from one port to another. When traffic was heaviest, it was these vessels which crowded the wharves, their lines sometimes stretching across one or two luckier ships before they were secured.

The dockside scurry reverberated with the city's other business, to which it was closely bound. And wharf owners acknowledged those ties in their own investment patterns. More than half of those who owned stock in wharves had bought into city banks and insurance companies as well. When they were offered railroad stock, a third of them were ready buyers, anticipating both direct and indirect returns from the new form of transportation which would expedite shipments to and from the interior. A quarter of them acknowledged shipping's reliance on the textile trade by investing capital in Chicopee and Lowell mills. And one out of five subscribed stock for city land development, which was often a by-product of the new transportation facilities.[8]

Not surprisingly, the men who controlled major wharves were wealthy men accustomed to wielding economic power. Seventy percent of the directors of the Central Wharf and the Boston Wharf companies were rich, and a minimum of two out of three of them also sat on the board of at least one other company—usually a bank or insurance company, whose collective capital resources were so vital to commerce. And two out of five wielded even broader corporate power. These were men who moved easily in the world of business and finance. Thus were the directors of Central Wharf able to link its board to at least twenty other corporations.[9]

Yet even without the affiliations of the wharves' directors and investors, the cotton trade by itself would have tied wharves to hinterland. Not only did raw cotton create the trade balance enabling importers to pay for their purchases abroad, but it also fed the textile mills which, in turn, provided a substantial portion of the goods Boston traded south for fiber. In 1830 over 45,000 bales of raw cotton were shipped through Boston to be spun and woven in New England. Five years later the amount had almost doubled.[10]

Intermediary in the exchange of raw materials and finished cloth were Boston merchants—prime among them Abbott and Amos Lawrence. Using their credit and contacts to control most of Boston's importation of New Orleans cotton, they were also major wholesalers of New England–made textiles. Key to both roles was the Lawrences' ability to act as private bankers, an activity both profitable and demanding when interest rates and money supply fluctuated sharply. By 1836 Amos reported that "A & AL & Co will have need of some millions of dollars" from textile sales to "supply . . . the companies whose business they do" with raw cotton.[11] The point was clear: shipping, trade, banking, and manufacturing were not just interlocked; they were symbiotic.

Boston's involvement in textile manufacturing was, moreover, broad. Her capital resources built factories at water power sources throughout northern New England and integrated them into the city's commercial economy. Investment patterns in the Merrimack Company alone illuminate much of the Boston style. The thirty-five merchants who held 560 Merrimack shares (worth $1,000 each at face value) in 1833 and another nineteen "capitalists or retired men" who held another 240 shares controlled and voted half the company's stock. Between two-thirds and three-quarters of all known Boston textile investors were engaged in commerce; half of them had invested also in banks and insurance companies; and a third of them owned wharf and railroad stock. Naturally they were wealthy—almost half worth at least $50,000; one in seven worth over $150,000.[12] And the investments which enabled Boston to integrate her economy with the manufacturing backcountry also served the investors' interests. During the mid-1830s, textile dividends averaged 11.8 percent per year.[13]

Yet even by 1836 Boston had not achieved a fully integrated trade. She had yet to develop as an entrepôt for western and other southern agricultural products, which an increasingly industrial and densely populated New England needed. She had yet to control the trade of Yankee manufactured products with the expanding American interior around the Great Lakes or in the Ohio River basin. That business, especially in grain and flour, centered in New York, where the developing Midwest traded its products for the manufactured goods its citizens sought.[14]

• • •

Nonetheless, with a flourishing cotton trade, extensive shipping, and the most industrialized hinterland of any American city, Boston's economy was exuberant from the upturn in 1831 until the ensuing bank war blighted the credit on which it rested. Real estate prices soared, increasing as much as 20 percent in a matter of days, 50 percent in a matter of weeks; William Appleton, who regularly analyzed the state of his soul and the prosperity of his purse in year-end diary entries, noted in December 1831 that his capital invested in real estate had returned a good 20 percent during the year. Though money was occasionally tight, the problem lay not in the city, so business leaders believed, but in the Bank of the United States and its Washington politics.[15] Appleton's friend William Sullivan wrote him in May 1832 that more business had been done in Boston the previous month than in any previous April on record and, just a year later, the *Morning Post* reported the consensus of local merchants that business had not been "so brisk for many years . . . the public houses are full of lodgers.—The countrymen are in fine spirits and good credit, and the Boston traders all politeness and accommodation." All meshed to produce that "extraordinary quantity of business in Rail Roads[,] wharfs[,] stores &c. going on in all quarters of the town" over which Frederic Tudor gloated.[16]

Mechanics, like capitalists and merchants, flourished during these years.

Dependent less on capital resources than on their own artisanal skills and practical knowledge, dispersed in many small shops and in a few large ones employing twenty-five or thirty workers, they turned out a hundred different kinds of products: bread and beer for daily consumption, balance scales and blank books for local commerce, ships and sails for seaborne trade, hats and mantuas to clothe fellow citizens, chairs and cabinets to furnish their homes, clocks and watches to tell the time, hammers and lasts for other artisans, pianos and philosophical instruments to enhance culture. In 1833 more than thirty-five hundred men and women were employed in these shops, both large and small, at a time when the distinction between mechanic and manufacturer was at best unclear.[17]

Their products, like those of the capital-intensive factories and skill-based craftsmen of interior Massachusetts, had from 1826 to 1833 been displayed at semiannual sales sponsored by the New England Society of Mechanics and Manufacturers. These widely advertised and widely attended auctions in Quincy Hall did lure buyers from the South and West. Yet their very success pointed up their potential danger to Boston's economy. The sales of $400,000 at a single fair in 1831 threatened both merchants and shopkeepers, who complained that they were losing their regular custom to the Quincy Hall auctions. Consequently the society abandoned the undertakings after 1832, only to generate complaints that, without such auctions, Boston could not compete with New York.[18]

If this disharmony of mercantile and mechanic interests could not be veiled, neither could that between mechanic-artisans and manufacturer-capitalists. There was no head-on clash, but the tension was clear. Mechanics worried about their declining status as they competed with capitalists who became manufacturers by investing in machinery rather than by utilizing the traditional skills and technical know-how of craftsmen. Urged on by the Democratic *Post,* which proclaimed that artisans were thus "excluded from privileges which were emphatically their own" and "exposed . . . to ridicule and contempt," master mechanics lamented that their sons preferred commercial careers.[19]

Nonetheless, mechanic-manufacturers increased and dominated the production of goods in Boston. Much was made of the local mechanics who undertook a cooperative steam factory in Pitts Court—installing a steam engine in a large building and transmitting its power by belts, shafts, and pulleys to the individual rooms where independent mechanics employed the most modern of power sources. Although that venture was short-lived, it symbolized a tenuous balance. On the one hand, manufacturing in the city remained largely the preserve of craftsmanship, individual skill, and expertise with hand tools and small machines. Yet on the other, Boston had, by 1838, more than forty-six steam-powered manufactories—principally print and machine shops. To be sure, the steam power thus generated was only 429 horsepower; nevertheless it was a token that mechanics could and would experiment with modern technology. Moreover, they used their skills to invent still more machines: in 1831 alone a leather-cutting machine, one to make hooks and eyes, and a hemp- and flax-spinning machine.[20] And, like other Bostonians, they prospered as they embraced change.

• • •

Boston's economy was, by circumstance and choice, tied to the nation's. However strong her own resources, therefore, she could not avoid being sucked into the crisis provoked by President Jackson's 1834 decision to remove federal deposits from the Bank of the United States. Even though the local branch provided but little of the city's credit or currency, Nicholas Biddle's and Andrew Jackson's battles, which strangled finances elsewhere, also shook Boston. In the six months from August 1833 to January 1834 the interest rate on prime business notes jumped from 6 or 7 percent to a range of 12 to 18 percent per annum. With that, the business community chose sides. Impatient with both but inherently more sympathetic to Biddle the banker than to Jackson the politician, a meeting of commercial men (the primary recipients of bank loans) at Faneuil Hall damned the latter's course. Proclaiming that Boston's economy was basically sound and that local banks were in good shape, they asserted that only a revitalized Bank of the United States could control the national proclivity to "speculation and over-trading."[21]

Inextricably involved in a nationwide credit contraction, Boston businessmen lamented the near panic it had brought their city. The "continuance of the existing embarrassments" caused by the "deranged state" of money would, they warned, "check the future operations of the farmer, merchant, manufacturer, and mechanic, and consequently lessen the employment and wages of the laborer." Harrison Gray Otis, sure that he had not seen "greater apprehension . . . about money matters" in years, likened its pressure to that of an "hydraulic machine." Small depositors withdrew their funds from the Provident Institution for Savings so rapidly that for the first time in its history it reported an absolute "diminution of depositors." Once again business failure stalked small traders and frightened large ones. Charles Francis Adams found it curious that the most visible bankrupts were "all small fry," whose public acknowledgments of failure in the closed shops lining Washington Street "shew the state of affairs more distinctly to the eye than the greater failures." Although only a few large houses succumbed, Abbott Lawrence believed that the panic racing through downtown offices was worse than anything he had seen in his entire business career.[22]

For great and small, however, the slump of 1834 vanished almost as quickly as it had come. By May money was again available, sales of domestic manufactures were good, and jobs so plentiful that Lowell mills were short 600 hands. Nonetheless, this short-lived panic focused the mercantile community's attention on the vagaries of Boston's banking system as it drove home to artisans and laborers the insecurity of their jobs.[23]

Twenty-eight banks served Boston in 1834, seven of them new since 1830. Private investment provided their capital, ranging from the new Franklin Bank's $100,000 to the old State Bank's $1,800,000; total bank capital, amounting to more than $12 million in 1831, rose or fell as established banks gained legislative consent to increase or decrease their capitalization and as rising entrepreneurs received charters for new banks. In 1836 alone, five banking institutions opened their doors.[24] Small for the most part, they nonetheless were an important avenue for men on the make to gain credit for themselves and to take part in the financial decision-making which a bank directorship promised. Indeed, the importance of supplying credit and exchange facilities to the business community not infrequently overshadowed bank directors' pursuit of profit for their own institution. They lent traders money by discounting their promissory notes; they provided merchants with drafts on banks in other American and in foreign cities; they backed the bonds which importers posted against customs duties owed the federal government. Thus by providing—or withholding—their varied services, banks wielded power throughout the commercial community.[25]

If, as was the case with their fellows in other enterprises, they broadened their economic influence, bank directors also enjoyed special access to the credit which they daily extended or refused to others. The actions of the Tremont Bank were not unusual. When director Ebenezer T. Andrews found himself embarrassed by $16,000 in debts he could not pay late in 1836, he applied to Tremont's president, Samuel Armstrong, for a $16,000 loan and an extension of his outstanding $4,000 note the bank already held. Uncertainty that he could promptly repay either one probably lay behind Andrews's reluctance to present his request directly to the regular board meeting. But even more revealing of the special consideration individual directors expected and received was his observation that, after all, four other directors already had loans at the bank amounting collectively to half its entire capital.[26]

Although state law precluded serving on more than one bank board at a time, a bank directorship was often a stepping-stone to other economic power. Three out of every five bank directors serving between 1828 and 1836 sat on at least one other corporate board, and close to one-third served three or more corporations.[27] Among Andrews's associates at the Tremont Bank, for instance, fifteen directors exercised economic power through seventeen other corporations, including six insurance companies, two wharf companies, and two railroads. And at the city's largest financial institution, the State Bank's twenty-two directors served on the boards of twenty-six other corporations, and nine of them had, at some time, served on other bank boards.

This interlocking activity and information network formed a web of economic power to which few outsiders were privy. On the other hand, the Suffolk Bank's clearinghouse system was visible to all. Boston-centered since its inception in 1819, the Suffolk system had rationalized banking throughout northern New England by controlling member banks' issuance of bank notes. Participating banks throughout the region maintained a substantial deposit in the Boston institution to avoid having to settle unfavorable balances with any Boston member bank on a daily basis. By so doing they avoided both a drain on their scarce specie reserves and the interest which Suffolk otherwise charged nonmember banks for short-term loans to cover their deficiencies. By insuring a stable currency and facilitating low specie reserves at member banks, the system not only benefited the region but rewarded Suffolk shareholders with steady profits. Throughout the 1830s Suffolk stock sold usually 10 to 20 percent above par; without exception, its yearly dividends ranged between 6 and 9 percent.[28]

More significant for the city as a whole, the Suffolk system protected local banking from domination by the Philadelphia-based Bank of the United States (BUS). Indeed, the latter's business had so dwindled in Boston that the branch bank produced, in 1831, only a paltry $18,000 in profits. Thus the real issue of the 1834 bank war in Boston proper was the adequacy of the federal government's new depositories—the Commonwealth and Merchants banks—to manage the government's money as well as the BUS had formerly done.[29] Once the national contraction had ended, therefore, Boston's financial institutions could proceed much as they had done before. It is true that some two thousand Bostonians, following the lead of free-trade advocate Henry Lee and Biddle's protégé, Peter Paul Francis DeGrand, proposed a "Bank of Ten Millions," half of whose capital would be furnished by the state, to supplement the public role the BUS had customarily played. Its supporters argued that only by mingling public and private funds would the capital needed for the transition from an agricultural to a greater "commercial, manufacturing and mechanical" economy be provided.[30] Boston's commercial leaders, however, clung to their preference for privately owned, locally controlled banks. Nor did the state legislature respond any more favorably when it turned down the petition for a new bank.

So strong, in fact, was the commitment of city business to a privately financed, profit-oriented economy that even public regulation of banking was challenged. Some city banks in 1834 and 1835 evaded the state usury law by initiating service charges for loans; others allegedly denied loans to local merchants to cash in on New York's higher interest rates. Merchants, preferring to pay 7 or 8 percent interest rather than suffer the ruin which faced them if they could not secure short-term loans, vigorously protested the commonwealth's 6 percent maximum interest rates and its 1 percent tax on bank capital, which they believed drove local resources southward. Although they could not impose their preferences on the legislature, some Boston banks faced down its investigations and prosecutions for malpractice. It may have been true, as ice dealer Frederic Tudor lamented, that country people had yet to become "sufficiently enlightened to understand [that] by allowing every one to get as much for his money as he can" interest rates would be driven down "by increased competition amongst lenders." But knowledgeable men in town certainly thought they understood. So, though both bank tax and usury laws remained on the books, bankers got 'round them. Pragmatic city values eventually triumphed. Within the year, the legislature rechartered the State Bank, whose original charter it had revoked on grounds of usury.[31] In this, as in rejecting the proposal for a state-subsidized bank of $10 million, the commonwealth endorsed Boston preferences for a privately owned and profit-oriented banking system.

· · ·

If the banking crisis revealed tensions between city and country values, low wages and unemployment sharpened cleavages within the city. And if the 1834 recession pinched businessmen, it clamped still harder on labor. Yet the problems made visible in 1834 had been interwoven in the prosperity which preceded it. In the first five years of the decade, Boston's population grew from 61,400 to 78,600. Probably two out of three of those entering the city were of working age. As many as one out of four was an immigrant. And disproportionately they were male. They joined a labor pool in which 40 to 60 percent supported themselves by manual labor.[32] Even in good times many of them were subject to changing modes of production, to increasing distance between employer and worker, to wages they found inadequate, to long hours and enervating working conditions.

The average family living in an American city in 1830 spent about

$1,000 a year exclusive of the cost of housing. In Boston, bank clerks and bookkeepers earned yearly salaries close to $1,500. By contrast, the standard wage for an unskilled male laborer was $1.00 a day. The most highly skilled journeyman earned no more than $3.50 daily, and most brought home somewhere between $1.25 and $1.75 a day. Women fared still worse. Their most common employment, as seamstresses, seldom paid more than $1.00 or $1.50 a week; the luckiest among them earned $2.50 or $3.00 a week in textile mills and bookbinderies. The social order nonetheless allowed wealthy import merchant William Appleton to complain bitterly that, in mid-decade, the price of labor was wholly out of hand when "journey men Mechanicks get from two to three dollars a day and the girls in the Factories at Lowell get two dollars and a half a week beside their board."[33]

Their relative disadvantage impelled Boston workers to organize. Yet they protested less their wages than their hours. Caught up in a national movement, mechanics and workingmen met in the good times of March 1832 to discuss the ten-hour day. Carpenters, masons, painters, slaters, and shipwrights met separately in craft groups and also united to form a local auxiliary of the New England Association of Farmers, Mechanics and Other Workingmen. If their first goal was "altering the number of hours . . . constituting a day's work," they soon broadened their program when merchants and shipowners broke a ship carpenters' and caulkers' strike and vowed not to employ workers "thus combined." Then at the association meeting in September, Boston workingmen endorsed a platform going well beyond hours, demanding the abolition of imprisonment for debt, the enactment of journeymen's lien laws, and the substitution of free public education for child labor.[34]

Although their goals were, in 1832, largely political, the 1834 crunch produced greater concern for strictly economic issues and reinvigorated support for creating a general trades' union. In January a mechanics' circular proclaimed that the American working class would not fall victim to the "cruel and heartless policy towards the Mechanics" which prevailed in Europe. Later that month a group of workingmen met in the old Common Council Room to address the "difficulties and dissentions, between employers and employed" in Boston. Building on that base, workingmen organized until at the July 4th celebrations they turned out a 2,000-man delegation for the annual city parade and then, at their own meeting, heard an oration on wages and hours. What New England Workingmen's Association spokesman Frederick Robinson proposed to them was no Luddite attack on manufacturing but a pragmatic program to tie wages and hours to consumer demands. Arguing that in good times labor could set "any reasonable price" for its work, Robinson attributed bad times to glutted markets, which left laborers without their "natural and rightful control over the price" for which their work sold.[35]

Traditional in orientation yet sensitive to conservative fears of labor organization, Robinson lambasted municipal court judge Peter O. Thacher. Already in 1832 Thacher had charged a grand jury to investigate the "combinations" of "mechanics, journeymen and apprentices" formed "to raise the price of wages or to diminish the usual number of hours of work." Yet as labor saw it, the bar itself was but "a secret Trades Union of lawyers . . . that has always regulated the price of their own labor, and . . . contrived to limit competition by denying to every one the right of working in their trade. . . ." While Judge Thacher thundered on about "conspiracies . . . indictable at common law," Robinson warned against aristocratic treason to the public. Nonetheless, Thacher shared Robinson's underlying premise that there was an inherent hostility between those "who pass their lives" organizing "insurance companies, manufacturing companies, turnpike, bridge, canal, rail-road, and all other legalized combinations" and those whose "personal labor" provided their "subsistence."[36]

However clearly the lines were drawn, the conflict was largely confined to words. It is true that in the spring of 1835 journeymen stonecutters voted to leave the city rather than work more than ten hours a day. And the following fall, bootmaker journeymen formed a society to maintain, if not to raise, wages. Nonetheless, the trade-union movement lagged in Boston. While strikes occurred in Philadelphia and mobs and riots reputedly disturbed New York "every half hour," "old Tri-Mountain" remained "quiet as a lamb." In the spring of 1836, wharf laborers who attempted to strike for higher wages were subdued "before noon" by the wharf owner.[37]

Whatever the apparent calm, endemic tension between employer and employee marked a partial collapse of the premise that worker and boss shared a common interest and a harmony of purpose sufficient to insure mutual sympathy and fair rewards to each. Former mayor Josiah Quincy might argue that it was Boston capitalists who gave "life and support to the industry of the labouring and mechanic classes." Master printer J. L. Homer might testify that the interests of aspiring journeymen were "identified with those of their employers—that what [was] advantageous to one [was] beneficial to the other." But master mechanics and conservative politicians alike dug in their heels against worker demands for a ten-hour day. Meeting in December 1835, master mechanics from forty-six trades proposed addressing those demands with a counterproposal to change the dinner hour from 1:00 P.M. to noon and thus to increase work time by eliminating the traditional morning beer break which the later dinner hour made necessary. As the old comradery between master and journeyman disappeared, city missionary Joseph Tuckerman saw evidence of its demise in the depersonalization of work relations. Increasingly the laborer was employed "by those, who hardly know his name, who never know whether he is married or unmarried, whether he is working only for himself or for a family. . . ." With an employer who had no thoughts for his employee except about "the service for which he may occasionally be wanted," the old mutuality foundered before the new instrumentality.[38]

• • •

For all the unease which the 1834 banking fracas laid bare, it seemed in hindsight only a "fluctuation." Rich William Appleton, conceding that the "eventful" year of 1834 had brought losses to some commercial men, believed that 1835 dawned on a "country . . . prosperous beyond all calculation." For him the observation was surely true. The following twelve months increased his property by $100,000. And his own well-being reflected the boom tempo to which the city's business danced. Wharves were prosperous. Central Wharf had never returned higher profits. Bank and textile stock prices spiraled upward. The Merrimack Company stock paid 18 percent in 1835. Withdrawals from the Provident Institution for Savings now signaled "success, by which small savings of our depositors" were withdrawn to start new businesses. And seventeen of the city's twenty-eight commercial banks paid dividends of 6 percent or more in 1836.[39]

On Beacon Hill and in the commercial center, "a vast quantity of building" was going on. Indeed, the "pulling down & building up" made it "inconvenient to get through the streets." So evident was urban development that Charleston's *Southern Rose* reported on Boston's physical ebullience: "Houses that many other places would be proud to possess, or be years in building, are pulled down, and palaces rise in their stead in as many months. . . ." From morning to night screeching saws and stuttering hammers echoed to make mechanics in the construction trades the richest of their peers. The very face of the city changed. Hills were leveled, coves became dry land, and wharves extended ever farther into the channel. Prestigious old mansions fell before the juggernaut of progress. Gardiner Greene's Pearl Street house overlooking the waterfront was sold in 1835 for five times the sum he had paid for it in 1795, only to be torn down and replaced by stores and warehouses. The pressure of harborside business construction drove Bostonians across the Common to buy residential land on Beacon Hill, where even in 1833 lots had sold for $3 to $4 a square foot.[40]

With all the relocation, the city's various commercial sections became more homogeneous and specialized. State Street, known also as the Exchange, housed the banking and insurance business. Faneuil Hall and

Quincy Market remained the heart of the food trade. Dry goods dealers clustered along upper Washington Street where it met the North End. And still farther north, on Fulton Street, leather dealers carried on their rank-smelling trade. At the foot of State Street and to the south, new four- and five-storied warehouses abutted the largest wharves. Interspersed among them, the dealers in hardware and textiles sold their vast stores.

Pressed by commercial building, the middling interests and the poor had to move. Pushed out of downtown tenements by soaring rents and property values, tenants were dispersed to new housing on the city's edge or further crowded into already densely occupied buildings in the North End, in streets south of the Common, and along Broad Street as it ran down to South Boston. The Fatherless and Widows' Society warned that a housing crisis loomed over the city in 1836. "While many are basking in the sunshine of prosperity, the overflowing tide of wealth, is threatening to exclude from domestic comfort those who have all the dependence of infancy, without its attractions to win for them sympathy and protection."[41]

That very crisis further spurred land speculation to develop suburban housing and commercial facilities in neighboring Chelsea, little more than a mile away, and on Noddles Island, separated from the North End by only 1,800 feet of water. Here, as in the oozing marshland south of the Common and in South Boston, a mere bridge span from old Boston, visions of mixed-use land development fed dreams of fortunes to be created overnight. Few investors in these schemes owned more than $30,000 of assessed property. Indeed, at mid-decade over half of them had no more than $10,000 of taxable property. They were, in short, a different group from those who reaped textile dividends from $1,000 shares or developed high-priced lots in the central business district.[42] The difference was primarily one of smaller capital and greater derring-do, of opting for quick capital gains rather than diversified investment and steady income.

Typical of city land operations was the Winnisimmet Company. Taking advantage of the regular boat service which had, for more than a century, made commuting between Chelsea and the North End feasible, the company undertook to improve ferry service and develop Chelsea land simultaneously. Somewhat atypically led by a few well-established Boston gentlemen, China merchant Thomas H. Perkins among them, the speculators chartered their corporation, bought out the city franchise for exclusive ferry rights, and purchased the Shurtleff lands and Mr. Williams's farm and ferry slip in Chelsea. Hiring Antonio Domingo's services and sailboat to ply the mile-and-a-quarter run until they could put steam ferries into operation, the directors laid out lots and began building company houses and subsidizing private builders who bought lots. Successful in encouraging settlement by laying out streets at once, donating land for a church and a school, and providing transportation to the city even in off hours, the company made residence attractive to many who worked downtown. And by encouraging factories and building a shipyard they also enhanced local employment opportunities. Thus, even though night service was too costly to continue and the damage done by winter ice ate up potential profits from the ferry operation, the company fared well in its early years. Its land increased in value from six cents per front foot in 1831 to a high of forty-five cents in 1838. And during the decade Chelsea's population grew from 771 to 2,390. Nonetheless Chelsea's distance from Boston—nearly four times as far as Noddles Island—put it at a disadvantage, and after 1838 Winnisimmet's profits declined.[43]

By contrast with the public-spirited aura which surrounded the Winnisimmet, the East Boston Company appeared self-serving from the beginning. Led by William H. Sumner, whose family had owned much of Noddles Island since 1800, the company was incorporated in 1833 to buy and develop what was then no more than farmland. Wheeling and dealing, Sumner and his principal associates (Stephen White and Francis J. Oliver, insurance company and railroad president respectively) issued stock for the capital to buy Sumner family land at very high prices and then had to borrow $6,000 to begin building operations. Losing no time, they turned an old farmhouse into a barracks for construction workers, who erected houses on company lots even before roads were laid out. The island lacked an established ferry, but Sumner and Boston businessmen Ammi Lombard, Daniel G. Brodhead, and Robert Gould Shaw provided for it by chartering the East Boston Wharf Company, which established facilities for various kinds of shipping in addition to commuter service. Within two years Noddles Island was transformed into East Boston, boasting a substantial hotel, a sugar refinery, a cast iron foundry, a shipyard, and an array of stores and shops. Whether or not it was by "hocus pocus," as Frederic Tudor believed, or by "honesty & integrity of dealing," which he very much doubted, Sumner and friends had turned an original issue of 1,300 East Boston Company shares in 1833 into nearly 30,000 by 1841 and had made the island home for many middling-interest and working-men's families.[44]

Both the Winnisimmet and East Boston companies bought and sold solid land; the South Cove Company created land by filling mud flats with earth and gravel stripped from sixty-seven acres in nearby Roxbury and Dorchester. Planned as the terminal for the Boston and Worcester railroad, South Cove was to be the new meeting ground of hinterland trade with long-distance shipping. As important as its landfill, then, was its waterfront, created south of the old wharves which lined Boston's eastern flank. Within seven years after its 1833 charter had granted it the right to hold as much as $1 million in real estate, the South Cove Corporation had filled in some fifty-six acres of Boston Bay with about 1.5 million cubic yards of earth. Its 53,000 square feet of wharf were secured by 4,900 tons of stone ballast, which was held in by 3.5 square rods of Quincy granite to form a 380-foot-long seawall. On its dry land, in addition to passenger station, freight depot, and warehouses, were a major hotel, shops, stores, professional offices, and small houses. Even by 1836 its total assets approached $700,000; and in its first three years, before most of its major facilities were in place, it had generated profits of $168,000—an average annual return of over 8 percent.[45]

Still farther south, and as dependent on the newly built free bridge as the Winnisimmet and East Boston ventures were on ferries and the South Cove on the railroad, was South Boston. There a group of Democratic politicians, headed by David Henshaw, collector of the port of Boston, chartered the Mount Washington Association to develop a highlands resort. There too, the Boston Wharf Company was at work by 1836.[46] Collectively less successful than the other land companies—the Mount Washington Association (better known as the Warren Associates) failed in a major scandal in 1838—the South Boston projects nonetheless furthered that area's emergence as an industrial area manufacturing iron, chain, glass, pottery, and similar goods.

• • •

Thus did Boston grow physically. Thus did her property and prosperity increase. Thus did her population swell as those who arrived to seek new starts more than replaced those who left with ambitions unsatisfied. Fluctuations in fortune, movement within the city, out-migration as well as in-migration were all part of Boston's evolution. For those who achieved their goals, who made the economic decisions, who determined the city's course, the years from 1830 to 1837 were good indeed. Men on the make as well as those of the old order acquired and increased their power and wealth.

Of those who directed the city's corporations at mid-decade, more than half paid taxes on less than $30,000 worth of property, even after their directorships had expanded their resources for gaining wealth. On the other hand, an almost equal number could count themselves rich—and nearly 10 percent would rank as millionaires if their wealth, which reached six figures in 1836, were translated into late-twentieth-century currency. Yet these wielders of wealth and economic power were not necessarily men of old families and distinguished social connections. Fewer than a quarter of all corporate directors belonged to the clubs and churches or shared the educational and occupational patterns which together marked upper-class standing. What did characterize them as a group was their dedication to profitable economic activity. They seldom acted visibly in the public sector. Indeed, over 70 percent of them wielded no direct political power and only 4 percent participated notably in city and state government.[47] In Boston, it was clear that the driving power behind the city's growth was overwhelmingly private. Expecting little from the public sector beyond acts of incorporation, Boston's economic leaders—be they directors or independent merchants and manufacturers—relied on entrepreneurial skills and private capital to guide and finance urban development.

Moreover, while Bostonians did invest in far-distant land speculations like the New England Mississippi Land Company, the Galveston Bay and Texas Land Company, and the Brunswick, Georgia, Canal Company, most of their exported capital returned more than individual dividends to the city. Textile manufacturing fed coastal and foreign shipping; railroads brought products from the hinterlands for exchange within the city. Private investments largely tallied with the needs of Boston's economy. Without an explicit or public policy, its economic leaders utilized the city's material resources and its human skills as they also integrated a manufacturing hinterland with a Boston which remained primarily a commercial city. Thus they shaped and profited from Boston's boom years.

4

Charleston's Dream of Prosperity

If Boston's boom years were characterized by the pragmatic pursuit of private profit, Charleston's drive to revive her economy was marked by a public rhetoric of growth and a private practice conducive to stasis. Her time pulsed not to the frenetic beat of Boston progress but to the slow rhythm of agricultural seasons. In October, when the harvest peaked and mosquito-killing frost made the city safe from fevers, the year began. Country shoppers flocked into King Street to stock rural stores and make individual purchases. Boats carrying six bales, or six hundred, came down the rivers and up the coast bringing short- and long-staple cotton to city docks. Schooners laden with rough rice destined for Charleston mills and cleaned rice ready for sale streamed into Charleston harbor from Georgia and Carolina tidal lowlands. Yet shipping, like the harvest, depended on nature, on rain sufficient to fill shallow streams with enough water to float cotton and rice to market. Droughts could delay shipments for weeks. But once the streams were full, commerce bustled until Christmas when, once again, business slowed almost to summer lethargy. That, however, was only the pause preceding the trading year's peak.

From January through April, ocean-going vessels jammed the harbor, their captains competing for freights. If their ships were to make two successive high-profit runs to Liverpool or Havre, they had to be loaded and off by mid-January to return, at the latest, by mid-April for a second cargo. Under such pressures, factors bargained for low rates when freights were short; captains charged what the market would bear when bales towered high on the wharves or when individual shippers lusted for the high prices the first European deliveries usually brought. In these months, business and profit reigned supreme.

By June, however, the city waterfront languished. Coastal packets which, in winter, touched weekly or biweekly ran biweekly and monthly schedules in the summer. Occasional ships, loaded with rice for the Caribbean trade, sailed out of a nearly empty harbor to which only pleasure and fishing boats gave life between June and September. And, when the harbor emptied, so did the city. Agents and traders unacclimated to Carolina summers fled the steamy heat and fevers. Merchants and shopkeepers, be they native or stranger, combined pleasure with business on trips to the North or Europe to buy stock for the coming season.

Thus for Charlestonians Boston's time was foreign, her dedication to constant activity perverse. It was not that they did not comprehend; they simply rejected. Sometimes they envied the northern city's forward thrust, her progressive energy. But in charting their own course they looked backward to an imperial trade and colonial greatness long gone. And that very yearning, that remembrance of things past, constricted their calculations for the future and gave them a dreamlike quality.

• • •

Charleston's immediate economic difficulties had begun in 1824–1825. In that brief period, soaring cotton prices had raised hopes higher than they had been since the 1819 depression had smothered the commercial revival which followed the War of 1812. Yet that precipitate rise in prosperity only made the subsequent decade of hard times more difficult to bear. Seeking a way out of defeated hopes and economic frustration, Charleston and the state of which she was part organized a prolonged attack on the new national tariffs which, they believed, sacrificed the agricultural and commercial prosperity of the South to protect newly established manufacturers in the Northeast.

It was true that after 1825, when the tariff of 1824 had gone into effect, Charleston's profits from the trade in domestic produce plummeted. Not until 1834 did her exports to the North and Europe equal the $11 million mark which her 1818 and 1825 records had set. No matter how much cotton and rice Charleston shipped out, low prices kept her annual sales of domestic produce between $6 and $8.5 million. And her imports plunged equally, not regaining their 1825–1826 levels until 1835 and never regaining the proportional share of the nation's total imports which they had previously enjoyed.[1]

The priorities of Charlestonians, furthermore, only worsened the city's economic plight. More likely than Bostonians to think in terms of community coherence than of individual success, more ready than their northern counterparts to engage government in economic enterprise, more often placing the drama of the public political forum above the demands of countinghouse and workplace, Charlestonians, with remarkable southern vigor and no trace of Yankee prudence, diverted their commercial energies into four long years of numbing political battle to attempt to nullify the tariffs of 1828 and 1832. In so doing, they discouraged innovative private ventures at the very time when most of the United States experienced increasing prosperity. Whether it was the tariff itself or the political controversy it engendered that isolated the Carolina economy was subject to dispute. Senator-planter George McDuffie attributed Charleston's economic "ruins" to the "shackles of unconstitutional restriction." Visiting journalist Anne Royall laughed "to hear these South Carolinians making such a noise about the Tariff. . . . If they had all the trade in the world at this moment, the Yankees would seize it all in less than a year."[2]

While her economy languished during the years of the nullification controversy, Charleston's press chronicled commercial news to serve partisan purposes. The *Mercury,* nullifier to the core, insisted, even at the peak of political crisis, that trade in agricultural staples throve along the wharves. The Unionist *Courier* found in that feverish activity only a flurry of quick sales before political disaster. Whatever its editorial comments, however, each paper painted a uniformly gloomy picture in its news columns. It is true that the *Courier* had hailed the *Henry Ewbank*'s launching in 1832, when such events had become a rarity in the seaport city, as a sign "that Charleston [was] about to awake from her lethargy." But the good omen reversed itself in subsequent reports that the *Ewbank* was so damaged by gale winds on its first voyage that it had to be sold for scrap only eight months after its launching. Similarly, press reports of a new sugar refinery in 1832 barely covered the ugly reality that it was no more than a reorganization of a refinery which had failed. Even the enthusiastic advertisement that, politics and rumor notwithstanding, some two dozen local merchants intended "to pursue [their] business . . ." and "meet the demands of our Customers as fully, and as satisfactorily as heretofore" rang hollow with the appended qualification "unless prevented by causes not now anticipated."[3]

Indeed, efforts to put a good face on things were sparse. More usual than optimistic projections were reports that real estate prices were tumbling, that stores and houses stood empty. Population diminished. Merchants were "disheartened." Trade flagged until the "spirit of commercial enterprize was completely checked." From 1830 onward the *Courier* elaborated Charlestonians' despair at the "alarming decline of that prosperity which in times past had animated and cheered their industry. . . ." By January 1833, when sane men feared impending civil war, the firm of Pitray & Viel cautioned against doing business in the "present critical & alarming situation of public affairs." The *City Gazette* reported that banks feared to lend money because of the revolutionary state of things. And Brown Brothers' financial agent, James Adger, refused to take on any consignments "at the present moment."[4] Thus did politicizing her economic plight serve Charleston's commerce.

• • •

What had set Carolinians against protective tariffs was their reluctance to engage in manufacturing. Why they should have rejected an industry utilizing local agricultural produce while Massachusetts built a textile empire on the southern staple was a matter of economics as well as culture. Plantation owners believed that cotton and rice planting paid them well. In the early 1830s low-country rice planters reported 8 percent average returns on investment above and beyond maintaining themselves and their families. Along the Savannah River, where Langdon Cheves, James Petigru, and James Hamilton all planted, profits ran as high as 12 percent. In the mid-1830s Petigru's rice operations more than doubled his already handsome annual income of $6,000 in legal fees. On up-country cotton plantations, where profits were less, owners were either satisfied or moved their increasingly valuable labor force west to cultivate new, more productive land in Georgia, Alabama, and the Southwest. Moreover, for Charleston's merchants, professionals, and other potential capitalists, manufacturing sparked no such enthusiasm as it did for their Boston equivalents because planting was not only profitable, planting was socially preferable.[5]

There was, nonetheless, significant mechanic-manufacturing in Charleston. Largest in scale were the rice mills. Before 1800, rice had customarily been threshed at plantation mills, and much still was. In 1801, however, Jonathan Lucas and his son had begun to centralize rice processing, first in tidal-powered mills and, by 1817, in steam-powered operations in Charleston. By the early 1820s Jonathan II and his chief competitor, Governor Thomas Bennett, each created extensive milling empires on the upper Ashley, which were ultimately pooled sometime after the marriage of Bennett's daughter to Jonathan III. Even together theirs was not a monopoly, for there were other mills, among them Chisholm's at the west end of Tradd Street and Norton and Carroll's on Gadsden's Cooper River wharf. But these were small and relatively unstable businesses. Chisolm's mill, which opened in 1830, sold out in 1836; Gadsden's wharf mill passed through at least three owners in five years. Not surprisingly then, Bennett and Lucas—whether separately or together—milled about 70 percent of the rough rice brought into Charleston for sale.[6]

With all their potential for dominance, however, Charleston's rice mills did not keep up with the trade. Hampered by city fire restrictions enacted in the wake of past fires, entrepreneurs were limited to locating their steam-powered machinery in marshland or outside city limits. Planters denounced city millers for charging high rates and suspected them of short-weighing as well. And, over time, Charleston's rice shipments to other American and foreign ports were less likely to have been milled in the city.[7] Neither city nor hinterland proved able to build a strong manufacturing base on Carolina's two great staples.

Not only did large-scale manufacturing fail to grow, the mechanic trades languished as well. Those mechanics who flourished were concentrated in the construction trades or the production of consumer goods such as carriages. Iron foundries, sawmills, sugar refineries, and machine shops were generally short-lived. Even shipbuilding in this seaport city so abundantly supplied with local lumber did not develop significantly. Thomas Bennett, his son, and his son-in-law operated a viable shipyard which produced vessels largely for their own shipping business.[8] Of the four other notable shipbuilders, three—William Bird, James Marsh, and James Poyas—rather than enlarging or diversifying their businesses drained their profits to buy plantation land at various times during the 1830s.

The extensive slaveholdings of these millers and shipbuilders illustrated another specter haunting the mechanic-manufacturing syndrome of Charleston. Of eight master shipwrights in the city in 1833, each owned between seven and nineteen slave carpenters but employed collectively only a total of twenty white carpenters and another twenty-seven white journeymen. The result, as Poyas himself testified, was that "many . . . young mechanics have left Charleston to seek employment elsewhere." Doubtless the situation was no different in the rice mills, where, in 1830, Bennett employed 90 slaves and Lucas 107.[9]

Moreover, those white mechanics who stayed in the city confronted a series of paradoxes. On the one hand, it was generally agreed that wages paid white labor were higher in the South than in the North—a situation, it was also said, which forced up local prices. Yet commodity price indices do not support that contention. Rather, the higher wages demanded by white mechanics to differentiate them from black workers both resulted in a clear preference for slave and free Negro workers in Charleston and made white labor costs there higher than they were in the North. Where, for instance, a slave ship carpenter hired out for $1.50 a day to do work for which a white man was paid $2, and where white blacksmiths earned $7 to $10 a week while black men with similar skills could be had for $3 to $3.50, white journeymen were at a clear disadvantage. Yet if they could survive long enough to employ black craftsmen themselves or to accumulate capital sufficient to buy slave artisans, they profited from the double wage standard. Not surprisingly, master mechanics were tempted, even when prices were as high as $1,000 for a prime skilled worker, to make an investment on which a comfortable annual return of at least 10 percent could reasonably be anticipated.[10]

Whatever effect this paradox had on the mechanic arts in Charleston, it was further distorted by the declining labor pool of both whites and blacks. A perceived white migration out of the city during the early 1830s was paralleled by a steady decline in the slave population, which between 1828 and 1834 diminished by 800. Furthermore, a quarter of the free black population also abandoned the city at the same time, perhaps as a response to the deliberate wooing of white labor during the nullification controversy.[11]

The net result, however, was not ambiguous. All over the city slaves worked as painters, carpenters, bricklayers, wheelwrights, millwrights, and coopers to an extent which made at least one visitor believe "almost the whole of the working population are Negroes." Without question, white mechanics resented the reality which lay behind this appearance. Calling for yet higher taxes on owners who hired out slave artisans, they appealed to their fellow citizens to save them from wage competition with black workers.[12] All told, differential wage rates—black and white, North and South—discouraged both artisanal and industrial manufacturing. And, as a result, Charleston's prosperity was impeded by an unattractive labor market and negative population growth.

• • •

Nonetheless, in the spring of 1833, when the worst of the political crisis had passed, the economy began to look up. The new compromise tariff promised a progressive lowering of duties while the state's retreat from nullification promised public stability. By fall the *Courier* was announcing that, in spite of a shaky cotton market, business was good in the best fall trading season the city had enjoyed in "many years." "Auspicious activity," Unionist Richard Yeadon called it. Yet no sooner had Charleston's economy emerged from a locally induced political crisis than a punishing national one struck. In February 1834, John Kirkpatrick & Company reported that President Jackson's war against Nicholas Biddle and his bank had created a "distress for money so great" that cotton sales were in disarray.[13]

Happily, as in Boston, that distress was short-lived, and little more than a year after Jackson's controversy with South Carolina had been resolved, the impact of his war with the Bank of the United States was mitigated. Only two months after Kirkpatrick's lament, Yankeephile Charles Fraser assured Boston's Robert Winthrop that business in Charleston was normal, credit good, money available. The city had weathered the storm, albeit only weeks before the inevitable summer lethargy set in. Even so, the trading season closed with real estate prices up a third to a half, every store on King Street occupied, and plans afoot to open several new and "extensive Mercantile Houses" in the fall. Surely East Bay would soon resemble New York's Pearl Street, as a revived King Street already did Broadway.[14]

That Charleston was on the way to recovery—even growth—upcountry merchants attested when they came to town for their fall purchases. "[S]tocks of goods [could now] be purchased in Charleston so low, and on such favorable terms" that buying trips to the North were superfluous. During the next three years, income produced by commercial sales and professional practice increased 11 to 14 percent a year; the value of commodities available for sale rose 15 to 18 percent a year. And Charleston's prosperity increased so much faster than the rest of the state's that her proportion of state taxes rose from 18 percent of the total in 1834 to 22 percent in 1837. A mood of ebullience now gripped the city as her citizens ventured on a massive pursuit of profit. "Lawyers, Physicians, and even Clergymen, abandoned the pulpit, the lancet, and the bar, for the Ledger and Day Book" in a frenzy which "for a brief period, made our merchants, like those of Genoa, princes, and inflated every broker into a millionaire. . . ." In 1836 "the old City" was more crowded "than for the last 20 years" as King Street teemed with shoppers and the harbor with ships.[15]

Grasping for their share of the new prosperity, Charleston's five banks, in addition to her branch of the Bank of the United States (BUS), were hard pressed to meet rapidly increasing needs. All four private banks—the Union, State, Planters and Mechanics, and Bank of South Carolina—had been founded before the War of 1812. Each had a capital of $1 million in shares ranging from $25 to $100 face value. So much were they the handmaidens of commercial interests that even the Planters and Mechanics, despite its name, never had more than one planter and one mechanic on its board of directors at any time from 1828 to 1838.[16] Like the other three private banks, its board was dominated by merchants and traders.

The fifth bank was the publicly owned Bank of the State of South Carolina. Established in 1813 when the state government withdrew its funds from the State Bank, the Bank of the State was designed to serve agricultural interests.[17] Yet even it was directed by a publicly appointed board which, throughout the 1830s, was between 50 and 75 percent mercantile in primary occupation.

However well-established and commercially oriented these state chartered banks were, Charleston could ill afford to lose her sixth major financial institution to Jackson's war against Biddle. On this there was consensus, even though the BUS depository had been a bastion of Unionist sentiment during the nullification crisis. Consequently, in a mystifying series of political moves nullifier leaders undertook to replace the depository with a new bank designed to absorb its former business and responsibilities. At their behest, in December 1834 the state legislature chartered the Bank of Charleston, capitalized at $2 million. It was to be twice the size of any South Carolina bank then in existence and had the additional advantage of being permitted to double that capital at its own pleasure. Its position was still further strengthened by its rapidly developing ties with the national bank. Because, as former governor Robert Hayne wrote Nicholas Biddle, the new bank was "designed to supply the vacuum which will be created by the discontinuance of your Branch," Hayne invited Biddle to invest the old depository's share of BUS capital in the new venture.[18]

Biddle played an active role in the subsequent speculative firestorm, and the BUS branch, like every other bank in Charleston, authorized unlimited loans to those who sought funds to subscribe for Bank of Charleston stock. Contracting for ten times as many shares as they actually anticipated buying, individual investors—including lawyer-politician Isaac Holmes, who subscribed for 4,000 shares, or one-fifth of the entire authorized stock of $2 million—borrowed up to $500,000. The Bank of the State pledged its entire capital to subscribe, in its own name, for 18,000 shares. For insiders who sold short the rewards were sweet. Biddle and the BUS cleared $20,000 on their speculation; the Bank of the State, $34,000.[19]

Characteristic of Charleston, however, this flurry was as much political as financial. Behind the mania which produced subscriptions for 894,000 shares when only 20,000 were available lay the competition for the new bank's control. Vying for the presidency were two former governors of the state and intendents of the city. One was Thomas Bennett, ardent Unionist and conservative entrepreneur; the other, James Hamilton, arch-nullifier and flashy politician.[20] With more supporters willing to overbid for stock, Hamilton won out. Without delay, he opened the new bank in the handsome depository building it had purchased from the BUS and, from the president's office, courted Nicholas Biddle. Within months the Bank of Charleston had not only assumed most of the branch bank's local business but was acting as agent for the Philadelphia bank. And, with the talent for intrigue which had shaped his political rise, Hamilton simultaneously induced the Jackson administration to deposit federal funds in the Bank of Charleston, which thereby replaced the Planters and Mechanics Bank as the city's "pet bank."[21]

Subsequent efforts by former directors of the depository to reopen a distinctive BUS agency in the city failed, because Charleston's largest and most conservative businessmen had moved their business to the Bank of

Charleston. Soon it was not only the city's largest but her strongest bank. And that very fact is a commentary on the differing economic styles of Charleston and Boston. In the northern city, the older banks provided the community's principal financial control as they also attracted the most prestigious businessmen to their boards of directors. New banks were smaller and directed primarily by aspiring entrepreneurs who used their position and access to capital to forward their rise into the established business elite. In the southern city, by contrast, the stripling Bank of Charleston was governed by directors half of whom were either wealthy or already accustomed to wielding substantial economic power or both.[22] This new bank, unlike its Boston equivalents, rarely provided access to economic power for new men on the make nor was its vast capital (larger even than that of Boston's State Bank) primarily dedicated to the needs of new and small businessmen.

• • •

If the most dramatic sign of a new prosperity was the speculative enthusiasm which drove men like Dr. Samuel Dickson and lawyer Isaac Holmes into business ventures in which they had little previous experience, its most reliable indicators were the growth rates of trade and commerce and the development of facilities to serve them. The florid language of wishful thinking which appeared constantly in the local press attested to a popular consensus that Charleston's economic woes had resulted from the "want of a direct commerce with Europe." That trade's near-demise in the panic of 1819 had, it was commonly believed, triggered the city's decline throughout the 1820s, allowing northern merchants to usurp the shipping and importing business and skim off profits legitimately belonging to the South. Why should not Charleston ships carry Carolina cotton directly to Liverpool and the British textile industry? And why, asked "Go Ahead," "Importer," and "Friend of Improvement," should their stores not be stocked with commodities shipped directly from Europe? They exhorted local agents to scour European markets for bargains and to ship them home directly on locally owned ships. To attract buyers for these goods, "Solon" proposed a wide-ranging plan to beautify the city and construct facilities to serve the visitors and merchants from the southern interior who would thus be lured into town. Rejecting the centrality of assured profits in attracting capital, he sought support by appealing to "that glorious disposition which is willing to risk something for the welfare of our city." Charlestonians, motivated by pride and patriotism, would build a new hotel, develop roads, improve the harbor, and provide entertainment for visitors. In rhetoric as in substance, "Solon's" appeal drew no line between public and private interests. All the plans for civic development echoed common nullifier assumptions: that Charleston was unnecessarily tributary to another port, and that political action was necessary for economic growth.[23]

Within this context, projections for a Charleston-Liverpool shipping company emerged. Outsiders differed about the wisdom of the direct transatlantic line it proposed. Baltimore's Brown Brothers, shrewd bankers with a strong interest in Charleston commerce, once believed the line could compete successfully against similar service via New York. On the other hand, reported William Ogilby, British consul in Charleston, northern cities' proximity to supplies of food and manufactures gave them a clear advantage and justified the familiar triangular trade routes. A Boston ship, Ogilby concluded, "can lay in all her stores at home[,] come to Charleston and take on board a cargo of cotton or Rice for Liverpool and there obtain a freight to return to her own port where she can be reprovisioned for a *new* voyage at a cheap rate, and free of all commissions and . . . the freight[s], which a ship provisioner at Charleston would be obliged to pay on most of her supplies."[24]

The records of actual trade from 1832 to 1838 support Ogilby's analysis. Charleston's imports, it is true, doubled in those prosperous years. Proportionately more of them arrived in American rather than in foreign-registered vessels. But most of that increase was brought by northern-owned ships, since the increase in Charleston-owned tonnage suitable for foreign trade could not possibly accommodate such growth, while the number of northern ships calling at Charleston increased markedly during those six years.[25]

If Charleston's dreams of a thriving system of direct imports were only minimally fulfilled, her exports of cotton and rice nevertheless soared, topping $10 million annually from 1833 to 1839. For five successive years total sales surpassed even the frenetic heights reached in the fabulous winter of 1824–1825—and it was on the price paid for cotton rather than the number of bales handled that factors made their 2.5 percent commissions. But Charleston's commerce in staples, even at its best, was only holding its own. Her share of the nation's rapidly increasing trade in short-staple cotton actually fell from 28 percent of national production in 1824 to 18 percent in 1830 to only 16 percent in the 1837–1838 peak season. It was only her continued monopoly of the highly valued but limited supply of long-staple which gave her cotton exports their special edge.[26]

What changed most visibly in the staples trade from the mid-1820s to the mid-1830s was its location within the city. Traditionally, upland cotton had been traded along King Street, where heavy wagons piled high with bulky round bales had lumbered in from the country. Here in the city's northwestern reaches the cotton trade had its roots. Here young men eager to make their fortunes as factors had started their businesses in the boom years after the War of 1812—Ker Boyce from a poor farm in the Newberry district, or Henry Gourdin with the resources of a Georgetown planting family behind him.[27]

By 1830 all that was changing. Shallow boats suited to navigating inland waterways increasingly brought upland cotton directly to Cooper River wharves, where Sea Island cotton had always landed. Moreover, predictions were rife that, within a few years, a railroad would eliminate the wagon trade altogether. As transportation changes reshaped the trade, factors moved their warehouses and counting rooms across the city to East Bay, leaving King increasingly to the wholesalers who supplied upcountry storekeepers with their stock-in-trade and to the retailers who sold dry goods, hardware, and sundries to local residents and fashionable visitors alike. Although that shift occurred largely in prosperous times, King Street traders nonetheless feared decline, envied public efforts to develop the waterfront, competed for city funds to improve streets, and acted out the frictions between those who dealt primarily in manufactured goods from the North and those whose chief livelihood was tied to the staples trade.[28]

• • •

Charleston's venture on "an age of improvement" began, nonetheless, with general agreement that it was "high time it should be so." Visiting Yankee cleric Samuel Jackson had observed during his 1832 visit that houses were "dingy" and there were "[n]o new buildings, no appearance of thrift & enterprise; everything [wore] the aspect of age & decay." Swedish traveler Carl Arfwedson agreed that the city looked "old and dilapidated." Still more telling, however, was an 1834 survey by the local historical committee which testified to the city's limited residential and business buildings. More than 30,000 residents within city limits lived in just over 3,200 houses—albeit many had separate "kitchens inhabited by servants." The business districts contained an additional 226 stores to accommodate the trade not carried on directly from residences. Housing, already in short supply, was the next year further reduced by fire. In February and June 1835 the mechanics' shops and modest houses of the third ward were swept by fires which burned over a hundred buildings and uncounted outbuildings.[29]

Coming just after the 1834 banking crisis had been resolved, however, those fires actually spurred plans for economic recovery. Almost before the ashes had cooled, dreams of urban renewal beguiled visionaries who anticipated a commercial utopia. To replace tawdry rookeries incinerated by the fires which had leveled Philadelphia Alley and Cock Lane, an oriental bazaar was proposed; and along burned-out Ellery Street, an arcade "on which [would] open the stores of taste and fashion." Lots leveled on Meeting Street could be pooled into a site for a "great and commodious hotel," while Pinckney Street would become a showplace of "ornamental and comfortable habitations." If this monumental transfiguration was not, in fact, achieved, there was significant new building. Within a year of the fire, five new stores were under construction at the corner of Market and State streets, and elsewhere other new business blocks were going up fast.[30] Throughout the third ward new houses appeared and old ones were refurbished. And simply to beautify the city, the facade of City Hall was restored and the Battery rebuilt so as to permit its transformation into a handsome city park.

The gratification for some was simply that "our city looks quite smart again." To others this resurgence presented a carnival of speculation. Cooper Jacob Schirmer reported the most extreme real estate transactions in April 1836, in which prices of land and houses jumped as much as 25 and 50 percent between morning sale and afternoon resale. They were indicative of a soaring market. The Godard house and Ravenel's tenements, both on the Bay, sold for previously unthinkable amounts. Lawyer, planter, and now banker James Hamilton had already bought Crafts' wharf for $46,500 and begun his career as merchant and factor. Ker Boyce, who had moved his factorage business from King Street, purchased Kiddell's wharf for $85,500 and had money left to extend the pier even farther out into the channel. Isaac Holmes snapped up Mey's wharf for a reported $35,000, and some dozen men pooled resources to buy Chisolm's wharf for $100,000. Few stood so aloof as wily James Adger, who, despite rumors that he had acquired an interest in Hamilton's wharf, waited to buy his wharf until the speculative bubble had burst.[31]

Occasionally visionary plan and profit-oriented speculation intersected, as they did in plans for a new hotel, a new theater, and a totally new commercial street. In regard to a hotel, there had long been agreement that the city needed more and better facilities for visitors. Most available accommodations were marginal, some intolerable. One of the biggest and best, the Planters Hotel near East Bay, offered an appallingly "filthy" bedchamber to at least one guest. Another traveler was better satisfied with Mrs. Johnson's small, old-fashioned, and remote hotel on King Street, but even he complained of swarms of mosquitoes, which sang like a teakettle in his bedroom. Seeing the demand, Angus Stewart sold his coffeehouse and opened the Carolina Hotel in several adjacent Broad Street buildings formerly used by the Fellowship Society. But in October 1835, even before this extensive hotel had been fully remodeled, it was severely damaged by fire. And the well-endowed Hibernian Society, which had seriously considered building a hotel, concluded late in the same year that its needs would be better served by a "Beautiful Ionic Temple" only large enough for a meeting hall.[32]

Thus the prospects for a major hotel seemed bright indeed. Among the Charleston Hotel Company's first directors were James Hamilton and Isaac Holmes, who had both participated in the spectacular creation of the Bank of Charleston. Its president was Alexander Black, active in promoting the Charleston-to-Hamburg railroad and the major force behind developing real estate in the newly created Princes Street. Captitalized at $150,000 in $1,000 shares, the company was committed to building not only a hotel at the corner of Meeting and Pearl streets but a range of wholesale stores and attached warehouses along Pearl to expand the growing East Bay business area.[33]

Despite the flurry of construction and land speculation, the city's actual territory increased almost not at all. It is true that minimal landfill occurred along the Ashley River marshes. At the western ends of Tradd and Broad streets, new sites were created for steam-powered operations on marshy locations, as required by the city's severe restrictions on this potential fire hazard. Farther out, landfill along Rutledge and Montague streets provided lots for new mansions. But these hardly paralleled Boston's growth. Charleston failed entirely to tie its minimally expanding transportation system to the creation of new real estate. Because it barred the Hamburg railroad from entering the city proper, it excluded the reciprocal interchange which made Boston's South Cove venture so profitable. Because its one bridge company failed to do more than operate a single ferry, Charleston remained the virtually insular city it had always been. The economic diversity which fed Boston's physical expansion throughout the 1830s remained a stranger to the southern city.

So it was that, while Charleston strove for economic growth, the values which shaped her culture and society produced a different entrepreneurial style from that of Boston. Fewer than half of the Charlestonians who wielded economic power in the ten years between 1828 and 1838 were steeped as merchants in the world of commerce. Over a third of them were planters and professionals; a quarter were as accustomed to wielding political as economic power; half viewed the world through the prism of high social status.[34] In all these ways they differed from Boston's economic decision-makers, who were but minimally oriented to negotiating political solutions and only slightly more attuned to the restraints imposed on self-conscious members of a socially defined upper class. Far more than Bostonians, Charlestonians were willing to conduct their business affairs in public meetings; far less were they willing to limit their projects to the demands of profitability or their imaginations to commercial development. Neither did their city have an economic structure able to offer venturesome but unknown men outlets for their business shrewdness, such as Boston's many new banks and small corporations offered that city's ambitious young men. Finally, when Charleston sought the support of small entrepreneurs to fulfill her dream of urban growth—as in the building of the South Carolina railroad—her leaders looked as much to the political process as to the economic.

And she suffered accordingly.

5

Hub and Hinge

Nowhere did Boston's and Charleston's economic styles diverge more sharply than in developing their transportation systems. Each city had long appreciated the value of the coastal and oceanic shipping which enlivened her port. Each grasped the potential which steam-powered railroads promised. Yet in applying these perceptions, Boston developed a complex network while Charleston pursued a simpler model. Preoccupied with the benefits of a direct trade with Europe in which southern staples would be exchanged for products manufactured abroad, Charleston pursued, in a publicly subsidized western railroad and an eastward shipping line, the means to expand her function as a hinged tollgate through which imports passed in one direction and exports in the other. Thus would the city revive the thriving commerce of her colonial days.

Charleston's efforts, therefore, had to be double-edged. In addition to constructing a railroad, she had to rebuild her fleet, which had so declined that, in 1831, the *Mercury* mourned the sale of the last locally owned ship to "strangers." Her harbor, crowded though it was each winter, was filled with "northern or foreign ships," which monopolized both interregional and transatlantic trade.[1] And until 1834 even the regular packets—whether sail or steam—which brought commercial news as well as passengers and low-bulk freight from New York, New Orleans, Boston, Philadelphia, and Baltimore were entirely owned and controlled at the other end of the run.

There were sound reasons for Boston's General H. A. S. Dearborn's belief that "[n]avigation is a different business from planting & Philadelphia N. York & N. England can do it best." The South lacked the saltwater farms, the fisheries, and the independent coastal shipping which, from

Maine to Long Island, were a training ground for skilled mariners and sea captains. And although shippers in every port complained that too few Americans would ship before the mast, common sailors were in still shorter supply in Charleston than in more northerly ports. Crews often could be gathered there only by costly collusion with boardinghouse landlords who, for a fee, delivered drugged or drunken seamen. State law required that out-of-state black seamen be jailed during their vessel's stay in South Carolina. And harbor pilots, so captains and shipping agents complained, held vessels captive to favoritism and special fees for navigating a harbor whose tricky winds and shifting bar excluded ships drawing more than sixteen feet and accommodated those of more than twelve feet draft only at or near high tide.[2]

Not surprisingly, oiling Charleston's seaward hinge to encourage direct trade with Europe proved troublesome. In 1833 city merchants did provide a steam towboat to free loaded vessels from their customary long waits for the coincidence of good winds and high tide which they needed to cross the bar. The next year Charlestonians began investing in locally sponsored steam packet ventures linking their city to Norfolk, Philadelphia, and Savannah. And in 1835, the Charleston and Liverpool Line Packet Company was chartered to initiate a locally owned transatlantic shipping firm with as many as five vessels.

This major effort to achieve the eastward swing of her hinge function embodied as well a second major component of the city's distinctive political economy. A private corporation, the Charleston and Liverpool Line was chartered by ten men, four of whom either had been or would be state governors. Just how important the political connection was the Act of Incorporation made clear. The company was granted a special five-year privilege by the state exempting merchandise imported in its vessels from all taxes on commercial stock in trade.[3]

Behind all these activities lay still another understanding, that Charleston was satellite to New York City. Her imports and her exports were transshipped there for Gotham's gain, her premiums on insurance and her interest on loans were paid there as northern profits. But control of her own economic life demanded the impossible: the markets of a populated hinterland and a trade in products more diverse than Carolina could offer.

The same physical and economic realities which limited Charleston's shipping potential also shaped her railroad venture. Her agricultural hinterland promised it only one major cargo—cotton. The paucity of manufacturing throughout Carolina limited the demand for two-way transportation of raw materials and finished products as it also restricted Charleston's potential to become a center for diversified regional marketing. Indeed, proponents of railroad development often promoted the use of steam power for transportation as a means to avoid industrialization. By importing goods produced outside the region more cheaply than they could be manufactured at home, Southerners could remain free from the necessity to "drive the shuttle and watch the piston in foetid atmospheres [,] stunning noises, and cheerless cells." Consequently, proposals for a complex railroad network did not appeal to Charleston railroad promoters, because interior towns had few distinctive products to trade among themselves. Although planters and inland factors jockeyed for conveniently situated branch lines on which to ship cotton, the only meaningful debate about routing centered on whether a single long-distance western railroad line should lead toward Georgia or Tennessee.[4] Either route would take it through sparsely populated areas of few villages, fewer towns, many plantations, and more farms. All argument turned back upon one thing: cotton. And when it was decided to build the line to Hamburg, the principal justification came down to diverting Savannah's cotton trade to Charleston.

. . .

When the South Carolina Canal and Rail Road Company was chartered in 1827, Carolinians had had little experience with privately owned and profit-oriented transportation systems. Their toll roads and most of their canals had been publicly funded. The state's major private venture was the canal, which, when it had opened in 1800, had indeed shifted the valuable Santee cotton trade from Georgetown to Charleston but had never proved profitable to investors, who received at most a 3 percent annual return on their capital. Its directors were predominantly wealthy men, and they profited indirectly from the service the Santee Canal provided them as planters and merchants rather than directly as investors.[5]

The stage was thus set for Charleston to justify the South Carolina Canal and Rail Road Company as a civic project, designed primarily to generate mercantile profits by stimulating commerce in the city rather than to produce dividends for investors. So much was it a device to fill Charleston's "deserted warehouses" that when railroad stock first went on sale, not a single subscriber was to be found either at Hamburg, the line's terminus, or at Columbia, the state capital, or at Camden, a major center of inland cotton trade. Indeed, even in Charleston it took six months to secure subscriptions for the 6,000-share minimum capitalization required to organize the company. Nonetheless, corporate reports and the public press retained the company's initial appeal to civic responsibility. Chiding Carolinians for their "entire apathy and indifference," which left "a few individuals . . . to struggle with the difficulties" of the undertaking, they praised the "public spirited individuals" who for "the future prosperity of Charleston" undertook a "hazardous" speculation "in the patriotic hope . . . of reviving the drooping fortunes of [the] city."[6]

Perceiving railroad building as a patriotic venture, appealing to public spirit rather than private profit, and operating in a state whose transportation system had been built with public monies, the new railroad company unhesitatingly sought funds from city, state, and national governments. Indeed, even before it had been incorporated, its projected route had been surveyed at government expense by the United States Corps of Engineers. Further federal aid was, however, stifled by the politics of tariff and nullification. When in 1829 the company petitioned the national government to subscribe for 2,500 shares of its stock, Congressman James Hamilton spoke for his state on the House floor to forswear such federal funding for internal improvements as absolutely as his colleagues rejected protective tariffs. Undercut by one of its own, the South Carolina company was in 1830 even more unlucky in making its second appeal through Massachusetts senator Daniel Webster, who, at the very time he presented their petition, was hotly debating South Carolina senator Robert Y. Hayne on the nature of states' rights, internal improvements, and the Constitution itself. And when Charleston Unionist William Drayton refused to press his constituents' cause in the House of Representatives, the railroad surrendered to political reality and shifted its sights from federal to state support.[7]

Indeed, in 1829 the legislature had already agreed to lend the railroad $100,000—but that was less than half the amount the company needed. Whether because it seemed too small to bother with or because accepting it might jeopardize the larger request it was then pressing in Washington, the company did not activate the state loan until 1831. Thereafter a whole series of accommodations evolved that confirmed the mutual interest of state and corporation in building the line. Even in the original charter the state's theories of political economy had played a role. The right to raise a capital of $200,000 had been linked to the company's issuing modestly priced $100 shares and selling them at offices located throughout the state. The directors were to be elected by a system which gave disproportionate weight to the votes cast by small stockholders. Its power to set freight and passenger rates was circumscribed by state-set maximum charges. In return for these democratic limitations, the state had granted the company a thirty-five-year monopoly. Subsequently, corporate prospects were enhanced by further state concessions. In 1832 all responsible railroad employees—from chief engineer to conductors—were exempted from jury and militia service. The next year the legislature granted the railroad all state land abutting its track to the depth of one mile on each side and, in addition, empowered the company to obtain privately owned land by eminent domain. But until the road was constructed, the state declined to buy railroad stock. Only Charleston's city council, which had subscribed for 200 shares in 1829, provided any public ownership.[8]

Most stock, therefore, was held by private investors who, whether for direct profit or the promise of indirect gains, had (with some exceptions) purchased only a few shares each. Thus Charlestonians of varied occupations, from merchant to grocer, from lawyer to boardinghouse operator, shared the risk and served the city's revitalization. Although full capitalization was never achieved, the railroad's 136-mile single track running from Charleston to Hamburg on the Savannah River was completed in October 1833. In addition to the $951,148 garnered from city and private investment, the state loan, and operating revenues, the company relied on credit. And when the full line was completed, the company still owed $150,000 in construction costs.[9]

The saga of building what was, in 1833, the longest railroad in the world was one of innovation and frustration, hard work and boondoggling. After fruitless efforts to import labor gangs, the company relied primarily on off-season slave crews—an arrangement which was not altogether satisfactory. The workers were unused to nonagricultural work schedules; their owners often exacted control of construction in exchange for leasing their slaves, or recalled their farm laborers unpredictably before the job was completed. Nonetheless, it was these crews who transported raw materials to building sites; constructed earthen roadbeds where the route traversed dry land; drove the piles—from five to twenty-five feet in length—on which the track bridged numerous creeks and swamps; set wooden ties in place; and laid across them wooden tracks topped with thin iron bands.

As the chief engineer experimented with roadbed and track construction, he also tried out various designs for passenger and freight cars and the engines to power them. Seeking to keep costs down and efficiency up, he sometimes had to settle for on-the-spot innovation. By the time the full track was laid, the railroad had settled on the smallest possible wood-stoked steam engines, whose weight was distributed on eight wheels. These little engines-that-could pulled three or four passenger cars or a short string of freight cars at speeds of up to ten, twelve, even fifteen miles per hour.[10]

Magnificent feat, the new railroad expanded the pride of Carolinians and Charlestonians as less than a decade earlier the Erie Canal had done for New Yorkers. Riding the line brought varied responses. In July 1832, when only the first thirty miles were functional, young lawyer Randall Hunt enjoyed the "great rapidity & ease" with which the cars glided along the "regular & level, & . . . nearly perfectly straight" road. But the full eleven-hour run was more trying. Passengers rode the first 120 miles from

Hub and Hinge

Charleston to Aiken without changing cars. Then for the steep descent to the Savannah River they and their baggage were transferred to a cable car which was eased down the inclined plane, dropping 200 feet in 1,200. Operated at first by man-powered cranks and later by a stationary steam engine which winched up and let out the heavy ropes serving as cable, the inclined plane was never a satisfactory part of the route.[11] But thereafter the route ran smoothly into Hamburg.

Nonetheless, both as a curiosity and as a comfortable and speedy alternative to travel by stagecoach or horseback, the line attracted as many as a thousand passengers a month before the entire route was completed. But the critical question was whether planters and farmers would opt for higher costs to get the speed and convenience of shipping cotton by rail. In September 1833, before the line was fully operational, the omens seemed favorable. In the first week 19 bales of the new crop came down to Charleston on the cars. But the next week only 7 arrived. Then, with the line open as far as Aiken, a sharp increase occurred, 65 bales coming down in a single week—44 of them from Georgia. The full 1833–1834 trading season signaled success: 7,500 bales—3 percent of the entire upland cotton sold in the city that year—had arrived by railroad. Thereafter throughout the decade the Hamburg line carried between 13 and 18 percent of the total upland crop sold through the Charleston market.[12]

But the railroad returned no generous income from that freight to its stockholders. Their meetings had long been rife with protests against cost overruns and denunciations of the high salaries paid company officials. The promise of the line's completion, it is true, had boosted the flagging market price for railroad shares and thus enabled the company to float another 2,000 shares at or above par in 1833. And in July 1834 the company paid its first semiannual dividend of 2 percent. But the road's "highly successful operation," as it was touted in the spring, had turned sour by the fall as roadbed and track began to deteriorate. Piles crumbled, earth settled, and the thin ribbon of iron tracking regularly tore loose from its wooden base, often curling upwards to rip through the floors of the cars passing over it. By October 1834, twenty-seven miles of piling had already had to be replaced, at great expense, by earthen embankments. And that was just the beginning of repair costs which ate into profits year after year.[13] By 1839 the repair and improvement of the original construction had more than doubled original costs, and total building expenditures stood at $2,500,000. In addition, repeated accidents and the paucity of engineers competent to operate the company's dozen and a half engines sharply diminished popular trust in the line's safety, while the 1836 Creek War and sporadic epidemics periodically reduced passenger traffic in unpredictable patterns. Commenting on two years of operation, Charleston attorney Robert Gilchrist sadly observed that the road was "in ill repute, and seldom used except for business purposes & transportation of property."[14]

The road's high costs and low returns might have been acceptable, even to the shareholders, had it fulfilled other expectations. It did not, however, enable Charleston to catch up with the growth of other old Atlantic ports or of the new Gulf ports. It attracted few skilled mechanics and no significant manufacturing to the city or the state. Indeed, while it is not clear how extensively local artisans were employed in building passenger and freight cars, it is clear that the most complex and sophisticated equipment, the steam engines, were purchased largely from England and northern foundries. Of the thirty-five engines in service between 1830 and 1837, only nine were Charleston-made. And while the Hamburg line's completion and early operation coincided with boom years, there is no evidence that the cotton brought into Charleston by rail significantly increased her trade.[15]

The anticipations of private profit and urban progress had rested on the assumption that a railroad would tap the rich hinterland of the Savannah river basin and beyond to bind its trade to the low-country capital. But those anticipations were misplaced, at least in part, because its intervening route traversed land so thinly settled that it produced little cotton and provided a minimal market for goods either produced in or imported into Charleston. In addition, Charlestonians balked at the ominous side effects of steam transportation. Though proponents of the east-west trade axis spoke glowingly of a continuous route from America's interior to remote European destinations, that route fractured with the city. Its citizens resolutely refused to join the two wings of the hinge on a common pin, blocking construction of tracks from the parish lines to the East Bay wharves. Not only did their decision add to freight costs, disadvantaging the railroad's competition with cheaper river and coastal shipping, but it smothered land development for new wharves, passenger and freight depots, warehouses, and the other facilities which a unified transportation complex demanded.

Although the company's charter stipulated only that the railroad must run to the northern boundary of St. Philip's and St. Michael's parish at Line Street on the Neck, there had been no question in the minds of its sponsors that the tracks would ultimately reach the Cooper River wharves. All that was needed, they believed, was formal city approval of the exact route. So, early in 1831, as construction crews built westward toward Hamburg, other workers broke ground to lay track into the city. Company officials had been informally assured by the commissioners of main roads that they would extend "every facility" to aid the construction. No one, therefore, was ready for the irate indignation of the rural and suburban residents, whose protests were so impassioned that the railroad, lacking a formal agreement with the commissioners and taken aback by citizen hostility, tore up the tracks just laid and relied on drays and wagons for shipments to the wharves.[16]

The next year, railroad officers petitioned the state legislature for explicit authority to extend their tracks from Line Street to the incorporated city's northern edge at Boundary Street. In return for permission to pass between the Neck's two major arteries, King Street Road and Meeting Street Road, and down through the center of Citadel Square, they renounced using steam engines unless the Neck commissioners granted express permission for them. Additionally, they promised to create "no obstruction or inconvenience in the public and ordinary use of the said streets and squares." With that, the legislature granted their request in December 1832, but reserved to the city of Charleston the right to authorize any further extension southward into the city proper.[17]

Now conflicting sets of values met head on. Wealthy planters and proud mechanics organized to protect their homes, land, animals, and persons from trains which might soon hurtle through the city's main streets. Simultaneously, merchants and other businessmen whose well-being depended on a commercial prosperity for which they believed the new railroad essential demanded that the hinge of east-west trade not be snapped apart at the critical juncture of land and sea.

The impasse called for resolution in the best Charleston style. Intendent Henry Pinckney called on a citizen's meeting to solve this critical problem through political channels. Expressing his own misgivings about the railroad in the public letter which announced the meeting, Pinckney precipitated a largely pseudonymous exchange of views through the press, according to the city's custom. Railroad opponents pled the well-being of mothers worried lest their children become "bleeding victims to the cupidity of an interested Corporation," of draymen who stood to lose their carting business, of wharf owners fearful that competitors would reap an unfair advantage from being the railroad terminus, and of King Street wholesalers, retailers, and hoteliers who had already suffered from the shift of the city's business toward East Bay. To counter these concerns, railroad enthusiasts condemned giving draymen a monopoly on moving city freight, either because most of them were black or because it was unfair to protect 1 percent of the people at the expense of the other 99 percent.[18]

Finally, when all stops had been pulled and all emotions tugged, the city council appointed a special committee of twenty-five to resolve the issue. Studded with names of important men, including that of South Carolina Canal and Rail Road Company president Elias Horry, the committee recommended that the railroad should lay tracks along specific streets but also assume responsibility for returning those streets to their original condition. The city had, they asserted, a paramount interest in bringing the tracks into the city. But, deferring to citizen protest, the committee concluded that only if the tracks on either King or Meeting and on Boundary streets did not disrupt city life unduly should the city authorize, at some later date, extending the tracks all the way downtown.[19]

For all the apparent compromise, Charleston citizens had blocked a continuous east-west trade axis. Thwarted in its plans, the railroad built only to the city's edge, and even then opted for a circuitous route on its own land lest citizens delay construction by challenging the railroad's use of established roads in the courts. If Charleston's commercial prosperity depended on her cotton trade and if increasing that trade depended on luring cotton away from the river and coastal shipping which took it to competing ports, Charlestonians had written their city's epitaph. In actual practice, carting cotton from railhead to wharf imposed a surcharge of between 12 and 20 percent on the transportation costs of every bale of cotton brought down to the city by rail. As an Augusta, Georgia, merchant warned, if avaricious Charlestonians did not stop "com[ing] 'Yankee,'" inland factors would ship their cotton to Savannah.[20]

Thus commercial and professional Charlestonians, the most numerous occupational groups among railroad investors, were little more rewarded by a spin-off of increasing business than they were by actual dividends paid on their stock. Moreover, even within the corporation, the business-oriented interests of two-thirds of its shareholders conflicted to some extent with the overlapping city and Neck real estate interests of four-fifths of the railroad investors as they wrangled over bringing the tracks into town. Another conflict of interest spawned controversy over freight rates between the one-third who owned plantation land and the two-thirds who did not and thus lost dividends but gained no compensating advantage when freight rates were lowered.[21] The directors of the South Carolina Canal and Rail Road Company, caught by shareholders' diverse priorities, failed to balance these competing economic pressures either for the greatest benefit to the company or the greatest stimulus to the city's economy. Thus did their venture fail to realize its promise. By 1836 the hopes originally vested in the Hamburg line were already shifting to another route stretching across North Carolina, Kentucky, and Tennessee to the Ohio River.

• • •

Boston faced the nineteenth-century transportation revolution from a far more advantageous base. It is true that in 1828 she had yet to achieve the viable packet service to England which New York enjoyed. Moreover,

Hub and Hinge

she had fewer ships engaged in transatlantic and interregional trade than did her major rival. Nonetheless, Boston's harbor was big and relatively easy of access. And, most important, many of the vessels serving her commerce were home-owned. Furthermore, while the War of 1812 had ruined her shipping, in its aftermath she had rebuilt a commercial fleet which sailed to California, Canton, and Calcutta, St. Petersburg and Smyrna, London and Liverpool, Havana, Hamburg, and Hawaii. And throughout the 1830s her tonnage grew at least at the same rate as did New York's.[22]

It was New York's inland water route up the Hudson River and westward over the Erie Canal to the Great Lakes which seriously challenged Yankee trade. To compete with it, Boston needed an inland transportation system to connect her with the West as well as to exploit commercial potentials closer to home. Thus her preoccupation with railroads. The lines her entrepreneurs projected in the 1830s stretched north, south, and west to tie Massachusetts's major port with towns and cities throughout the state as they also reached out toward New York and the rest of New England. These early roads were not just to link the interior towns with shipping facilities or merely to provide them local transportation. They were also to insure that the interior towns' trade went through Boston. In providing the locus for a mutual exchange of raw materials and finished products among inland towns, Boston would become not just a hinge but a hub city, battening on the diversified production and substantial population of Massachusetts, the most densely populated and industrialized state in the Union. Her position at the very heart of this complex trading network made it certain she would profit from the regional and national trade that that network extended, as would also the more than fifty towns in the immediate hinterland which manufactured shoes, textiles, and machinery.[23] But particularly Boston, for it was her bankers, her investors, her entrepreneurs who orchestrated the exchange of raw materials and finished products within New England, as it was her shippers and merchants who took their commission on trade outside it. In this way Boston's location and economic potential shaped a railroad system which became the prototype for the new transportation networks associated with early American industrialization.

Boston's genius, however, lay in seizing the opportunity which her manufacturing hinterland and her regional control of banking and credit offered and in applying to railroad building the managerial experience of her merchants and capitalists. Even so, her first railroad projections were as broadly and patriotically drawn as Charleston's. From 1828, by which time Nathan Hale's *Advertiser* had long since been campaigning for "an easy and cheap communication with the interior," until July 1830, the explicit focus of railroad enthusiasts was the public merit of "one or more

Railways from this city to the interior of the State." Merchants Nathan Appleton and Thomas Handasyd Perkins served on a publicly appointed committee "to accelerate [its] construction." Mayor Harrison Gray Otis pressed its importance in his first address to the city council. Suffolk County representatives in the state legislature backed appropriations for a railroad survey. And Democrat David Henshaw joined National Republican Nathan Hale to insure that the Massachusetts Board of Directors of Internal Improvement supported the proposition that a railroad from Boston to Albany was a "public accommodation" so essential that it "should be under the control of the government of the state." Boston's city council went even beyond its support of state sponsorship to petition for permission to buy stock if the state failed to sustain the venture.[24]

In January 1829 a proposal for a state-built line to Providence failed to win the support of the general court. The next month a group of wealthy Boston citizens sought to charter a private railroad to the west for which the state would provide one-third of the capital—only to have the legislature delay all consideration of railroads until the 1830 session. Then, decisively, a coalition of coastal and inland representatives whose constituencies would not be served by a road from Boston to Albany killed the pending bill for state subsidies.[25]

Defeated in their appeals to the state, Boston citizens then considered Mayor Otis's tentative proposal that the city take a financial interest in a western railroad. It was to assess that option that a "Great Railroad Meeting" was held in Faneuil Hall on a hot mid-July evening in 1830. Judge Lemuel Shaw rehearsed the benefits the railroad would bring the city: her warehouses would be filled, her western trade recaptured, her exports increased, her trade in Massachusetts manufactures enhanced. Yet city property owners were not convinced. Led by Marlboro Hotel owner Alexander Townsend, they denounced the increase in taxes which city investment in a railroad threatened. After wrangling that pitted the rich against the poor and the propertied against the unpropertied, the meeting finally adjourned to let tempers cool. When it reconvened a month later, however, stalemate ensued. In spite of a four-to-one endorsement from its twenty-five hundred participants for city aid to a railroad, Townsend blocked action by threatening a court test of the plan's constitutionality. By January 1831, city investment in a western railroad was doomed. Responding to some three hundred wealthy property owners who petitioned against the city's projected use of tax funds, the general court voted by a large margin to refuse Boston the "liberty . . . to subscribe $1,000,000.—for a rail road to Albany."[26]

As a result, while Charleston's railroad enterprise began with some federal and significant state and city assistance, Boston's initial recourse

Hub and Hinge 65

to the public purse was nipped early. Her first railroads were privately owned and controlled corporations more intent on making profits than cultivating political postures. The Boston and Lowell set the style. Linked to, indeed almost identical with Lowell manufacturing and its principal Boston investors, it was from its inception in 1830 a model of a tightly integrated and competently managed transportation venture which in satisfying its investors also served public ends.

In 1829 the state legislature had allotted $250 to survey a railroad route to Lowell, and that manufacturing center's chief corporate developer of power and land, the Proprietors of the Merrimack Locks and Canal, appointed a committee to assist the surveyors. By providing the funding necessary to assess potential building costs and to project demands for freight and passenger service, they assured that the initial report was a full feasibility study. Thus even before the Boston and Lowell was chartered, the highly profitable Locks and Canal Proprietors, a corporation whose dividends from 1827 to 1845 averaged nearly 16 percent per annum, had seized the opportunity to link the railroad to its own interests.[27]

Yet when the new line was incorporated in June 1830 and its stock was put on sale, there was little public response. The terms of incorporation, it is true, were generous. Although its thirty-year monopoly was subject to the proviso that the state could buy the company out after twenty years, the charter guaranteed stockholders a 10 percent annual return should the state take such action. Additionally, the railroad was empowered to set its own rates unless its profits exceeded 10 percent annually for four consecutive years, in which case the state could, if it chose, set limits.[28] Even though the state in both cases condoned notably high rates of return, railroading proved too novel to inspire investor confidence.

Without capital, the company was powerless to organize. In Charleston this combination of public reluctance and private apathy would have stifled the project. But Boston had the resources to overcome both deficiencies. The Locks and Canal Proprietors acted to launch the Boston and Lowell almost as a subsidiary. It chose Patrick Tracy Jackson from among its own directors to take charge of the new company. It solicited the boards of directors of all Lowell textile companies to purchase sizeable blocks of the railroad's initial 1,000 $500 shares. The Locks and Canal Proprietors set the example by having already bought 250. So successful was this form of stock salesmanship that those who had bought shares when they were first offered could sell them a year later for a 20 percent profit.[29]

Speculative gains on stock, however, were not the goal of the Locks and Canal Proprietors, either individually or as a corporation. The company owned much Lowell land whose value would soar with improvements in transportation. Likewise, textile manufacturing profits would climb as raw materials and finished products were shipped faster and more cheaply. Additionally, the railroad's need for a Boston terminus triggered complex land speculations in which Jackson and his associates bought up flats from the Mill Pond Wharf Company for a depot site, marshes in East Cambridge on which to develop manufacturing sites, and old estates on Pemberton and Beacon hills to be quarried for gravel and then leveled for development as high-priced residential lots.[30]

A master manager as well as a venturous speculator, Jackson oversaw construction at every step. Traversing terrain very different from Carolina's first railroad route, the Boston and Lowell's solid iron rails were laid on well-ballasted, solid granite roadbed. Only a fifth as long as the Hamburg line, the Lowell road was both better constructed and more heavily used. When, in late June 1835, service commenced over its entire twenty-five-mile single track, the capital had already been raised and the roadbed prepared for a second track. When the double track was completed in 1836, the company had spent over $1.3 million for construction and owed a mere $100,000 more against assets of $60,000 in land and $1.5 million worth of track, rolling stock, and installations. Those funds had built a viable operation able to pay a 3¾ percent dividend in its first year of operation, and to return 2 percent on the 3,000 outstanding shares in its second year. Thereafter dividends increased until in 1839 they struck a plateau of 8 percent paid without fail for the next twelve years.[31]

The Boston and Lowell thus demonstrated the profitability of railroads. Its sound management, careful planning, and utilization of local resources also contributed a critical dynamic to urban growth. It furthered manufacturing by providing needed transportation and, in so doing, enriched both Boston and her hinterland. It created jobs by turning early to native mechanics to build engines and other equipment—often in the Merrimack Locks and Canal's own shops. Serving a series of towns between its termini, the railroad fed both commerce and industrial growth along the way. By connecting downtown Boston to outlying areas, it met an unanticipated demand for commuter transportation. By undertaking complementary real estate ventures, it changed both land contours and land use in ways that Charleston's railroad and land developers never dreamed of. And, with it all, the Boston and Lowell was only one of Boston's railroads built in the early 1830s.

More immediately attuned to the early campaign for a state-financed western railroad was the Boston and Worcester. Nonetheless, it too was chartered as a completely privately owned company in 1831, capitalized at $1 million. The line was designed to tie Worcester's myriad small mills and manufactories and its busy local markets to Boston and, only secondarily, to be the first link in the Albany route. Its charter differed from the Boston and Lowell's in two significant ways. Its shares were valued at a low $100 instead of $500, and the state was denied the power to set either passenger or freight rates unless corporate profits exceeded 10 percent for a period of ten (rather than only four) years. Taken together, these provisions seem less an effort to democratize ownership than an attempt to attract investors. For the rest, the provisions were similar. An 1832 supplemental act gave the state the right to buy out the railroad after twenty years, but only if it assured investors a 10 percent per annum return.[32] Mute on the number of votes which large stockholders might cast in making corporate decisions, its charter, like that of the Boston and Lowell, implied that every share entitled its owner to a vote—a very different provision from that of the South Carolina Canal and Rail Road charter, with its weighted voting system. Thus Massachusetts investors were more clearly enabled than were Carolinians to protect their financial stake in proportion to its size.

Even so, shares sold slowly. Deliberately offered in small units to attract the widest field of investors, Boston and Worcester stock needed an imprimatur similar to that which the Locks and Canal Proprietors had given the Boston and Lowell. Thus wealthy citizens like Harrison Gray Otis were pressed to buy shares and make their purchases public that others might be reassured by the *"shrewd capitalists"* who endorsed the investment. Those with limited purses, however, were not warned, as was Otis, that 3 to 5 percent rather than 10 percent was the likely rate of return.[33]

The difficulties, however, were not all financial. When the first section of track was opened in 1834, the celebratory excursion for investors and public officials was a fiasco. It took four hours to make a nine-mile round trip punctuated by breakdowns and unexplained delays brought on by malfunctioning and rusty equipment operated by inexperienced superintendents. Nonetheless the forty-three-mile double track was completely laid between 1832 and 1835 and, despite early operational difficulties and a roadbed subject to frost heaves, the Boston and Worcester proved viable. Laid out to maximize passenger and freight business, its route meandered through nine different towns from Brighton and Newton near Boston to Southborough and Grafton just short of Worcester.[34] And, at the Boston end, the railroad tied the South Cove Company to its own interest by developing land for warehouses and depots as well as by building wharves to link its tracks directly to the waterfront.

That the docks along the South Cove wharves were, in fact, too shallow for the largest transatlantic vessels illustrates the Boston and Worcester's limitations. Its accomplishments were not as easy as the Boston and

Lowell's. Its initial stock issue never did sell at face value but was, instead, sold by installments, with purchasers subject to a series of small assessments over time. Stockholders, worried about high costs, once tried to stop construction altogether. And when the road opened for full operation in 1835, freights fell considerably below projections. But these were disappointments, not disasters. Passenger revenues were much higher than had been anticipated. During its first six months of operation, the road earned more than $72,000 in fares, whereas the South Carolina railroad took in only $36,000 from fares during an equivalent period. And although freights had started slowly, they steadily increased so that by the end of 1839 its per-mile income was 80 percent above that of its first full year of operation; the southern railroad's freights increased only 30 percent over the same period. All this added up to respectable dividends: 2 percent in 1835, 4 percent in 1836, 8 percent in 1837, and in subsequent years returns as high as 10 percent and never lower than 6 percent.[35]

Even more than the Boston and Lowell, the Worcester railroad changed the topography of the seaport city. If its causeway dammed up and polluted Back Bay, its landfill operations at South Cove opened new areas of the peninsular neck to housing, commerce, and manufacturing.[36] And, equally important for Boston business interests, it overwhelmed the Blackstone Canal, which, in linking Worcester to Providence, had threatened to make New York rather than Boston the outlet for the sizable agricultural and manufacturing produce of Worcester County.

Still, however important this regional shift, Boston herself needed a swift link with New York. Thus she reinforced her position as a hub city by building a third railroad south to Providence, where it connected with regular steamboat service to Gotham. Although the Boston, Providence, and Taunton Rail Road, chartered in 1830, never came into being, its successor, the Boston and Providence, was readily capitalized in 1831 at $1 million. Its $100 shares were traded far more speculatively and in larger blocks than those of either the Lowell or Worcester companies had been and were largely subscribed by New Yorkers. Even though the Boston and Providence met significant transportation needs so well that it began to pay dividends even before it was completed and thereafter paid 6 to 8 percent annual dividends, it had in fact less impact on Boston than did the other lines. Its depot was far from the wharves near the southwest corner of the Common—a site which provoked much criticism but no city veto of railroad land use—while in fixing its terminal on the edge of the stagnant Back Bay, it engendered no significant land development.[37]

With a northern, a western, and a southern spoke in place, Boston's hub pattern was already clear. Thereafter those lines were lengthened and new lines were projected to reach an ever growing perimeter. Indeed, be-

Hub and Hinge

tween 1831 and 1835 a total of eleven railroads were chartered. The Boston and Ontario was organized in 1831 to push on beyond Lowell across New Hampshire and Vermont to the distant outpost of Ogdensburg, New York. Competing enthusiasts sought lines running to Brattleboro or Montpelier, Vermont, or, more remotely, Windsor and Whitehall. Some planned a westward route through Keene, New Hampshire, and Brattleboro to Troy, New York.[38]

But the last railroad actually to be built out of Boston during the decade was the Eastern, which was to follow the North Shore to New Hampshire and Maine. Reversing the usual pattern, it began as a land development scheme evolving from competition between the Winnisimmet and the East Boston companies. Each group sought the stimulus to land use which a rail terminus would produce. When the East Boston group won out in 1836 and the directors broke ground for the line, they celebrated with a twenty-six-gun salute. Their euphoria, however, ended abruptly with the panic of 1837. Unable to collect the assessments due on stock already subscribed, the Eastern then turned to the state, which lent it half-a-million dollars to complete its line to Salem and thus burdened it with a debt which made it somewhat less profitable than its predecessors.[39]

The commonwealth's new financial commitment to railroads, however—both the Eastern and the projected Western from Worcester to Albany—came only after the first three lines had clearly demonstrated not just their utility but their profitability. Private investors and the public as well had resisted railroad investment until it could be demonstrated as a probability if not "a moral certainty that it would produce regular and sure dividends."[40] But although city government neither lent them money nor invested in their stock, it did enhance their attraction by allowing the railroads to reach the wharves. Unlike Charleston, Boston assented to tracks running through the city to reach waterfront terminals. Although this decision was made easier because the terminals were located on reclaimed land at the city's edge—the extreme west end, South Cove, Back Bay, and Noddles Island—steam-powered railroads nonetheless had to cross Washington, Tremont, Front, and other major streets on their way to the South Cove yards. Thus did railroads make Boston a hub city. Thus did entrepreneurial vigor outweigh environmental protection.

• • •

If different expectations of profit, different roles for public investment, and different receptivities to railroads' entering the city created divergent transportation and land use patterns in the two cities, Boston's and Charleston's divergent hinterlands played even more important roles. The 108 miles of railroad which served Boston by 1836 fanned out in three directions into the most densely populated metropolitan area in the country. These roads fed not only Boston's economic growth but that of the towns which bought and sold in Boston.

Charleston, with conscious planning and public support unmatched in the Massachusetts capital, had built a single long railroad which went through no important town and served but a minimal population until it reached a terminus 136 miles distant. Thus the possible uses of their lines differed profoundly. The chief business of the South Carolina Rail Road was carrying high-bulk freight of the sort the Massachusetts lines found least profitable. Nor did Charleston produce equivalent freights to ship out in return for the cotton brought into the city by rail. In addition, its passenger traffic comprised principally long-distance travelers rather than a steady two-way passage of commuters.

Moreover, projecting into the future, railroading promised no returns for the southern city equal to those which Boston enjoyed. Even were an alternative railroad built from Charleston through North Carolina, Tennessee, and Kentucky to Cincinnati, it would still serve a sparsely populated region more likely to lose than gain inhabitants and almost devoid of manufactories. If Bostonians, on the other hand, should realize their Western Rail Road connection with the Hudson River, they would, on the way, tap the businesses of 189 factories, 91,145 people, 311 stores and warehouses, and 368 tanneries and mills producing goods worth $5 million a year.[41]

The economic development of each city was defined by conditions which no exchange of investment alternatives, management styles, and political strategies could have reversed completely. Boston could be a hub city despite her perch on a small and precipitous peninsula because she was surrounded by a populous and growing hinterland whose manufacturing potential was stoked by the immigrants and commodities which ships brought into her fine harbor. Charleston, by contrast, was an urban oasis in an agricultural land whose soil was deteriorating and whose population was leaving. Charleston's backcountry, no less than her social values and her remoteness from shipping lanes, limited her ability even to be a hinge city.

PART III · STRUCTURING PUBLIC
RESPONSIBILITIES

6

Pragmatic Politics and the Politics of Passion

At the peak of the 1834 banking crisis and almost exactly a year after the compromise which had ended South Carolina's open defiance of tariff laws, the *Imperial Gazette and Washington Court Journal* was alleged to have reported that Boston and Charleston were the last remaining holdouts against King Andrew's despotic rule. "[T]he present unnatural rebellion against our rightful sovereign . . . is fast drawing to a termination," as resistance is confined to the "rebel forces" entrenched "within the limits of the principal cities" of Massachusetts and South Carolina.[1] That Boston's *Daily Advertiser* could thus lampoon politics only underlined the wide differences separating the two cities' styles, however.

Each had suffered a major economic crisis, to which each responded politically. Boston used politics to produce pragmatic solutions for national banking problems. But politics served to distract attention from Charleston's economic issues. The evils of the Tariff of Abominations were almost lost in the pursuit of state sovereignty. The federal tax, believed to protect northern manufactures at southern expense, produced not a tariff crisis but the nullification crisis. To Washington's attack on her economy, Charleston, like the rest of Carolina, responded with passionate partisanship and revolutionary rhetoric.

Following hard upon the 1825 collapse of the cotton trade and descending on a city already preoccupied with its economic decline, the tariff of 1828 simply had to become a major issue. Charleston's response had already been fixed in 1824 when her business and political leaders had condemned the tariff of that year as "a system of monopoly and bounties . . . inconsistent with every idea of equal rights and sound policy."

The city's congressman, William Drayton, fought the 1828 tariff bill in the House of Representatives and, when it was passed anyway, denounced it as he had the 1824 measure on the practical grounds that a schedule of high import taxes "fetters our industry, cripples our commerce, and taxes the many for the benefit of the few."[2]

But the economics of the tariff was not really the issue at home, for few Charlestonians defended it. What was decisive was how the tariff should be countered, and in Carolina that was a central political concern. As early as 1827 Robert Turnbull, writing as "Brutus" in the Charleston *Mercury,* had advocated that the state declare the tariff null and void. So, too, James Hamilton, already charting the nullifiers' course in 1829, raised the tariff issue to the level of demanding "reform of *principles* as well as *practice."* And while Congressman Drayton gave hard-nosed attention to finding some practical means to lower the tariff, Senator Robert Hayne appealed for a return to a romanticized past, urging Charlestonians to recapture *"those good old times,* when commerce [was] essentially free."[3]

Underlying the nullifiers' response was not simply a defense of the agricultural economy on which the city's commerce rested, but a firm rejection of an industrializing future as well. Their perception was that the exorbitant levies imposed by the growing manufacturing interests in the North betokened a shift in power that boded the "wreck of all [Carolina's] hopes." Emerging in the tariff was political confirmation of a new national economic network in which manufacturing, like a hungry spider, occupied the center of the web while Carolina was doomed to its periphery. An heir of the American Revolution, Mrs. Harriott Pinckney Rutledge Holbrook enthusiastically greeted the independence which she believed nullification would bring. It would, she smiled, restore her state to "single blessedness" in which "the desert will blossom as the rose, and all the waste places be made glad." On the other hand, Unionist judge Daniel Huger wrote emphatically to William Drayton that he "would not have felt [himself] called upon to make great sacrifices, if these nullificators, [did] not mean Disunion."[4]

Charlestonians, however, faced a dilemma. If as Carolinians they were out of step with national trends, as city folk they were also losing power within their own state. The tensions between low-country and up-country as well as those between urban commerce and rural agriculture stretched back to pre-Revolutionary days. But recent events had exacerbated them. By 1790 Columbia had replaced Charleston as the state capital, but only in the late 1820s did the legislature try to end the last duplication of state offices and thus remove from the coastal city the surviving vestiges of its colonial dominance. Although that legislation failed, the debate over retaining the low-country state treasury office only heightened Charleston's awareness that the burden of taxation was shifting from agricultural property to commercial.[5] As the city had grown, so too had the taxes exacted on her citizens' real property, income, and stock-in-trade. Yet taxes on agricultural property were still levied on assessments made in 1784, and the sale of agricultural staples had never been taxed. City people, who contributed an ever increasing proportion of the state's income, were unable to gain a hearing for their special needs in a legislature dominated by up-country and rural interests. That this was already so made Charleston's citizens cautious about espousing a politics which would set them further at odds with those who wielded power in Columbia.[6]

Charlestonians therefore were warned against supporting anti-nullification candidates for the legislature in 1830. If they won, "the prosperity of the City of Charleston" would be "in a great measure destroyed; For . . . our City would lose the [state] appropriation allowed for the transient poor, which would visit a *new* and *heavy* taxation on real Estate; and . . . nothing thereafter will be done for the Rail-Road, or any other public work in which Charleston may be interested." Caught between a northern-dominated congress and a rural-dominated legislature, Charleston had to make her choice. If she did not seize this opportunity to vote solid support with the rest of the state, she faced ruinous isolation.[7]

. . .

Charleston was not yet cowed by such threats in 1830, and her city and state elections showed it. Both were fought over South Carolina's right to declare a federal law null and void. In both the city voted nay. James Pringle, collector of the port, a Jackson appointee and a Unionist, headed the September ticket, which trounced the nullifier candidate for intendent (mayor), Henry Pinckney. Though all his ticket did not win, Pringle brought in with him a sufficient infusion of Unionist wardens to create a majority in the city council.[8]

The October state election, which followed a hard-fought campaign and produced some challenged victories, also went to the Unionists.[9] But the narrowness of the margin and the bitterness of the contest announced the cleavages which would soon divide Charleston into two warring camps. In the city and on the Neck 2,562 people had cast ballots, but what they did for a living—40 percent of them laborers or mechanics or persons of unknown occupation; nearly a quarter of them low-prestige white-collar men; a quarter merchants, professionals, and bank or insurance company officers; the rest (a mere 7 percent) planters—had little to do with how they voted.

Nonetheless, economic interest did shape the partisan affiliations of some voters. Factors who traded the planters' rice and cotton were slightly more nullifier than the planters themselves. All other merchants, however, like all retailers except grocers, were somewhat more likely to be Unionists—perhaps because they traded many goods manufactured in the North. And the grocers' strong support for nullification doubtless bespoke their opposition to prominent Unionists who advocated temperance and strict enforcement of the laws prohibiting the sale of liquor to slaves. Mechanics, too, sometimes voted special economic self-interest. Although carpenters generally were evenly divided between the two factions, shipwrights (whose products tied them to national commerce) were pronouncedly Unionist.

Among still other voters, social factors shaped politics. Ethnicity influenced recently arrived immigrants, although it played little role among groups long established in the city. San Domingan French inclined to the Unionists, less assimilated Germans and Irish to the nullifiers. But well-assimilated Huguenots and Scots-Irish were about evenly divided. Additionally, among prominent voters the quest for power per se was a major force in shaping partisan allegiance. Those accustomed to wielding economic power in the city were disproportionately Unionist and ready to uphold the old order. On the other hand, upper-class men who had been excluded from economic power but who were likely to expect it as their right disproportionately affiliated with the nullifiers.

While politicians seeking votes played heavily on appeals to class, occupation, or ethnicity, voters' attention was probably equally attracted by the hoopla, the rowdyism, and the skulduggery which not only made elections exciting but garnered votes for one side or the other. Indeed, it was charges of bribery and illegal voting which led to the contemporary investigation of just who had voted in the October 1830 election. Because twenty-eight voters were consequently disqualified and because the Unionists had carried only a scant 51 percent of the votes for the six actively contested seats, one of their number lost his narrow victory. The subsequent by-election, in which he was defeated by a nullifier, demonstrated how tenuous were the Unionist claims to victory and how vital their hold on every voter.[10]

Aware that gaining only slightly more than 1 percent of the vote would secure them victory in the city's elections, in which every candidate ran at large, nullifiers for the next two years cultivated all the devices of partisan warfare. Their opponents, because they were either too self-assured or fatally accustomed to power, failed to make such persistent exertions. Rather, too many of them looked back on the last election and lamented the style by which nullifiers had almost won. Unionist James Petigru, however, betrayed his party's claims to strict electoral probity when he complained that in the 1831 city election "Nullies" not only bought votes but bought votes "that were sold before" to the Unionist side. Yet even he was shocked at an opposition which "kept men drunk, locked up, broke [into] houses and carried them off and, in fact, did everything that was audacious." Half admiring the "impudence" by which Nullies won that election, he also wished his associates had themselves been more "audacious." But J. S. Colburn doubted Unionists' will to win, rather than their methods: "[W]e have the numbers . . . [and] we have money—but do not spend it," while nullifiers "have little but that little they spend freely."[11]

Nullies not only spent with style, they organized with effect. Their Fourth of July celebrations attracted young and old alike. Wrapping states' rights in the rhetoric of the American Revolution, they appealed to hoary veterans in the Order of the Cincinnati and the '76 Association as well as to youth-filled militia companies. Their lively speeches and endlessly available refreshments generated an enthusiasm which staid Unionist celebrations could not match. "I never expect to see again," William Dukes wrote, praising his party's abstemious 1831 Independence Day celebration, "such an assemblage of talent and respectability."[12]

It was not that the nullifiers lacked talent and respectability; they simply doubted that respectable assemblages would either rouse enthusiasm or win converts. Rather than cringe when Unionists condemned their States' Rights and Free Trade Association as a Jacobin conspiracy, "a secret conclave . . . removed from the restraint of the public eye," they organized a Young Men's auxiliary. Those who were already old enough to fight and almost old enough to vote would, after all, find such a political "conclave" rather exciting. So their rallies were fun and their meetings crowded.[13] When the galleries were opened to the ladies, "all the beauty and fashion [of the town] were present." After the speeches, good food and ample supplies of "sour Claret & Punch" were served. And they sang all the old songs—all, that is, except "Yankee Doodle."[14] Indeed, Yankee-baiting was a staple activity, not just because the tariff was a Yankee device or even because most Yankee merchants and traders in town were undoubted Unionists, but because nullifier politics required cultivating loyalty to state over that to nation. Therefore King Street traders and the city's strong Unionist press—both A. S. Willington's *Courier* and William Gilmore Simms's *City Gazette*—were uniformly damned for being "the property of Northern Capitalists."[15]

Thus did the nullifiers prepare for the critical state election of 1832. If Charleston was to have a positive voice in the legislature when it considered calling a state convention to nullify federal tariffs, nullifiers must carry the city. Surrendering to a new urgency, their leaders, who had earlier joined Unionists in calling for election reform, dared not sacrifice any stratagem that might bring victory. As the 1832 elections approached, James Hamilton, who was then state governor, committed his side to meet bribery with bribery. Charleston Unionists, he warned, had the money to buy "300 Swiss votes." "[I]t will be a struggle between our management with small resources & their length of purse who shall obtain a majority of them." And so both sides undertook to use the September city elections to prepare for the more important state contests, just as they had in 1830. Nor did either side trust to bribery alone. This time both sides kidnapped potential voters and locked them up until they could be marched to the polls and voted. Only after Peter Staunton, sequestered in a Union house on Queen Street, had become either so drunk or so desperate that he jumped from a third-story window to his death did both sides agree to empty their lockups.[16]

Equally able, at the critical moment, to use every device available to their opponents, the Unionists lost the city election neither by indulging in moral scruples nor by lacking "resources." Their narrow majority of 1830 turned into a narrow minority in 1832 because of nullifiers' constant exertions throughout the two intervening years. The nullifiers' constant organization and recruiting garnered 54 percent of the vote, to make Henry Pinckney intendent and install a city council entirely of his party. At this juncture the polite constraints of the Charleston style weakened under the increasing pressure of political crisis. As the state elections approached, and Charleston's last chance either to block or to join the state's surging nullification movement hung in the balance, violence threatened social order. Gentlemen hurled insults, recipients issued challenges, duels were fought—all in the name of politics. Yet it was on the gentlemanly code that the peace of the city relied. "Were the leaders Demagogues . . . ," wrote one Unionist, "we could have a civil commotion in a week."[17]

Therefore the men of property and standing on both sides, social equals whatever their political differences, met in emergency session to preserve the safety of their community. Representing the nullifiers was a delegation led by former senator Robert Y. Hayne, a man of "engaging manners" and "the ease of the gentleman." Speaking for the Unionists were Congressman William Drayton, the "very best surviving specimen of the Carolina Gentleman of the old school," and James L. Petigru, whom even his enemies praised as "a man all parties should cherish." Together these men and their associates arranged a truce limiting the political practices which threatened their city's peace. They agreed to stop buying votes, kidnapping voters, and offering refreshments at party rallies. They limited both the places and timing of political meetings.[18] But the question remained, could a gentlemen's agreement control the passions which their politics and rhetoric had loosed?

On October 20 it seemed for a while that it could not. Unionists had convened that evening in Seyle's rooms between King and Meeting streets. Shortly before they were to adjourn, Drayton received a message from Hayne that nullifier crowds in an ugly mood were swarming on King Street. But when Hayne's suggestion that they adjourn by the Meeting Street exit was put to the assembly, Union men refused to turn tail. Instead they shouted their approval of a plan to march down King Street as a body. That bloody riot was avoided can be attributed only to their collective pledge of obedience to Colonel Drayton and Mr. Petigru, whom they chose to head their demonstration. In good order behind their leaders, hundreds of proud men marched through a screaming mob—but one which was too cowed, with few exceptions, to use violence. Some bricks were thrown—one missed Petigru, only to hit nullifier "Skilly" Bee's head and draw blood. But neither side resorted to fists or dirks or firearms. Weighing pride against prudence, Petigru later observed that his followers could "have cleared the street and it would have been policy to do so, but doubtless the parties would have met the next time with muskets."[19]

With violence thus narrowly averted, the election was held; and voters returned every single nullifier candidate to the state legislature. The Unionists, counting 47 percent of the votes but losing every seat, acknowledged defeat. They had put forth their strongest candidates. They had gotten out their voters—for this election, like its 1830 predecessor, had drawn probably the maximum number of voters. Again, the 2,735 who cast ballots may have exceeded the number of those legally eligible. But at the polls the nullifiers showed the same discipline which the Union men had displayed in King Street. The least popular nullifier candidate received only thirty fewer votes than the most popular. Their party lines held tight. So it was that Charleston voters had approved nullification as the state's proper response to federal tariff laws which, so they argued, exceeded Congress's constitutional prerogatives. There was little likelihood that the electorate would soon reverse itself.[20]

The newly elected legislature met almost at once to call a state convention which would, in turn, meet to nullify federal law. In the subsequent election for convention delegates, Charleston Unionists ran not a single candidate. Thus the city voiced no opposition to the convention which, on November 24, voted that both the 1828 and the 1832 tariffs were null and void within South Carolina.[21] By December 1832 Charleston commerce was at a standstill, and her people, however much they were ostensibly at one with their state, faced the possibility of civil conflict. In contemplating the arrival of federal troops they knew that only a bare majority of her white population supported state sovereignty over national loyalty, and that almost half would give their primary allegiance to the Union. In evolving a politics which had elevated an economic question to a constitutional issue, they had watched their city stagger to the brink of armed violence. Thus had nullification shaped the new realities of Charleston's politics.

• • •

The preparation for civil war, as 1832 gave way to 1833, took its toll. Most militia companies had already openly identified with the nullifiers, and the Fourth Brigade, of which these citizen soldiers were part, was now commanded by James Hamilton. Conscious of their minority position, Unionists had, since early fall, looked increasingly to Washington for their own and their city's security. Shortly after the October election Joel Poinsett had warned President Jackson that the nullifiers were prepared to storm the customhouse. But even before that, Jackson had appointed Captain Jesse Elliott, unquestionably loyal to the Union, to command the federal vessels and installations in Charleston harbor. He was also transferring unreliable army officers out of the district and, with Port Collector Pringle's help, purging the customs service. Moreover, he had dispatched a secret agent in the guise of a post office inspector to "see the F[or]ts and revenue cutters in [the] harbour" and "to obtain the real intentions of the nullfyers [sic]."[22]

When, on December 16, the president of the United States issued his "Proclamation to the People of South Carolina," telling them flatly that "disunion by armed force is treason," he was prepared to meet treason. Pringle had been charged to use revenue cutters to collect duties—or to secure the usual bonds for their future payment—from all ships entering the harbor, even if they must be stopped in the stream. If violence threatened on land, Pringle was to move the customhouse facilities from the vulnerable Exchange building to small Castle Pinckney Island, which could better be protected by the Navy.[23]

The likelihood of armed confrontation spiraled upward as each side prepared for it. The Young Men's Free Trade and States' Rights Association pledged itself "to repel any act of aggression" and "to march at a moments warning to defend . . . Carolina and the cause of Liberty." Robert Hayne, acting assistant adjutant and inspector general for the state, was organizing an emergency military force of 10,000 men to defend Charleston from federal invasion. On the other side, and less openly, Joel Poinsett channeled arms from Washington to some 1,500 local men recruited to defend national interests in the city. Prominent Union men went about armed with "deadly weapons," and many agreed with Mitchell King that "War, civil, servile war, seemed inevitable."[24]

During the three long months of crisis, however, resolution wavered. Men of property acted cautiously, while men of temper waxed wroth. By mid-January merchants were pressed so hard that even some nullifiers indicated a willingness to pay duties. Neither ship captains nor consignees backed British consul William Ogilby's diplomatic protest against the revenue cutters' stopping British vessels under sail to collect customs. Nor did practical men back General James Hamilton and Miss Maria H. Pinckney in their publicly staged refusal to pay duties on the Cuban sugar they had imported specifically to defy federal law and thereby demonstrate that Carolinians *"would go even to the death"* to defend free trade.[25]

Neither by late January 1833 was Joel Poinsett the least assured that Union men would stay their course without support from federal troops. Divided and frightened, "a majority of the Union party in Charleston" declined to join in the posse comitatus proposed by the federal marshal to defend U.S. property. Anxiety ran deep, and the dilemma was personal. "There is scarcely a family wherein some member is not in the opposite ranks," Poinsett wrote President Jackson, "and it is certain in such a contest father would be arrayed against son and Brother against brother."[26]

Searching for some solace in these bleak days, William Simms thought that by late January most nullifier hotheads had begun to show "a disposition . . . to claw off from the issue & crisis they [had] provoked." And in early March, though Henry Clay's compromise tariff was received in Charleston with no enthusiasm, nullifiers did "hail [it] with gratification" as "decided evidence of a disposition on the part of Congress to do justice" to the South.[27]

Yet the residue of passion had not been fully vented. Years of living in "the very center of a dormant volcano" bequeathed a legacy of "constant fear that it would burst forth [again] with irrepressible fire and spread utter ruin and desolation around."[28] Reason required that this anxiety find a new object. And thus, after almost three solid years during which the possibility of slave insurrection was hardly mentioned publicly and virtually never in print, overt consciousness of Charleston's black majority surfaced again just as it had after the Denmark Vesey affair in 1822.

It came into the open not just because nullifiers needed to find a new issue—despite James Petigru's conviction in the summer of 1833 that their intention was "to pick a quarrel with the North about negroes," and Mitchell King's that they were seeking "a better engine for effecting their unholy purposes." There was a credible rationale for the fear's new guise. Antislavery sentiment was growing ever more visible. After the Nat Turner uprising of 1831 the Virginia legislature had debated ending slavery in that state. In May 1833 the British Parliament voted to abolish slavery in the West Indies. Since 1831 William Lloyd Garrison had published unrestrained attacks on slavery in his weekly newspaper, the *Liberator;* and for more than a year the New England Anti-Slavery Society had been openly holding meetings in Boston to advocate immediate and uncompensated emancipation throughout the United States. Moreover, Charlestonians not only knew all this but knew as well that abolitionist propaganda reached their city. Already a sailor had been apprehended for peddling copies of David Walker's violent *Appeal* against slavery on a waterfront street.[29]

In July 1833, then, the South Carolina Association's first public meeting in years recalled familiar fears as it celebrated the tenth anniversary of its founding in response to the Vesey revolt. Simultaneously the *Mercury* published a series of editorials and a plethora of letters all exposing the dangers of abolitionism; even the *Courier* played indirectly on the new uneasiness by proclaiming that it would print nothing more on the "West India Question," as British emancipation in the Caribbean was called.[30]

Unionists were clearly uncomfortable in this atmosphere. The next summer it was rumored that Joel Poinsett's political enemies had toasted him as "the Denmark Vesey of 1834." Yet he and his friends were as much a part of slave society as any nullifier. "Can anything surpass such utter desolation," Alfred Huger fretted at the same time, as he described his personal isolation and despair. "[D]eserted by friends . . . [and] abandoned by kindred," he and his associates anticipated becoming the objects of the "merciless brutality" of a "demonic gang" both "infuriated" and ignorant. Their only recourse, they believed, was to seek reconciliation by ending the political schism among kith and kin. Consequently, they had proposed in the fall of 1833 a bipartisan slate for the city election. In returning government to "good men" regardless of political faction, they had hoped to restore "confidence . . . to the people" and to secure "peace and quiet" for themselves.[31]

But neither nullifier leaders nor their ragtag followers were ready for compromise, and the independent ticket of gentlemen went down to utter defeat—except for the four candidates who also ran on the nullifiers' ticket. Although the tariff controversy per se had been settled by South Carolina's revocation of nullification, the commitment to state sovereignty persisted. The state convention which accepted the compromise tariff had also, on the same day, nullified the federal Force Act. And in December 1833 the legislature reimposed the Nullification Convention's requirement that all militia officers take an unqualified oath of allegiance to South Carolina. At once Unionist officers resigned and companies threatened to dissolve rather than brook constraints on the election of their own officers. Challenged in the state courts, the oath requirement was soon ruled to be in violation of the South Carolina constitution.[32]

The nullifiers could then have let the issue die, but they chose to replay the old issues of state sovereignty. In their 1834 platform they proposed a constitutional amendment requiring an unqualified loyalty oath from all state officials. In so doing they finally loosed the violence so narrowly avoided in 1832 and so ominously threatening ever since. On October 13, 1834, a mob some three hundred strong rushed Unionist headquarters on Boundary Street. Attacked, Unionists fired into the crowd. Nullifiers fired back. But only a few were armed, and almost at once the crowd surged toward the state arsenal to get more weapons. Shortly after they arrived, so too did Governor Hayne and General Hamilton. Finally the rioters— persuaded by rhetoric, reasonable reflection, or the realization that further violence would inflict still more casualties on both sides—were convinced to stop. It took this "great row" to shock nullifier leaders into political compromise.[33]

Thus it was less important who had won the 1834 canvass—it was another nullifier landslide—than that the legislators chosen acted at once to restore their city's sanity. Although he had lost election to the House, James Petigru went to Columbia, where he was invited to give that body his views on the pending loyalty oath. What he said on the floor, however, was less important than his conversations the next day and the following week with James Hamilton, his political arch-foe and his former law partner. Hamilton had sought the interview. Newly elected to the state senate, the former state governor and federal congressman had already urged conciliation on his chamber. Then, meeting in a private but impersonal hotel room, he and Petigru forged their strategy for compromise. They knew each other well. Their rice plantations lay close together on the Savannah River. Their daughters attended the same finishing school in New York. Both had started adult life on the fringes of Charleston's legal and social world, and both had gained professional and political prominence and a place in the city's upper class. As gentlemen they were adept at accommodation. And when they emerged from their final session, the deed was done.[34]

Each side was allowed its dignity. Opting to enshrine the loyalty oath in a simple law rather than a constitutional amendment, the legislature also passed resolutions that the avowal of allegiance to the state was in no way intended to conflict with citizens' obligations "to the Constitution of the United States." Rather the new law "expressly provid[ed] for [its] support," although it "maintain[ed] the sovereignty of South-Carolina."[35]

By formulating words of little meaning and an act without substance, two men had ended the political battle which, for four years, had divided Charleston into warring camps and threatened her very stability. Powerful individuals meeting in private had decided what public bodies and electoral polls then legitimated. What had seemed in 1832, 1833, and 1834 to be the emergence of a clearly defined two-party organization turned out to be only a short-lived departure from a politics of deference because, in the end, Charlestonians preferred public order to partisan ideology. The ability to pull back so completely reflected the reality of power in a city where one-half of the politically powerful were also members of the upper class, and where one-half of all political leaders and major officeholders were, if not personally wealthy, at least accustomed to wielding economic power.[36]

Politics did not, of course, revert to the status quo ante. Among "little men" the nullifier-Unionist division remained for a decade the most important political distinction, although it lacked practical meaning. Political debts, both great and small, incurred during the crisis years were paid off in the patronage and electoral support on which former nullifiers thrived. Occasionally, but only occasionally, national distinctions emerging elsewhere between Whigs and Democrats affected local politics. No new political excitement replaced the old. And yet Charleston, however alert she was to the dangers inherent in the politics of passion, still retained an emotional public style on issues connected with slavery. The saving grace was that, on that subject, the entire white community was presumed to agree. In 1835 the issue was abolitionist literature arriving in the mails, and the response a short reign of vigilante justice. The next year Congressman Henry L. Pinckney was tarred with heresy because his support for the Gag Resolution, which buried all antislavery petitions in a House committee, was understood at home as tacit recognition of federal power to tamper with slavery. No matter what his nullifier past, Pinckney failed of reelection in 1836. Slavery had replaced state sovereignty as the key political issue. But it was, on the whole, more a unifying than a divisive issue politically.[37]

• • •

While Boston politics similarly reflected community values and historic principles, they were, especially on economic issues, pragmatic. The Revolution was venerated, but revolutionary rhetoric was not. Public issues were addressed as matters demanding practical results. Political passion was tolerated only as long as it threatened neither property nor public peace. Economics should not be politicized, however much politicians and legislatures might be asked to forward local interests. And politics should remain subservient to the community's economic well-being.

Within this framework the commercial city of Boston made the transition from firm opposition to protective tariffs in 1816, when they threatened her postwar trade revival, to equivocal support in 1828. Underlying that shift was the growing importance of textile manufacturing in Massachusetts, in which so much Boston capital was invested and on which so much Boston trade depended. It was, however, only in 1830, two years after the state's congressional delegation had helped shape the Tariff of Abominations, that Boston resolved her persistent ambivalence between her merchants' commitment to free trade and their trade's reliance on domestic manufactures.

Throughout the preceding decade, Senator Daniel Webster had often acted on behalf of the Boston Associates, incorporators of the first textile manufactories at Waltham and Lowell. Not surprisingly, then, it was at a meeting attended by Webster, one of the Lawrences, and Patrick Tracy Jackson, among others, that Bostonians with sizable textile interests decided to back a congressional candidate committed to protection. They chose one of their own, Nathan Appleton. Against him ran Henry Lee, a long-time merchant and supporter of free trade—but also Jackson's brother-in-law and a frequently disgruntled investor in textile stock. Except for the tariff issue, little separated the candidates. Thus when the votes were counted and Appleton carried the election with 56 percent of the vote, the city was believed to have spoken on protection. In an address to his fellow citizens, Mayor Otis, who had been widely criticized for using his office to endorse Appleton, excoriated those who challenged the verdict. Revealing more than he intended about the underlying framwork of Boston politics, he condemned those who would "excite the middling classes against the supposed rich" and their tariff. After all, many of the city's "most opulent individuals" had been in the "anti-manufacturing party." Now was the time to close ranks and heed Appleton's claim that protection guarded the interests of both labor and capital. The issue was settled by 1833, and the Free Trade party had completely disappeared.[38]

So simple a resolution of the tariff question left Boston's economic leaders scornful of Carolina's traumatic political drama. The Southrons were unreasonable in rejecting compromise and misguided in valuing price more than industry. Indeed, Yankee contempt for "treason & rebellion" overcame political difference, and all parties praised Jackson's firm course in proclaiming that federal law would be enforced. Congressman Appleton looked behind the façade of nullification to discover deeper economic troubles than the tariff could possibly create. Carolina's problem was, he believed, exhausted land, which would produce only three bales of cotton where new land in Louisiana could produce six. If that was true—and the population shift out of the Palmetto State testified that many farmers and planters believed it was—free trade could avail little, while moderate protection would enhance national prosperity with benefits for both South and North. Thus rather than "stoop" before nullifier demands, Bostonians held firm—even though some investors sold their Lowell shares, believing that inevitable tariff reductions would drive prices down.[39]

Perversely, it was the Bank of the United States, despite its limited activity in Boston, that shaped politics and generated new partisan divisions in the northern city. In Charleston either its financial role was too central—it furnished half the currency circulating in Carolina—or its style too accommodating for it to be divisive. Consequently, throughout the tariff controversy, although the local branch office was headed by Dr. Joseph Johnson, a prominent Unionist, it retained nullifiers on its board and struggled for institutional impartiality. In 1832 Nicholas Biddle himself ordered sizable loans for James Hamilton as well as James Pringle and Joel Poinsett, just as he cultivated the support in Congress of George McDuffie as well as William Drayton.[40]

The BUS was, however, no monster in Massachusetts, where it furnished only 3 percent of the currency in circulation. The Boston branch was directed by elderly and very rich gentlemen who used it, so Biddle's advisors warned him, primarily as their private brokerage office. Gardiner Greene, worth about $3 million and crowding eighty, was president. Advising Greene, the cashier, and everyone else in the bank was Thomas Handasyd Perkins, nearly seventy and living on the income generated by the enormous fortune he had made in the China trade. Both men were slow-moving targets for Democratic charges that the bank was a monopoly of wealth and a bastion of the old order.[41]

Except to Democrats, the Bank of the United States was, in Boston, nothing special, nothing more than another bank, to be judged on its utility to the business community. It generated no special loyalty among the economic elite or among Jackson's political opponents. Nonetheless, the BUS did affect Boston's prosperity because it was the only institution which provided a stable currency and credit system nationwide. It thereby made trade between different parts of the country easier and more predictable. When Jackson vetoed the bank's recharter, when Biddle contracted credit, when Jackson curtailed federal deposits and Biddle again counterattacked, when together they disrupted credit and drove up interest rates, Boston's commerce fell victim to the rents their bank war created in the national web of commerce.[42]

Boston's businessmen grew frantic as interest rates soared to as much as 20 percent in February 1834. Bound neither to King Andrew nor to King Nicholas, they damned the partisan game both were playing. Even William Appleton, Gardiner Greene's successor in 1833, disdained his bank's heady political preoccupations. Looking back on his first months as president of the local branch, he concluded that the bank war was "unnecessary" and that the bank's fatal flaw was that "like most great monied Institutions [its] Managers feel their power more than they should or think they have more power than they have." Loyal to Boston rather than the central office, Appleton pressured headquarters to stem its unreasonable contraction of credit—at least in Boston. Things had simply gone too far when, by early February, nearly three-quarters of the branch's outstanding loans had not been renewed. Appleton went to Philadelphia and put it to Biddle bluntly. If the main office did not reverse its contraction policy in Boston, Boston would withdraw all support from Biddle in Washington. And Abbott Lawrence, whom Boston had sent to Congress the year before, backed Appleton to the hilt. By February 19, Biddle surrendered. He would give special treatment to the Boston branch because, as he wrote Appleton, he knew it would be judicious about extending credit. But it was not to financial wisdom but to political reality that he had made his concessions. He still believed the Yankees erred in sidestepping a confrontation which could bring Jackson to his knees. But, so he wrote Lawrence, he would "rather err with you than be right with many others."[43]

The about-face came none too soon, for on March 6 a large public meeting in Faneuil Hall debated what action would best address the banking crisis. Appleton, who had feared its outcome, saved the day. When Appleton's trip to Philadelphia and his subsequent ability to accommodate hard-pressed debtors became known, Biddle and his bank were safe in Boston. Within ten days of the meeting nearly seven thousand citizens signed a petition condemning the financial policies of Jackson—not Biddle.[44] Appleton and friends could congratulate themselves. They had not only addressed the city's financial crisis, they had opened the way for an anti-Jackson political consolidation. They had brought together great merchants and corner grocers, as commercial interests of all sorts turned out to provide two-fifths of the signatures. That the petition was broadly representative and popular is attested by the one-third of the signers who were mechanics, the five out of six signers whose occupations lacked particular prestige. Indeed, only a tenth of the petitioners could be said to exert any economic power, and fewer than a twentieth could be called rich.[45]

That this was no blind commitment to the Bank of the United States Appleton's course had already made clear. That bank, like any other, was acceptable only as it served Boston's economic needs. Boston had avoided a public battle over the Bank of the United States only because Appleton, in his private war with Biddle, had made certain it would serve local and practical concerns. He had threatened to resign unless he had "controul of the business . . . and a Capital, not to be withdrawn" and had exacted from Biddle a promise that, as branch president, he "might do any thing [he] pleased in relation to the Office in Boston." Biddle was, he concluded, "a man of talent . . . but too fond of power. . . ."[46] Neither he nor his bank could be allowed to unleash that power on Boston. Instead of holding the city's economy hostage to the bank's political ends, Biddle's bank became at last only the instrument for building the Whig party in Boston—a party which, like the branch office, would serve local interests.

The Bank of the United States created a two-party system in Boston less by dividing a prevailing consensus than by forcing an amalgamation of small parties and factions into two broad coalitions. In the years before Andrew Jackson became president, the city's dominant party had been the National Republicans, which in 1828 had supported native son John Quincy Adams by a margin of three to one. After Adams's national defeat, however, the party fissured into its constituent parts: the followers of Daniel Webster, the old-school Federalists who hated the entire Adams family only slightly less than they feared Jackson, and the moderate Federalists and personal coterie loyal to the former president. The old party could, it was true, be patched together for specific elections—Appleton had won his seat in the House of Representatives as a National Republican in 1830—but whatever cohesive program it had smacked of the past.[47]

But in the interval between Adams's and Biddle's defeat, new parties sprang up to reflect current frictions and address current issues. By mid-1830 the Anti-Masons had parlayed tensions between rich and poor into a local political organization whose attacks on secret societies were indictments of all the ties which allowed those in power to manipulate government and defy the electorate's will. Like other single-issue parties, this association injected new life into local politics by challenging established politicians regardless of their national affiliation. On the one hand, they blasted old Federalist Mayor Otis for violating freedom of speech in denying them the use of Faneuil Hall and then defaming their collective character. On the other, they denounced powerful Democratic leader and Mason David Henshaw. Nevertheless, their growing numbers lured old politicians who needed new support at the polls. Ex-President Adams, Congressman Edward Everett, and mayoral candidate Samuel Y. Armstrong—National Republicans all—sought their endorsement. So too did Otis's brother-in-law William Foster, who, as a radical Democrat, stood much closer to Anti-Masonic attacks on monopoly, aristocracy, and secret power.[48]

Nonetheless, their party's concentration on the Masonic conspiracy and their reluctance to embrace money and banking as central issues limited Anti-Masons' potential to become a meaningful national party. Yet their visibility in several states in the early 1830s gave them far more significance than most of Boston's other single-issue groups—the Free Bridge party, the Anti-Imprisonment for Debt faction, and the Grocers' group among them. Nor did ties with a similar organization in New York enable Boston's Workingmen's Party to build either a local coalition or a national party. Although it was strong enough to run or endorse candidates in city and state elections from 1833 to 1835, its platform, promoting more numerous schools and more equitable taxes and opposing monopolies, attracted too few votes to give it a significant voice. In the 1835 city election it garnered only 500 votes. Moreover, the candidates it endorsed were frequently National Republicans, even though the Workingmen's party had more in common with the other splinter groups who explicitly opposed "aristocratic institutions & manners."[49]

If the futility of single-issue parties tells much about the nonideological nature of Boston's politics, the emergence of the Democratic party again demonstrates politics' subservience to economics. In the days of Jackson's presidency, some of the city's most prominent Democrats had drifted into the party from the arch-conservative Old Federalists. Theodore Lyman, the only Democratic Republican elected mayor from 1828 to 1836, was of this number. Even the party leaders were little different from their opponents, except that they held few elective posts. So it was less by egalitarian rhetoric that they challenged the establishment than by their use of federal patronage to feed their entrepreneurial aspirations. Heading the list was David Henshaw, collector of customs and a former apothecary. Almost equally visible were his brother Charles, also a druggist; Daniel Brodhead, a merchant tailor; and John Simpson, an upholsterer, all of whom held major federal appointments while they secured for the Commonwealth Bank, in which they were all interested, the federal deposits removed from Boston's BUS branch office. Other Democrats sought similar favors for the smaller and newer banks of which they were officers. John M. Fiske at the Middling Interest Bank pressed Secretary of the Treasury Levi Woodbury for federal deposits because he and his associates were *"active friends* of the Administration, and as such [*might*] *be opposed by the Bank aristocracy of State Street."* Editor Charles Greene urged that the Hancock Bank be made a pet bank so that it could "afford young democratic merchants the same favors that their federal neighbors receive. . . ."[50]

Indeed, the Democracy in Boston was so self-serving that it comprised a faction at odds with Democrats elsewhere in the state. As economic power seekers its leaders exuded none of the Jacksonian image. Relying on patronage rather than votes for their power base, they ignored the mechanics and laborers of the North End and South Boston who were loyal to the party's ticket and who elected its few councilmen.[51] Yet paradoxically their very banking connections joined them to the radicals in condemning the BUS.

Thus the bank stalemate of 1834 offered to Jacksonians the same opportunity to consolidate as it had to anti-Jacksonians. As the latter had collected their seven thousand signatures, so some three thousand other Bostonians signed a counterpetition supporting Jackson's course in his war with Biddle and drew thereby the clear line which henceforth separated voters into two camps of roughly the same proportions at the polls as they had been in signing the two petitions. Moreover, because the antibank position attracted almost twice as many mechanics and half as many businessmen as had the probank document, the division also cleared the way for merging splinter parties into one or the other of the two emerging principal parties.[52] Consequently, from 1834 onward, the city's political contests were fought out between Whigs and Democrats. And because the 1834 economic and class divisions held relatively firm, Whigs dominated Boston's political life for the next decade.

As a minority in the city, Democrats could gain power only by forging an alliance with their counterparts statewide, whose rural priorities were not infrequently at odds with Boston's economic growth. Such an alliance, however, created fewer problems for either Whigs or city merchants than did Charleston's efforts to tie her interests to a party with a rural majority. Unlike the southern city, Boston was and remained the state capital. Both within and outside the State House her persistently Whiggish delegations defended urban and commercial interests.

Thus the apparent similarities with which the *Imperial Gazette* had vested Charleston's and Boston's defiance of King Andrew were no truer than the reported demise of the American republic. How the cities' politics differed lay finally in their electorates' priorities and the representation each chose. If occupation be a guide, voters' economic interests in each city were remarkably similar in their distribution. Men engaged in commerce comprised nearly one-third of the electorate in each city—although in Boston they were slightly more numerous and in Charleston slightly less. Mechanics, laborers, and those of unknown occupation numbered just half of Boston's electorate and only slightly less than half of Charleston's. The crucial difference lay in two relatively small groups. Professionals' share of Charleston's electorate was twice their share in Boston. Nor did Boston have any equivalent for the 7 percent of Charleston's electorate who were planters. Indeed, in the southern city close to one of every five voters was either a planter or a professional. Thus in Boston, where professional voters were but one in twenty, this generally prestigious group failed to provide the influential counterweight to commercial interests which they did in Charleston.[53]

The men each city elected to her state legislature confirmed the differing political influence commercial interests generated in each. During the nullification crisis only 12 percent of Charleston's representatives in Columbia were engaged in commerce. It was planters and professionals who

Pragmatic Politics and the Politics of Passion

dominated her legislative delegation, two out of every three representatives being drawn from those occupations. By contrast, while one of every three legislators whom Boston sent to the State House during the early 1830s was also professional, a good half were men of mercantile and entrepreneurial outlook.[54] Thus it was that Boston ensured that politics remained the handmaiden of economics, while in Charleston a vitally important economic issue generated a politics of ideology. The one was prudently pragmatic, the other passionately dramatic.

7

Policing the City and Providing Welfare

Antebellum city governments had two principal responsibilities: to assist the destitute and to insure the public safety. Their ability to achieve those goals effectively depended, of course, on having the requisite resources. Yet individual cities also had distinctive styles, and Boston and Charleston defined their municipal practices quite differently. In so doing, the southern city gave highest priority to maintaining a socially cohesive community; the northern, to public efficiency.

Boston's municipal government, created in 1821, set a pattern for modernity. Its form and structure, unlike the traditional town-meeting government Boston had just abandoned, was well suited to meet the new problems and potentials of incipient urbanization. Consisting of a mayor and a two-chamber city council made up of eight aldermen elected at large and a common council of forty-eight chosen equally from the twelve wards into which the city was divided, Boston's executive and legislative branches mimicked those of state and nation. In addition, because the city (excluding only tiny Chelsea) was identical with Suffolk County, her judicial system was her own. The state-financed county probate and municipal courts and jail served the same population as did the city's police court and House of Correction. The scope of governmental authority was as a result well defined. Likewise the boundaries of governmental responsibility were more clearly charted than in Charleston. Those areas immediately adjacent to the city clearly lay in different jurisdictions, for both Dorchester and Roxbury were organized towns and parts of another county.[1]

In his seven years as mayor, Josiah Quincy could therefore shape the

Policing the City and Providing Welfare

new charter to a well-defined municipality. When he left office in January 1829, after being defeated in a hard-fought election, he had accomplished much. The city's business had been rationalized, her real estate surveyed, her voting lists updated, her streets straightened, her avenues "enlarged," her public places—including the new market—"ornamented," and her common sewers "regulated" and repaired. All this had taken money, and the city debt had climbed during his mayoralty from $100,000 in 1823 to over $900,000 in 1828. Quincy's drive toward modernity had created dissent—much of it about fiscal affairs. But for many, the loss of the personal satisfactions customarily derived from public service bound to a village mentality was the chief bone of contention. Quincy had valued public safety over the cheapness of citizen bucket brigades and the good will of volunteer and entirely independent fire companies. Pursuing that goal, he had dismantled the board of fire wardens, which had previously overseen fire fighting, and replaced it with a single, salaried engineer, who by 1828 was supervising new city-owned engines and an up-to-date hose system manned by 1,200 at least minimally disciplined volunteers. Though friction persisted between the fire companies and city hall, the results were clearly beneficial. Fire insurance rates dropped by 20 percent.[2]

Similarly, Quincy had put safety from vermin and rats ahead of the profits which unsystematic and unreliable private scavengers had formerly reaped from carting the city's offal into the country. He instituted regularly scheduled pickups by city employees and an annual spring cleansing to remove unusual accumulations of trash. However primitive the state of medical knowledge, the mayor well understood that filth and disease were linked, and found justification for his policy in the declining mortality rates which accompanied the new system. Concerned to protect public order as much as public health and private property, Quincy oversaw the creation of a House of Reformation for Juvenile Offenders and the construction of a new House of Correction for older offenders, where inmates were separately housed according to the severity of their crimes and where the less hardened were to be rehabilitated.[3]

Old ways, however, die hard, and by uprooting established traditions and building new institutions Josiah Quincy drew to himself criticism and widespread enmity, so much so that in December 1828 his fellow townsmen turned him out of office. The strongest of three candidates running against him was Thomas C. Amory, an assistant city engineer whom Quincy had refused to promote to chief engineer. Losing the firemen's vote to Amory cost Quincy his customary majority and reelection. But Amory no more than Quincy threatened the established social or economic order. Rather, conservatives feared that the failure of either to receive the majority required for election and the refusal of both to run again foretold a major change in city politics. Charles Francis Adams worried that the "people [were] for taking power into their own hands," while cagey Harrison Gray Otis, observing the "violent commotion" Adams feared, let himself be persuaded out of retirement by the pleas of "various parties and interests in the city." With little real competition, he was handily elected mayor.[4]

Although his inaugural address promised strict economy, Mayor Otis followed in his predecessor's steps.[5] His ability to do so lay partly in the hierarchy of power and prestige which the bicameral city council enshrined. Throughout the decade, mayors and aldermen were twice as likely as common councilmen to be merchants and were notably more likely to enjoy wealth, upper-class standing, and the broader political power derived from service in the legislature. That this composition fueled their ability to lead rather than kindled conflict between upper and lower chambers is explained by the consistent commercial and non-Jacksonian majority in both chambers. Despite the presence of mechanics and Democrats in the common council—and their near invisibility among aldermen—the city council as a whole and each house alone were, throughout the 1830s, controlled by commercially oriented majorities in which storekeepers and traders joined wholesalers to insure that mercantile interests were steadily supported. Nor did annual elections erode the special power of the upper chamber, for mayor and aldermen stayed in office notably longer than did common councilmen, half of whom retired with each election.[6] In addition, the city's growth eased the strain created by a growing debt, which doubled again in the 1830s. Increasing income in the pre-panic years assuaged anxiety about that debt, as a 20 percent rise in tax rates and a 44 percent increase in assessed taxable property combined almost to double annual tax returns between 1829 and 1836.[7]

Yet the tax structure itself remained unaltered. The city turned over to the state a portion of the poll tax levied on all males between sixteen and seventy years of age. All other tax revenues remained in the city. Most productive was the real property tax, rates for which were set by three salaried assessors, whose expert judgments were tempered by political wisdom after 1836, when two unpaid associate assessors appointed in each ward helped to insure neighborhood equity.[8] Even so, establishing the value of real property was more difficult and subject to debate than was the uniform tax on all males of a certain age. But such value judgments were mere child's play compared with assessing personal property (which the city also taxed), at a time when personalty was the fastest-growing and most underassessed property in the city. Traditionally a citizen either submitted an exact list of his commercial stock-in-trade and his other investments, which could not be challenged, or else chanced an unchallengeable assessment by town officials. Preferring to risk a blind assessment rather than reveal their business assets, Bostonians not only refused to submit reports on personal property but were undoubtedly undertaxed as a result. In 1827 only 26 of the city's 12,000 taxables submitted a list, while the rest benefited from assessors' reluctance to evaluate property at which they could only guess.[9]

In spite of these deficiencies, tax collections and the city's ability to borrow provided the resources requisite not just for regular policing and civic improvements but for meeting crises. In 1832 the Asiatic cholera, which first entered North America through Canada, tested the city government's ability to respond. Mayor Quincy had replaced the old lay board of health with a board of five distinguished consulting physicians. But their acumen had been untested, except by the city's free vaccination program for schoolchildren, the customary quarantine regulations, and an isolation hospital for contagious diseases on Rainsford Island.[10] Now, as the cholera moved southward and public pressure mounted, the city council realized that public authority as well as professional expertise was needed to enforce rigorous regulatons should the epidemic reach Boston. Therefore a new board of health made up of the mayor, four aldermen, and six councilmen was created in June. It was given extraordinary powers—even the authority to order inspection of private houses for health menaces, at a time when the sense of emergency pressed hard. Only days after the board was created the dread disease, which was killing between thirty and a hundred Montrealers daily, reached "the interiour of New York & Vermont."[11]

Although Boston acted knowledgeably and firmly and was, in the event, spared the worst ravages of the contagion, the public response did reflect class distinctions. Because cholera was almost uniformly believed to be a class disease, afflicting the "degraded and suffering poor, the superannuated, the exhausted, the intemperate, [and] the debauched," the board of health concentrated its work in the hovels and tenements along Broad Street and south of the Common. Persons living in filth and likely to cause "nuisances" were removed from their homes, by force if necessary, as were the fifteen families who, with a large sow, lived in a single Broad Street house devoid of toilet facilities. Public health officials now condemned—as they had not earlier—buildings which lacked "suitable vaults and privies, and drains under ground for waste water." Yet informing the attitudes which underlay these sensible measures and the creation of emergency hospitals was the reluctance of the privately managed Massachusetts General Hospital to treat potential victims unless "all the other hospitals [should be] filled so that no adequate accommodation [could] be had elsewhere. . . ." So, too, Dr. George Parkman's neighbors successfully blocked his proffer of his Bowdoin Square "mansion house" for a cholera hospital. Nonetheless, Boston did police the public health effectively, combining the expertise of consulting physicians with the authority of elected officials. The cholera epidemic claimed only eighty-six lives. And, just as important, the city council thereafter extended the drain system, as it also continued the annual cleansing which laid the groundwork for a modern public health system.[12]

Boston dedicated notably fewer resources to policing the city against crime. Indeed, its chief law enforcement officer, the city marshal, was burdened with a multitude of responsibilities, being charged with overseeing street and vault cleaning and enforcing all city ordinances, as well as detecting and reporting crimes, arresting and testifying against alleged criminals, and using "all lawful ways and means, for the effectual prosecution, and final conviction of offenders."[13]

It was an awesome task to enforce all laws in a city of sixty thousand inhabitants with a force of but twenty-four constables and eighty night watchmen, of whom only eighteen were on duty at any one time. Yet these arrangements generated no perception of impending crisis like that which had prompted reorganization of the fire department and innovations in public health. Constables, it was true, did little more than serve court orders, for which they received their pay in the form of fees. Indeed, until 1838, even with two pay raises for the watch (who were universally believed to be inefficient), regular police expenditures in Boston did not exceed 6 percent of the annual city budget. And neither in 1838, when Boston finally appointed its first modern police force of six full-time paid officers, nor in 1845, when the force boasted twenty-two men, did it add more than about 1 percent to the public order's share of the city's operating expenses.[14]

When it came to providing a water supply of sufficient quantity to fight fires and of adequate quality to maintain public health, however, a paucity of resources did impose a long delay in meeting a major urban problem. But an equal obstacle was the prolonged debate about whether bringing fresh water into the city was more properly a public or a private concern. The Boston Aqueduct Company, founded in 1795, supplied the older part of the city with water from Jamaica Pond. But its pipes served only the main streets; it lacked facilities to pump water up Beacon Hill; and seasonal variations in the pond's water level often left regular customers totally dry. But until 1840 the company overhauled its equipment only once and extended service not at all.[15]

Not surprisingly, then, Mayor Quincy had commissioned the first public survey of the city's water supply in 1825. Because the city already used an estimated 1.5 million gallons of water a day, Quincy deemed formation of a municipally operated water system an urgent matter. But in the end he simply launched a twenty-year debate. Sometimes the battle raged fiercest over the best source for a pure and reliable supply. Should it come from Long Pond in Natick, Farm Pond in Framingham, Spot Pond in Stoneham—or even the Charles River? But the most critical issue was whether public authority or private enterprise should be charged with meeting a need about which all agreed. The Aqueduct Company justified its refusal to undertake renovation and enlargement as long as the possibility of a city-owned water system jeopardized the investment which expansion would require. And another private corporation, the Boston Hydraulic Company, chartered in 1836, came to nothing when the city council rejected its invitation to subscribe one-third of its capital.[16]

Growing population, increasingly brackish well water, and diminishing reserves for fire fighting all generated popular pressure for action. In August 1836 a public meeting in Faneuil Hall voted overwhelmingly that the city "in its corporate capacity, with its own means and credit" should provide abundant soft water for her citizens. The issue was debated in the fall elections. In January 1837 the just-elected city council authorized another feasibility study and an experiment with drilling artesian wells. But then the panic and subsequent depression brought plans to seek legislative authority for a municipal water system to a halt.[17]

Nonetheless, the issue did not die. In 1838 four massive petitions favoring a city water system and four opposing it streamed into city hall. Perplexed, the city council resorted to an advisory referendum in April, in which some four thousand citizens collectively and in all wards but the Aqueduct-supplied North End favored a municipal waterworks three to two. Still, nothing was settled. Public meetings discussed and discussed while the city toyed with buying out the old Aqueduct Company or buying into yet another private corporation, the Spot Pond Aqueduct Company.[18]

Lured by lower labor costs, the old Aqueduct Company even began to improve its facilities without the assurances it had previously insisted on from city hall. But citizens, long annoyed by the company's high prices and bad service, gave it little support. Ultimately it took the return of prosperity and the election of the second Mayor Josiah Quincy in 1845 to build the city waterworks which his father had proposed in 1825.[19]

Less amenable to the centralized efficiency which shaped the changes made in exercising the city's police powers was municipal government's second major responsibility: assisting the destitute, the sick, the handicapped, the very old, and the very young. Mayor Quincy's efforts to rationalize these duties had run up against the popularly elected Overseers of the Poor, a remnant of town government which had not been made subservient to the city council. This board, with loyalties to the wards which had elected its members, doled out the income from a fund of over

$100,000 that it alone controlled. Challenging the overseers' traditional largesse in giving monetary assistance to worthy natives and shelter in the old almshouse to sick transients was the new House of Industry, which opened in 1824.[20] Under directors responsible to the city council, the House of Industry's operation was guided by the popular belief that paupers could be reformed if they were first made to feel a social stigma for their economic deficiencies and then acclimated to regular industry. It followed that they should be institutionalized, taught skills, put to work, and made to absorb the work ethic while, incidentally, they helped pay the costs of their own confinement.

Perversely, the new approach was simultaneously promoted and balked by the growing numbers who sought public assistance. On the one hand, in-migration and immigration made the city's poor more numerous and less native—even though their numbers grew at a much slower rate than did total population. Consequently, city taxpayers complained of high welfare costs even when costs per inmate went down, especially as the Overseers of the Poor channeled funds formerly given the almshouse into outdoor relief, which they controlled, rather than into the House of Industry, which they did not. Moreover, state government cut its traditional subsidy for the cost of sheltering transient paupers in the city institutions.[21]

On the other hand, the House of Industry soon discovered that many of those who entered its care could neither leave nor work because of infancy, old age, permanent physical disability, or incurable insanity. Its mission was only further complicated by an 1834 state law which directed police court judges to alleviate crowding in the House of Correction by sentencing vagabonds, drunkards, and prostitutes to the House of Industry. Often sick when they entered to serve their short terms, they left having learned nothing and contributed nothing to the institution's operation. And since the mingling of petty criminals with the poor implied that "poverty itself [was] a crime," the compassionate were persuaded to continue outdoor relief. Thus until panic and depression pressed hard on the city's ability to offer relief, the Overseers of the Poor successfully defied various mayors' efforts to rationalize welfare and bring its funds under the oversight of the city auditor.[22]

In sum, Boston approached city governance as pragmatically as she did national politics. Functional efficiency and the availability of resources were the formal standards against which new governmental forms were measured. But it is also true that tradition, entrenched social institutions, and community-oriented values limited the extent of change—albeit their role was notably less powerful in Boston than it proved to be in Charleston.

• • •

In the Carolina city a small, single-chambered city council shaped an informal operating style among the twelve wardens and the intendent. Not only did they meet in City Hall every week or two to transact public business; they also met in clubs and in church on Sunday. Virtually every member of the council belonged to some social organization, and over 85 percent of them belonged to at least five such groups. On the sabbath a quarter of them worshipped at St. Philip's Church, 10 percent at St. John's Lutheran, and another 10 percent at Scots Presbyterian.[23]

There were, of course, similar contacts in Boston, but their occurrence was more limited. The distinctive social and economic composition of each chamber, the rarity with which the two chambers met together as the full city council, and the large size of the common council, forty-eight men altogether, impeded informal interchange. The Second Unitarian Church, where councilmen were most likely to worship, claimed but one in twenty of their number. And one out of three members of the lower house appears to have belonged to no club at all. So even if Boston's aldermen were more likely to meet each other socially—one-eighth of them attended King's Chapel on Sundays and one-half belonged to three or more clubs—they were no more likely to encounter councilmen in social situations than in council chambers. And even the common economic perspective they shared as commercial men probably failed to bind Boston's councilmen and aldermen together as tightly or as imperatively as slavery united Charleston's wardens and intendents in their determination to maintain public order. Five out of six of them were slaveholders, and half of them owned ten or more slaves.[24]

Nevertheless, the camaraderie and social unity which characterized Charleston officialdom did not provide either mechanism or incentive to develop the sort of efficiency and centralized control that marked Boston's growth. Its intendent and twelve wardens, elected at large although representing in their residence each of the city's four wards, assumed responsibility for a city whose boundaries were less distinct than Boston's. Charleston abutted the unincorporated Neck, not organized towns. Together the city and its northern suburbs comprised St. Philip's and St. Michael's parishes, which state government treated as a single unit. So, while elected commissioners of crossroads and of the poor administered much of the Neck's business, state-appointed commissioners of main roads and public buildings oversaw both city and Neck without distinction. Moreover, both parishes were part of Charleston District, a sprawling, fan-shaped land mass which combined eleven parishes into a single judicial system furnishing jurors and cases to the state-financed courts and jail in Charleston. Finally, the problems caused by ill-defined responsibilities and overlapping authority were exacerbated by the state government's location 120 miles distant in Columbia. So even when Charleston sought to centralize and rationalize her government, she was at a disadvantage compared to Boston, where city and county were virtually coterminous, where neighboring areas operated under discrete authority, and where the state legislature met only a few blocks from City Hall.

Power was also dispersed within Charleston, where some nine annually appointed commissions bore major responsibility for policing the city and providing welfare with but minimal control by the city council. The board of health was key among them, for in addition to all the diseases which threatened northern cities, Charleston was also plagued by endemic malaria ("country fever") and epidemic yellow fever ("strangers' fever"). Nonetheless the board was distinguished neither by professional expertise nor by special political power. Of the 134 health commissioners between 1828 and 1843, only eighteen were M.D.'s and only twenty-eight held any additional political post. Lacking wealth and high status as well and serving without pay, they were selected to be broadly representative of the city's population and were rewarded only by the personal satisfaction they derived from increasing the public safety. Because most of them belonged to a club or a benevolent society and because those who were churchmen represented various denominations, they were accessible not only to their neighbors in the wards they were chosen to serve but to associates throughout the city. Moreover, their home and business addresses were regularly printed in the press.[25]

Like other contemporary health authorities, they were charged with maintaining a clean, well-drained environment which would be free from "foul air" and "noxious effluvia." Consequently they were empowered to order the removal of "nuisances" by city scavengers—but only through the board of street commissioners which employed them. When necessary the health commissioners could also order property owners to drain their cellars and low-lying lots; they could even demand admission to private property when noxious gases signaled inadequate vaults or defective cesspools, and could then order repairs made at the owner's expense. Nonetheless, the system was not effective in preventing epidemics. Seven times from 1828 through 1843, "strangers' fever" struck the city and claimed over six hundred lives. In addition a smallpox epidemic in 1830–1831 infected nearly eight hundred persons, of whom nearly sixty died—mostly blacks, who apparently were not fully included in an emergency vaccination program.[26]

In a city regularly visited by epidemics whose virulence was associated with pervasive warm climate and fetid air, the Asiatic cholera was especially threatening. When reports of its spread southward from Canada reached Charleston, the city council at once appointed a battery of assistant health commissioners to help the regular board in inspecting lots and identifying places where cleansing or nuisance removal was needed. Anticipating the worst, the council also committed itself to allocate $10,000 for four special cholera hospitals should they be needed to meet the emergency. Finally, the board of health ordered all citizens to ventilate their buildings, whitewash their cellars and outbuildings, avoid indigestible foods like cucumbers and cabbage, stay out of drafts, dress properly, and, above all, remain sober.[27]

Spurred to extraordinary precautions, Charleston remained calm until, on October 30, 1832, the *Amelia* ran aground off Folly Island just south of the city. Sailing out of cholera-plagued New York, the *Amelia* had a steerage crowded with laborers and mechanics, and twenty of her passengers had already died. So when Captain Dickenson rushed into Charleston, he reported a double disaster to a city already rent by the turmoil of nullification. Acting firmly, the city council quarantined not only the vessel but the whole island. Unhappily, wreckers had by then already left to salvage the disabled vessel; and one young man, a looter perhaps, broke into the ship's stores, got drunk on the wine, slept in wet clothes, came down with cholera, and died—all within twenty-four hours. Subsequently the islanders, hearing the news, tried to flee to the city's presumed safety.[28]

To aid the sick, the city council sent physicians to the island. To protect public order and health they sent a contigent of the city guard. Subject to quarantine as soon as they reached the island, both were refused permission to return. Within days guard officers could stifle mutiny only by removing their men to the far end of the island after they had refused to guard the stricken vessel, while in town private citizens patrolled the wharves to block escape into the city. Even so, at least two resolute fugitives eluded detection.[29]

The island a powder keg of discontent, the city rent by anxiety, Intendent Henry Pinckney ordered the *Amelia* burned to the water line. Whether or not that was ultimately the critical precaution, the cholera soon abated. But fear of a real epidemic remained. For each of the next three years, special assistant health commissioners were again appointed until, in 1835, the board itself was enlarged. And a lazaretto was built on one of the harbor islands for more effective quarantine.[30]

Then in 1836, despite all the preparations and precautions, cholera struck with full force. About six hundred cases were reported, and nearly four hundred people died. Again city officials ordered precautions by then familiar: cleansing, restricting the sale of foods likely to be contaminated, providing ambulances and hospitals for the sick, coffins and swift burial for the dead. Sharing the class assumptions about cholera common in northern cities and thus believing Negroes to be especially susceptible, the city set aside the Medical College buildings on Queen Street for their care.[31]

By late fall the epidemic had run its course. Charleston did not break down as New York had during its 1832 cholera epidemic. Nor was she as rigorous as Boston in enforcing preventive measures. While individual citizens reported nuisances to the board of health, who then acted on their complaints, the peculiarly neighborly relations of the board to its constituents impeded the use of its investigative power. Thus Charleston's blurred lines of authority and responsibility worked, in fact, better in routine health care for the poor than they did in a major epidemic.

Where Boston left most such care to private philanthropy, Charleston mixed private and public funds as it did private and public control to create a complex, municipally supervised health care system. Shirras Dispensary, founded by private bequest, provided, as did the privately funded and managed Boston Dispensary, both drugs and medical treatment to the sick poor of the city. But unlike the Boston institution, Shirras was overseen by a quasi-public board of three trustees, one of whom was, ex officio, the intendent, and was actively managed by commissioners whom the city council appointed. Its two visiting physicians were nominated by the commissioners but were paid by private income derived from the bequest. Those sick poor who needed institutionalization were treated in the poorhouse by a physician and an apothecary employed by yet another public commission.[32]

And, finally, should the sick be sailors, they were cared for in the Marine Hospital, partly suppported by federal funds but operated by yet another autonomous city commission. Unlike the Chelsea Marine Hospital, which served Boston but was operated by the United States government, Charleston's original facility had been a city venture to which Washington made compensation for services rendered. When in 1834 the new hospital, built with federal funds, opened on Back Street near the other city buildings serving the sick poor, it was still operated by the old board of commissioners.[33]

If Charleston's overlapping policing of public health was moderated by the accommodation of public to private interests, its policing of public order was not. Ever mindful of its biracial population and the possibility of slave revolt, which the 1822 Vesey episode had laid bare, Charleston maintained a varied and substantial protective force, which was substantially increased during the nullification turmoil. Where formerly the city had vested responsibility for enforcing city ordinances in a marshal (who reported directly to the city council) and his two assistants; in 1831 it provided a salaried marshal for every ward, giving each direct access to city hall. In addition, its two dozen constables, who patrolled the wards by day

Policing the City and Providing Welfare

to enforce the peace, were rewarded for their diligence by receiving a commission on all fines levied against the individuals they arrested. At night the hundred-man paid, uniformed, and armed guard took responsibility for the city's safety in two watches, while a third watch of six guards was regularly posted to daytime duty. Whereas the Boston night watch's prime concern was tipplers, prostitutes, and other disorderly persons, Charleston's guard was specially charged with controlling the black population. To insure citywide coverage they operated from two bases, the Main Guard House in the center of town and the Piquet guard quarters on the northern boundary. For their services, privates were paid $15 to $43 a month while officers earned $45 to $100 monthly. Thus the guard alone commanded between 9 and 13 percent of the city's total yearly budget.[34]

The equivalent of its control work was carried out on the Neck only by citizen patrols until, after 1832, the state-financed Citadel Guard assumed partial responsibility for protecting the whole of St. Philip's and St. Michael's parishes as well as the state arsenal and powder magazine. Authorized in response to the 1822 Vesey threat, its complement of sixty men was not actually assigned to duty until the nullification crisis pressed its urgency; some citizens even then believed it insufficient and sought a state guard double its size with cavalry as well as foot soldiers.[35]

While Charleston's policing of public order resembled New York's and London's in the priority it gave to social order over the apprehension of criminals, it differed in its preoccupation with slave control. So too its court system differed from that of most American cities, although it shared the customary division of cases, trying misdemeanors in a locally supported police or recorder's court and felonies in the state-operated Court of General Sessions. It was its third criminal court which made Charleston distinctive, for the Magistrates' and Freeholders' Court tried only blacks. Similarly reflecting racial lines was the workhouse. Differing from the jail, which housed debtors, witnesses, and those accused of felonies, it was a penal institution both for disobedient slaves sent by their masters to be worked on the treadmill and for disorderly Negroes sentenced by either the Recorder's or Magistrates' and Freeholders' courts to detention and whipping.[36]

Charleston's no-nonsense approach to preserving public order did not extend to protecting property from fire, albeit much of the city was built of wood. Unlike the city guard, the marshals, and the constables—all of whom were directly responsible to the city council—the fire fighting forces were largely volunteer and supervised by yet another appointive commission, the board of firemasters. The city did, it is true, have its own fire engines, which were operated by slaves who earned 25 cents an hour fighting fires under the supervision of part-time paid white engineers. But these city engines were only supplements to the volunteer, traditionally independent, and highly competitive private companies, which differed little from those with which Mayor Quincy had struggled in Boston.[37]

The whole fire department was characterized by dispersed authority and limited expertise. The fire companies used city-owned equipment, but under the direction of officers they elected. The firemasters had had little experience in the volunteer companies, but were charged with taking over all command at fires. The chief engineer, whom they appointed, was in charge only of the slave-operated engines and the explosives used to create fire breaks. Constables were in charge of organizing bucket brigades. Militia companies turned out to prevent looting at major fires. And the intendent and any wardens who arrived on the scene were entitled to assume command from the firemasters. The result was "a *very evident* want of concert and discipline" which allowed fire after fire to get out of hand. In February 1833 a fire on East Bay and Market streets destroyed thirty to forty buildings. Two years later almost to the day, another fire spread north and west from Cornel June's brothel on State Street to consume sixty-three buildings, one of them St. Philip's Church. Barely four months later yet another fire raced north from Market Street, destroying from three to four hundred buildings. After each fire citizen criticisms of the whole firefighting system mounted higher, until General James Hamilton, who had himself been burned out in an 1830 fire, proposed clearing the lines of authority by turning fire fighting over to the militia. But committed as they were to the value of the volunteer companies, firemasters and wardens hesitated even to try to assert more centralized control.[38]

Controversy haunted the Charleston fire department in the same way as similar friction plagued Boston's public assistance program. But the southern city's welfare system generated no such tensions. In part, at least, that was so because its activities came under the unified direction of the poorhouse commissioners, who both oversaw institutional relief and administered grants to those able and permitted to live on their own. The commissioners were men drawn principally from professional life, though over time they came increasingly from commerce. Not surprisingly, they were guided in part by a commitment to noblesse oblige, since almost half of them came from the upper class, and a third also wielded political power beyond the poor house.[39] They were, therefore, disinclined to demand industry from those they aided or to force the elderly or small children and their mothers into institutions.

Nonetheless, their practices did have some parallels with those of Boston. Native Charlestonians, for example, were three times as likely to be given outdoor relief as to be institutionalized. Irish immigrants were three times as likely to end up in the poorhouse as to receive subsistence grants.

Furthermore, the poorhouse did require labor from those who could perform it; able-bodied men broke stone to macadamize the streets or made coffins for the poor, while women were expected to spin and weave. But how little such work was instituted to reform the attitudes of paupers is revealed in the proportion of inmates the poorhouse admitted as patients. In 1830–1831, 85 percent of all new admissions were sick when they entered the house.[40] Mostly mechanics, laborers, and seamstresses, they needed hospital care of the sort which in Boston would have been rendered, if at all, by private institutions—Massachusetts General Hospital or the Lying-In Hospital in particular.

So, too, Charleston's care for orphans filled a role chiefly left to private philanthropy in Boston. The Charleston Orphan House, founded in 1790, was an institution inspiring particular civic pride and attracting a sizable private endowment as well as public funds. Its commissioners, to a degree unmatched by any other city board, were well educated, wealthy, and upper-class.[41] Their charges, accordingly, were well financed, well taught, and well cared for. Although most boys were apprenticed to a trade, those with exceptional talents were trained for the professions. The girls were prepared for the domestic arts and "female occupations," and, if they did not rise as high as the luckiest boys, they generally at least "turn[ed] out well."[42]

• • •

However comfortably familiar were her patterns of operation, her reliance on volunteer public service, and her dispersal of authority and responsibility, by the mid-1830s Charleston's governmental inability to modernize produced pressures for reorganization. Explicit proposals first appeared in the press—characteristically as pseudonymous letters from insiders who were familiar with proposals already pending. Thus it was only a week after the first writer suggested paying the intendent a salary that the city council voted in mid-August 1835 to hold a referendum on that very question. Although framed as a device to provide a "more effective Police," and coming when fears of arson and incendiary abolitionist propaganda agitated the city, which had barely recovered from a destructive fire, that proposal was resoundingly turned down at the polls. Yet persistent demands for greater efficiency and expertise in city government pressed the council to act again. In the spring of 1836 it adopted ordinances to raise the salaries paid the city guard, the city clerk, the assessor, and the principal fire engineer, who was also given two paid assistants by the same measure.[43]

With that much change already accomplished, the city's opinion formers advanced from letter writing to invoking that other popular device for stirring up the citizenry—the public meeting. One meeting, convened in May

1836 ostensibly to consider railroad affairs, appointed a committee of economic and political leaders to address once again the question of paying the intendent a salary. James Hamilton and James Petigru represented the nullifier and Unionist factions. Charles Edmondston spoke for East Bay merchants, as Alexander Mazyck did for the planters and those with extensive interests in city land and the railroad. They agreed that their city needed a full-time executive able to take on the extended duties required to centralize authority and render government more efficient. And they proposed he be paid $4,000, which was $1,500 more than Boston's mayor. Like earlier backers of a similar proposal, they urged the special need for immediate action because an outbreak of riots in the North created circumstances requiring "more than ordinary vigilance" to ward off the "lurking danger" presented in a "country like ours, with two distinct classes."[44] All their proposals, however, came back to paying the intendent adequate compensation for assuming and coordinating a broad spectrum of duties.

One of the intendent's new responsibilities was to hear much of the city police court's routine business, relieving the recorder from many customary activities and reducing his salary accordingly. After the report's proposals had been enthusiastically endorsed by a second public meeting in June, another aspect of the Charleston style went into play, accomplishing that judicial change in a ritual procedure which insured that no person was demeaned and no insult given. First Samuel Prioleau, long-time city recorder and James Hamilton's father-in-law, resigned his post on June 27. The next day the city enacted the ordinance which lowered the recorder's salary. Then, within the week, the council appointed a new recorder, Jacob Axson, a man in his forties with a strong nullifier past. Then, in early August, just before the city voted on the referendum to adopt a paid, full-time intendency, a prestigious group of planters, merchants, and politicos publicly invited Robert Hayne to run for the office if the proposal were adopted. The next day Hayne accepted because of "the general and cordial support" he anticipated from the citizenry "in the great cause of 'City Reform and Improvement.'" Thus in smooth style was change arranged and announced almost simultaneously.[45]

In this atmosphere Charleston voted two to one to endorse a salaried intendent. Less than two weeks later the city council adopted the requisite ordinance, and in two more weeks Robert Young Hayne, former United States senator and South Carolina governor, ran unopposed and was elected intendent. Swept into office with him as wardens were men who made the new council no ordinary one. Among them were James Hamilton, the former governor and congressman and currently president of the Bank of Charleston; George Henry, partner of the powerful factor Ker Boyce, who was soon to succeed Hamilton at the bank; Henry W. Conner, a Bank of Charleston director destined eventually to succeed Boyce; and John S. Cogdell, president of the Bank of South Carolina.[46]

For Hayne the election returns were a clear mandate. Without delay, he and his associates undertook to alter not just the operation of the government but the shape of the city. Yet his latitude was limited, first by the 1836 cholera epidemic, then by the onset of the 1837 panic. Nonetheless, once the health emergency was over, the intendent went into operation. Hayne moved swiftly to coordinate the city guard and the Citadel Guard into a bulwark against domestic insurrection and riot as well as an "efficient arrangement, for the detection and arrest of criminals."[47]

Compiling an integrated plan for city improvements, he gained endorsement for the whole program at yet another public meeting held in February 1837. With that evidence of citizen support, Hayne and his colleagues laid out a timetable for paving all city streets and draining and filling city-owned lowlands. From his office came also a prospectus for turning the city's southernmost tip of land into a handsome public park. To make fire fighting more effective as well as to speed up traffic, alleys were to be closed and major streets widened into throughways, with street signs erected at intersections. To further public safety, more extensive street lighting was planned. And to address public health, the city adopted a tight ordinance requiring that private drains connect with the municipal sewer system and regulating the construction of privies and private drains. Hayne even envisaged a tidal flushing system to clean the principal sewers twice a day.[48]

Hayne, who had the experience and the political contacts to get action from the state legislature, went to Columbia for power to extend the board of firemasters' control of private volunteer fire companies and to enable the city council to draft stricter regulations for the fire department's operation—albeit still under the firemasters' control. With permission from the state legislature, the city moved to curtail further extension of wharves into the channel, where they already obstructed navigation and caused silting. And, in recognition of Charleston's drive to modernize her government and comport with the practice of other American cities, the state granted her the right to change the titles of intendent to mayor and warden to councilman.[49]

More critical than nomenclature were modifications in fiscal matters. The payment of accounts was centralized and rationalized. Henceforth budget-making was to precede the making of appropriations; and appropriations, the expenditure of city funds by the treasurer. More difficult to arrange was increasing city income sufficiently to pay for the manifold improvements which Hayne projected. Because the state engrossed direct property taxes on both land and slaves, the city was left to raise funds from the alternative revenue sources available to her: taxes on the income of professionals and on the commercial sale of all commodities except rice and cotton; taxes on the means of transportation, be they drays or carriages; levies (however designed they also were for social control) which taxed free blacks according to their ages and occupations and charged owners fees for the badges which the slaves they hired out had to wear. Mayor Hayne groped to find the revenue sources which would detract least from his program's popular support and found them principally in taxing nonresidents. Anxiety about the size of the city's black population—and especially the numerous slaves living unsupervised in town—drew support for an ordinance increasing the fees which nonresidents paid for slave badges. And, after the state gave permission, the city levied a tax on all incomes earned in the city by nonresidents—a measure directed at those who lived in the minimally taxed Neck but enjoyed the city's services and amenities.[50]

For all the activity, the vigor of Hayne's mayoralty came to an end even before his single term expired. Whether or not the halt was a response to the 1837 panic, it is clear that by spring rising city expenditures and the imposition of new taxes had created a backlash. The one new tax levied on residents—a steep surtax on owners who hired out more than six slaves—roused enough opposition to force its immediate repeal. And as early as April, the city council forced postponement of projects already authorized.[51]

Whether Hayne could have carried his full program had he sought and gained a second term can only be speculated, though the evidence suggests that the mayor himself may have doubted it. He had not ruled out a second term when he took office, and the offer of the presidency of the new Louisville, Cincinnati, and Charleston Rail Road in mid-May might have appealed to him less had reelection to public office offered more opportunity for service to the city. In any case, his official report upon leaving office explained that the city had spent only 10 percent of the funds authorized for improvements because "the sudden change in the condition of the country from a state of the most palmy prosperity, to one of great pecuniary embarrassment" had occurred at just the moment the city was "preparing to enter vigorously, upon an extensive system of public improvements."[52] It is clear that when Hayne left city hall so too did his program for modernization. But even that program had not addressed the heart of traditional forms and practices. All the old commissions remained, and the cause of efficiency had stopped short of blunt actions likely to abrade the city's smooth style.

Succeeding Hayne in the mayor's office was Henry L. Pinckney. A former intendent, he returned to city hall on a platform of retrenchment. His council contained no one equivalent in stature or influence to the men of economic and political power who had served with Hayne.[53] His official conduct suggested his understanding that the office had changed little except in name—and financial rewards. And by 1840 even the mayor's pay was drastically reduced, and with it his power and responsibility to coordinate all the city's business. Hayne's income tax on nonresidents had backfired. Instead of inducing Neck residents to seek annexation to the city, it had generated a counterproposal for separate incorporation as Upper Charleston. But that measure too was doomed by residents' opting for low taxes over increased services.[54]

It is ironic that Hayne, who undertook, as had Josiah Quincy fifteen years earlier, to modernize his city and her government, achieved such different results. Like Quincy, he understood the need for basic change and guided Charleston's path into new forms which seemed to promise new substance as well. Perhaps it was that Hayne's mayoralty came at a less propitious time; but if that were so, when would it have been more propitious? Was Charleston ready to pay the cultural price for a city governance which valued expertise above public service and clear lines of authority above the compromises necessary for community cohesion?

8

Education, Work, and Cultural Values

If the style and substance of government are shaped by community values, no public documents can reveal more about cultural assumptions than the appropriations a city makes for education. Throughout the 1830s, from one-eighth to one-quarter of Boston's steadily increasing annual budgets went for education. Taxed in 1829 to operate 9 grammar and 57 primary schools, by 1843 Boston taxpayers funded 15 grammar and 104 primary schools. And the children who attended those schools were one-third the entire population under twenty. On the other hand, Charleston's sole financial contribution to publicly financed primary or grammar school education was to the orphan house school. The city's five free schools—three primary and two grammar—were state-funded parish schools primarily reserved for the children of the poor. Serving a student body which ranged annually from a low of 377 pupils to a high of 557, the free schools enrolled a scant 11 percent of all white young people under twenty.[1]

This is not to say that education was not valued in Charleston, but rather that differing cultural values produced different educational structures. There was in Boston, for instance, no public college, and that city entered the 1840s (as it had left the 1820s) with but two public high schools, the Latin School and English High. The city's priorities revealed themselves, however, in the near doubling of primary and grammar schools during the period. The public's educational responsibility was to provide the skills of verbal and quantitative literacy and the fundamentals of physical and social science, which all young people needed to prepare themselves for citizenship and productive labor. In 1838 Charleston, by contrast, expanded her public support for education by turning the moribund

College of Charleston into the first municipally funded college in America and then by providing a city-sponsored high school to prepare local boys for college or for business and professional careers. City funds were thus provided to subsidize higher education for the few, to make prestigious occupations and economic and social mobility more accessible to the talented.

The paucity of public schools was largely compensated for by private schools, and Charleston parents supported at least seventy-two proprietary establishments at various times between 1828 and 1843, which provided education ranging from primary to college preparatory levels and offered specialized commercial and language instruction as well. Many wealthy parents sent their children to boarding schools outside the city. Sons attended Moses Waddel's declining academy at Willington or Philip Gadsden's school in Summerville; daughters, the South Carolina Institute at Barhamville, near Columbia. Others chose out-of-state Episcopal schools, like the Muhlenberg Academy for boys in Flushing, New York, or St. Mary's Hall in Burlington, New Jersey, for girls. The more innovative might choose the secular and very progressive Round Hill School in Northampton, Massachusetts; the more conservative employed tutors, who educated children under the family roof.[2]

For those unable to afford substantial fees, local societies provided various kinds of schools for members' children—and sometimes for other youngsters as well. Among the latter, the Fellowship Society had since 1796 used income from an endowment which had reached nearly $50,000 by 1832 to provide free primary schools for orphans and children of the poor. The prestigious South Carolina Society, after it closed its charity school in 1827 because of declining enrollments, opened separate male and female academies which offered a general English education for modest fees to the children or orphans of members and, if there was room, to others at somewhat higher fees. After 1828 the German Friendly Society sponsored similar academies to serve the boys and girls of its ethnic community. Churches, too, offered educational programs. Bishop John England's Classical and Philosophical Seminary led a precarious existence because of the controversy it generated by training young men for the priesthood in the same classes where Protestant youth were instructed in Greek and Latin. That the issue was not simply hostility to a Catholic education was attested by the popularity of the girls' schools operated by the Ladies of the Retreat, the Ursuline Sisters, and the Sisters of Our Lady of Mercy. Episcopal St. Philip's for a while ran a competing classical school directed by the rector, Christopher E. Gadsden, and taught largely by his assistant, Daniel Cobia. Somewhat later St. Peter's church opened a parochial school for boys.[3]

However many and varied these schools, they were private and no child had the right to attend them. And entry to the free state schools was controlled by a means test. But why, in a community where citizens supported using tax funds for such varied endeavors, did they exclude elementary schooling from their city's public responsibilities? And why did the city fund a classical high school and a college while it ignored its abecedarians? At least part of the explanation lies in hierarchical assumptions about education's varying utility. For the children of the wealthy, education was most valued as a cultural adornment and a means to enrich leisure—albeit it might also prepare them for the professions or a political career. For the children of the middling ranks, education was, at its best, the vehicle for individual upward economic and social mobility. In both cases, therefore, parents were motivated to pay school fees. But to the children of the poor, the state and eleemosynary societies provided the rudiments of education only as they provided charity to adults. There was no widespread commitment to functional literacy and "useful knowledge" as a public good, as the requisites for the economy's prosperity and the republic's survival. Indeed, state law forbade teaching half the city's youth to write and, later in the decade, even to read. And because slaves did so much of the city's labor, making education the prerequisite for hard work or hard work the prerequisite for upward mobility was simply unthinkable. Consequently no clarion call for universal free public education rang through the city.[4]

Charleston's justification of education was therefore largely put in individual rather than communal terms. Fathers of high as well as of middling rank, like their Yankee equivalents, urged their sons to study that they might, in future, support themselves. Planter and wharf owner Elias Vanderhorst pressed his sons to use their school years well that they might avoid the "great difficulty in getting into any business" which ignorance brought. Planter and railroad president Elias Horry provided in his will for his sons "to be educated in such a manner as to gain their livelihoods, by their talents." Nonetheless, most general discussion of higher education accentuated the personal fulfillment to be derived from literary accomplishment and cultural improvement. And this was sometimes the case even when appeals to study were made to mechanics and apprentices. As Dr. Samuel Dickson told them, he who failed to cultivate ennobling knowledge would be "something less than a man."[5]

Yet it is also true that lecturers to the Apprentices' Library Society more often stressed the upward mobility which schooling promised young artisans. Dr. Joseph Johnson, the society's president, repeatedly reviewed his own humble origins as the son of a craftsman who, through diligent study, had elevated himself first to professional standing and then to a bank presidency. The much younger William D. Porter, the son of a grocer, who became a lawyer after he had attended the College of Charleston, praised education as the gateway to an "honorable career." Urging the inclination to improvement on apprentice mechanics, Porter promised them that "respectability, fortune, influence—all prizes of the social state, [lay] within the reach of [their] well directed efforts."[6]

It is in this context that public support for a municipal college is to be understood.[7] The College of Charleston had been chartered as a private institution in 1785 but had operated only sporadically and as a secondary school until 1829, when it was revived to encompass a collegiate course as well. Private contributions for a new building and an endowed professorship attracted a new president and new faculty members. But the college remained primarily a grammar school, unable to lure advanced students and generating so many feuds among faculty, trustees, and president that, in 1835, it faced total collapse. Responding to the impending disaster, the trustees pledged themselves "not to suffer [the college] to go down," and took their problems to city hall.[8] With little delay the city council voted $2,000 to pay the salaries of one or more professors during the coming year.

That, even so, the trustees decided to suspend college operations in 1836 was testimony that the problems went beyond finance and that public money alone could not solve them. What was essential was reshaping college policy to conform to the societal role which Charlestonians expected education to play. Dedication to improving the quality of intellectual life was insufficient. The college must be made to provide the access to education through which Charleston youth could enhance their social and economic opportunities. It must serve the needs of families who either could not afford to send their sons to distant colleges or who feared that boys educated far from home would be corrupted or, still worse, would never return to their native city. It must reinforce the image of Carolina democracy as a society which included the interests and addressed the needs of its total white population. "All classes of our citizens," the city council insisted, must be given access to the classical education which promised the son a chance to improve on his father's condition.[9] The special consideration which the orphan house gave talented boys must be extended by the college if it was to gain lasting public support. Indeed, that the college had previously failed in this respect was made clear by an 1831 tiff between trustees and faculty over admitting orphan house students free of charge. The city council had sought their free tuition as a quid pro quo for funds it had already furnished the college library. The trustees had agreed in the spirit of public relations. But the faculty balked, arguing that the proposal would infringe their control of admissions and reduce their incomes by the amount of fees not paid.

Before the college could reopen with a municipal subsidy, therefore, the trustees had to demonstrate that "[t]his College belongs to Charleston" and establish the "proper basis" which would make "its advantages to our citizens . . . inestimable."[10] In pursuing the theme of broad inclusiveness when it did reopen as a publicly supported institution in 1838, the college admitted qualified orphan house boys free of charge, and, in addition, reduced the tuition charged other students and transformed its board of trustees from an Episcopal enclave into a multidenominational assembly willing, in 1843, to appoint as president a Baptist minister.

Having lost its largest grammar and classical school when it limited the college to teaching college-level courses, the city council then voted, in a time of great budgetary stringency, to establish a high school which would be under its direct control. Opening in 1839 with only a Latin course, by 1840 it had added a commercially oriented English track as well. Charging a modest tuition—only students from the orphan house paid no fees—the high school, like the college, was understood to serve "all classes" by offering "an efficient education at a cheap rate."[11]

. . .

Certainly Bostonians shared Charlestonians' eagerness to offer their children the means for upward mobility; and even more surely they offered their city's youth extensive access to free or cheap schooling. But no similarity can hide their fundamental disagreement about the social and economic function of education and the consequent imperative for public schools. In Boston, no matter what one's rank, the primary value of knowledge was its utility. It was knowledge of "men and things" which was most valued, for that was the practical knowledge which gave power. And the test of education's practicality was not just the power and prosperity it promised the individual but the economic and social well-being with which it endowed the community.

Harrison Gray Otis loved to recount George Washington's legendary discussion with a Yankee aide-de-camp. The general fretted lest Revolutionary success destroy New England by excluding her from British markets. The young officer, incensed at the suggestion, replied, "Sir we never had any thing but our heads and our hands, and having those left we shall find something to do with them." And sixty years later, Yankee inventiveness was still the region's major natural resource. Young or old, rich or poor, Yankees honed their skills and informed their minds as they studied "men and things." Traveling in England at seventy-one, Thomas Handasyd Perkins was just as fascinated as was Amos A. Lawrence at twenty-six with the "workings of . . . *European machinery.*" Over thirteen thousand tickets were sold in a single year to adults eager to learn from the twenty-six lecture series which Boston offered that season. The popular Lyceum alone drew weekly audiences of two thousand to absorb its fare of geography and philology, science and technology. No wonder that South Carolina planter William Elliott attributed Boston's many improvements to the extraordinary "mechanical skill possessed by [its] people."[12]

The belief that skilled and informed citizen-workers underlay Boston's economic viability was the cornerstone on which the city's commitment to public education lay. Mayor Quincy had justified extending the city system only if it "put every necessary branch of elementary instruction within the reach of every citizen." Moreover, Quincy led the fight to close the recently opened girls' high school in 1829 on the grounds that because girls were not being prepared there for future occupations or professions, it was "impracticable" for the public to fund their education beyond grammar school levels.[13]

While knowledge might enable a man to climb up the social and economic ladder, and was valued for so doing, education was also expected to instill the attitudes recognized and enshrined in the Franklin medals with which Boston rewarded its best grammar school pupils. "They declare to the children of the city," explained the school committee, "that the public sentiment which supports [the grammar schools] sets a value upon excellence"; and they kept before every pupil the model of Ben Franklin, "self-made . . . by industry, frugality, and common sense." So closely were these values held that critics of the Franklin awards opposed them because the fierce competition they engendered produced "violent and spasmodic effort" rather than the "patient and moderate labor" by which the prudent workman succeeded.[14]

In the face of such commitment to public education, the number of Boston's private schools diminished between 1829 and 1845 and attracted proportionately fewer children. It was true that well-to-do parents seeking special advantages for their offspring continued to patronize such excellent day schools as Chauncey Hall or to send their sons to boarding schools, among them the Phillips academies at Exeter and Andover and Northampton's Round Hill. But their patronage of private schools did not in the least impede the steady growth of public education.[15] Indeed, it had been a recognition of the inadequacy of private dame schools to prepare the city's increasingly numerous children to meet the public grammar schools' entry requirement of basic literacy which had led, in 1818, to the first city-operated primary schools. Rapidly expanding, they numbered twenty-five hundred pupils in 1825, about five thousand in 1840. Here boys and girls between the ages of four and seven received their first two years of instruction in reading, writing, and, increasingly, arithmetic. Over time, innovations were made: recesses to allow for alternation of mental and physical activity, free school books to make the schools completely available to all.

Salaries for their female teachers were raised in 1835 from $200 to $250 a year; three years earlier, for the first time, the city had also provided the fuel teachers used to heat their schoolrooms. Gradually, too, city-built schoolhouses replaced hired rooms of varying size and appropriateness.[16]

Not all, however, ran harmoniously. The number of masters each grammar school should employ was fiercely debated until a system of one master with both male and female assistants was adopted. Then reformers, in 1838, proposed appointing a professionally trained school superintendent for the more efficient management of the growing system. But Boston's cultural commitment to public education was too deeply emotional to permit transferring the control of its schools from elected neighborhood representatives to a single appointed bureaucrat. Indeed, the importance of representatives per se had been signaled in 1835 when the autonomous primary school committee, which had originated as an appointed subcommittee in 1818 but had continued as a self-perpetuating group, was placed again under the control of the school committee. Thenceforth its members were appointed annually by the only agency of the city government, except the Overseers of the Poor, which was directly elected, albeit it continued to act as though it were still an autonomous board.[17]

The vigor with which the voters protected direct popular control of the school system in 1835 and 1838 had been foreshadowed when the city council had tried to institute election at large for school committee members. But in 1834 citizens had turned out to defeat the proposal two to one, thereby defending their traditional practice of electing committeemen to represent the individual wards. And the next year, when they approved the referendum to consolidate control of all schools under the annually elected committee, they also approved enlarging each ward's representation on the committee from one to two. Subsequent proposals to shift students from one school to another to equalize numbers and segregate boys from girls in single-gender grammar schools were opposed—unsuccessfully, however—on the grounds that neighborhood was the most appropriate basis for pupil assignment. But what was most important about all these heated debates was that they demonstrated the importance of public education to Boston's citizens.[18]

• • •

"We are," wrote Massachusetts educational reformer Horace Mann, "an industrious and a frugal people." In saying so he was not exhorting Yankees to follow the work ethic but implying that they already embodied its very substance. For articulate Bostonians of all ranks this was no empty cliché—it was self-evident truth. Nor was it confined to a declining remnant of Puritan Calvinism, for the consociation of Unitarian charities assumed that it was "God's will that man should provide for his own subsistence" by hard work and firmly condemned all and any attempts "to live with as little labor and self-denial as possible." So, too, liberal reformer William Ellery Channing argued that only labor gave "energy of purpose and character." Episcopal minister William Hague, who for a while superintended the House of Industry, asserted that those who could and did not work both should and would be poor. Thus did liberal and high church religion reinforce the more orthodox Congregationalism of the Society for the Prevention of Pauperism, which would address the problems of poverty by "facilitat[ing] the communication between those who need[ed] employment, and those who [could] supply it." And even a Christian vocation did not assuage Congregationalist cleric William Jenks's perpetual self-doubts: Did he work sufficiently hard? Did he do his duty? Did he employ his time "aright"?[19]

Secular success manuals similarly exhorted young merchants and aspiring shopkeepers to cultivate the substance and the form of "industrious habits": Always look busy even when no one was there to see. Be diligent. Avoid the snares of sensuous indulgence. Keep clear of the ignorant and the turbulent. Pick a prudent wife who would conduct the home as a business was run. Lawyer Rufus Choate, who assessed the matter as an insider, celebrated that labor which was "the condition—I will not say, of our greatness, but—of our being." Thomas Grattan, a British consul with Irish roots, grimly observed that even young men in Boston were shriveled hulks, driven by work to old age before they could enjoy their youth.[20]

Merchants, even when they talked among themselves, connected both business success and personal well-being with the work ethic. China trader Thomas Perkins warned wealthy John Cushing, only recently returned from long years in Canton, lest he drift into the unhappiness which a complete retirement from active business would bring. Drawing from his own experience, he advised that "the remainder of your time will be more happy from being [each day] engaged in some business." Congressman Abbott Lawrence almost rejoiced when his brother's illness forced him to assume the mercantile responsibilities which Amos had increasingly shouldered during recent years. He was, he assured his ailing brother, "a better and happier man for constant and arduous employment." And it ran in the family, for Amos never ceased reminding his schoolboy son Amos Adams that success came only from hard work and seldom graced "geniuses, who can learn without effort, and are idle when they ought to be at work."[21]

By contrast, Charleston's enunciated ethic was mute on the elevating potential of work. Indeed, it discussed work primarily as a function of slavery. An anonymous pamphleteer writing in the mid-1830s argued that manual labor was an "agony" so burdensome to thought that, if persisted in, it would "exhaust the very source of . . . perception," kill the intellect, and leave the worker a "mere animal . . . brutalized and besotted—a slave—a tool—an instrument in the hands of a master." Because the security of property and society both required that labor per se be firmly linked to race, upward socioeconomic mobility could scarcely be vaunted as the reward for hard work, whatever its nature. So much was this separation maintained that even children in the orphan house did none of the regular chores which northern children of all circumstances performed. "[T]he prejudice against work," so English traveler Harriet Martineau observed, "appears as much here as anywhere. No active labour goes on; the boys do not even garden. No employment is attempted which bears any resemblance to what is done by slaves." That most boys in the institution would be trained as mechanics created no apparent contradiction in values, for then success would bring them slaves. And southern mechanics, as Dr. Samuel Dickson assured an audience of apprentices, were especially fortunate because they could leave to slaves all the work suited to "mere animal effort" which northern mechanics were forced to do for themselves.[22]

Those few Charlestonians who explicitly championed the value of work were likely to be outsiders. Irish Catholic bishop John England defended the dignity of labor in sermons directed largely to working-class immigrants. Scottish Presbyterian Thomas Smyth extolled the virtues of Christian industry to the prosperous merchants who assembled weekly in his Second Presbyterian Church. But not even an outsider, not even Boston-born Unitarian minister Samuel Gilman, would choose a hot July day on which to preach, as did his Boston colleague Cyrus Bartol, from the text "In the sweat of thy face shalt thou eat bread." Nor was any Charlestonian likely to extol the "obligation of man to labor" on a day when the mercury reached ninety-five degrees.[23]

• • •

As surely as Boston's support of elementary education was rooted in the work ethic, so its cultivation of upward mobility encompassed not just hard work but the education which prepared the gifted as well as the privileged for the professions. And Charleston's public dedication to a city high school and college, as well as her support for a private medical school (and for a while two), portrayed at least equal commitment to making available that education which would meld an aristocracy of talent with a democracy of professional opportunity. At first glance, a comparison of the College of Charleston, which in 1834 enrolled only 39 students to Harvard's 217, suggests that here too Boston's enthusiasm for education outshone Charleston's. Moreover, those Charlestonians who could generally did send their sons to South Carolina College—or even to Harvard and Yale—in preference to their local institution. But if one compares the proportions in which each city's young white males enrolled in their local institutions, it is clear that white male Charlestonians were about twice as likely to attend college as were their northern counterparts. And, in numbers at least, the Medical College of South Carolina outranked the Harvard Medical School with at least twice as many students—despite its having the same number of teachers.[24]

But professional preparation was not simply a matter of numbers, and each city faced the ambiguities inherent in maintaining high standards in a self-consciously democratic era. In Boston, where economic and political leaders often held Harvard degrees, physicians had the power of the state's oldest and largest college behind their efforts to exclude the ill-trained from practice. When, in 1803, the state legislature had ordered the Massachusetts Medical Society to open its membership to all physicians in the commonwealth, Boston doctors had formed their own exclusive Boston Medical Association, which admitted Harvard M.D.'s automatically and others rarely and only on examination. Critics believed it operated as a monopoly because it compelled its members to abide by a fee schedule and a code of ethics which regulated referrals. But even the Massachusetts Medical Society continued to be controlled by Harvard-educated Bostonians, who resisted public pressure to admit all medical college graduates as automatically as they did Harvard M.D.'s and who resolutely barred competing medical schools in the western part of the state from gaining the licensing power. Not even a legislative investigation in the mid-1830s, triggered by a Thomsonian physician's complaints against the society's monopolistic control of medicine and pressed by the Democratic party, could break the society's hold on admission to practice. In resisting political pressure to recognize these practitioners of botanic medicine, the regular physicians proved themselves stronger than Suffolk county lawyers, who in 1835 lost their bar association's power to license attorneys.[25]

Charleston physicians, fighting the same battle against Thomsonian or botanical medicine, were less successful. Their South Carolina Medical Society had already eroded its licensing power first by transferring it to the South Carolina Medical College, which it founded in 1824, and then by wrangling with its faculty, who finally resigned to found their own school. Drawn into the battle between two competing medical colleges, the state legislature gave the licensing power to the old faculty operating the new school. But then came the court battle between the medical society and some Thomsonian practitioners which, in 1838, led the legislature to vote to end state-imposed penalties for unlicensed medical practice—though whether they conceded to the leveling principle or simply to sheer exasperation is debatable. In either case, by 1841 it had also stripped Charleston's bar association of its licensing power, which was thereafter exercised by the courts, as it was in Boston. If the end of licensing made holding a diploma even more critical for professional recognition, as medical professor Samuel Dickson insisted it did, it also, in both cities, limited education's control over professional opportunity.[26]

• • •

The cultural values and the social realities implicit in the interrelationship of education, work, and mobility are further clarified by the education each city offered her daughters. In both cities it was fairly common for primary schools to teach basic literacy to boys and girls in the same classes. But in grammar schools, Charleston practice agreed with the Boston School Committee precept that there was an "impropriety and danger of girls and boys, at an age approaching to that of maturity, going every day, for years, to the same school." And neither city took high school education for young women very seriously at all. In Boston the explanation remained as it had been in Quincy's day: that the reason for publicly supported high schools was to "enable every individual in the community, however poor, to have his son educated for the particular profession, . . . for which his talents destine him." Since the only profession for which females could be destined was teaching, a girls' high school could not be justified. But also because the growing school system needed teachers, the girls' grammar school course was extended to a nine-year maximum to allow them to study natural philosophy, astronomy, algebra—some but not all the subjects "of a substantial character" which boys normally studied in high schools.[27]

In Charleston there was not even debate about public support for a girls' high school. The issue of upward mobility was not a consideration, as it was for a boys' high school, because women's status was established by that of their fathers or husbands. Thus the best preparation for their adult occupations—be they privileged daughters or inmates of the orphan house—was the mastery of domestic skills which might be put to use when necessary to earn an income by nursing, operating a boardinghouse, or making clothes. Nor was preparing women for teaching perceived as a public obligation, for only a few taught in the free schools and other teachers were privately employed.

Thus those who could afford to pay up to $200 a quarter might send their daughters to Mme. Talvande's fashionable school on Legaré Street. Others patronized the academies operated by religious and eleemosynary groups at various levels of sophistication. The German Friendly Society offered science classes requiring a philosophical apparatus; the Ursuline convent school provided a broader liberal education than many young men received. But when all was said and done, it was fashion which was the prevailing concern. James Petigru might express remorse that "fifteen is not an age to finish one's education," but he brought his daughter back from a New York finishing school at that age nonetheless. Young Harriott Horry Rutledge might prefer Latin and Greek, but she spent her summer studying French and dancing.[28]

And when the matter came up for discussion, it was generally conceded that Carolina's daughters were less well educated than their Yankee equivalents. Young "Pickwick," defending Charleston's young ladies from an attack on the quality of their education which a northern schoolmate had launched, countered rather chivalrously that they "read well, dance[d] well and converse[d] as brilliantly as your Boston favorites." But "Caroline" minced no words in her retort to "Pickwick": "You cannot more easily provoke the laugh of derision than to ask a man, who sincerely wishes his daughter to become an accomplished scholar, why he sends her away to school. He invariably asks, in which of the *female seminaries* [here] would you have me place her?"[29]

• • •

Whether considered as an adornment for leisure hours or a practical preparation for life, women's education differed from men's in both cities. Conversely, education served both purposes, regardless of gender and geography. Charleston, like Boston, had instructive and utilitarian lecture series. Charlestonians by the hundreds, like Bostonians by the thousands, listened to lectures on religion, philosophy, and literature as well as on political economy and applied chemistry. Both cities provided night classes and specialized libraries for mechanic apprentices. Both cities had libraries replete with current novels and classical literature. Both had collections of textbooks and handbooks. On a per capita basis Charleston's society and circulating libraries probably served their readers more plentifully than did Boston's, though Boston's libraries all told had at least two or three times as many volumes. Intellectuals, both north and south, wrote articles, read journals, and discussed the affairs of the day and the things of the mind. Nonetheless education, more clearly for men than for women, more pervasively in Boston than in Charleston, served economic ends. How it did so embodied each city's most deeply held cultural values about the nature of work, democracy, individual opportunity, and community obligation.

PART IV · BALANCING SOCIAL INTERESTS

9

Class, Family, and Church

In Jacksonian America, wealth, economic power, and political position could be gained—or lost—in ten or twenty years. Few, it is true, rose from penury to great riches even in a lifetime; still fewer made the reverse trek. And how much property men owned was directly related to their age, as most Americans owned significantly more at fifty than they did at twenty.[1] Nonetheless, wealth, economic power, and political position altered more swiftly than class standing, and to a large extent status determined the social though not the economic and political structure of the city.

Exactly what placed a person in the upper class and what separated the middling sorts from the lower orders puzzled even astute observers and was seldom elaborated by those who, as members of a particular society, knew—or thought they knew—intuitively. Social standing was too complex a mixture of substance and symbol to be readily defined. The outsider might judge hastily by observing individuals' apparent wealth or noting the prestige of the occupations they followed. Yet a number of less visible attributes were critical to judging a person's status. Not least of them: Who were one's kin? Where had one gone to school? What church did one attend? In which clubs and with what associates did one pass one's leisure time? So determined by the past was it that status was a more conservative force than either wealth or power, both of which could be gained or lost more quickly. Nonetheless it was possible not only to move through the middling ranks but to enter the upper reaches of society within a lifetime, though it was more commonly a question of generations.

So it was that Charleston's class structure was notably less rigid than her self-conscious preoccupation with aristocracy would imply. Her educational system explicitly provided for upward social and economic mobility. Distinguished at the bar, James Petigru, the son of a small farmer, achieved great prestige; Ker Boyce, a man of yet humbler origins, sat in the state senate after having gained wealth in trade and power as a bank president. Nonetheless these men were exceptions; however tolerant she was of internal inconsistencies, Charleston did define her patrician core by linking high status to landed wealth. Planting, or owning a plantation, symbolized a continuity with the country gentry of England—even though planting land was subject to purchase by anyone with the cash or credit to pay for it. Its importance is reflected in the fact that while fewer than one-fifth of the Charlestonians with high status were wealthy, nine-tenths of them had some planting interests and one-half owned large plantations. No other kind of property, no matter how productive, had such social power[2]—a fact James Petigru recognized in buying a Savannah River rice plantation.

But even being able to call oneself a planter was insufficient to make one a member of the upper class, as auctioneer and real estate speculator Mordecai Cohen found out. Similarly, James Adger and Ker Boyce, who had far greater economic resources than either Petigru or Cohen, did not plant and remained men of only modest social status. Nor did owning the right kind of property eliminate other ambiguities of status. Petigru was a college graduate, a lawyer, and an Episcopal vestryman. Adger was an Irish-born Presbyterian, a merchant, and largely self-educated, as was Boyce, who was a factor and a Baptist. And Cohen was a Polish Jew who dealt in corn. Petigru was clearly a man of the upper class; the others comprised the upper reaches of the middling ranks who engaged in trade and enjoyed modest but not high social position. Yet a merchant could become a self-made aristocrat, even in Charleston, by displaying talent and conforming to aristocratic values, as did Irish-born Simon Magwood, who reared his son as to the plantation born. Nonetheless, very high status was largely reserved to the old planting families with names like Huger, Manigault, and Middleton.

The differences which set Charleston's class structure apart from Boston's reflected their distinctive social theories. Charleston defined her structure in terms of an underlying duality. All inhabitants were divided first by race, with all whites enjoying social advantages which all blacks lacked; then whites were further divided into a small aristoi and a broad demos arrayed by various combinations of property, occupation, family, education, church, and leisure-time activities. Yet if the rank ordering of these combinations was consciously blurred by an egalitarianism bred of race, the proffering of upward mobility primarily through education limited it to those singled out for advancement in early youth.

Class, Family, and Church

Bostonians, by contrast, enunciated a more flexible social theory. They defined social class within a triune hierarchy of the poor, the middling interests, and the rich. But while their social structure was both static and rigid, place within it was not. Rank order was perceived less as inhering in a personal combination of attributes than in a person's location on a ladder up which the diligent might climb by hard work first to acquire property and then to achieve positions of prestige and power. In actual practice, of course, neither the sequential rise nor the coupling of wealth and status was quite so direct or automatic as popular myth would have it. Neither was their connection with hard work inevitable, and inherited wealth had to be justified as the work of past generations. And while one-third of Boston's upper class were men of great wealth, only one-fifth of the city's wealthiest citizens enjoyed high social standing.[3]

The contrast with Charleston was sharp. Social distinctions did not depend on the kind of property in which wealth was invested, for Boston operated within a cash nexus, measuring the value of productive property by the income it produced or the value it was likely to gain over time. Ralph Waldo Emerson was, after all, writing as a critical outsider when he complained that "things [were] in the saddle, and [rode] mankind." But he was right in insisting that property was not inert. It was not just the fruit of labor; it required still more labor. Properly understood, it was utility which gave property its value. Property vindicated itself only when it created more property, by the work of its owner, or of those he employed, or of those whose employment his investments made possible. Farm land had no inherent worth different from other property. As early as the eighteenth century, Massachusetts had broken with the traditional British practice to which South Carolina still adhered, and in probate inventories it valued real estate just as it valued all other property.[4]

Nonetheless, even in Boston, property was no monolith. It varied in kinds. Some was enjoyed and displayed for aesthetic and status-oriented reasons. Ann McLean Lee, in addition to $53,500 in cash bequests, left silver, paintings, prints, musical instruments, and other special objects to thirty-eight different friends and family members. And the wills of Bostonians, if they almost uniformly bequeathed property of equal value to their various sons and daughters, did sometimes make distinctions by gender in the kind of property left each. Sons were somewhat more likely to inherit the stores and wharves of wealthy fathers or the tools and stock-in-trade of middling-rank sires. William Phillips divided his extensive real estate holdings so that sons and grandsons inherited his stores on Kilby Street, his daughters residential property and bank stock. Rufus Barrus left his medical library and surgical instruments for his son, to be given him only when he was qualified to use them. Clearly the inheritors of business and professional property were expected to improve on the value received by further work.

By contrast, daughters were more likely to be preferred in gifts of jewelry (except for their fathers' watches, which universally went to sons), furniture, silver, china, and other household items, while the property assigned the widow usually included the family home and its furnishings. Even John Whitney, laborer, who divided the rest of his estate equally among his three children, provided that Catherine, his only daughter, receive the furniture she wanted. If, on the one hand, such bequests acknowledged women's domestic role, they also reflected the expectation that women would display their fathers' or husbands' status by using their most luxurious goods. The reverse implication was that they could not manage business property. Stocks, bonds, and other liquid assets—most often divided without distinction of gender—were put in trust only for women and minor or spendthrift sons unlikely to manage them profitably.[5]

In both South Carolina and Massachusetts, the law governing the property of intestates provided equal distribution to legitimate sons and daughters. That relatively few people in either state made wills is evidence that the law accorded with widely held assumptions just as did wills, which generally contained similar provisions. Yet if a wealthy Charleston father had not already provided plantations for his sons during his lifetime, he almost always left his planting land to one or more of them, even when there was no equivalent for daughters and other sons. John Parker left his single plantation to his eldest son, while four other sons and two daughters were to enjoy the rest of his estate when it was distributed on his widow's death. Harriott Maxwell, on the other hand, left her plantations to her daughter because her late husband had already left their son all his land. Only when the testator owned a number of plantations, as did Elias Horry, were daughters as likely to inherit plantations as their brothers. And when they did, if they were married, management of the land generally passed to their husbands, even when the wives retained actual title or when it was left them in trust for their children. Thus that property which most displayed status passed to male use, albeit women were given, as they were in Boston, more of the family furniture, silver, jewelry, and, much more conspicuously than in Boston, horses and carriages.[6]

Finally, slaves were a form of property totally lacking in the North. With them Charlestonians could actually bequeath future as well as past work; with them they could endow their heirs with leisure as no Bostonian could. Yet the various ways in which wills treated such property betrayed considerable ambivalence. Some decedents, like bricklayer John McKee and widow Anna Carpenter, ordered that their slaves be sold for cash, with the proceeds to be distributed among the heirs in a manner which complied as fully with the cash nexus as any Boston practice. For them slave property was no different from any other kind. Planters passed on field hands as part of bequeathed plantations, although they occasionally divided ownership of the work force among several children as they would not divide the land. Others, like physician-planter Paul Weston, allowed slaves to choose new owners from among the heirs, with other property being used to equalize discrepancies in the will's intended distribution of the whole property. Possessors of smaller estates, like pump and block maker Moses Andrews and the illiterate Mrs. Lavinia Benson, left slaves to be hired out to provide income for their heirs.[7]

Then there were those who treated slaves as heirs. British-born merchant Adam Tunno left $12,000 to be distributed among his house servants. Others ordered that some or all of their servants be emancipated if state law were ever changed to permit it; many more, that favored servants be given the use of their own time and the fruits of their labor, living as free as the law could be stretched to allow. Such testators may be understood to have placed humanity above property or to have donated part of their wealth to a philanthropic purpose. A few, like Captain James Bean, were by so doing only providing for their slave families as men generally did for wives and legitimate children.[8]

Because relatively little Boston property displayed the intrinsic values implied in the testamentary disposition of slaves and the general veneration of plantation land, it is less useful as a gauge of social attitudes. The houses of the rich might display their luxuries—but they were not family seats. Thomas Perkins gave his turn-of-the-century Pearl Street mansion to Samuel Gridley Howe's school for the blind after he had built a still grander mansion on Temple Place so filled with objets d'art that it shocked the Reverend John Pierce. Gardiner Greene's heirs sold his great house on Pearl Street to be leveled for commercial development. And Harrison Gray Otis moved from his first Bulfinch house on Cambridge Street to his second on Mt. Vernon to his third on Beacon.[9]

In Boston that which sanctified wealth was family origin, about which nothing could be done; marriage, which blessed new money despite upper-class proclivity to marry in; and education, if not for the professions, at least for the social ties which a few years at Harvard could build. Thus Josiah Quincy II's property of $140,000 in 1841 accompanied rather than caused the high status which he had derived from his family. Yet neither Frederic Tudor's fortune of at least $80,000 in 1841 nor his distinguished father and brother nor his sweet young wife could do much to enhance social standing injured by sly business dealing in his national and international ice trade and by an unusual liaison which continued after his marriage. On the other hand, young Amos A. Lawrence adorned the great wealth he would inherit by a social style cultivated more in Harvard clubs than Harvard classrooms, while his less promising older brother William secured his social standing by studying medicine in Paris and becoming a physician in the years following his marriage.[10]

Social rank was thus something quite different from wealth, however much associated with it. And if wealth did not automatically mean the direct exercise of power, no more did social standing. Indeed, it promised less, for no more than two out of five of those who enjoyed some mark of social status in either city also held political office or exerted economic power. Thus it was their own and their families' style of living which characteristically displayed upper-class privilege. In Charleston the very great dwelt in mansions which, if they seldom contained more than twelve rooms, were graced by large piazzas and lovely gardens. In Boston, where climate made indoor space more important, Perkins's four-story Temple Place house required twenty-three fireplaces to heat it. Yet few in either city lived on that scale. In Boston even Otis, Lee, and Brooks townhouses were filled to their limits with large families whose children doubled up in bedrooms.[11] And in Charleston, where the first floor and half the second of the two- and three-story houses were customarily public rooms and where sleeping quarters must have been equally crowded, there was little private space.

Nonetheless, Boston's upper class and her rich lived very differently from William Taylor, barber, whose total assets amounted to $74 when he died in 1832. Owning no real estate, he had lived in sparsely furnished rented housing, probably a good deal less comfortably than Thomas Moore, master carpenter, who had put his money into a home and other real property worth over $7,000 at his death in 1833. Yet both these men possessed sufficient property to inventory—and, however humble, doubtless lived better than George Berry, laborer, who in 1834 left his wife only his claim to her own back wages of $31 and to the $43 which his employer owed him for labor performed.[12]

Small traders were somewhat better off than George Berry, but not necessarily better off than master mechanic Thomas Moore. Samuel Boyden, provision dealer, left an estate of only $410. Ellis Cook, while he did leave some silver and a few stocks, had assets amounting to little more than $1,000, and his $200 worth of household effects suggests a meager domesticity. Even Stephen Dix, whose store was stocked with $17,000 worth of the oils and paints he sold, rented his shop and residence; but he furnished the latter with more than $600 worth of household goods. Yet if he and his wife, Cecelia, had lived comfortably before he died in 1832, they knew nothing of the style of a truly great ménage such as old John

Amory had kept up before he died the same year. The cellar of his Tremont Street mansion was stocked with fine wines worth $2,000, his sideboard with silver worth $1,500. He insured his widow's convenience by bequeathing her the horses and carriages which made winter calls pleasant and the cool comfort which a summer estate in Roxbury provided.[13]

It was doubtless in a house like Amory's, one furnished with "stately, solid . . . expensive" furniture, that bachelor Frank Gray lived in "splendid state" and served the seven-course dinner which planter William Elliott reported with pleasure and some amazement. "[F]ricaudeaux, & french unnameable dishes," fruit of ten varieties, and six kinds of wine marked its profusion and elegance. Indeed, the dinner party was the forte of upper-class men's entertaining. Served at midafternoon or early evening, often with no women or only the hostess in attendance, they were meals of incredible size and variety, enlivened, at their best, by witty dialogue and probing discussions of social and political issues.[14] Nor did Boston outdo Charleston in the style and substance of such parties. Visiting Englishman James Stuart reported a feast gotten up for twenty gentlemen and ladies which ranged from turtle soup through fish, game, poultry, and mutton to a course of "pastry and puddings" followed by desserts of fruit and ice cream, all of which were accompanied by "Champagne, Madeira, sherry, port, claret, porter, lemonade, &c." That entertaining in this style was urbane and something to be learned young planter John Grimball attested. It was only after six months of attending Charleston dinner parties and recording guest lists, seating arrangements, table settings, service, and menus that he essayed his first five-course dinner for eight.[15]

If men liked the dinners best, upper-class women's special social form was exchanging calls and fostering the festivities of particular interest to the young: suppers, balls, soirées, and the other evening parties whose size and success were measured by the number of rooms which were "opened up" for dancing. These were elegant and sophisticated affairs in a country still 90 percent rural, most of whose urban population lived in small towns. But these were also styles of life foreign to most city folk. Ann Amory McLean Lee, daughter of one wealthy Bostonian, widow of another, and wife of a third, might in bequeathing six dozen silver spoons transmit the potential for gracious elegance. Rebecca Tolman, whose whole estate amounted to $23, had neither the silver nor a particularly desirable way of living to transmit. And even though the relatively humble in Charleston could bequeath the leisure that slave ownership implied, Louisa Cabeuil's bequest of two wenches, who accompanied her $85 worth of household furnishings, and Sarah Clement's of four, who accompanied her $39 worth of domestic furniture and implements—albeit in a house she owned—meant something quite different from the social style which Harriet

Hockley Bampfield passed on with the distribution of her thirty-six slaves, including Nat, the coachman, who drove her carriage and horses so well.[16]

The display of wealth in either city, however, had little to do with the exhortations which addressed Boston's imperative to improve one's economic and social rank by hard work. As printer-publisher Joseph Buckingham advised aspiring mechanics, "A middle station in the order of society—a position removed at a suitable distance from the extremes of mendicity and wealth—is usually believed to be the happiest."[17] Whether or not they were the happiest, Boston's middling interests were a stabilizing force, mediating and buffering the vast reaches between the unpropertied poor struggling for bare survival and the "idle rich" to whom elegance, conviviality, and taste were so essential. And in Charleston, the blurring of class distinctions among whites served the same purpose.

. . .

> I thank thee, Lord on bended knee
> I'm half Porcher and half Huger . . .
> For other blessings thank thee too—
> My grandpa was a Petigru.

Thus eloquently did doggerel bear out the familiar likening of Charlestonians to Chinese, both of whom ate rice, spoke a language intelligible only to themselves, and worshipped their ancestors. It also epitomized the conservative force of family. Except as Pettigrews became Petigrus, nothing could alter one's ancestry. And that fact shaped the property and prestige to be transmitted across generations, the rearing and education of children, and the preparation of youth for particular kinds of occupations. So too it shaped the options for marriage partners and the way in which family would shape the next generation, given the common preference for cousins as spouses. Generally parents encouraged their children to marry for their own well-being. But matrimony was also a way to cement existing family ties, to establish links with like-situated families, and, especially in Boston, to provide that ballast which would pressure adult children to work, save, and be prudent.[18] Wealthy parents provided daughters with bridal gifts of substantial sums to furnish their new homes and endow them with some independent income, and, in Charleston, with servants. Middling ranks joined their social betters in attempting to prevent their daughters from wedding men who would not or could not support them comfortably, and, especially in Charleston, in negotiating formal marriage settlements to protect a wife's interest in a few household furnishings as much as in considerable fortunes.[19] In both cities, too, husband-fathers tried to insure their children's future by conveying only a life interest in real and other property to a surviving widow. Similarly, Charleston marriage settlements often provided that a wife-mother's property would pass directly to her children whether or not she died before her spouse. And if in their wills fathers, when they made distinctions among their children, sometimes favored sons over daughters, so women often favored their daughters, daughters-in-law, and nieces.

Thus in both cities marriage and the transmission of property within the family was, in part at least, a conservative socioeconomic institution, favoring continuity and preservation of resources in many ways. But once again the peculiar nature of some southern property added yet another dimension to the intersection of family and material possessions. Marriage patterns for most blacks differed markedly from those of whites. Because slave-owners' economic self-interest demanded they retain the right to sell or otherwise dispose of their property, society could not demand that slaves' marriages be the lifelong bond they were among whites. Yet the commonly perceived relationship between family and social stability reinforced religious teachings that marriage was a practice much to be encouraged. Thus as church doctrine was altered to teach that slave marriages were something less than bonds unto death, so wedding forms developed to sanctify those commitments which could be made. Customarily a white minister or black class leader presided over ritual solemnities which resembled but were not identical with those of whites.[20] No less celebratory in form, they created in substance families with minimal paternal power and no recognized provision for the transmission of property within the family. Children of formal unions inherited, just as did all other slave children, the slave status of the mother; and no matter how formal the marriage bonds, it was that matrifocal structure which was most likely to be recognized when slave families were sold as a unit.

Less distinctive, but nonetheless different from the union of whites, were marriages of free blacks. They could and did involve legal settlements protecting the wife's property. When they linked a slave to a free spouse who bought as well as married the slave partner and thus owned their children as chattels, they involved quite different property relations. In addition, the ties resulting from the union of white men with black women created yet another amalgam of family and property. Although marriage across race lines was uncommon, long-term relationships were formed. When such unions transgressed divisions between slave and free, there is little record of the man's making provision for his children and their mother except as he might bequeath them the use of their own time, the fruits of their labor, and the limited freedom it was in his power to give. When, however, the liaison linked free people across race lines, some men—both poor and rich—provided that their property be transmitted within their families. And the probate court did, sometimes with the consent of other heirs and always with that of the executors, oversee the distribution of property to the common-law wife and her children.[21] But it was only in such rare circumstances that family ties and the transmission of property from one generation to the next challenged the status quo and the cultural values which underlay it.

• • •

Perhaps because religious affiliation was more a matter of individual choice than either family or class, churches were of all traditional institutions the least conservative. If they acted as ballast amid felt crises, they also adapted to shifting pressures. In so doing, they changed as they conserved and embraced the new as they clung to the old. By these apparent contradictions, they simultaneously expressed social tensions and bridged them in cities where ethic hostility, racial heterogeneity, and class division were often disruptive.

While the Calvinist denominations may have nourished the Protestant ethnic customarily associated with the rise of capitalism, those who had risen by its application, in Boston at least, increasingly opted for Unitarian liberalism or Episcopal ritual over Congregational orthodoxy. Nonetheless, in both cities it was evangelicalism which challenged prevailing Protestant orthodoxy and in so doing reached the humble as, with few exceptions, liberal religion did not.[22] It served simultaneously as a bastion against the social change which threatened native mechanics and as a means to direct the earthly discontent of slaves heavenward. By contrast, recent immigrants, whose social and economic aspirations were even less sure, sought solace in churches of ritual whose cultural bonds united them with old-country practice as it cemented ethnic awareness in the new.

In Charleston, ethnic churches also provided a secure institutional base from which to embark on the process of assimilation. Most Germans in the city belonged to St. John's Lutheran Church. Founded by and for immigrants in the 1750s, by the 1830s it was so strongly assimilative that pastor John Bachman abandoned giving even the single monthly sermon in German. But by so doing he triggered a movement among recent immigrants to organize the German-language parish of St. Matthew's in 1840.[23]

Less clearly a question of assimilation but clearly linked to it was the split within the Jewish congregation. Beth Elohim's distinctive services had been shaped by its Sephardic members, who in the 1820s had challenged some Talmudic practices and the use of Ladino through their Reformed Society of Israel. After 1836 the synagogue's new Ashkenazi rabbi, Gustavus Poznanski, went still further in reforming ritual by extending the use of English. Yet congregational unity survived until it came to installing an organ in the new synagogue, built after fire had destroyed the old one in 1838. The last straw, it opened the way for orthodox Jews to fight all departures from tradition and, when they lost, to form the conservative Shearith Israel.[24]

Indicative of still other ethnic and generational tensions among immigrants was the experience of Charleston's Catholics. By the 1830s the San Domingan French, who had arrived after the Haitian revolution of 1803, were firmly established in St. Mary's Church; the Irish, whose numbers were steadily increasing, worshipped at St. Finbar's, only blocks away. The origin of St. Finbar's lay in Bishop John England's experience when he had first taken up his see in Charleston. He had confronted, in 1820, a controversy common to Catholic churches elsewhere in the United States— whether the lay vestry or the priests and bishop controlled the parish's physical assets. St. Mary's vestry chose to model their church governance on the prevailing practice of all other Charleston churches, and the bishop had built St. Finbar's and made it his cathedral church when they would not conform to traditional Catholic polity. There the Irish-born and -educated bishop and priests of similar origin served the steady flow of Irish immigrants into the city. And by 1838 there was a similar congregation worshipping at St. Patrick's on the Neck.[25] Thus Lutherans, Jews, and Catholics all reflected the adaptive capacity of churches. Each distinctively ethnic denomination had both an assimilative branch comprising mainly earlier immigrants and a more traditional institution which served primarily the most recent arrivals. But in creating that option, Lutherans and Catholics avoided the public conflict which Charleston's Jews experienced.

Among Boston's still heavily English and homogeneous population ethnic churches played a more limited role. Essentially it was the Irish who were served by the city's three Catholic churches, and despite Bishop Benedict Fenwick's American birth, they were not assimilative churches. They served a population isolated and despised as Charleston's Catholics were not. The institutions, like their memberships, were subject to prejudice. Their parishioners knew well the nativist violence and arson which in 1834 destroyed the Ursuline Convent in neighboring Charlestown. They were thwarted by the prejudice which excluded the Irish-born from serving in city fire companies and denied them the privilege of organizing militia units. Thus their churches, in offering the consolations of faith, hewed largely to the old ways and provided a stable institutional bulwark against a hostile environment. The only notable clash within the church was a riot at St. Mary's, whose parishioners were divided over whether temperance was a church issue and whether the bishop or the laity should choose their priest. Those seeking church autonomy rather than behavioral reform backed their temporary pastor, Father O'Beirne; their opponents supported O'Beirne's replacement, Father Thomas O'Flaherty, Bishop Fenwick's protégé and a vocal teetotaler. On February 20, 1842, O'Flaherty was jeered from the chancel by O'Beirne's supporters in a demonstration which some attributed more to demon rum than to a preference for lay control. In any case, when neither priest nor laymen could quiet the congregation, the city marshal was called to restore order—which he did by arresting a dozen parishioners for disturbing the peace of the sabbath.[26]

The upheavals which evangelical revivals caused, however, could neither be written off as the emanations of an inherently unruly people nor controlled by duly constituted authorities. Indeed, in Charleston they penetrated even into Episcopal churches. Born-again lawyer-planter William Barnwell, who had taken up the Christian ministry in Beaufort, came to Charleston and held the revivals which, in 1833, led to the formation of St. Peter's Church—Episcopal but also evangelical. Young Daniel Cobia, as assistant minister at St. Philip's, also preached a simple gospel of Christ Jesus the Lord, using the unsophisticated language which had earlier attracted sizable congregations of humble folk to the mission Chapel of St. Stephen's. Viewed ambivalently by conservative clerics, these enthusiastic ministers were disruptive to old ways but also appealing to church officials. On the one hand Bishop Nathaniel Bowen wished to correct the lamentable "absence . . . of the poorer classes" from the churches of his diocese. Yet he was also sure that "revival enthusiasm, going on for several days at a time, interrupts normal activities of life & are probably not expedient or useful or desirable. . . ." Still, it was by these methods that other sects attracted converts, and without them that Episcopal churches failed to grow.[27]

It was, of course, primarily among the nonritualistic churches that evangelicalism prevailed, nourished by the camp meetings which Charlestonians attended throughout the 1830s. Comfortable among the poor and middling country folk, many Charlestonians of lesser rank found in camp meetings the religious commitment which subsequently propelled them into new denominational affiliations in town. But religious enthusiasm did not guarantee harmony, and in Charleston's Methodist churches the prevalence of black members led to overt clashes. Statistically, at least, the Methodist Episcopal church was primarily a black church. Moreover, by mid-decade its 3,629 black and 632 white members were crowded into three churches whose combined pews could accommodate scarcely half their number at one time and whose resources were inadequate for an extensive building program. As in other Charleston churches, tradition had confined slaves to the galleries of Trinity Methodist Church—but it had also permitted free people of light color and decrepit blacks to take their seats in the rear of the main floor. Under the pressure of growing numbers, however, more and more Negroes of whatever condition were occupying first-floor pews.[28]

In the late summer of 1833 white resentment at these incursions came to a head. A group of mechanics and small tradesmen, regarding the situation as a racial affront, asked their presiding elder, William Capers, to confine all nonwhites to the balcony and to keep black and white parishioners separate even in the churchyard. But Capers's commitment to black Methodists was long-standing, and there ensued a prolonged internecine battle, which ended only with the dissidents leaving the Methodist Episcopal denomination to form their own Methodist Protestant church. But their departure only revealed another division, this one among the Negro parishioners, who would still have been overcrowded in their three extant churches even had all white Methodists seceded. Again in 1837 black slaves challenged the special seating afforded free people of light color, touching off a minor riot in front of Trinity Church.[29]

However much caste divided Methodists—and even the seceding Methodist Protestants had their black parishioners—their churches served the humble, directing their aspirations to the next world, feeding their emotional strength to exist in this one. William Capers, who had molded his mission work among plantation slaves to satisfy their largely Episcopal owners, was proud that he ministered to "the poorer of the people." But he also implied some doubts: "Everything about the [Methodist] denomination partook somewhat, perhaps too much, of the cast of poverty." Yet the church which was predominantly a black and a slave church had few options. Even those with greater resources met similar problems.

All other Charleston churches seated the races separately. And even when slaves were guided in their religious affiliation by the preference of their masters, as were most black worshippers at St. Philip's and St. Michael's Episcopal churches, St. John's Lutheran, and the Second Presbyterian, they attended services so eagerly that they overcrowded the galleries set apart for them until these churches provided special lectures and religious services for black adults and Sunday schools for all age groups. So the city's other churches adopted the Methodist system of classes in which black leaders offered instruction, imposed church discipline, and preached and prayed with their fellows. To be sure, the city council monitored the classes and services to enforce the city ordinance requiring white supervision. But church practices as a whole both bridged and accommodated the caste system as no other institution did.[30]

More easily resolved was the division within Charleston's Baptist community over conflicting preferences for an educated as opposed to an enthusiastic ministry. Founded by Mainers, the First Baptist Church had held to the New England tradition, calling to its pulpit educated ministers only minimally given to revivalism. Its pastor until 1837 was Basil Manly, whose background had prepared him to assume the presidency of the University of Alabama. His departure that year released a controversy long brewing between traditionalists and those affected by the prevailing revivalism. Its resolution involved establishing a second Baptist church uptown, whose members ultimately chose the enthusiastic but well-educated James Furman for their pastor.[31]

Such resolutions were not for Boston, in spite of the systematic founding of new churches by all denominations to serve the city's rapidly growing population and its physical expansion. Three waves of revivals had indeed swept the city between 1823 and 1833; and it was alleged that Lyman Beecher's fiery preaching during the last of them had furnished the spark which ignited nativist determination to burn Charlestown's Ursuline Convent, which Beecher had damned for corrupting the minds and bodies of Boston girls. But it was only after the 1837 panic, and in the hard times which reached their low point in 1841–1842, that Boston experienced revivals which equalled—and even surpassed—Charleston's in intensity. In Park Street Congregational Church, evangelist Edward N. Kirk introduced a new enthusiasm even to that evangelical bastion—especially to its women. And Charles Grandison Finney, famous for his prolonged revivals in New York, came to town and for weeks stirred the souls of middling-interest folk. But neither generated the extremes of religious excitement which Jacob Knapp stirred up among the Baptists or the public denunciations which his energetic preaching inspired. So intense was his style that converts succumbed to raving insanity—or so their families said. Mobs surrounded the Bowdoin Square Church where he preached, throwing stones at the windows, ready to attack the radical within could they but lay hands on him. Damned in the press for "blasphemous levity," Knapp but spoke the language of common men, assuring them that a Universalist could "no more go to heaven, than a shad [could] climb a May-pole tail foremost."[32]

And if these three evangelists—one Congregationalist, one Baptist, and one supported by various denominations—converted the four thousand sinners they claimed, their combined impact was overshadowed the following winter, when many Bostonians prepared for the end of the world. With Millerites announcing the impending millennium, the faithful began to construct a five-thousand-seat auditorium in which they might gather to be taken into heaven. Meanwhile they crowded into Marlborough Chapel to hear Brother Himes and the Reverend Hawley rouse "the many sleepy sinners" with their *"Midnight cry."*[33]

But the world did not come to an end, nor did perfection dawn. And if at the peak of their fervor Boston's sectarian enthusiasms seemed, more than Charleston's, to loose all constraints and to threaten social stability, the shrewd observations of Democratic politician David Henshaw were probably correct. "[T]he benefits of public worship are not so much in the preaching," he argued, "as in the association of men at the altar. Congregate men of all ages in a church at stated periods—assemble both sexes, dressed in clean habiliments," and "even if error be preached to them, they will still improve in their kindly and social feelings. . . ."[34]

Evangelicalism, when it was organized into institutions, fed the social feelings so necessary for community cohesion as well as did ritual, traditional orthodoxy, or liberal dissent. Different churches served as anchors for different sorts of people, and the limited interchurch mobility in both Charleston and Boston made this clear. Among Catholics, Methodists, and Baptists, as among the much better documented Presbyterians, Congregationalists, Unitarians, Lutherans, and Episcopalians, there was little apparent raiding of rival sects for new members. The goal of all was to bring the unchurched into the fold or to renew the commitment of backsliders. Movement from one church to another was most likely to occur within a denomination. While such movement often veiled a choice among significant substantive differences, it was at least as likely to reflect the worshipper's change in residence or a preference in pastoral styles. Religion, like class and family, established rather stable boundaries, although it did so without eliminating the possibility of subsequent choice. And it was the churches associated with wealth, power, and high status which most attracted the members of other denominations.[35]

It was not surprising that religious affiliation among the rich, the upper class, and the powerful often reflected their social circumstances as clearly as did those of more humble folk. In Charleston, a quarter of wealthy churchgoers and a quarter of those with economic power worshipped as Presbyterians and Congregationalists. Although in Boston half of all rich church members were Unitarians, rich Unitarians were negligible in Charleston. But two Episcopal churches in each city attracted a third of the rich and the prestigious. In Boston they went to St. Paul's and Trinity churches. Moreover, the Unitarian church which attracted the greatest number of rich and prestigious Unitarians was King's Chapel, where liberal theology was dispensed in forms drawn from the Book of Common Prayer and the days when King's Chapel had been an Anglican church.[36]

Nonetheless, there was a significant difference between Boston's Episcopal churches and St. Philip's and St. Michael's, which attracted Charleston's rich, powerful, and prestigious in still greater proportions. In Charleston the two churches also attracted those who exerted the greatest economic and political power in similar numbers.[37] The implications of such concentrations are nowhere better seen than in the way in which St. Philip's overcame public opinion and city government in a head-on test of wills.

There was no question that St. Philip's would rebuild when the old church was destroyed in the 1835 fire. And after some discussion, there was no question that it would be rebuilt much as it had been. And it had, in the past, protruded well beyond all other buildings on Church Street—so much so that the street bowed in a great arc to accommodate its portico.

The city council, however, had voted that, in the public interest, the street should be straightened and the new church moved back on its lot. Thus the vista up Church Street would be unbroken and its easier navigation would make the city safer. The powerful vestry and building committee demurred. To move the building back would not only increase costs but disturb the graveyard. Each side was adamant, agreeing only to seek a resolution from the state-appointed Commission for Opening and Widening Streets. The commission's decision largely favored the church, influenced perhaps (as the press alleged) by the majority of its members who were not only Episcopalians but also members of St. Philip's.[38] To this day, although the church was moved back two feet from the original plan, its portico still protrudes markedly, and Church Street still bows to get around it.

• • •

More flexible than either family or class, church and religion illuminate the dualities which allowed tradition to be tempered by change. In both cities, religious fervor was principally the concern of the powerless, while the church as institution either enforced social stasis or negotiated orderly change. In both cities, too, communicants and those who had made confessions of faith were overwhelmingly female,[39] while the officials and pewholders who voted on the churches' business and wielded their power were almost exclusively male. Generally the two were compatible because institutional organizations reinforced the faith and morals they enshrined.

Most churches were governed by laymen, who were likely to be preoccupied six days a week with secular affairs. Vigorous clashes therefore sometimes occurred between them and their spiritual leaders. And when the laity were accustomed to wielding power, they often had their way. Charleston's St. Michael's vestry rejected young Paul Trapier's efforts to bring church practice into conformity with Episcopal church teachings. Its powerful wardens and vestrymen clung to unusual but traditional practices—tolling its bells for the dead of other faiths, admitting unconfirmed adults to communion, baptizing infants from a bowl on the altar instead of from the font—and Trapier resigned. Similarly, Boston's Trinity Church was so split that rector Jonathan Wainwright resigned after four years of stalemated dispute in the vestry on almost all major issues, from the use of church funds to the election of bishops. Conflict over church discipline and supervision of the Sunday school led to Benjamin Palmer's resignation as pastor of Charleston's Congregational Church. And most famous of all, John Pierpont's reform enthusiasm and especially his temperance advocacy so infuriated the proprietor-pewholders of the Hollis Street Church—some of them liquor dealers—that it led to a church trial involving nearly all of Boston's Unitarian clergy before Pierpont, having been exonerated by his peers, finally resigned.[40] In all cases, where lay governors had the resources of wealth and power, lay practice and interests finally overwhelmed ministerial propagation of the faith at odds with secular commitments.

There was no easy resolution to the clash in matters religious between the powerful and the powerless, any more than there was between the radicalism of religious enthusiasm and the conservatism of long-established churchly institutions. Nonetheless, it does seem plausible that while Charleston's powerful Episcopal and orthodox Calvinist churches reinforced the traditional values which, in large measure, limited the city's ability to seize and exploit new opportunities, the theological liberalism of Boston's powerful Unitarian establishment encouraged innovative responses to new economic forces without at the same time threatening social or political stability.

10

Play and Philanthropy

Charlestonians, who made no special moral virtue of work, savored unoccupied time more openly than did their Yankee cousins, who thought of time as money. Charlestonians' dedication of resources to servants was but part of that conspicuous consumption of leisure which justified the maxim that if Boston was a state of mind, Charleston was a state of being.[1] Yet however different their degrees of "frivolity and mirth,"[2] the two cities' forms of recreation were remarkably similar.

Citizens in both cities celebrated holidays actively. Their Independence Days were enlivened by parades, band music, military hoopla, speeches, and dinners. Nonetheless, at least one Charlestonian found the Boston festival tame. Yankee boys simply did "not seem to enjoy themselves . . . with the lightheartedness and gaiety which is observed at the South. . . ."[3] And that observation carried over to other occasions. Washington's birthday, little more than a midwinter political occasion in Boston, introduced the height of Charleston's social season: race week with its sports, parties, and fancy balls. It was followed, just a month later, by the political and ethnic observance of St. Patrick's Day, unknown in the northern city.

Perhaps it was a matter of seasonal climate, for Boston's special holidays came not in late winter but in late summer and fall. Near the end of August, Harvard commencement unleashed what one Carolina visitor called a "Carnaval [sic] season." Then on fall militia day in early September resplendently clad troops maneuvered on the Common, captivating the crowds of children dismissed from school to watch the event. The "feasting, visiting, [and] recreations" of Thanksgiving completed the annual round of holidays before Bostonians dug in for the winter.[4] But not for them the week-long Christmas celebrations of the southern city.

Play and Philanthropy

The privileged of both cities enjoyed vacations as well. Indeed, summer social life in Charleston was largely shaped by that city's being a refuge where planters could escape the country fevers. Conversely, city denizens who owned plantations often spent spring and late fall vacations in the country. Others summered for weeks or months on nearby Sullivan's Island, just a twenty-five-cent ferry ride from a downtown wharf on the Cooper River, so conveniently located that businessmen could commute and day-trippers could turn the trip itself into a special outing. For Boston, Nahant served a somewhat similar role. A craggy promontory visible from the city on a clear day, Nahant boasted summer cottages and a good hotel. But because for most of the decade it was accessible only by carriage or a two-to-four-hour sail it was primarily a rural retreat for the rich, some of whom built extensive estates there.

Other Bostonians less ostentatiously visited surrounding towns which could be readily reached by omnibus, coach, steamboat, or railroad. Quincy, Woburn, Brighton, Brookline, and Hingham were near at hand; Northampton, Rhode Island's Newport, and Hampton in New Hampshire, farther away. According to the distance to be traveled and the length of their purses, they made either one-day excursions or extended stays at rural inns and resort hotels. For Charlestonians, too, the coming of the railroad extended vacation options and eased traveling. Mountain summer homes in Pendleton or Greenville and in Buncombe County, North Carolina, were readily reached; Aiken was consciously developed as a resort. Additionally, many of the affluent, like their Boston counterparts, made long trips to spend vacations at nationally fashionable establishments in Newport, Saratoga Springs, and Northampton or, somewhat closer to home, at the spas of the western Virginia Piedmont.

Sports, which could be enjoyed closer to home and, with the exception of yachting, were less expensive, drew many participants and spectators. In Boston, at least by the late 1830s, the Cambridge Trotting Park offered horse racing as a seasonal event. Several gymnasia catered to men wishing instruction in sports or the discipline of regular exercise. Their facilities popularized both boxing and fencing. But the most popular sports were connected with the sea. Small boys skinny-dipped, while grown men patronized bathing establishments. And if the yachting regattas off Nahant were the playthings of the upper class, mechanics and sailors rowed competitively in pulling races which were scheduled regularly off Chelsea and East Boston.

Charleston's sports were more heavily shaped by the rural preoccupation with horsemanship and the ready opportunity for hunting which the surrounding countryside offered. Race week in February, sponsored by the socially prestigious Jockey Club, attracted both rural and urban participants lured to the Washington race course by substantial prizes and the chance to test their fastest horses against national favorites like Bonnets of Blue and Clara Fisher. Watched by "fashionables, and the laboring class, the curious and the idle, the sharper and the flat, the dandy and the *sans culottes,* the gay and the grave, old age and puling infancy," these races were, as well, gambling events with stakes so high that once nearly half a million dollars reputedly rode on a single race.[5]

More regularly scheduled and available during much of the year was a variety of participant sports. The Carolina Archers acted out their romance with bow and quiver in colorful uniforms. Others organized fencing and boating clubs. Still others patronized the gymnasium on King Street or the nine-pin alleys which gave rise to complaints that balls "thunder[ed] . . . along the floor" well into the early hours of the morning.[6] No less noisy, and common to both cities, were the crowds of loiterers and tavern patrons who filled back alleys watching unscheduled cock, dog, and human fights.

Distinctly more respectable was music, whether privately made or publicly performed. In Charleston, John Siegling's music store rented between fifty and one hundred pianos annually in addition to the many pianos, guitars, harps, and violins it sold.[7] Obviously, interest in music making was extensive, yet public performances were largely the province of paid professionals rather than of local amateurs. Societies of singers and instrumental players did occasionally emerge to give concerts, then disappear from public view—the Hebrew Harmonic Society, the Musical Association, and the Instrumental Association among them. But Charleston lacked the variety as well as the persistence of musical organizations which kept so many Bostonians singing and playing and promoting music. While the southern St. Cecilia Society had long since exchanged musical performances for balls and other social activity, Boston's Handel and Haydn Society, formed in 1815 to improve church music, boasted, in the 1830s, a chorus of 150 men and women and an orchestra of 25.[8] These amateurs, sometimes employing professional soloists and directors, performed regularly in public.

In addition, the Academy of Music, organized to "diffuse the knowledge of music, in its most beneficial forms throughout the community" rather than give "musical exhibitions," had by 1838 a chorus of nearly two hundred voices and an orchestra of thirty, which staged series of concerts in Odeon Hall.[9] In addition, however, the academy actively pursued its original purpose of instilling the rudiments of music appreciation so widely that singing might offer "innocent indulgence" for youthful emotions and become a "substitute for drinking and riot" among the poor.[10]

So effective was its campaign that in 1838 the school committee voted to include music in the curricula of all city schools.

Thus over the years Bostonians sang, played, and listened to a purpose. "Our good Boston people are all for music," Charles Francis Adams wrote his mother, describing the summer concerts on the Common. Conducted amidst the "outcries of boys and the noise of public ways," they were paid for by "the gentlemen who live round the Mall who must from their houses have *great* enjoyment of it." Still more informally, on summer evenings young men bedecked in romantic fashion serenaded their ladies; one strolling tourist reported that "very fine music and many excellent voices" poured out the open windows of house after house. Yet these tunes and airs bespoke irrational abandon no more than did the harmonies of the Billings and Holden, the Gregorian, and the Education societies or the Flute Club or the brass band. The *Musical Gazette* proudly boasted that while the city was "without dispute, a musical community" it did not allow music to "interrupt the course of business."[11]

Perhaps because of the theaters' customary basement bars and the third-tier balconies where prostitutes solicited, acting was almost exclusively a commercial enterprise in both cities. While established stars like Edwin Forrest and Fanny Kemble drew packed houses, bad acting, thin or hostile audiences, and inadequate financing more often than not kept theater directors on edge. Charleston's single theater had short seasons and often seemed threatened by financial disaster. Boston, which occasionally operated three houses, was frequently reduced to a single theater. Legitimate theater also competed with a circus, in which equestrian performances, tightrope acts, and animal shows featuring Bengal leopards, laughing hyenas, jackals, and pelicans were staged. Moreover, traveling magicians, aerial balloonists, and displays ranging from freaks to stuffed mermaids always found eager audiences, at least for a while. Panoramas of stirring scenes—Napoleon bombarding Moscow or Washington crossing the Delaware—drew crowds hungry for visual imagery, while annual art exhibits displaying copies of old European masters and originals from the brushes of modern Americans—George Catlin, Charles Fraser, and John Audubon among them—attracted the more serious patrons.

Both as commercial ventures and as fund-raising events for good causes, bachelors' cotillions, masked balls, military promenades, and dancing assemblies supplemented private parties and offered amusement to rich and poor according to their purse and preference. Fayolle's in Charleston and Papanti's in Boston were the best-known dancing schools, whose semipublic subscription assemblies were eagerly anticipated from year to year. Young gentlemen might host a brilliant affair like that in Charleston's St. Andrew's Hall, at which the Tyrolean Minstrels provided the music. Once

Boston's young bachelors filled fourteen "very beautifully ornamented" rooms at the Tremont House with two bands, a supper table, and an attendant crowd of party makers.[12] But more commonly Bostonians danced to raise money for fuel for the poor, as Charlestonians danced to honor military units or assist fire companies. And for the less fastidious, there were the dance halls, the taverns, the gambling houses, and the brothels, which made both cities' waterfronts and the back side of Beacon Hill unsavory and unsafe. Thus did city folk amuse themselves in ways both suspect and envied among their rural fellow countrymen.

• • •

Voluntary associations were, so Tocqueville observed in 1835, a hallmark of American life.[13] Organized for profit or mutual aid or philanthropy, they served both serious and trivial purposes. Their memberships and their beneficiaries could range from small exclusive groups to all mankind. Charleston societies were, more often than not, broadly inclusive and served the cause of community cohesion by a sociability which augmented the philanthropic and cultural activities avowedly their purpose. Boston's associations were far more likely to be exclusive in membership and specific in purpose—whether it was moral uplift, social reform, intellectual stimulation, or just plain fun. Thus while both cities had business associations, ethnic clubs, do-good organizations, religious societies, and cultural institutions, they operated in distinctive ways.

The old stereotype would have us believe that Bostonians seldom made merry. It is true that during anniversary week each May, earnest New Englanders gathered in their chief city to attend the simultaneous conventions of as many as forty different benevolent societies. They heard elected officers of the Temperance Union, the Education Society, the Seaman's Friend, the Prison Discipline Society, the Peace Society, the Convention of Congregational Ministers, and many more lament social evil and proffer plans for human redemption. In their lightest moments, the delegates were said to converse seriously at staid tea parties or attend concerts confined to sacred music.

Yet just as Charleston's upper-class youth gathered in theatrical and gaming clubs, their Boston counterparts ate and drank together in private clubs formed largely of Harvard classmates or boyhood chums. When marriage first and then the responsibilities of middle age eventually restricted their club nights, they continued to meet weekly or monthly in exclusive societies, among them the Wednesday Evening Club and the Anthology Club.

Equally important, Charleston had its do-good organizations. Though it lacked the endless variety of Boston's reform groups, Charleston's benevolence soberly embraced the Protestant Episcopal Society for the Advancement of Christianity in South Carolina; the Charleston Bible Society; the Protestant Episcopal Missionary Society of Charleston; the Unitarian Book and Tract Society; the Methodist Missionary Society; the Episcopal Female Bible, Prayer Book, and Tract Society; the Young Men's Bible Society; the Young Men's Education Society; the Young Men's Temperance Society; and the South Carolina Sunday School Union.

It was thus style rather than substance which differentiated associational life in the two cities. Charleston associations were usually eclectic. Typical was the Hibernian Society, which, despite its name, was open to adult males of "any nation or religion." Beyond its chartered purpose of aiding Irish emigrants and their descendants, as well as the widows and children of members, its extensive endowment allowed it to assist other needy individuals and even render aid to public projects. Charity, however, was not its major function. At jolly monthly meetings in the Carolina Coffee House members socialized over punch, and at the annual banquet over one hundred men ate extravagant dinners and offered extravagant toasts to Carolina, Ireland, and one another.[14]

Such easy familiarity was not narrowly restricted. Though the Hibernians' officers were men of wealth and power, the more than eighty initiates during the 1830s included young professionals, accountants, retailers, and mechanics, as well as scions of elite and prestigious families. To what purpose these men from varying ranks met and mingled is revealed by a pattern they shared with the South Carolina Society, the German Friendly Society, and the French Benevolent Society. All four sharply expanded their membership in the years following nullification, drawing members from both political factions to heal its lingering divisiveness.[15]

Bridging political rifts was but part of the assimilative role played by Charleston's ethnic societies. The Huguenot South Carolina Society and the Scottish St. Andrew's Society had, like the Hibernians, surrendered their original ethnocultural restrictions on membership. The Hebrew Orphan Society aided non-Jews. And in 1834 the German Friendly Society almost dropped its ethnic restrictions. So despite their tolerance of the societies which served the most recent immigrants' interests exclusively—the St. Patrick, Emerald Isle, and French Benevolent societies—most Charlestonians opted for white solidarity over ethnic exclusiveness.

Such easy inclusiveness and diverse function did not, however, characterize Boston organizations, whose goals were narrower than community cohesion. Its ethnic associations—the British and Scots charitable societies excepted—all served recent immigrants and were restricted both in membership and activity to nationally or culturally defined groups. But the city's preference for exclusive membership and purpose extended beyond the rationale of its Irish, German, and Italian societies. The Harrison Club is a case in point. Its constitution limited its life to nine months, its purpose to the election of the Whig presidential candidate in 1840, and its membership to one hundred people. No Bostonian who was not a member could attend its meetings. An arm of the majority party, it was no secret political conspiracy, as its published constitution and open action demonstrated. The Harrison Club merely applied to political organization the limitations on membership and activity which most other Boston organizations—whether the Massachusetts Historical Society, the Athenaeum, or the Natural History Society—imposed on themselves.[16]

This exclusiveness extended to occupationally based organizations as well. When those Bostonians who engaged in trade sought to operate a mercantile library or to reach certain markets, they restricted membership to that single purpose and to those it would serve. Although they included all ranks from great merchants to shopkeepers and clerks, little more than 10 percent of their collective membership came from other walks of life. And, similarly if not so intensively, two-thirds of Boston's various mechanics' associations' membership comprised those actively engaged in a craft, whether as journeymen or as masters.[17]

In Charleston, except for the chamber of commerce, mercantile groups were twice as likely as their Boston counterparts to have noncommercial members. Practicing artisans comprised less than a third of its mechanics' associations' listed membership. And even resident Yankees were absorbed into the southern pattern. The New England Society, largely businessmen, was virtually indistinguishable from all other Charleston mercantile associations except for its members' place of birth.[18]

Perhaps these characteristics explain the intense Anti-Masonry in Boston and its total absence in Charleston, where Masonic lodges continued to operate unchallenged. The very inclusiveness of Charleston's visible organizations made Anti-Masonry's deep anxieties about secret societies largely irrelevant in the southern city, just as white Charleston's fears of slave insurrection seemed excessive in Boston.

• • •

"Men," observed Henry Pinckney, addressing the Methodist Benevolent Society in 1835, "should be kind to each other, because man is essentially a dependent creature." It was an unexceptionable comment. Few Bostonians would have challenged it outright. But Pinckney's further elaboration revealed the premises which set Charleston's philanthropy apart from that of the northern city. "The whole social system" was, he averred, "but a chain of reciprocal dependence, the poor hanging upon the rich, and the rich upon the poor." So linked, the rich were obliged to ameliorate the condition and promote the comfort of the poor by "employment, counsel, or gratuity"; and the poor were expected to "manifest their gratitude" to the rich.[19] Responsibility for the poor and needy was thus immediate and personal, and in a slave society its primary obligation rested on masters, who were expected to care for their servants in infancy, sickness, and old age. At least half of Charleston's population was thus to be succored directly within the patriarchal system rather than by any system of organized charity.

Charleston did not, of course, lack charitable organizations. But even its structured philanthropy was largely based on personal ties. Virtually every society in the city—ethnic, occupational, or religious—made some provision for its members or for special charges who fell into distress. Charity was thus a function of many organizations, though in most cases not their only one. Nor was this benevolence pro forma or niggardly. Sundry societies in the city disbursed upwards of $25,000 annually to the sick and needy, in addition to the donations for these purposes made by the various churches.[20]

That Charlestonians prided themselves on the personal warmth inherent in their good works author-editor William Gilmore Simms made clear in describing how alms were distributed in northern cities: "The poor are made to assemble at set places, undergo examination and be fed on soup."[21] For all the acerbity in Simms's observation, there was also a good deal of truth in it. Boston's citizens contributed no less to the poor, the ill, the down-and-out than did their southern counterparts. It may be they contributed more. The difference lay in that successful appeals to their pockets were less likely to be personal, were more likely to stress the donors' social obligation to maintain a stable society or their religious obligation to act as stewards of the Lord's plenty.

What more fitting topic could Richard S. Fay, Harvard graduate, lawyer, member of Trinity Church, touch upon in his Fourth of July oration than the role of charity in maintaining social stability and protecting property? Warning the rich against extravagance and the conspicuous display of their "gifts of fortune before the eyes of poverty," Fay then insisted that as an absolute minimum the wealthy serve their community through "quiet and searching benevolence."[22] Most Bostonians who carried out this obligation directed their benevolence through organizations specifically designed to render charity. By 1830 they had already poured over $750,000 into charitable institutions. Fifteen years later they had given more than twice as much again to philanthropy of this sort, in addition to the $10,000 they gave annually through their churches.[23]

Surely Bostonians could be forgiven their pride in the scope of their generosity. Yet like so much of their economic activity, their benevolence was made easy by growing wealth in the form of liquid resources. At a time when a merchant prince and his family could live comfortably on $15,000 a year yet could accumulate three times that much—as did William Appleton—the proper uses of wealth rather than its availability was the major issue.[24]

If there were those in the South whose consciences were tortured by slavery and assuaged by patriarchal kindness, so in Boston there were those for whom the constant accumulation of wealth created similar dilemmas. No one was more conscious of them than William Appleton, who admitted that he gave money to good causes with considerably less pleasure than he enjoyed in getting it in business.[25] It was only after he could record his total worth at over one million dollars that he finally could assure himself that, after all, he was as much interested in good works as in profits. Even then, however, it was to demonstrate "that a man may be . . . zealous in business [and] successful in his undertakings without the desire of increasing an ample fortune," that he was, in short, "able to strive to make money to distribute the same for the good of his fellow beings beyond his own blood." Less introspective and more uneasy at publicizing his generosity, Amos Lawrence also readily admitted to the personal satisfaction his stewardship gave him, whether through small gifts to deserving individuals or large benefactions to worthy institutions.[26]

Thus in Boston as in Charleston, charity was an instrument which validated the worth of the donor as it added to the well-being of the recipient. Whether as part of patriarchal slavery, noblesse oblige, Calvinist stewardship, or capitalist success, self-conscious benevolence legitimized wealth and privileged position.

• • •

While Charleston boasted humanitarian concern and public responsibility for the sick and the needy, Boston structured its private charity, as it did its public welfare, to distinguish between the worthy and the unworthy poor according to their adherence to the work ethic. Its voluntary benevolence was therefore largely directed to those who could not be expected to support themselves because they were sick, or young children, or women whose age, widowhood, or maternal responsibilities precluded their being economically self-sufficient.

It was to the cure of the sick that Boston dedicated its most impressive philanthropic institutions. The privately supported and operated Boston Dispensary performed services similar to Charleston's publicly governed Shirras Dispensary, treating up to two thousand patients a year in their own homes—sending them its physicians and providing them medicine. In addition, the dispensary completed the education of many recent Harvard

M.D.'s by offering clinical experience through short-term appointments to its staff. Its much needed and valued services attracted substantial donations from Bostonians of wealth and high status.[27]

Still better endowed was the Massachusetts General Hospital, which, by 1841, was caring annually for over four hundred patients of modest means, many of whom were admitted free of all charge through the tickets which the hospital issued to wealthy donors to distribute as they would.[28] Serving as Harvard Medical School's teaching hospital much as Charleston's publicly supported Marine Hospital and poorhouse did its medical colleges, Massachusetts General's philanthropic purposes embraced professional education as well.

Boston's third major health institution for the poor was more specialized than any Charleston facility. Devoted exclusively to the care of women in childbirth, the Lying-In Hospital was founded in 1832. Its services, even more clearly than the Dispensary's or Massachusetts General's, were denied the unworthy; its rules excluded from its care all but married or recently widowed women "who may need the benefit of the Institution. . . ."[29] In Boston, as in Charleston, unwed mothers were relegated to public institutions—the House of Industry in the former, the poorhouse in the latter.

The underlying difference was not only that in Charleston all hospital facilities received public subvention and were open without distinction to the white poor. The private agencies which supplemented them—except for emergency hospitals established during epidemics—were not institutions but societies whose members personally served the sick poor. Prime among these was the Ladies' Benevolent Society, which had been founded in 1813 and which by the 1830s raised and spent from $2,500 to $3,000 annually. But just as important, its members made an average of 250 calls a year to supplement the professional ministrations of the Shirras Dispensary physicians on whom they called for medical assistance. And, in addition to health care, the benevolent ladies provided for other wants which accompanied prolonged illness—fuel, food, and clothing among them.[30]

The second group for whom both cities made special provision was orphans and the children of the poor. But while in Charleston the quality of care offered in the city-operated orphan house was the town's pride, Boston provided no similar public institution. Juvenile delinquents were placed in the House of Reformation; poor orphans, like the children of the destitute, were accommodated in the House of Industry, which, after 1840, did add a children's annex in one wing of the House of Reformation. Thus it was the private Boston Female Asylum and the Boston Asylum for Indigent Boys, the latter in 1835 combined with the Proprietors of the Boston Farm School to become the Boston Farm School and Asylum, which specifically assumed responsibility to shelter, educate, and prepare for an occupation the orphans and abandoned youngsters of the city. Even they, however, assumed that the children in their care shared the stigma of their parents' failure to provide. Therefore the asylums offered those opportunities "suited to their [inmates'] condition and prospects" as "idle and morally exposed children" rescued in the nick of time from "vice and danger."[31] Despite their otherwise differing assumptions, however, both cities' orphanages bore a Protestant orientation so clear that non-Protestants felt obliged to provide otherwise for the parentless young of their religious persuasions. Boston had its Catholic orphanage; Charlestonians made special provision not only for Catholic but for Jewish children. In addition, Boston founded the Samaritan Asylum for Indigent Children in 1835 to serve its black population—a provision Charleston saw no need to make.

Religion was also an issue in the infant schools, established primarily as day-care facilities to aid working mothers. Providing children from eighteen months to six years of age "employment and amusement, not less than instruction,"[32] Boston's two infant schools were differentiated at first along liberal-orthodox lines—the Unitarians operating one, Congregationalists, Episcopalians, and Baptists joining together to operate the other. But when the Unitarians, mindful of the needs and preferences of the Irish North Enders whom they intended to serve, hired a Catholic teacher, the lines were redrawn as the orthodox charged Unitarians with increasing the "influence of Catholics in [the] City." Ultimately, sectarian warfare destroyed support for these schools and thus the assistance they promised those mothers trying both to work and to care for their young. Charleston's infant schools, one in the fourth ward and the other on the Neck, met a similar fate amid resentments that the Infant School Society was dominated by Episcopalians.[33]

Beyond these, Boston operated myriad services to shape children's present and thus their future. The Children's Friend Society housed and taught children neglected by their parents. The Society for the Prevention of Pauperism, believing in the power of a rural environment to reform the unruly, found jobs in the country to which it sent vagrant youths. The New England Asylum for the Blind addressed the needs of the handicapped, preparing them to become self-supporting as cabinet makers, mat weavers, and handicraftsmen of various sorts. Churches operated sewing classes for girls and work programs for boys, all with an eye to insuring that they would not, as adults, join the unworthy, nonworking poor. Henry C. Wright, city missionary in charge of orthodox Sunday schools for poor children, epitomized such organizations' intention to shape attitudes as well as provide the skills for useful employment. Children naturally busied "their little fingers about something" and might just "as well have their ac-

Play and Philanthropy 149

tivity so directed as to produce something useful"—to gain thereby a "sense of *responsibility* for the use of [their] time, talents & opportunities."[34] The relative paucity of similar programs in Charleston Sunday schools reflected a more limited attachment to instilling the work ethic in the young, just as its philanthropy generally was less rooted in distinguishing between the worthy and unworthy poor on the basis of their willingness to labor.

Women whose condition did not permit them to be self-supporting were the third group singled out for special benevolence in both cities. Not surprisingly, the societies which served their needs were also more likely than others to be comprised of women, who by their very gender best understood the hazards and limitations associated with the female condition. Even Charleston's most privileged ladies knew well that however much society might define woman's place as "the guardian angel of the household shrine,"[35] that place was also in shops, schools, and boardinghouses as well as in the kitchens, washhouses, and sickrooms of households not their own. Indeed, a Charleston clergyman actively defended women's participation in organizations precisely because they had ample servants to help them with their own housework.[36]

Their activity was not, of course, confined to the female poor, as their constant fund-raising bazaars for many good causes and their succor to the sick attested. Nor can the pensions which most men's organizations and various churches provided their members' widows and orphans be overlooked. Nonetheless, it was women who, in the Charleston Fuel Society, provided cheap wood to female-headed households. Selling it at or below cost, they solicited donations to cover their costs, which amounted to as little as $400 in the early 1830s and to more than $1,500 by mid-decade. A Ladies' Industry Society flourished for a time to provide employment to "poor and industrious white women."[37] And after 1835 the Ladies' Garment Society both sewed and collected clothing for distribution to the poor of either sex and all ages, as the Juvenile Industry Society had earlier done.

Boston women were considerably more diverse in their organizational activity. Like their southern counterparts, they were diligent fund raisers for religious, philanthropic, and even patriotic causes. Yet they too gave special attention to the needs of females. Since 1803 they had run the Boston Female Asylum for orphan girls. Their Fragment Society had since 1812 assisted pregnant and newly delivered women as well as children and the elderly. The Fatherless and Widows' Society had, since its founding in 1817, aided "poor infirm widows, and single women of good character."[38] In the 1820s the benevolent women of the Society for Employing the Female Poor in Boston established a house in which women could wash and iron as well as sew, knit, and sell the articles they made. Later the Boston

Seaman's Aid Society provided facilities for poor women—even those who were not sailors' wives or daughters—through which they were taught to make sailor's clothing, which they then sold through a nonprofit store.

Additionally, Boston women moved beyond the charitable activity for which their ministers thought their meek and humble nature was especially suited. And although some of their reform-oriented societies, like the Female Anti-Slavery Society, extended well beyond the bounds of sisterhood, most did not. Having early organized a women's auxiliary to the Penitent Females' Refuge Society, in 1835 women founded a fully independent Female Moral Reform Society, dedicated not only to sheltering the penitent and redeeming the fallen but to taking preventive social action to protect young women from falling into the toils of "specious and intriguing libertines" and small children from being exposed to obscenity.[39] The American Female Home Education Society also protected young women from sexual exploitation both by operating a temperance boardinghouse for them and by offering classes designed to make them economically self-sufficient. Other women organized in the Odd Ladies Mutual Aid Society. Imitative of men's organizations and rejecting dependence for cooperation, groups of this sort challenged the prevailing definitions of women's place as no Charleston group did. Nonetheless, in both philanthropy and reform Boston women hewed to the value their society placed on work and individual exertion just as much as Charleston women reflected their culture's insistence on a social system of reciprocal dependence and immediate personal obligation.

• • •

Ironically, it was those Bostonians most engaged in charity who most feared creating an extensive dependence of the poor on the rich—for to do so would negate the underlying purpose of their philanthropy: to insure a stable society within which individuals could rise from poverty by their own efforts. They were haunted by the possibility that growing numbers of the poor had learned to thrive on alms and live without labor. Among the first to react were the Unitarians, who in 1826 had responded to increasingly visible urban poverty by sponsoring Joseph Tuckerman as a missionary to their own city. They read his prize essay on the drastic effects of the meager wages paid most working women, and they also knew through his reports about the transient "families which . . . are never more than a few months in a place . . . [,] compelled to remove by inability to pay their rent; and, to escape from the little debts which they have contracted in the neighborhood. . . ." They supported his conclusion that, while most could ultimately be salvaged by work, some, even the unworthy, must be aided for long periods.[40]

Nonetheless, they also fretted that Tuckerman's careful charity might encourage enduring pauperism. They heeded Artemus Simonds, master of the House of Industry, who warned against that "injudicious alms-giving" which lacked coordination and dispensed aid to "unworthy objects" who ultimately became a permanent charge on the city. It was bad enough that intemperance filled the House of Industry with chronic paupers, but that well-intended benevolence should have the same effect was intolerable. Simultaneously, the long-established Fragment Society discovered that it was distributing aid to the grandchildren of those whom it had first assisted. "Thus we, republicans, who refuse to tolerate hereditary honors of nobility," the Seaman's Aid Society observed in reporting that fact, "encourage the establishment of hereditary pauperism."[41]

The resolution was not to abandon charity but to coordinate it, to make it yet more like Simms's description of northern almsgiving, for which the poor must first "undergo examination" before they received meager assistance. So it was to control the unworthy, who lived too well on overlapping claims, rather than to extend assistance by pooling their resources that a dozen charitable organizations and the principal Unitarian churches formed the Association of Benevolent Societies. Appalled that "the moral sense of the poor . . . [had] been deadened by the course which charity [had] taken," the founders lamented that past generosity had led recipients to expect assistance as a right. Indeed, it alleged in 1834, families poured into the city just to receive charity, while fathers of families already there fled "into the country, but [were] sure to return . . . in the spring and tarry through the summer" to partake in the assistance which their families received.[42]

Within a year all Unitarian charitable groups channeled requests for aid through a central office—a system which worked so well that orthodox groups followed suit, through their own Society for the Prevention of Pauperism. This *"central* society" kept "a Register of those who really *need* & of those who *receive* assistance so as not to encourage idleness by maintaining it, & to prevent imposition by obtaining charity from various sources, for the same cause." Boston was thus committed in her prosperous mid-decade years to rationalizing private charity. The structure worked well enough until 1842–1843, the worst winter of the depression which began after the 1837 panic. Only then did Boston do-gooders establish a Soup and Bread Society whose benevolence was available to all without test. Even then the society justified its decision to furnish "gratuitously to the poor, during the winter months, soup and bread" less by the massive crisis than by the fact that it was, in such circumstances, cheaper and more efficient to run soup kitchens than to provide food and the fuel to prepare it with on an individual basis.[43]

In Charleston no similar rationalization of philanthropy occurred. Her city missionaries were not social workers but religious proselytizers. Her various churches and charitable societies distributed their largess as they had in the past. It was true that even in Charleston there were those who questioned indiscriminate giving. Robert Mills, who subsequently went to Washington to pursue his architectural career, had asserted in the mid-1820s that aid should be "bottomed upon the broad basis of encouraging habits of industry and economy." A decade later the Ladies' Benevolent Society announced its intention to "guard against imposition." The German Friendly Society asked but never required its clients to declare their assets when they requested aid. But to insist or to investigate independently was to violate the reciprocal dependence on which benevolence was grounded. Making distinctions between the worthy and the unworthy was invidious and would erode the spirit in which charity was to be given. Henry Pinckney only spoke his city's cultural values when he told the Methodist Benevolent Society "that we must either aid the poor, or suffer them to perish. . . ." Even, he continued, if "charity has been sometimes misapplied, or acted as a premium to idleness and vice," it is not to be stinted, for it is "better that unworthy objects should deceive us, than that meritorious individuals should receive no aid." And even the Ladies' Benevolent Society, which worried about imposition, stressed the personal rewards inherent in giving without question: "You are not giving money to the idle poor, but necessaries & comforts to the helpless sick, & surely all must deem it a priviledge to administer to the relief of the sick!"[44]

• • •

Charleston's charity, like her organizations, was inclusive. The value her residents attached to leisure subverted using work to distinguish between the worthy and the unworthy at any level of society. Her stability was served by the patriarchal assumptions governing race and class relations. Her societies almost always served a variety of purposes and customarily undertook aid to the poor as one responsibility. Their memberships similarly bonded various groups to bridge political, religious, and ethnic divisions. Both play and philanthropy were cohesive forces assuring the city's future.

Boston's play and philanthropy were, in comparison, exclusive. Only the worthy poor were entitled to private benevolence. Almost all societies were dedicated to a single purpose and comprised only of those likely to aid in achieving their set goals—whether in music or sport, history or politics, care of the sick or support for the weak. Purposeful work was the summum bonum on which rested the city's continued existence. Neither charity nor leisure could be permitted to subvert that fundamental premise. But no more, either, were the wealthy and privileged free from a moral obligation to aid the worthy poor and maintain social peace.

11
Disorder, Violence, and Community Control

Staid nineteenth-century city dwellers believed themselves plagued by disorder. With a third of her male population between fifteen and thirty, Boston was preoccupied with rowdiness. Newspapers reported the activity of gangs like the Forty Thieves and the White Oak Club, whose members were hauled into police court for harassing the respectable, pilfering shops, and picking pockets. City officials put young truants and vagrants into the House of Reformation; do-gooders rounded up unruly youth and sent them to the farm school on Thompson's Island. When the adolescent sons of Boston's best families defied the authority of parents and school masters, they were rusticated to study with small-town ministers. And the few who sank into drink and degeneracy were shipped out before the mast. Charleston was no less harassed by youths who perpetrated "every kind of vice and wickedness," shouted obscenities at "unoffending white female[s]," and roistered about to endanger the peace and safety of the less exuberant, but the southern city made little institutional provision for their control.[1]

In addition to the delinquencies of ever-present youth, there were the seamen who drank, brawled, and patronized the disorderly houses which crowded the waterfronts of both cities. Because their unrestrained activities consigned them to the lockups and disrupted the shipping on which seaports depended, both cities encouraged efforts to provide them honest—preferably dry—boardinghouses, "moral and religious instruction," and harmless recreation. Boston's Seaman's Friend Society organized an employment agency and offered classes in navigation. Its Savings Bank for Seamen provided patrons protection from "improvidence and prodigality."

The Port Society of each city supported a full-time minister for sailors. Charleston's Bethel Union not only held prayer meetings but managed a job registry and a library, and maintained a roster of acceptable boardinghouses.[2] And Windward Anchor societies, both north and south, buttressed whatever temperance principles could be instilled in mariners.

Yet either because their rowdyism was a constant or because the young eventually grew up and sailors eventually went back to sea, neither group stimulated the crises which made city dwellers plumb their deepest fears of disorder or assert fully their commitment to social control. It was rather in their city's growing population of foreign-born and the nativist violence it generated that those Bostonians who shaped public policy in the 1830s perceived the major challenge to social order. Characteristically, they responded by modernizing governmental institutions. But in Charleston fear was race-borne, fanned in the 1830s by growing abolitionist activity, which exacerbated a persistent anticipation of black unrest. Pressing, on the one hand, for ever more legal restraints upon Negroes, free or slave, the city tolerated, on the other, white vigilantism to stifle dissent.

• • •

"Five hundred men have been under arms every night, since Monday last," Warren Dutton of Boston wrote his fellow townsman Nathan Appleton on August 15, 1834. "Eight hundred police men, patrol the streets. The draws of the Bridges are all raised after nine O'clock, and guards stationed at all the avenues—at the arsenal, at the Catholic Church and at Cambridge . . . Men collect in the streets, in the day time, in great Masses to talk—bayonets gleam by moonlight, and women are frightened by day and by night."[3]

Such was Boston's response to the midnight arson which had leveled the Ursuline Convent in Charlestown immediately across the Charles River. Her citizens were deeply involved in the fire, the rioting, and the looting. Contributing to the outburst were fears, stirred up by evangelical preachers, that Boston women were held in the convent involuntarily and that Boston girls were educated there in vile corruption. On August 11 Protestant, native-born Boston truckmen, sharing Charlestown laborers' resentment of Irish Catholic job competition, had joined a mob of nativist rowdies gathered in the main square. Disguised in the fashion of the Boston Tea Party, they had marched on the convent and, once there, signaled their intention by first burning barrels of tar. Yet Charlestown's selectmen took no action to protect property, and her justices of the peace had not turned out to read the riot act. And when Boston fire companies responded to the flames clearly visible across the river, they, like the Charlestown companies, were harassed by the mob and refused to fight the fire.[4]

Disorder, Violence, and Community Control 155

Nor were things under control at dawn. Rumor embroidered on the embattled mother superior's threat to the mob that, if they persisted, Bishop Fenwick would call up twenty thousand Irishmen to retaliate. Indeed, the bishop's first action was to defuse that possibility, enjoining the faithful against seeking revenge, exhorting them to let justice take its course. Simultaneously Mayor Theodore Lyman called a public meeting in Faneuil Hall at which the better sort condemned the "base and cowardly act" against the Ursuline sisters and pledged themselves "collectively and individually, to unite with [their] Catholic brethren in protecting their persons, their property, and their civil and religious rights."[5]

The mayor went still further, forbidding the fire companies to leave the city, ordering a full militia patrol for the six following nights, urging each ward to form its own citizen patrol. The Protestant clergy, repenting their contribution to the prevailing hysteria, joined with Bishop Fenwick to deplore mob action. Political leaders of both parties investigated the entire affair and reported their findings with little gloss. Charlestown's selectmen had been derelict in their duty. The public was obliged to indemnify those who had lost property because the social contract, which guaranteed "security of life, liberty and property" to all citizens, had been breached. It is telling that for ten years prominent Boston men pressed the Ursuline claims on the state legislature and that the legislature, reflecting its constituency's will, refused to pay an indemnity.[6]

While technically the destruction of the Ursuline Convent was not a Boston affair, it was undeniably part of its ever escalating ethnic tensions. As early as 1826, Broad Street's dense Irish population had been the target of nativism. Other tumults had occurred in South Boston and in the North End. Some of the riots which occurred during the period were not, it is true, ethnic in origin. The alleged immorality of theaters periodically sparked crowds intent on destroying obscene property and driving out immoral individuals. But the principal precipitant of mob violence was Boston's Irish and the prejudices their very existence ignited. Nor did official Boston act to stem nativism. In 1835 Mayor Lyman publicly linked rising institutional costs in the House of Industry to a 100 percent increase in its foreign-born inmates during a five-year period in which native inmates had in fact declined in number. In 1837 the state imposed a special tax on immigrants to meet these costs, and at the same time threatened sea captains with substantial penalties for bringing lunatic, idiot, maimed, aged, or infirm aliens into any Massachusetts port.[7]

It was not, however, deliberate intention but happenstance which led to further violence. Indeed, the origins of the 1837 Broad Street riot resembled farce. On a hot June Sunday Fire Company No. 20, returning to its East Street engine house after fighting an early afternoon fire, encountered an Irish funeral procession moving along Sea Street. For reasons unclear, a couple of firemen tangled with a couple of mourners. It was only a short scuffle, however; and the firemen quickly retreated to their station, where one of them rang the fire bell. At that very moment—and quite by chance—the bells of New South Church began to toll. Mistaking this second bell for another alarm of fire, Fire Company No. 9 roared down Summer Street to find and fight the new blaze. Careening around the corner onto Broad, the engine, pulled by eager volunteers, lurched into the same funeral procession, still on its way to the Charlestown cemetery. By luck no one was hurt, but the mourners, sure they were once again under attack, struck back. Up went the shouts, out came the fists. And from nearby houses came a flood of Irish immigrants to face down the growing crowd of firemen. Soon a full-scale riot was under way. The young firemen carried the day, stout sticks and paving stones their heavy weaponry. As the Irish retreated, the firemen followed them into their homes. Then for two hours fighting and looting reigned supreme; men were wounded, houses destroyed, and furnishings thrown, torn and broken, into the street. Only then did the militia appear and restore order.[8]

Public response was more mixed than it had been after the Charlestown riot. Frederic Tudor blamed the Irish, who were "becoming a sore" in Boston. Horace Mann blamed "the educated, the wealthy, [and] the intelligent" for allowing "the ignorant, the vicious, [and] the depraved to form . . . public opinion" into popular prejudice. And he predicted aright that the Irish would "suffer all the punishment," albeit in his eyes "the Americans had about all the guilt." Yet in the event the results were muddled. Only two of the fourteen Irishmen arrested were convicted of rioting, and even they were treated leniently because the "whole affray . . . grew out of . . . unavoidable errors." And although none of the four Americans arrested was found guilty—one having jumped bail—a citizen's group was established to raise $3,000 to relieve the twenty-nine families who had lost everything in the disturbance.[9]

More significant still was the common council report on the fire companies involved. It chided the first company for stopping for "refreshments" immediately before the initial encounter with the funeral. Then, although it absolved the native firemen of "particular ill will" against the Irish and in turn chastised foreigners for their clannish proclivity to live "in groups together" and to retain "their own national usages," the council placed ultimate responsibility on volunteer companies' failure to control their members' behavior. Indeed, such lack of discipline was a threat to the city's safety. Public interest demanded a reorganization of the department. When, threatened with a city-enforced professionalism which would throttle their high spirits, curb their clublike camaraderie, and weed

Disorder, Violence, and Community Control 157

out underage members, some firemen protested the city's plans, they were dismissed from duty unceremoniously. Others, incensed by the dismissals, resigned en masse. Thereupon the mayor retaliated by establishing temporary volunteer companies to fill the void until the department could be completely revamped. No more than Mayor Quincy nine years earlier was Mayor Eliot to be stayed by appeals to the rights of citizen volunteers or defenses of that "youthful spirit" which dared what "older heads and colder hearts" did not in fighting fire.[10]

Only six weeks after the riot the city council enacted the mayor's proposal for a thirteen-company fire department whose members would be paid a yearly salary of $50 and its officers up to $100. All were placed under the command of a paid engineer and his eight assistants. The mayor and aldermen retained their power to discipline the company as a whole, to approve new members, and to veto the election of officers.[11] Thus did Boston's fire department move still further from independent companies of citizen volunteers toward paid civil service. Public safety, public order, and the protection of private property—not sympathy for the Irish—demanded that rational and reliable service be placed above the personal and social rewards of voluntary civil participation.

No sooner had the fire department been reorganized than that bulwark of social order, that last defense against riot and tumult, the militia itself was torn by nativism. Indeed, the traditional and legal obligation of all males between sixteen and forty-five to maintain arms and drill regularly had long since lost its force, and the whole militia system was under attack. By 1830 state law had exempted persons over thirty from its service. The annual muster was, more and more, a farce at public expense. The only units Boston officials could rely upon in the 1830s were the named companies, whose fancy uniforms, regular drills, clublike admission and election procedures, and elaborate social programs built an esprit de corps which alone kept them prepared to meet emergencies and control violence.

It was as much within this context that for ten years Massachusetts governors had regularly refused requests to form an all-Irish militia company as it was that Edward Everett approved such a petition in January 1837. Whether the governor sought thus to woo a growing part of the electorate, or to mold a new spirit of toleration, or to strengthen a dwindling militia in the face of general indifference is unclear. Nonetheless the Montgomery Guards, comprised "principally of Irish & persons of Irish descent," all of whom were either birthright or naturalized citizens, staged its first review without event in the same month as the Broad Street riot.[12]

But when the new guard marched onto the Common on September 12 for the annual review of all city militia units, the privates and noncommissioned officers of the Washington Light Infantry, the Lafayette Guards, and the City Guards all left the field in a mass protest. Whether this mutiny or the subsequent pelting by a "gang of miserable vagabonds and boys" when the Montgomery Guards retired to headquarters offered the greater insult was hard to say. Either way, nativism had taken on the militia. Proper Bostonians might find "such dastardly meanness" both "deplorable & disgraceful." But the priorities of public order, public safety, and the protection of private property again prevailed. In April 1838 Governor Everett dissolved the Montgomery Guards, thus ending the fifteen-month existence of an Irish unit.[13]

The city fathers, perceiving dangers from an unreliable military, acted even more swiftly. Mayor Samuel Eliot and the city council sought a new and more "efficient means of enforcing the laws." Their city's rapid growth had not only put Boston "lives and property at the mercy of the incendiary, the burglar, or the lawlessly violent" but now threatened the very "social bond" of civilization.[14] For her safety and security Boston needed a system of paid police officers to enforce the law and relieve her total reliance on fee-paid constables and volunteer militia. Although it took seven months to obtain permission from the state legislature, the mayor and aldermen did gain authority to appoint such officers in April 1838.[15] Perceptions of steadily growing disorder, highlighted by three major riots in which traditional forces of law and order had either failed to act or had contributed to that disorder, thus forced the modernization of law enforcement through full-time salaried policemen.

• • •

If open riot was an expression of ethnic and class tensions, so too was temperance. More than any other issue in Boston, temperance revealed an interwoven matrix of attitudes about public disorder, social welfare, upward mobility, class conflict, and social control. A Boston grand jury only echoed myriad reports about convicted criminals when, in 1833, it asserted that "a great proportion of the crimes" it had investigated could be "traced, directly or indirectly, to the excessive use of intoxicating liquors." Both the House of Industry and city missionary Joseph Tuckerman offered a similar explanation of pauperism, reporting that institutional inmates demonstrated alcohol's power to destroy families, create debt, induce destitution, encourage crime, and inflict sickness and death.[16]

It would be easy to attribute these analyses to class prejudice had not mechanics and laborers, especially those who owned property, fervently supported temperance as a means for upward mobility. Native-born workingmen who found in temperance an agency for self-respect and a support for economic security actively joined the crusade to control the liquor trade—although in smaller numbers and proportions than did men of more prestigious occupations.[17] But opposing them and their goals was a similarly mixed group. Grocers, hotel keepers, distillers, and others with an economic interest in the liquor trade joined Irish immigrants, Yankee journeymen, and upper-class topers to oppose restricting the sale of alcoholic beverages.

Early on the respectable had appealed only for individual and voluntary moderation or, at most, some governmental restraint in issuing licenses to grog shops and grocers. But by 1838 the Massachusetts legislature, under pressure from its rural majority as well as from urban drys, enacted a law which limited liquor sales to quantities not less than fifteen gallons, allowing the affluent to buy in quantity. The law was praised by its supporters, who boasted publicly that it made it "more difficult for the poor and laboring classes" to waste their substance on alcohol.[18] But even then class lines were not clearly drawn. Harrison Gray Otis headed the petition of 17,000 citizens who protested that the law, because it declared illegal in small quantities what it permitted in large, set rich against poor in "odious" fashion, and thus violated the imperatives of simple justice. So fierce was the contention and so politicized the issue that in 1838 and 1839 Boston Whigs split into two factions over the law, ran opposing slates, and thus stalemated Boston's election of legislators when, in three-way elections with Democrats, only twenty candidates could secure a majority. As a result, for two years Boston had less than half its customary representation in the general court.[19]

At the same time Boston citizens evaded, defied, and challenged the law. Entrepreneurs operated "striped pigs," where patrons paid to view a remarkable animal and incidentally picked up a free glass of gin as they passed the display. Other opponents shunned such ruses and sold liquor as openly as they always had. Temperance societies and individual teetotalers, unwilling to rely on normal law enforcement procedures, planted informers, undertook "sting" operations, and instituted legal action.

Thus the municipal court, presided over by an ardent dry, Judge Peter O. Thacher, was flooded with fifteen-gallon law cases. Benjamin F. Hallett, a dedicated Democratic wet, served his party's purposes and his own political ambitions by freely offering his services as defense counsel to the accused. Judge Thacher, a Whig, refused to impanel jurors who admitted to doubting the law's constitutionality, rejected verdicts which considered constitutional issues, and, when thwarted in his rulings, dismissed troublemakers whose refusal to heed his directives hung the juries on which they served.

Before long Thacher's behavior provoked public disorder. Fed by the

Democratic *Post*'s excoriation of this "daring attack upon the rights of jurors," rowdy crowds surrounded the courthouse and once invaded its inner precincts in a manner so menacing that the trial of victualler Gilbert Cummings was halted and the witnesses against him spirited out a rear door lest they be assaulted. Other informers, however, were not so lucky. Two months after the Cummings trial, a mob nearly demolished informer John Manley's dry goods store, while another caught paperhanger Asa Savells at the Chelsea ferry wharf, beat him up, and then tarred and feathered the miserable man. In the face of such violence the legislature backed down. In February 1840, less than two years after it had passed the temperance measure, it repealed the fifteen-gallon law.[20]

The issue was not resolved, however, for the old licensing law was still on the books, and the mayor and aldermen, charged with issuing only so many licenses as "the public good may require," limited their number. Moreover, the city hired spies to replace the volunteer informers in ferreting out those who now sold without licenses. Once again municipal court dockets were filled with liquor cases. Once again Judge Thacher excluded all who questioned the law's constitutionality from the jury box. Once again law enforcement as much as the law itself agitated the city. The *Post* continued to challenge the whole operation of Thacher's court. Five hundred citizens petitioned the board of aldermen "against the City Government['s] appropriating their portion of the city tax to pay hired informers to enforce the license law." Finally, even the mayor and aldermen denounced the law as "unwise, inefficient, and impracticable" and sought its repeal.[21]

More subtly, the municipal court, tainted by its reliance on paid spies and informers as well as by the blatant bias of its sole judge, was modernized. Indeed, Peter Thacher's sudden death provided the opportunity for swift change without engendering any further friction. Under the new law a panel of five magistrates rotated the duty of presiding over the municipal court, which was thus protected from the vagaries of any one judge.[22] But if Thacher's summary challenges to jurors were thus eliminated, the fact that jury selection itself overrepresented those with high-prestige occupations, mercantile interests, and corporate power went virtually unrecognized and altogether unchallenged.[23]

If, for a while, it appeared that the judicial process itself was under popular attack, all it took for that perception to vanish was the removal of a single judge, rather than a fundamental restructuring. What had been established was that even social control had its limits and that those limits had been reached when city and state government intruded into the private lives and personal habits of economically independent citizens. Thereafter temperance was returned to the private sector, and the Washingtonians,

Disorder, Violence, and Community Control 161

who dominated the battle against demon rum in the 1840s, were committed *"wholly and solely* to moral suasion."[24] Assertively a society of reformed drunkards and avowedly representative of as well as dedicated to working-class folk, it promised, at least for a while, to brake its members' descent into alcoholism, pauperism, and crime and to bring to temperance the support of those classes which the premises of the fifteen-gallon law had precluded. At the very least, temperance had once again become a force for public order rather than a rallying point for challenges to law and public authority.

• • •

If the conflagration which destroyed the Ursuline Convent marked Boston's most fearful encounter with mob violence, the bonfire which lit Charleston's night sky on July 30, 1835, illuminated a similar pressure point but very different pressures. The crowd which had assembled at Citadel Square to destroy a United States mail sack stuffed with antislavery tracts was a respectable one, asserting its will to maintain the city's biracial culture as it was. Its actions were defended by the highest public officials. If it was technically illegal and appeared disorderly, it acted on the priorities which white Charlestonians expected law and order to enshrine. The key to all apparent contradictions lay in the descriptions they applied to the burning propaganda, which was called interchangeably "insurrectionary" and "incendiary."[25]

Only the day before, postmaster Alfred Huger had spotted the suspicious sack amid mail brought from the North by a New York steamboat. Discovering its contents, Huger had decided at once not to deliver the pamphlets. Later he had checked out his decision with several leading gentlemen of the city, who had, in turn, spread the news and insured the ease with which, the following night, the offending pouch was spirited from the post office and burned alongside effigies of arch-abolitionists William Lloyd Garrison and Lewis Tappan. Yet even Postmaster General Amos Kendall in Washington recognized the special circumstances involved, and later concurred in Huger's initial decision to detain the mail. Technically it was illegal. But, after all, the postal service had been created to "serve the people of *each* and of the *United States,* and not [to] be used as the instrument of their *destruction.*"[26]

Huger, a Unionist, blew up his own crisis into one even more severe than nullification. "The Whole Civil authority were in favor of arresting the Mail, and no power could have protected it, but a military force greater than the Undivided population of Charleston." And the powerlessness of civil authority to do otherwise was played out in subsequent days. On August 10 a public meeting in City Hall resolved to control the flow of dangerous people and ideas. Until the state should pass a law banning it, citizens demanded that the courts sanction the seizure and destruction of "incendiary publications" arriving in Charleston. The harbor master was charged with recording the names of "all the persons arriving to and departing from" the port to guard against incendiaries and other "evil disposed persons" entering the city. The very next day the city council acquiesced to public pressures by posting a $1,000 reward for the arrest and conviction of any person bringing incendiary literature into the city, or for publishing or circulating such material with the intent or tendency to "disturb the domestic quiet and good order" of the town.[27]

But that was weak medicine for those who had already fought fire with fire, and for a while no authority dared check the turn to vigilante justice. On August 21 barber Richard Wood (alias R. W. Carroll) was kidnapped from his shop near Queen and East Bay by a crowd which charged him with receiving stolen goods from Negroes. Frustrated by the "difficulty of proving the fact sufficiently to satisfy the *technicalities* of the law," the mob tarred and cottoned their victim before marching him triumphantly through the market to jail, where he was deposited, allegedly for his own protection. Shortly thereafter the Lynch Club warned the "most dissolute and abandoned" out of the city in widely distributed "cards." There were, of course, upright citizens who deplored this turn of events. Dr. Samuel Dickson was outraged by the Lynch Club even before it attacked Wood. "From all such misrule or anarchy Good Lord deliver us," he wrote. Yet even his indignation was tempered by the values of a slave society, for he damned the lynchers most of all for "fritter[ing] away our energies which ought to be kept under high pressure for movement upon the great questions that are pending and must soon be 'discussed by sword & gun' as well as by tongue and pen."[28]

In 1835 no institution, no judicial process, no governmental restructuring could be relied upon to meet the threat that insurrection might ultimately demand "sword and gun." Yet only five years earlier, when a Boston sailor had been apprehended on a Charleston street peddling David Walker's fiery *Appeal* for slave rebellion, the courts had handled the matter calmly.[29] It was the nullification crisis in the intervening years which had demonstrated that divisions within the white population could run deep enough to threaten civil war. Paired with a simultaneous outburst of northern antislavery, that knowledge brought home the realization that a society half slave and half free was, at best, a tenuous one unless all whites united to sustain it.

• • •

In 1823, after Denmark Vesey's plans for revolt had been fully exposed, prominent Charlestonians had joined other Carolinians to organize the

South Carolina Association as an aid to public authority in executing the "laws in relation to negroes and other persons of color," and to take "all lawful means for the prevention of disturbance or insurrection among them." Overshadowed by the political issues of the early 1830s, the association was minimally visible until 1834. Then, remembering the African Church affiliation of several Vesey plotters, the association demanded that the city council enforce the ordinance which prohibited black churches and add to it a requirement that all black religious assemblies be supervised by whites.[30]

The restrictions they demanded would add to an already extensive body of city and state legislation regulating slavery, slaves, and Negroes generally. South Carolina law had long since established the relationship between master and servant; more recently it had forbidden the one's freeing the other. It defined the legal rights of each—with many of the provisions for slaves applying also to free blacks—and provided for separate courts in which to try white and black offenders. The city's ordinances took up where state law left off in prescribing the minute details of black residents' lives. The curfew warned them to be off the street by 8:45 P.M. in winter, 9:45 in summer. The police were empowered to demand that slaves show passes from their masters or employers detailing their mission, their route of travel, and their destination should they be out after hours. Slaves not working on their masters' premises must wear one kind of badge. Adult free blacks must show another kind, which certified that they had registered and paid their annual head tax. Public peace required that blacks of any age be prohibited from following military parades or fire company reviews, as it also required that slaves have their masters' permission to buy liquor after curfew.[31]

Yet no matter how many regulations were already on the books—and they went on and on—tense times required still more. After 1835 blacks were forbidden to hold any religious services without white supervision. Their wakes could not extend beyond family members except with specific permission and under severely restricted conditions. Under no circumstances could they buy liquor to be consumed on the premises or without their masters' permission. If they worked as porters or day laborers, they must abide by city-mandated wage rates.[32] All these restrictions made little distinction between slave and free blacks.

As the law defined ever more misdemeanors and petty felonies, it created a trial burden which required some alteration in the court system. Thus in the mid-1830s the city supplemented the Magistrates' and Freeholders' Court, which traditionally tried all cases involving blacks, by granting the intendent power to hear minor charges against slaves and free Negroes. When the mayor's court was established in 1837 it assumed those same powers. This exceptional court, which handled both black and white cases, demonstrated uniquely the racial dimension of social control. Perhaps because there were more offenses punishable by law for blacks than for whites, there were two black arrests for every white one, although their proportions of the total population were roughly equal. And while four-fifths of all blacks brought before the court were held for trial, two-thirds of the whites were dismissed at once.[33]

Sensitive to growing repression or hopeful of improving their lot elsewhere, substantial numbers of free Negroes left the city. In 1832 nearly a hundred and fifty colonists sailed directly for Liberia, while others similarly destined went first to New York. In all probability others migrated north, for African colonization and death are insufficient explanations for the disappearance from the city of between one-quarter and one-half of its adult free Negroes every five years.[34]

Nonetheless, for all but a few slaves, as for most free blacks, ignoring or defying the law was the chief protest. The passage of new ordinances and renewed efforts to enforce the old ones did little to stem a steady stream of citizen complaints. The Battery promenade was never controlled enough for ladies to walk there "without being thumped from one side to the other . . . [or] inhaling the smoke of a nauseous pipe." No military parades graced the city without attracting "tumultuous assemblages of negroes." Blacks not only operated the stalls in the public market but loitered and slept there, "and in other respects abuse[d]" them. The informal Sunday morning markets on South Bay, which attracted "country negroes," were scenes of "cheap bargains and consequently no little noise!" Yet they continued unrestricted until a vigorous sabbatarian movement forced the city council to close them on other grounds in 1843.[35]

More serious was the question of literacy. Teaching slaves to write had long been illegal, lest they be able to forge passes. But the new dangers provoked by an increase in antislavery tracts and papers led South Carolina in 1834 to pass a law forbidding teaching slaves to read. Then in the summer of 1835, either to compete or to collaborate with the Lynch Club, the South Carolina Association insisted that church-sponsored schools for blacks—whether slave or free—be closed. Their first target was the Catholic school, which Bishop England, suspicious that religious prejudice lay behind the demand, shut down only with the understanding that all similar schools would be forced to follow suit.[36] Yet while all these actions might have a long-term effect, they could not alter the fact that slaves were already widely literate. Moreover, free blacks continued to operate schools of their own, while white Methodists, despite the law, continued their black Sunday schools.[37] Forged passes remained common and advertisements for runaway slaves frequently mentioned their ability to read. There could be little doubt that if they did not study antislavery tracts,

Disorder, Violence, and Community Control   165

Charleston blacks probably did peruse local press coverage of the Creole mutiny, the Amistad case, and abolitionist activity in the North.

Not surprisingly temperance, too, with few exceptions, was directed largely at controlling black behavior. It is true that in the early 1830s the Young Men's Temperance Society had addressed the physical damage which excessive drinking inflicted on the city's white population. And in the early 1840s, Washingtonians gained wide support for their efforts to redeem white drunkards. But the steady focus of restrictive action was to limit or eliminate black consumption of liquor and the behavior associated with it. State law and city ordinance established elaborate rules to insure that no part of groceries or grog shops be hidden from public view, so that every passerby might see whether blacks were drinking illegally on the premises. State law prohibited whites from purchasing cotton or rice from slaves, while city ordinance prohibited selling slaves liquor without their owners' explicit permission. The ban on both made clear the connection between the theft of cotton and the funds with which slaves purchased liquor.[38]

Yet these precautions were ineffective. Blacks not only continued to drink but were noisy and disorderly in so doing. When the city clamped down, Negroes crossed Boundary Street into the Neck, where city ordinances were unenforced and city police unauthorized. Even though the Neck's provisions for citizen patrols were the strictest in the state, these unpaid keepers of the nighttime peace were unable or unwilling to stop the increase of grog shops, gambling houses, and disorderly establishments. Negroes claiming to be free but lacking free papers abounded there; slaves without passes swarmed there after curfew. And if the Neck was wild on weeknights, it was sheer bedlam on weekends, as "idle and profligate" blacks promenaded and took public naps in daylight hours and at night behaved in ways likely to "lead only to riot, immorality, and ruin."[39]

Pressed hard by such disorder and its implications, the city strengthened the regular guard, whose principal responsibility was patrolling and protecting the city by night. In 1838 she temporarily enlarged the corps from 100 to 120 men. In 1839 she outfitted the guard in distinctive uniforms. By 1840 she was appropriating more for the guard than she had at any time during the previous decade.[40] Yet no action was satisfactory. Guard turnover remained high. Its privates lacked any stake in the city and took no pride in their jobs. They grumbled at long night duty and at daytime assignments like directing traffic around churches on Sundays. Citizens grumbled that guardsmen let "desperadoes . . . march the streets" at will, failed to protect "families and firesides," drank on duty, and connived with grocers and blacks who broke the liquor laws.[41]

What more could the city do? Made anxious by the lack of control over the day-by-day operation of the workhouse, the city removed it from the hands of the renters who had run it for profit and placed it under the direction of a paid city official. At the same time, addressing the potential danger inherent in Charleston's growing trade in slaves brought from the upper South and destined for new western plantations, the city created an official slave mart to be run by the workhouse master. By 1840 all public slave sales were to be conducted in the mart and all slaves awaiting such sales were to be billeted in the workhouse. But neither these measures nor the new three-dollar head tax on slaves brought into the city from out of state for sale discouraged the flow of transient slaves through the city. The number of large gangs brought in for sale increased so much that they overflowed the workhouse and had to be put in the jail as well. Yet slave brokers fought the new restrictions on housing and sales which the city imposed on their trade.[42]

In addition, none of this addressed the movement of the resident black population onto the Neck and beyond the city's control altogether. Burned out by a major fire in 1838, hundreds of blacks and whites sought new homes across Boundary Street, outside city limits. Although Mayor Pinckney acknowledged that "policy and courtesy" dictated that the city do what it could to meliorate the effects of this migration, it lay with the Neck to "have a police of its own, and a place provided for the custody of negroes arrested by the patrols. . . ."[43]

Neck residents, however, were ambivalent about the kind and degree of government they wanted. In 1840 the Charleston Neck Association, which had been organized in 1837, sought to strengthen government by instituting citizen vigilance committees, extending militia responsibilities, and ultimately incorporating the Neck as a municipality independent of Charleston. Other citizens toyed with making the Neck part of the city; many of them worked in the city, paid city taxes on property and income, and had the right to vote in city elections already. Denying both plans for major reorganization, the state legislature granted permission only for minimal change. Patrols were given yet more power to stop illegal liquor sales, close disorderly houses, and otherwise subdue "insubordination and depravity."[44] But if white complaints about noisy rowdiness be the measure, riot and disorder remained largely unchecked.

• • •

While neither Boston nor Charleston imposed the degree of behavioral control which respectable adults with property, station, and power would have preferred, neither experienced major social upheaval. Each maintained, in addition to her law enforcement force and her militia, courts to try the accused, jails to detain those awaiting trial, and institutions to punish the convicted. Yet the way in which they operated betrayed markedly different understandings of permissible behavior and the chastisement of that which was not. In 1834 Boston's police court, before whom all those arrested by city authorities first appeared, committed in a six-month period some 249 souls to stays of various lengths in the House of Correction as punishment for misdemeanors and minor felonies. Of those sentenced, five-sixths were prostitutes, drunkards, or vagabonds whose personal deportment, rather than damage to other persons or property, was at issue. The 223 blacks who were tried and sentenced by Charleston's mayor's court over a twelve-month period in 1838–1839 were also largely guilty of victimless crimes, though they were different in nature—"loitering in retail shops, purchasing liquor without tickets, sleeping out without tickets, keeping dogs contrary to law, gambling, depositing shavings or other combustible matter in the streets, improper riding or driving generally, [and] improper riding or driving on the Sabbath day." But of the entire list of misdemeanors, only one—placing combustibles in the street—accounted for all the whites sentenced in the same court. And as surprising as it must have been to contemporary Bostonians, no one was punished for prostitution—because prostitution was not a crime. Furthermore, in Charleston no one, black or white, was sent to a house of correction—indeed, the city had no such institution. Virtually all white miscreants and 77 percent of the black ones were fined; the remaining blacks were sent to the workhouse for corporal punishment.[45]

However revealing the differing understanding and treatment of petty crime, it was in the tolerance and punishment of personal violence that the two cities differed most. While Boston's crime rate climbed in the early 1840s, personal violence did not. Fewer than one-sixth of the crimes against property involved personal violence.[46] When the press reported assaults, which it did with enthusiasm, they were almost always associated with lower-class haunts behind Beacon Hill, along the waterfront, and in the homes, back streets, and alleys of the North End.

A fair proportion of Charleston's personal violence also occurred as brawls in and around bars and brothels. Yet its incidence was more stylized and more widespread, reaching into stores and offices, compromising apparently respectable folk, and involving the courts in a way unknown in Boston. In the southern city, assault charges were preferred by the victim rather than public authority. If it is true that over half the antebellum criminal cases tried in Charleston were for assault, it is also true that half the 131 complaints of assault brought to the grand jury in the 1830s were dismissed without indictment (no bill) and that nearly half the indictments were never pressed further (*nol pros*).[47]

In 1836 a grand jury complaining about the "numerous frivolous disputes" brought before it also recognized that "the object of many such cases . . . seem[ed] to be, something other than the attainment of Justice, or the prevention of crime."[48] The assault and the resort to law were both aspects of a quest to protect honor yet limit violence in a style resembling the code duello. The ritual appeal to the court in assault cases—indeed, it was not unusual for the accused to file countercharges—was an honorable end to a violent confrontation which otherwise might have persisted in an ongoing pattern of revenge. The court's chief role, like that of the second in a duel, was both to save honor and to avoid a fight to the death.[49]

Albeit in smaller numbers and in different sequence, Charlestonians persisted in fighting duels when their seconds failed in their initial charge to find a mutually acceptable solution. In spite of clerical and legislative efforts to end the practice, at least three men were tried during the 1830s for dueling, and at least eight other duels were reported. But neither warnings of mortal sin nor threats of heavy fines and restricted income could stay the manly stance and personal violence deemed necessary for the defense of honor. When the issue was clear-cut the courts favored honor over law, whether honor was defended by dueling or, where class differences precluded that gentlemanly solution, by assault. Thus when merchant Octavius Chisolm, a member of the Charleston Light Dragoons, assaulted editor Thomas Eccles for the latter's "low Scurrility" in his "vile and improper publications," he was tried and found guilty. But the jury, abhorring dishonor and its perpetrator Thomas Eccles more than assault and the assailant, petitioned Judge John O'Neall to set the punishment at "the lowest coin known to the Law." Octavious Chisolm was, accordingly, fined exactly one mill.[50]

The scurrility of the press offered no such justification in Boston. When young William Pelby confronted the editor of the *Daily Herald,* charged him with insulting both his sister and his father, and then proceeded to knock the editor down and beat him up, he was speedily tried and convicted. Perhaps because the son was an actor, the sister an actress, and the father the director of the National Theater, where the editor had been denied access backstage, different social ranks were involved than in Chisolm's case. But when Judge Thacher, noting Pelby's youth and relative poverty, fined him only $200, his mercy brought not sympathy but public outrage at his leniency. Here was no perception of a question of honor and its manly defense. Yet Bostonians did not lack a sense of honor; they only defined it differently. In Charleston dishonor centered ultimately on the appearance or reality of cowardice—the fear of violence in defense of honor. In Boston, as Thomas Sears defined it in his will, dishonor was most deeply to "live on the labor of [o]thers."[51] And if that was so, damage to honor could be calculated and compensated. In honor as in politics, Charleston flaunted fantasy and emotion; Boston cultivated pragmatism.

Central to honorable resolutions in Boston was retaining one's self-control and dignity. When socially prominent ladies were parodied in a satiric description of their 1833 bazaar to raise money for Samuel Howe's asylum for the blind, and young George Parrish confessed his authorship, no duel threatened. Feelings had been hurt, reputations trifled with, good will shattered. But since the damage could not be undone, Harrison Gray Otis, acting as intermediary, settled for Parrish's admission of indiscretion and an apology. Business disputes, where damages were more measurable, were, if possible, settled quietly by gentlemen unwilling to publish their private business in the courts. Peter Chardon Brooks and his rather prickly son Edward ignored the many invitations to personal challenge in their long dispute with the abrasive Frederic Tudor over a wall between adjoining commercial properties, and they also avoided legal action, quietly relying on their wealth and position to defeat a relative upstart. And when Horace Mann, as a lawyer-arbitrator, experienced a personal attack "belched out" by the opposing attorney in terms so vitriolic that "south of Mason's & Dixon's line, [it] would have been deemed fit cause for the duello," he prided himself on the "perfect self-possession" and "touch of dignity" with which he responded.[52]

Thus it was that in Boston the privileged and the propertied were expected to exert self-control, to support public safety, public order, and defense of private property by their own actions as well as by controlling the actions of others. Charleston's elite, no less concerned about order, safety, and property, nonetheless tolerated violence when it was used to defend personal honor, which, by definition, could not be satisfactorily assuaged in any other way. Tolerating illegal action as the defense of manly self-respect for themselves, they not surprisingly accepted it as well from the Lynch Club and from firemen rejecting civil governance—dangerous though they knew such action to be. And thus it was that they also cultivated a soft style to keep extralegal defense of honor within bounds.

• • •

Both Charleston and Boston struggled to subdue public disorder in the interest of maintaining a peaceful society. Boston, rooted in a homogeneous culture and a capitalist economy whose joint motive power and social cohesion went back to a Puritan ethic of hard work and self-denial, defined the limits of acceptable behavior more sharply and shaped the institutions to enforce them more rigidly than did Charleston. While different living styles were expected from different social orders, violence was acceptable from none. Charleston's heterogeneous culture, its biracial society, and its slave-bound economy propagated different norms. Not only different behavioral styles but different levels of violence were tolerable according to race and class. Limits were set, but they were flexible; the law which applied to one need not apply to all. Personal imperatives were often stronger, institutional restraints weaker. Charleston's citizens were readier to agree with the proposition that it was "problematical whether any police establishment is sufficient to keep *all* the inmates of a large city at *all times* in the sober ways of decency and order. . . . We wish not a despotism for the sake of order."[53]

Boston learned the limits of order and the dangers of policing despotism in the fracas over legally enforced and class-based temperance. But the city fathers should have recognized the limits of order well before when, in the same year that Charleston laid siege to the United States mail, burned abolitionist literature, and resorted to vigilante justice, Boston experienced its own antiabolitionist riot. First city government had denied the use of Faneuil Hall for an anti-slavery meeting, then it encouraged a massive anti-abolitionist rally, and shortly thereafter a mob led by "gentlemen of property and standing" sought to lynch William Lloyd Garrison. Originally their object had been George Thompson, a British agitator, who had already been warned to leave town. Gathered outside the lecture room on Washington Street near Cornhill, just next door to the *Liberator* office, the crowd milled around menacingly until two constables and Mayor Theodore Lyman arrived. The mayor convinced the ladies of the Boston Female Anti-Slavery Society who had assembled there to hear Thompson that they should leave. Jeeringly the men let the women pass through their ranks. But they were ready for action, and Mayor Lyman—he who had kept the whole town on alert for a week after the Charlestown fire—did little more to control the mob until Garrison had been seized from his office and marched through the streets with a noose about his middle—at which point Lyman intervened to take him to jail for safekeeping. He did not call up the militia. He did not summon more city officers to the scene—it was daylight, after all, and the night watch was not yet on duty.[54]

This reversal of Boston's usual pattern of action presents puzzling questions. Did Boston's demonstrable prejudice against its small black population and their abolitionist champions legitimate action intolerable even against the despised Irish? (After all, the Irish were not segregated into one or two public schools or listed separately in the city directories, as were Negroes.) Or did antislavery's potential for subverting national unity and Boston's trade legitimate the public violence necessary to crush so great a menace? Or did the presence of gentlemen of property and standing legitimate mob action not permitted crowds of lesser standing? Or did it all simply demonstrate, as did the fifteen-gallon fiasco, that, in the words of the Charleston *Mercury,* "It is still problematical whether any police establishment is sufficient to keep *all* the inmates of a large city at *all times* in the sober ways of decency and order"?

PART V · RESPONDING TO REVERSES

12

Charleston in Panic and Depression

In February 1837 news reached New York that Liverpool cotton prices had dropped precipitately. The great English cotton dealers Wiggin, Wildes, and Wilson had all failed. No sooner did word arrive than many New York firms engaged in the English trade faced ruin. Some failed almost at once. In January the British Baring Brothers had already cut back on credit for the American trade. In March New York interest rates reached 24 percent per annum. Even then lenders were few and reluctant.[1]

Two weeks later the panic reached Charleston. The "Money Market [was] very much embarrassed. . . ." Business ground to a halt. Top upland cotton prices, which were over fifteen cents a pound in early April, skidded to ten cents by mid-May, when the annual trading season customarily ended. But unsold bales still jammed wharves and warehouses, mute testimony that the season's sales were down one-third from last year's. In public trading, stock of the Bank of Charleston—the city's strongest— plummeted from 158 to 100. Merchants, fearing bankruptcy, called in all outstanding debts; banks scrambled for funds to afford them credit. Yet Judge John O'Neall saw only "commercial distress permeating this place." Some of the "strongest, and soundest" were in "very straitened circumstances"; others had already gone under. None would remain unscathed. "What a dreadful Revolution we have had in the money World!" moaned factor Alexander Robertson. "Ruin, Ruin, Ruin, stares many a man in the face." Cooper Jacob Schirmer announced why: the boom was over, "The Bubble [has] burst and great is the explosion[.]"[2]

Charleston's panic was not unique. Demands that banknotes be redeemed in specie pressed banks hard everywhere, and Charleston banks only followed the lead of New York, Philadelphia, and Baltimore when they suspended specie payments. A local citizens' committee chaired by David Alexander, president both of the Union Insurance Company and the Chamber of Commerce, recommended suspension but simultaneously denied rumors that any Charleston bank was about to fail and asserted that the city's banks collectively had sufficient resources to cover all their liabilities. Moreover, they agreed that during the crisis they would honor each other's notes, subject only to a weekly balancing of accounts.[3]

The banks could survive this way, but could the merchants? Their credit was already curtailed. The collector of the port insisted that customs duties be paid in specie, but no specie could be obtained. The district attorney, on orders from the attorney general, refused to extend the bonds which merchants customarily posted for future payments of tariffs after the imported goods had been sold until Washington officially permitted a change in policy the following October.[4]

Furthermore, when lesser traders, mechanics, and shoppers cried for small change, which was sucked up by the specie-hungry, the banks refused to issue small bills to fill the void. Workers were reduced to accepting pay in scrip, and all householders resented the disruptions of their daily business. As a *Mercury* correspondent put it, he and his fellow citizens did not want "specie for the paltry purpose of gain—any small currency will answer at present, if only for family purposes."[5]

But in September 1838 the banks resumed specie payments, and merchants espied omens that the cotton trade would revive. This was, however, a delusive hope, for Charleston was about to slip into a long depression whose aftermath stretched into the 1850s. The panic and the disruption in currency were painful enough in themselves. More importantly, however, they revealed persistent obstacles to economic development: the political motives which blocked construction of a viable transportation network, the limited capital available for nonagricultural investment, and the impediments to manufacture which a minimally educated and numerically declining labor force imposed. Less as a result of panic than of an underdeveloped hinterland minimally responsive to decisions made in Charleston banks and countinghouses, projects for economic growth lost momentum. Capital and population seeped out of the city and the state, and along with them, dreams of a revitalized commerce.

• • •

However sparse the early rewards of the South Carolina Canal and Rail Road Company, Charleston was radiantly optimistic in 1836 about a second railroad. Veering north from the Hamburg line at Branchville, the Louisville, Cincinnati, and Charleston would, so its charter provided, run first to Columbia, the state capital, then cross the mountains through a North Carolina pass into Tennessee and traverse Kentucky until it terminated at the Ohio River. In organizing and attending the Knoxville Railroad Convention, called to draw other states into this project, Charlestonians had rejected an alternative route, pressed by John C. Calhoun, for extending the Charleston-Hamburg route westward to follow the cotton belt through Georgia, Alabama, and Mississippi.[6] In so doing they also rejected a railroad based on the freights of a single though massively produced crop in favor of a trade based on exchanging western grain and livestock as well as Carolina cotton for European and northern imports brought in through the port of Charleston. At its completion the railroad would, by connecting with the Ohio River and penetrating the upper Mississippi valley, extend markets and products still farther. If Calhoun's motives in preferring to link Carolina to the delta were as political as they were economic, so too was Robert Hayne's espousal of the Cincinnati route. Both men were ambitious for national power; both men would willingly ride regional railroad networks toward their political goals.

But politicizing such decisions befogged economic analysis. Why, on the one hand, cotton which could be shipped cheaply by water from New Orleans and Mobile would instead be shipped by rail to Charleston or how, on the other, a railroad whose track ran largely through rugged mountains and minimally settled small farming areas would produce vast freights and markets was not seriously considered. Charleston enthusiasts clung to their dream that an extended transportation system would of itself produce the hinge city they sought. "Only once run our Rail Road to the Mississippi," claimed one early booster, "and half a continent of the richest agricultural country in the world will pour its produce into our ware-houses, and freight our ships with incalculable wealth." No one could find the bounds of Charleston's future prosperity, claimed factor James Rose, "if our great Western Road should be carried into effect."[7] Cincinnati citizens fed the delusion in a public meeting which celebrated joining the upper and lower South with the upper reaches of the Mississippi valley as far away as Michigan and Wisconsin. Southern commercial conventions in 1837, 1838, and 1839 continued the same theme even after panic and depression had struck.[8] Buying Louisville, Cincinnati, and Charleston stock when it was first offered in 1836 was urged on Charlestonians just as buying South Carolina Canal and Rail Road stock had been. Public economy and patriotism more than personal profit demanded investment. The pastor of the First Baptist Church, Basil Manly, stretched his clerical salary to buy a few shares "to encourage so laudable an undertaking, out of pure patriotism." The *Mercury*, an early booster, addressed the city's more worldly interest in subscribing large blocs of shares. It was "vastly important . . . that

Charleston should acquire an influence from the amount of stock subscribed" so that "her voice [would be] heard, and her interests . . . consulted in all the measures adopted by the Company."[9]

In truth, both political and economic determinants promised less to Charleston and urban development than did public discussion. When the state, in 1835, sponsored the survey to find a suitable western route, it was conducted by a board of six men, only two of whom were Charlestonians. True, it was headed by the man soon to become city intendent, but Robert Y. Hayne was much influenced by Abraham Blanding to choose a route which served Columbia's interests better than Charleston's.[10]

It is possible that Charleston's interests were not significantly diluted by the longer and more mountainous passage, because so vast a project along any route would demand sizable public subventions. Doubtless Columbians' weight was reflected in the state's decision, in December 1838, to lend the new railroad $2 million—more than twenty times what had been lent to the South Carolina Canal and Rail Road Company. Even so, Charleston's government and citizens bore most of the load. At its outset, the city had subscribed for more than nine hundred shares and, still believing that the road would stimulate both its foreign and its domestic trade, had bought another six hundred shares by 1838. Additionally, in December 1837, "believing that purchase to be essential to the success of the Great Western Rail Road," the city lent the road $100,000 with which to buy up the Hamburg line, which its shareholders had voted to sell at a $25 advance over par.[11]

Almost from the first, though it went long unperceived, the road was destined to fall short of its original purpose. It did not attract capital. By late 1837, although South Carolinians had paid in almost $225,000 for over $2 million of railroad stock, all out-of-state sources had paid in scarcely more than $40,000. Even when the state was willing to lend the company $2 million, railroad investors readily parted with their stock for less than half what they had paid for it. Only politics carried it on.[12] Hayne's charisma created faith in linking the South and West in a present exchange of agricultural goods and, in the foreseeable future, a trade in the industrial production which must eventually come from the otherwise barren mountains of North Carolina and Tennessee. As the company's president from 1837 to his death in 1839, he exhorted more than he managed. His priorities were not high efficiency, low costs, and profitable operation. Rather he enchanted the faithful with preserving and perpetuating "THE UNION . . . by establishing connexions in business, promoting friendships, abolishing prejudices, creating greater uniformity of opinions, and BLENDING THE FEELINGS OF DIFFERENT PORTIONS OF THE COUNTRY INTO

A UNION OF HEART."[13] Not bad for a nullifier; not particularly useful for a corporate entrepreneur.

More immediately useful for generating funds was the railroad charter's provision for organizing a bank. Railroad banks were common devices for tying the generally sure profits of banking to more speculative transportation ventures, offering banking privileges in return for an investment in social capital. Accordingly, Hayne and his longtime political associate James Hamilton pressed the formation of the South Western Rail Road Bank. Hamilton, who shortly resigned his Bank of Charleston directorship to serve the new bank in the same capacity, shared Hayne's extravagent expectations of an institution chartered to do business in three states. If, as they believed likely, Georgia and Kentucky would also charter the bank, it would soon become a "Southern U[nited] S[tates] B[ank]," filling the gap which Nicholas Biddle's institution had formerly filled.[14]

The bank was created amid the tentative optimism which followed resumption of specie payments in the fall of 1838, and its stocks sold briskly, though one could subscribe to bank shares only if one owned an equivalent number of railroad shares. Doubtless some subscribed because they believed the bank would make money—and for the first two years it did pay 8 percent a year on capital actually paid in. Others, perhaps, looked to it only as a hedge against total loss from the railroad stock they could not sell except at prices below the several $5 installments they had already paid on their $100 shares. But the same mismanagement which hounded the railroad dogged the bank, and it lost heavily on bad and partially unsecured loans when the economy turned sour again in 1841 and 1842.[15]

The bank really could not save the railroad, even though for a while it was profitable to investors. Like its mother corporation (though not so evidently until 1842 investigations into bad debts revealed it clearly), it put economics in the service of politics. The railroad's politics were fully bared, along with the failure of Charleston's economic strategy, at a September 1839 stockholders' meeting which voted to suspend construction when the track reached Columbia.[16] The finality of that decision was not known until a few weeks later, when Southwestern Rail Road Bank president Abraham Blanding and Louisville, Cincinnati, and Charleston Rail Road president Robert Y. Hayne both died of fever.

The old Charleston-Columbia coalition died with its leaders. So too did plans to connect Charleston with Cincinnati, if they had not already. Now the way opened not just for a full probe into the road's management and a reassessment of its finances but a reconsideration of the route which would best serve Charleston's interests. James Gadsden, an engineer recently returned from Florida and a long-time proponent of Calhoun's preferred route, had immersed himself in the affairs of the bank and the railroad before the Asheville stockholders' meeting made its decision to stop building at Columbia. Indeed, he helped propel his fellow shareholders to that decision, arguing that "the whole scheme has been made to bend to political influences & instead, as designed, a great commercial road, we have one twisting & turning as combinations of political & interested feelings may dictate." Gadsden yearned to set it right as the next railroad president—indeed, he eagerly eyed the chances of taking over the bank's management, too—not just to rationalize their interwoven finances but to realize both John C. Calhoun's program and Charleston's ultimate goal. He wrote to Calhoun's cousin and brother-in-law, "Secure for me one half of the confidence which was reposed by the State & Stockholders in Hayne & I will build your road to Columbia & find a shortcut through Georgia to the *far West*."[17]

In 1840 Gadsden did become president of the railroad—though not of the bank—after the brief interim term of Vardy McBee of Greenville. While his personal preferences encompassed a railroad built entirely at government expense and operated to enhance Charleston's trade (he had opened a factoring business in 1840) as well as a South Carolina link to railroads already projected across the lower South, his chief accomplishment was completing the line to Columbia in 1842. In doing so he reoriented the Louisville, Cincinnati, and Charleston Rail Road Company toward profits and efficiency. As an engineer he had assumed office impatient with the "Humbuggery practiced, and the little that [had] been done." He rationalized the uncertain assessments on company shares, which had provided capital only sporadically, into a system in which five-dollar installments were assessed each quarter. He guided the company through a consolidation of outstanding stock when the deepening depression made that necessary. He initiated machine shops to make the company self-sufficient in equipment. He brought the South Carolina Canal and Rail Road Company and the Louisville and Cincinnati under a common management. And he pressed to extend the railroad tracks all the way to Charleston's wharves—and got at least closer to them.[18]

Under Gadsden's dynamic management the rechristened South Carolina Rail Road Company began to show profits, and Charleston factors were heartened by the 33 percent increase in cotton shipped to the city during the road's first full year of operation. However reassuring that 1842–1843 development, Charleston's economy was still only stable at best. Its share of the Atlantic cotton states' crop remained relatively static throughout the 1840s. Indeed, as a proportion even in 1842–1843 it was down from its peak. Furthermore, almost two-thirds of the cotton which the Louisville,

Cincinnati, and Charleston Rail Road brought into the city actually came from sources along the old Hamburg line.[19] And even were Charleston's anticipations of attracting an ever greater proportion of Carolina and Georgia cotton from Savannah to be realized, its staples trade faced relative stagnation as cotton production moved west and world prices fell. Finally, Hayne's dream of drawing, alternatively, on a diversified southwestern economy was dead—even though it had probably always been a fantasy.

The Louisville, Cincinnati, and Charleston Rail Road was no more than the Branchville-to-Columbia line when its name was lost forever in the consolidation which, in 1842, produced the South Carolina Rail Road. Poorly built and heavily in debt from its inception, it was in the long run a disastrous investment. A major creditor, the Bank of Charleston, wrote off a half million dollars of its bonds as a bad debt in 1851—its worst antebellum investment. For all involved, it was a "bubble . . . expensive in its blowing and disastrous in its bursting."[20]

. . .

Remarkably, no Charleston bank failed in a panic and depression which sent banks reeling into insolvency throughout the country. Nor, on the other hand, did the Charleston banks curry favor with their fellow citizens or meet fully the banking needs of the city. Their failure in 1837 to issue small bills when they suspended specie was but one of the actions which drew sharp criticism. Throughout, the strongest banks—the private Bank of Charleston and the public Bank of the State of South Carolina—were least responsive to mercantile demands for accommodation.

Just before the panic broke, the Bank of Charleston had wilfully pursued self-interest at the cost of public image. Its original charter provided that it might double its capital from \$2 to \$4 million. But the method it chose for doing so confirmed the suspicions about monopolistic power which Andrew Jackson and Nicholas Biddle had cultivated. Its new shares were offered exclusively to those who held the old, on a stock option basis.[21] Once again the speculative whirlwind which had swirled around its original stock subscription blew hard, and the price of old stock soared. The message was clear. The bank, insensitive to prevailing values, kept profits and power for itself, letting outsiders buy in only at a price.

Though the sale of new stock, announced in February 1837, was soon postponed until the worst of the panic had passed, the press was filled with protests, to which the bank answered only that "the privileges of this corporation, like most of its kind, [were] paid for" by the fee which the state assessed the bank for increasing its capital. Those who paid the fees, it proclaimed, were entitled to the profits. But a democratic "plain man" damned the aristocratic tactics which barred "Mechanics and [the] poorer class" from privileges open only to those already growing rich on bank stock. Still more biting criticism came from the local merchants who were considerably more likely to make such investments. Their complaints, however, were less concerned with how the new stock was sold than with how the bank was operated. Its profits, they argued, were pursued at the expense of "accommodating" commercial interests. Indeed, said "Mercator," Charleston would be better off if it did not concentrate so much capital in a single monster bank but rather distributed resources among many small banks which, in competing with each other, would more readily provide the city's businessmen the credit they required. Then, two years later, Miller, Ripley & Co., a wholesale dry goods house with Yankee connections, hid behind no pseudonym in charging publicly that the Bank of Charleston played favorites among its would-be patrons. The bank, of course, denied the allegation, but its ledgers suggest that it, like most Boston banks and probably most Charleston banks, did just that. At least in the early 1840s, James Adger, an active and powerful director, was provided far more extensively with short-term business loans than any other person. Indeed, in a single and unexceptional month in 1843 he borrowed over $116,000.[22]

It was less any one particular practice, however, than the bank's size, power, and profits which stoked widespread animosity. It had regularly returned, during its first five years of operation, a 10 percent annual dividend. In the year following specie suspension, its ability to discount over $12 million in notes and provide some $6 million in exchange drafts on other banks made the difference between survival and collapse for merchants seeking its services. Moreover, during a period when Biddle's Pennsylvania Bank of the United States was engaged in major cotton speculations, the Bank of Charleston was its agent, as it was for various English banks interested in the cotton trade.[23] And its first presidents brought to it their own power as wealthy factor and politician Ker Boyce followed ex-governor James Hamilton in the front office.

Hamilton's resignation from the presidency—he stayed on until 1838 as a director—was connected with his opening his own factorage business and joining Nicholas Biddle's attempt to corner the cotton market, redeem southern trade, and regain for his state-chartered bank the financial might which the Second Bank of the United States had formerly exercised. Hamilton entered into the speculation for its "most *beneficial results to ourselves.*" Together the two men and their associates borrowed and bought, edging cotton prices constantly upward by engrossing ever more of the supply until, by early 1839, cotton brought seventeen cents a pound—close to peak pre-panic prices of eighteen to twenty cents.[24]

Charleston mercantile involvement in the scheme was mixed. Hamilton was, of course, an active partner. Patterson and Magwood sold regularly to Biddle—or at least advised him when to buy. Merchant Jacob C. Levy constantly warned Biddle that the city as a whole was leery of his scheme and uneasy about his ability to throw both the cotton and the money markets into confusion. Charlestonians resented the concentration of economic power it implied and feared that unchecked speculation by a Pennsylvania-controlled monopoly tied to shifting English economic conditions boded ill for their commerce. When the frenzied upward price spiral sagged, they, like other Southerners, were unwilling to back Hamilton's proposal to a Macon, Georgia, planters' convention that they withhold cotton from the market.[25]

Doubtless no action could then have stopped what followed. The bottom fell out of the British market. The previous year's high prices, which had been linked to a short crop, plummeted. Charleston exports, which had exceeded 300,000 bales in 1837–1838 but had dropped to slightly over 200,000 in the following year, once again reached 1837–1838 levels in 1839–1840. The problem was that it sold at prices "fully as low as they have been at any time for 20 years," hovering around ten cents a pound. "[U]nless we have the *United States Bank* again to come into the market," factor William Dukes observed in September 1839, "we must expect prices to settle down at about 10 or 12 to 12½ cents. . . ." But Biddle did not reenter the market. Nor did Hamilton. By October it was clear that Charleston was mired in depression, "the prospects of Trade . . . so gloomy that no calculation can be made what course things may take."[26]

At that very moment the Pennsylvania Bank suspended specie payments—and all but two Charleston banks followed suit. Then, once again, the arrogance and the strength of the Bank of Charleston stirred resentment. On the very day that all except the Bank of the State and the Bank of Charleston agreed on suspension—because Baltimore and Philadelphia had already suspended and New York was sure to follow—the Bank of Charleston resolved to call in the specie which other city banks owed it. On all sides hostility was its instant reward. Some banks feared pressures on their own limited specie supplies from those competitors who held their notes; others hesitated to issue the small notes needed for general circulation lest they be collected by the Bank of Charleston and likewise presented for specie redemption. Merchants, for their part, were angered by the customhouse regulation which again demanded payments in ever-vanishing specie.[27]

But it was the Bank of Charleston's last power play in the suspension crisis that rankled most. In June 1840 it undertook to force other banks to resume specie payments. The bank presented them with their bank notes which it had accumulated during the winter and offered them the choice of redeeming those notes in specie or having them treated as six-month loans bearing 6 percent annual interest. Their worst fears realized, city banks preferred to pay out the specie they had laboriously accumulated since suspension began rather than to acknowledge dependence upon the Bank of Charleston and its president, Ker Boyce. All but one of them resumed specie payments.[28]

The Bank of Charleston did not emerge unscathed. By paying specie when other banks declined to do so, it had diminished its own reserves—indeed, had watched them trickle into the vaults of competitors. In 1841, consequently, its annual dividend dropped below 8 percent for the first time. Its stock, which had customarily sold well above par, dropped to par in 1841 and significantly below in 1843. But the bank had preserved its power and its independence. Alone among Charleston's banks, it successfully challenged an 1840 state law requiring banks to accept a system of fines in cases of future suspension. Because it had not suspended in 1839, the Bank of Charleston successfully defended its charter from unilateral state amendment.[29] And if its power to do so soon involved its president, Ker Boyce, in a damaging political battle, the Bank of Charleston also came close to placing itself outside the reach of public opinion and state government.

• • •

The Bank of Charleston's survival, essentially uncompromised by the heady mixture of depression and politics, rested on a financial strength which the Louisville, Cincinnati, and Charleston never had. But the two corporations' different fates mirrored the earlier responses of the old Bank of the United States' Charleston depository and the South Carolina Canal and Rail Road to the buffeting of politics and the vagaries of the national economy in the early 1830s. After 1837 Charleston's government reflected a similar intersection, as the city experienced the impact of a new depression and the continuation of political patterns set during the nullification crisis and before.

In 1836 the Congressional district of which Charleston was part had sent Unionist Hugh Swinton Legaré to Washington to replace nullifier Henry Pinckney, whose Gag Resolution had offended his constituents. Thereafter Charleston's politics continued to bear little resemblance to the national consolidation into Whig and Democratic parties. In their stead, numerous factions—Independent Republican, United Independents, and the Equal Rights party among them—dominated local allegiances. If, however, Charleston had any semblance of a national party, it was the Democratic—for there were virtually no acknowledged Whigs in the city. Consequently Legaré, in siding with the Whigs and opposing President Van Buren's proposed federal subtreasury, designed to fill the role which the Bank of the United States had formerly played, undermined his support at home. But his failure to regain nomination was engineered by fellow Carolinian Joel Poinsett, Van Buren's secretary of war. Poinsett's opposition sparked an arcane battle among Charleston's Unionist Democrats—breaking old friendships, dividing families, and almost precipitating duels. Resolution was achieved only in an agreement to back moderate nullifier Isaac E. Holmes over any former Unionist as the Democratic congressional candidate. Thus in 1838 did Charleston's Democrats rally to run a ticket shaped by national rather than the old nullifier and Unionist divisions.[30]

If for a while a new Democratic consensus seemed to blur factionalism, it was only a passing appearance. In 1840, with few Whigs to back Tippecanoe and Tyler too, the critical race was for Charleston's seat in the state senate. In it Ker Boyce, president of the Bank of Charleston, ran hard against John S. Ashe, a planter from St. Paul's parish. Ashe had served his rural parish in both state house of representatives and senate; Boyce had represented his city in the lower house since 1832. Both had been nullifiers; both had opposed Pinckney in 1836; both were Democrats in 1840. Ashe was a gentleman of the old school, a college graduate, an officer of the Jockey Club, a pillar of the South Carolina Association. Boyce, known as the "cur of Newberry" in political doggerel, was a self-made man, an upstart who had gained his first capital in the King Street trade and become an East Bay factor and wharf owner, then a bank president. As an officer of the chamber of commerce he represented the city's mercantile interests. But the press resounded with allegations that his candidacy was just another Bank of Charleston attempt to mold government rather than be subject to it.

The canvass once again politicized economics. It was more a question of class and status than of partisan affiliation. Bitterly emotional in conduct and aftermath, it generated charges of corruption so intense that Boyce's narrow election provoked a senate investigation into alleged election fraud. But before its committee could hear testimony Boyce resigned his seat, came home, ran again, and won by a landslide. Both campaigns were testimony to the economic shift in the nature of city politics and government. Supporters and opponents alike saw in Boyce's bid for a senate seat an urban-commercial challenge to agricultural priorities. But that his election and reelection both occurred before he resigned the Bank of Charleston presidency suggests that the castigation of a dreaded monopoly carried little weight among the voters who elected him.[31]

Thus even though he had run in state elections at least since 1830 and won since 1832, Boyce's election in 1840 embodied the change which had been going on in city government as new people had come to power. Commercial interests had gained an ever larger voice. At the beginning of the decade, merchants had numbered fewer than one in four among city council members; in mid-decade they comprised about half the body; by the early 1840s they were a clear majority of two-thirds. In the process of gaining seats, they had eliminated the mechanics, who in the early 1830s had constituted about 12 percent of the council, and had nudged professionals down from occupying one-half the council seats to filling only one-fifth. Parallel with these occupational shifts was the declining social status of council members, as upper-class domination faded swiftly away. Politics increasingly represented city business interests, and economic self-interest pressed hard against self-proclaimed aristocratic values.[32]

In explaining the election of the personally unpopular Richard Cogdell, Esq., in 1839, one commentator quipped that he was voted in so "that there might be one gentleman in council, if His Honor the Mayor should die."[33] But in the next election not even the mayor was a man of high social status. And when lumber merchant Jacob Mintzing died in 1843, the city's first German ethnic mayor was followed at once by its second, John Schnierle, also a lumberyard operator. Control of the city council, which in the decade's early years had been in the hands of high-status professionals and was seized at mid-decade by a group of high-powered politico-economic entrepreneurs, passed in the depression years to undistinguished merchants preoccupied with narrowly defined local interests. The city they governed still did not march to the tune of national politics. Nor had it experienced the commercial renaissance which the Hayne-Hamilton group had promised. Its citizens had experienced a whiplash from entrusting their future to the politics of economics—both nullification and railroad. By the 1840s their economic vision was more parochial than ever before. And even at the city level the experiment in a publicly stimulated political economy turned sour as government was whittled down by depression.

Just how much of the city's resources had been committed to the blending of public with private funds is difficult to establish. Sure it is that, over time, the city both bought and sold stock as she also both borrowed from and lent to corporations. Her accounts with the railroad limn a dynamically complex interaction. To buy her first 939 shares of Louisville, Cincinnati, and Charleston stock the city had borrowed the down payment from the Bank of Charleston and repaid it with capital gains from selling 200 shares of South Carolina Canal and Rail Road stock. Shortly thereafter, in February 1837, Mayor Hayne, who was also already president of the Louisville, Cincinnati, and Charleston, arranged that the city borrow from his railroad, at a low 4 percent interest, all capital not immediately committed to construction. When, the following August, the council considered how the city would repay what she had borrowed in February, it resolved to issue $150,000 of city bonds at 5 percent. Then in December

1837, even though the city had yet to repay the railroad, the council further committed itself to increase municipal holdings of railroad stock by sevenfold should the railroad be unable to find capital elsewhere, and it simultaneously pledged to lend the company $100,000 at 5 percent. That in the end the city apparently bought only 1,539 shares was more a matter of good luck than shrewd choice.[34]

City government was no less entangled in real estate development. After two great fires in 1835 it had issued $200,000 of 5 percent bonds to buy up blocks of land in the burned-out district for resale or planned development. One sizable lot it sold almost at once for the Charleston Hotel, which was destroyed only three years later in another devastating fire. Qualifying in 1838 for a state-financed loan whose repayment the city guaranteed, the hotel company decided to rebuild. But when hard times made its venture unprofitable, the company failed, and the hotel was sold at auction. Bought up by the city for the knocked-down price of $84,000 in an attempt to avoid a complete loss, the hotel was refurbished at further expense to the city, to be sold as an operating business. Unhappily, by 1843 the council had still found no buyer who would pay the city's price and was reduced to renting it out to J. H. Nickerson, formerly the manager of Barnum's City Hotel in Baltimore.[35]

Development of the other fire land—for handsome residences on Princes Street and a mercantile block on Pearl (later Hayne) Street—which involved the city in smaller losses, did little to inspire taxpayers' enthusiasm. At last, when the rumor was rife that "a scheme [was] on foot to make [the] city responsible for the bonds of the Georgia Rail Road Company to the enormous amount of 500,000 dollars," taxpayers rebelled at city subvention of private corporations. In 1843 property owners petitioned the state legislature to prohibit city investment in "companies formed for constructing Rail Roads or other works of public improvement beyond the limits of the City."[36]

Although formal petitions protested only the use of municipal funds for private ventures outside the city, the bitter disillusionment with economic development based on public investment in private ventures was pervasive. Moreover, projects completely within the customary municipal domain were cut short by the severe depression—albeit not before the city's appearance had been markedly changed. By 1839 the four-acre White Point Garden on the South Battery had been completed, its "broad and serpentine walks," "beautiful pagodas," and "seats tastefully arranged amongst the trees" a notable contribution to civic amenity. Major arteries had been widened and paved for an easy flow of carriages on Meeting, Broad, and East Bay streets. Narrow ways and crooked alleys had been straightened and connected, making new through streets. A new porticoed guard house adorned the fourth corner of Broad and Meeting. But all these monuments to public progress became, after 1839, arguments for municipal retrenchment. Already during the previous year the number of adult male paupers seeking city assistance had soared by nearly 70 percent. The funded city debt reached $1 million in 1841. After 1840 commercial inventories declined and taxable income dropped. Priorities shifted, resources declined, and by 1842 the city budget had been cut to half its mid-1830s peak.[37]

Retrenchment took various forms. Taxes were lowered on real estate, but increased on slaves hired out and on slaves brought into the city for sale. The income of nonresidents working in town was taxed at the same rates as that of residents. Though they did not succeed, efforts were made to reassess all city property in 1842. Politicians seeking election curried favor by pledging to slash costs of government operation. Salaries of city officials were cut—even the mayor's, which dropped from $4,000 to $2,500.[38] The city development and governmental reorganization which Hayne had introduced in 1836 came to a halt—indeed, reversed. The mayor's office was shorn of many responsibilities which had permitted some centralization and professionalization of the city's operation. Plans to attract trade to the city by improving both public and private accommodations were cut short. Austerity reoriented the public's understanding of city government's appropriate functions.

• • •

To what resources, then, was the city to look for recovery? On what strengths was she to rely? William Gregg, a watchmaker who had come to Charleston in 1838, spent the 1840s urging Carolinians to build their own cotton mills, and thereby both diversify the state's economy and enliven Charleston's commerce by turning abundant supplies of raw cotton into finished products. Charlestonians had toyed with the idea as early as 1816—yet their state remained agricultural and their city continued to rely on the trade in agricultural staples. Why? The answer in 1845 differed little from the answer in 1825, even though its long-range implications were, if anything, less promising.

Charleston had about the same distribution of artisanal production, shipbuilding, and milling in 1843 as she had had in 1828. Civic leaders continued to look for political spurs to economic growth as they pressed again for a navy yard which would employ the city's skilled labor and utilize its lumber reserves, made even more accessible by the railroad. City government in 1843 concluded that "the public authorities should . . . afford a liberal encouragement to the mechanical pursuits of the citizens." Yet it adamantly prohibited the erection of steam engines except on marshy land or, if it did grant exceptions, stifled their utility by minute regulations. And while Dr. Samuel Dickson urged parents to take their sons "from the overcrowded professions" and enfeebling trade and to "make them artificers in wood, and brass, and iron," no one urged the city to support schools for their basic education.[39]

As a result, Charleston's pool of artisans did not grow, and probably shrank. Except for bakers, carpenters, and coopers, the absolute numbers of mechanics engaged in trades for which there are comparable data declined between 1826 and 1848. Without question the number of black males in the city also declined, from 7,500 in 1830 to 7,000 in 1840 to 5,500 in 1848. Given their key role not only as laborers but as bakers, blacksmiths, bookbinders, bricklayers, brickmasters, carpenters, confectioners, coopers, coppersmiths, engineers, fishermen, foundry workers, and so on through the alphabet, it is likely that their declining numbers, especially after 1840, explained part of the city's diminished number of skilled workers.[40]

A heavy Irish immigration probably met the needs for additional unskilled labor. But only the special demand to which skilled northern construction workers responded after the fires of 1835 and 1838 explains the unusual increase in carpenters while other crafts declined. The high wages which attracted construction workers were an aberration produced by catastrophe. The clear decline in slave hire rates between 1840 and 1843 was, in all likelihood, accompanied by a drop in most white wage rates—a situation which must have discouraged white mechanics, just as the drop in slave rates encouraged owners to remove workers from the urban labor force and place them on new, profitable Gulf Coast plantations.[41] In sum, there is little reason to believe that Charleston actually had the potential for the growing mechanic labor force necessary to increase artisanal manufacturing in the city.

What then of capital-intensive manufacturing of the sort William Gregg promoted in cotton mills? Did Charleston have the resources to invest in large-scale textile production? If, on the one hand, Boston had twice as much capital employed in commerce and manufacture as did Charleston, it also appears that Charlestonians on a per capita basis had about as much capital as Bostonians to invest in their city. Indeed, if one excludes slaves from the per capita count, they probably had more. But because Bostonians largely controlled textile manufacturing outside their city, the capital invested in hinterland factories is the more critical figure. In all of South Carolina there was but $3 million invested in manufacturing of any sort in 1840, as against Massachusetts's $41 million; and when Gregg's Graniteville Manufacturing Company was chartered in 1841, the state discouraged investment in it by making stockholders liable for twice the value of the stock they were to purchase.[42]

And in Charleston itself, much of the capital was not locally controlled. How much of her commercial capital was owned and controlled by Northerners and Englishmen is impossible to determine—but much was. Much of it also was invested in the staples trade and was thus a form of agricultural wealth. Nor can one say how much of the money available for manufacturing went into slaves instead of machinery or shops. Moreover, there is no reason to believe that planters, merchants, and professionals surrendered their preference for planting over manufacturing investments. The only new business arrangement to keep money in the city was the limited liability partnership in which the silent partner's responsibility was limited to his actual investment, and public records suggest that this arrangement was confined to a few commercial establishments, some of which involved no more than an aging man's interest in the busines success of a younger kinsman. Venture capital was still further discouraged by moves in the early 1840s to curb the limited liability even of corporations.[43]

In actual fact, individual Charlestonians may have had less capital to invest after 1840 than they had had in the 1830s. If owning slaves in the city symbolized their total resources, more Charlestonians of sizable property in 1830 saw their property decrease by 1840 than saw it increase or even remain the same. Nor is there evidence that the capital which had once been invested in slaves moved to other investments which would stimulate the city's economy. Rather, it is likely that those slaves or the capital they represented left the city for the country; indeed, that they left Carolina for more productive cotton land in the West.[44]

Moreover, the failure of at least forty-five men who had played visible roles in the city's economic life may have discouraged entrepreneurial adventure in a climate where planting was valued more highly than was commerce. Seven succumbed to the 1837 credit crisis, thirty-eight to the depression years 1839–1843. More than half of them were merchants and factors; one-third had wielded economic power associated with extensive capital investment; three-quarters were engaged in some sort of commerce; but no more than 12 percent had been planters before they failed. Their fate could be read as a warning against commerce, a testimony to the safety of planting. And the many who barely skirted failure—physician Samuel Dickson, factor John Kirkpatrick, even banker Ker Boyce among them—may well have taken that message to heart.[45]

• • •

The dream as well as the reality of becoming a hinge city slipped farther and farther away as the improved transportation on which it depended failed to materialize. Indeed, rapidly developing internal improvements elsewhere only disadvantaged Charleston's trade and her access to the business news on which successful commerce rested. As steamboats and railroads linked other cities in a national network over which the mails and business information moved swiftly, the city's relative isolation increased. The Southern Steam Packet Company, which had promised locally controlled regular steam packet service from New York, was defunct by 1842, leaving Carolina with direct, frequent steam packet service only to yet more remote Savannah and to Wilmington, North Carolina, whose connections farther north were slow and irregular in all but fine weather.[46]

For a short period in 1841 the city believed she might secure a direct packet connection with England. But time-consuming waits for the right tide on which to cross the ever-more-formidable bar and to penetrate the silting harbor defeated the new British line's willingness to interrupt its West Indies run. Projected inland rail lines from Washington south to Columbia threatened to lure the main domestic mail route away from the coast and delay still further Charleston's receipt of commercial intelligence. So the city council and the chamber of commerce, which had first struggled to speed up the boat mail, were ultimately reduced to fighting the shift to its transportation by rail.[47] But no success in either vein could change the reality that the New York and Boston steam packets from Liverpool brought those cities the international cotton news several days before it reached Charleston.

Old hopes were dashed. New opportunities vanished as soon as they emerged. Seemingly nothing could lighten the depression's impact as 1841 and 1842 dragged on, dreary and exhausting years. When, in February 1841, Biddle's bank folded for good, the specie supply dipped once again, stock prices slipped still farther, and dividends slid down along with them. A year later even Bank of Charleston shares had fallen twenty-two points below par. The staples trade, real estate—all business—was *"most awfully dull."* People wondered whether Charleston could be saved from "utter ruin," could revive from prostration, could survive the "melancholy gloom." Mayor Mintzing made the jeremiad official, announcing that the dreams of the 1830s were dead: "The illusion which flattered with the belief of great public and private prosperity, is now completely vanished. . . ." It was more crushing than the desperation of the late 1820s because the intervening high hopes had raised expectations. Even when 1843 brought a restoration of business, a revival in the stock market, and better times generally, the city was as riveted to the staples trade as it had been in 1828. In 1844 Thomas Bennett, who had watched the city's economy for over forty years, observed that cotton "compared with the cost of Labour which produce[d] it[, was] the lowest cheapest article in the world."[48] And Charleston's economic future was not only chained to that article but to a declining agricultural hinterland whose worn-out soil made its labor costs among the highest. Unwilling to turn toward manufacturing, unable to diversify her trade, and unsuccessful in linking herself to the growing steam-powered national transportation system, Charleston's aspirations for economic growth were doomed to disappointment.

13

Meeting Catastrophe

Misfortunes rarely come singly. Between the panic and the depression which laid low Charleston's economy, two steamboat disasters, a devastating fire, and two epidemics leveled one quarter of the city's buildings and took nearly six hundred lives. Cumulative in their effect, they drained physical resources as they tested the city's ability to adapt. Their psychic toll was less precisely defined, but no one can doubt that they also nourished an anxious insecurity which shaped citizens' responses to subsequent political and economic events.

Steam power, vaunted as a source of progress, was also a source of accidents—the result of both mechanical and human failure. So it was in 1837 when Captain Carleton White took the steam packet *Home* out of New York harbor for her mid-October run to Charleston and ran her aground near Sandy Hook. There he sat until the rising tide freed the vessel. Then, pressed by the tight schedule which characterized all steam packet service, he headed out to sea despite his fears that the engine was damaged. A violent storm off Cape Hatteras demonstrated his error. The engine failed. Sails could not hold the ship on course. The hull leaked faster than it could be bailed. And, so his critics charged, Captain White's seamanship was severely impaired by drink. In any case, trying to save her from sinking in deep water, he let the *Home* drift ashore, where she broke up in shallow water, drowning sixty-seven passengers, twenty of them Charlestonians.[1]

Stunned by the news as it filtered into the city, citizens recalled the "unfavorable opinions" about the *Home*'s seaworthiness which had recently circulated. Only three weeks before the *Mercury* had responded to them by printing a "card" from satisfied patrons, who had commended Captain

White's skillful navigation and the vessel's comfortable accommodations. Now, however, the paper was filled with allegations from Charlestonians angry at the deliberate deception practiced on their neighbors. They castigated James Allaire, "the rich [New York] proprietor," for his "unprincipled avarice" in operating a vessel he knew to be unsafe and for his criminal role in "induc[ing] the victims . . . to risk and sacrifice their lives. . . ." The mayor called a public meeting to consider what should be done, and the meeting appointed a committee to investigate the disaster. On its recommendation, the city council required that all steam packets touching at Charleston be examined for safety, and mandated a fine of $1,000 for any master who refused to permit inspection of his vessel.[2]

That the measures were ineffectual was only in part because no qualified Charlestonian would act as inspector. Its futility was born out only nine months later when, just hours out of Charleston, the *Pulaski* blew up, killing over 150 of its crew and passengers, 128 of whom had come aboard at a Cooper River wharf. Unlike the *Home,* the *Pulaski,* which the recently organized Savannah and Charleston Steam Packet Company had purchased in England, was in excellent condition. Here human error alone was responsible for the catastrophe. But whether blame lay with Captain DuBois for racing against a competing line's vessel to keep to his company's demanding schedule or with a second engineer for allowing the boiler to blow its steam and then filling the red-hot container with cold water, no one could tell. The explosion which resulted split the boat amidships and sank her within forty minutes. Since all the officers but the second mate were either killed in the explosion or drowned at sea along with most of the crew and passengers, subsequent explanations were largely guesswork.[3]

Once again, however, angry citizens, lamenting the loss of many who were "the flower of the Charleston circles," demanded safety precautions. This time their indignation joined that of others elsewhere to secure federal legislation requiring semiannual inspection of boilers aboard vessels operating in American waters and the provision of two or three lifeboats on each ship. Once again results were nugatory. Charleston engineers refused to be inspectors, fearing blame for the catastrophes they believed the measure's inadequacies made inevitable. Semiannual inspection was, they asserted, to little purpose unless equipment was constantly under an engineer's oversight and unless automatic safety valves were required on all marine engines.[4]

. . .

If steamboat explosions were a new hazard, fire was an old perennial. Yet despite two devastating fires in 1835, Charleston had made little headway in coping with their prevention or extinction. When on the night of April

27, 1838, fire broke out at the corner of King and Beresford streets, the city was little more organized to fight a major conflagration than she had been three years earlier.[5]

Driven by smart winds, flames raced north and east between Society and Market streets until they reached East Bay and the Cooper River. Devouring block after block of old and mostly wooden buildings, the fire also burned the brand new Charleston Hotel to the ground and consumed at least four churches. All told, the raging firestorm leveled 560 dwellings and stores and some 600 outbuildings, at an estimated loss of $3 million. Fighting the conflagration, four white and "several negro" firemen lost their lives. And when, finally, at dawn, the flames had finished their work, Charleston seemed "to be no more . . . the rude columns that once were chimneys, standing as thick as trees in the forest, and the piles of rubbish lying everywhere over the ground in most unsightly disorder . . . miserable memorials of our fallen state."[6]

Damaged also was community cohesion. As flames had leapt high in the night air, casting an eerie light and dancing shadows over the city, private and public discipline collapsed. For a while it was each man for himself. As the propertied sought to save what little they could, looters roamed freely, plundering the smoking ruins and the piteous piles of goods salvaged from the fire's path. Even firemen, discouraged when the shortage of water seemingly made their task impossible, deserted public duty for their families' safety and the rescue of their property. And it was rumored that Mayor Pinckney, immobilized by fear, skulked on the sidelines unable to take command. Social obligation had foundered and, in retrospect, it seemed that "the blood-thirsty tiger" of inhumanity had been loosed "upon the carcase of the torn victim."[7]

Nor were the catastrophes over yet. In the wake of fire came epidemic. On August 6 the Marine Hospital reported nine cases of yellow fever. Disease swept the city almost as rapidly as had the flames, incubating in tenements crowded with burned-out tenants and in vacant lots where wet cellar ruins and piles of rubble bred the mosquitoes which spread yellow jack. Moreover, the city was also full of strangers—northern workers lured by construction jobs which the fire's destruction had created. Unacclimated to the region, they were doubly susceptible to the disease known locally as "strangers' fever" and to the summer weather customarily deemed the "sickly season." With neither friends nor family to look after them, these workers were "not only predisposed to embibe" sickness, "but in the very worst position for its reception." Half of the city's white deaths that year were from yellow fever, and 40 percent of all those who died in the city that year were non-Carolinians. Doubtless the epidemic hit the Yankee workers hard, as it also struck down many recent Irish immigrants.[8]

So great was the fever's toll among the foreign-born that the Brotherhood of San Marino, recently formed as a Catholic workingmen's mutual aid society, opened a special hospital for them. The city too extended her care to them until the Marine Hospital, the poorhouse, and the lazaretto could hold no more. While the mayor urged strangers not yet sick to leave the city and private citizens subscribed funds to aid them in doing so, city hall also established a temporary hospital in the Medical College building on Queen Street. The special board of commissioners who operated it, embracing virtually all the religious organizations and benevolent societies in the city, represented yet another mutual endeavor of government and private philanthropy.[9]

If the response to epidemic was a return to the customary Charleston pattern of community cohesion and volunteer service, the response to the fire's entire aftermath was considerably more complex. Nonetheless, the city's measures for coping with immediate crisis were predictable from the past. Aware, even as the embers cooled, that the city must cope with dangerous rubble, mayor and aldermen at once appointed a corps of special assistant health commissioners to oversee rubbish removal, the dismantling of partially destroyed buildings, and the filling up of the holes where water and trash would otherwise collect. Within a week five aldermen took charge of official relief efforts while citizens organized committees in each ward both to solicit funds and to identify those who needed assistance. In a matter of days they had collected over $24,000, with pledges of more to come. And the city council, recognizing that much more was needed, voted $10,000 of public funds to supplement privately subscribed aid to the destitute. The homeless were sheltered in the poorhouse and in the federal barracks, which Washington permitted the city to use for emergency housing. To thwart looting and theft, special citizens' patrols were organized to supplement the militia units put on special guard duty.[10]

If all this activity blurred memories of the bloodthirsty tiger which the fire had loosed, if it testified to the community's ability to regroup its forces and reestablish social order, it did not address the long-range problems the fire had revealed or accentuated. Mayor Pinckney did seize the opportunity to centralize responsibilities for public health and replace volunteer assistant health commissioners with a paid city inspector charged with locating "nuisances" and seeing to their removal. The superintendent of streets was voted funds for a few more carts and horses to be used in trash removal. And propelled by the yellow fever and a subsequent scarlet fever epidemic as well as by the fire, the city undertook to develop a cemetery well out on the Neck to achieve a place of "inhumation" not "hurtful" to citizens. But like most other northern and southern municipalities, the city developed no efficient sewer system and retained, much to nearby residents' dismay, the practice of using street sweepings, trash, and vault offal for landfill and street foundations.[11]

For the resources with which to rebuild physically, the city turned to the state. Within weeks Governor Pierce Butler, tying Charleston's recovery to South Carolina's long-range "prospects of [her] great Rail Road, and of the noble scheme of direct importation," convened a special session of the legislature which then underwrote a $2 million loan "to reconstruct and put in operation, the great social machine which has been destroyed." The speed in actually doing so was slowed by the provision that the Bank of the State of South Carolina must first sell sufficient state bonds to provide the requisite capital for the fire loans it was charged with administering. In 1838, a year of national and international depression, money was tight. Consequently, even though repayment was guaranteed by the city, the bank moved slowly, while citizens were deterred from borrowing on the unusually favorable terms for a fifteen-year repayment period by the new building code, which required fireproof roofing and solid brick construction.[12]

At best, it was a full four months before the first reconstruction under the fire loan could begin, and even by November only one-sixth of the promised funds was available. Then early in 1839 Charleston succumbed to the deep depression which made the scheduled loan repayments a burden to many. By 1840 citizens were petitioning the legislature to simplify compliance regulations and by 1841, to modify mortgage foreclosure stipulations.[13] Moreover, funds which might have been used for transportation, commercial, or even manufacturing ventures to moderate the depression were instead tied up in construction. No wonder the city was soon saddled with the defaulted debts of the Charleston Hotel and the nearby residential development which its president, Alexander Black, had undertaken on fire loan money.

Financial contraction also made citizens ever more unwilling to abide by the costly building code—even though it was designed to insure their safety.[14] Arguing that private dwellings should be exempt or that residential sections should be excused from rules forbidding modestly priced wooden construction, they seemingly forgot the fears which the fire had generated. Ten years after the 1838 blaze, Charlestonians were still more likely to live in wooden than in brick buildings, especially if they were renters. Not even the fear of incendiarism seemed to make a difference, though after every fire the cry of arson echoed in rising volume and increasing frequency. In the four weeks following the 1838 devastation Mayor Pinckney reported that eighteen attempts to ignite the city had been uncovered. Predictably, in every case a black was apprehended as the suspect. Although five slaves were actually prosecuted for alleged arson, the only proven arsonist was Keating Laurens, who had set his planter brother's house on fire but was found not guilty by reason of insanity. Despite this reality the "Community [was] in great excitement." The city guard was reinforced. A special citizen force was organized to track down malefactors. The mayor's court was thronged with Negro arson suspects. Thus did fire sap the city's physical and psychic resources.[15]

• • •

Even the alarm which followed the devastating exposure of the fire department's deficiencies and the water supply's inadequacy soon gave way to inertia. However dangerous each might be, attempts at reform laid bare the danger of a social division so deep that it was preferable to endure the old rather than chance the new. Yet immediately after the April fire it had not seemed so. Press and public meetings were filled with charges that firemen had been inefficient, had neglected their duty, had even deserted their posts. The white volunteer companies, stung by the charges, blamed the board of firemasters for the chaos which others blamed on them. Appointed by the city council "not for capability, but for no other reason than that they are friends, whom they wish to screen from militia duty," the firemasters were, the rank and file believed, put in charge of fire fighting without a semblance of the experience and know-how possessed by fire companies' elected officers.[16]

At least for a while, city government was not to be distracted in its efforts at reorganization. Elected officials no more accepted volunteers' assertion of their rights to control fire fighting than the firemen would accept others' attacks on their manliness. Nonetheless the Aetna, Charleston, German, Phoenix, and Vigilant engine companies and the Fire Company of Axemen, all comprised solely of whites, perceived any moves to reduce their independence as an effort to equate them with the black operators of the city engines. They could not stomach Pinckney's reorganization plan, for to centralize the department's authority in a paid, professional engineer threatened to reduce them to the status of those slaves whose fire fighting was already done under the direction of paid white city appointees. Even more demeaning to their sense of volunteer civic service was a citizens' committee proposal that free blacks be allowed to form a volunteer fire company. Fiercely proud mechanics and the men from other middle- or low-prestige occupations who largely filled the companies resented being bracketed with Negroes. They would drop their spanners for rifles and take on the militia duty from which fire service exempted them if volunteer fire fighting crossed racial lines.[17]

In a rare turn of events, the city council, still determined to bring the unruly firemen to heel, stood absolutely firm. Despite the companies' protests, Charleston's mayor and aldermen took their plan to the state legislature, seeking permission to organize free black companies. Although they were turned down on this most controversial part of their reform, they nonetheless proceeded to implement the rest. Not just the white firemen but even the newly enlarged board of firemasters were now to be put under the command of the chief engineer at fires. Efficiency, order, and competence were to replace volunteer companies' clubbiness and the rowdiness it bred. To achieve the protection of public order and private property, the council was willing to exacerbate rather than mollify a growing social cleavage within the white population.

The firemen too held firm, refusing to give an inch. In a March 1839 meeting they denied that the chief engineer could possibly handle all the authority the council was loading on him. Implying mutiny, they asserted that no fireman would accept such authoritarianism. "[T]he eye of the taskmaster" would never replace "the high spirit of generous rivalry which has so far kept us in constant attention to our Engines and implements." Furthermore, they warned that the proposed reorganization violated the terms under which the companies were chartered and was thus patently illegal. Their final declaration left no doubt of their intent. If the city fathers persisted, firemen would *"resist* and *disobey* all laws passed in *violation* and in *repugnance* to *their charters."*[18]

The council responded in kind. The firemen had displayed "a spirit of insubordination." If they actually did resist and disobey, recalcitrant companies, who were thus breaking the law, would be summarily disbanded and replaced by new companies. But when the firemasters too revolted, the council began to waver. The firemasters—like all other city boards—were unpaid public servants. If they forced surrender on the firemen and if they surrendered their own power to a central authority, they would erode the very system they served. Like the firemen they presided over, they had little power or standing beyond that which their public service gave them in the eyes of their community. But they saw themselves as long-term solid citizens, for if few of them were men of means, three in four of them were property owners. They too wanted a stable community, one in which the slave property which almost two-thirds of them owned would be protected by a solid white phalanx supporting social arrangements as they were.[19]

At first the council attempted to thwart their opposition by packing the board with additional members, two aldermen among them, but on second thought it backed down. In a move to avoid increasingly open conflict, Mayor Pinckney proposed a referendum on reorganization. On July 1, 1839, Charlestonians gave their verdict in an election so dull that only one-third the voters who had recently turned out to choose a sheriff bothered to cast ballots. They voted to return to the inefficient but volunteer way of running the fire department. A month later the city council revoked the ordinance reorganizing the department and returned to the system which, only fifteen months earlier, had contributed to burning a quarter of the city to the ground. Charleston citizens had expressed a preference not just for voluntaristic government but for the complex network of personal contacts and the avoidance of confrontation on which social stability rested. The fire department remained as it had been, with six white volunteer companies serving the city on their own terms and nine slave-operated city engines directed by paid employees.[20] Neither private property nor public order was any safer than it had been on April 27, 1838, when the bloodthirsty tiger had been loosed. But then, it was no more endangered.

• • •

If it took Boston the whole second quarter of the century to achieve a public water system, and if reorganization of the fire companies in Charleston was balked by relatively few citizens, it is not surprising that the second item on Mayor Pinckney's fire agenda got no further than a statement of the city's desperate need for a reliable water supply. The matter was not simply insufficient water pressure with which to fight fires. The city's marshy location and the many cemeteries within its limits generated a situation in which inhabitants drank a decoction "not only [of] the soluble filth, and excretion of men and animals, but the very mortal remains of our citizens, who are interred in the city."[21]

Still, with the priority the city gave public health, something might have been done were not the economy so depressed, public funds so limited, and the need for reconstructing the fire-wracked city so pressing. But all these conditions prevailed; and when Col. Benjamin Hunt proposed to the city council that it move forward to build a city water system, the council voted it inexpedient to consider such a measure "under existing circumstances." The state, seeing no connection between Charleston's drinking water and the railroad, direct trade with England, or cotton prices, refused to vote funds for the project despite a Charleston petition that $400,000 of the fire loan funds be used to bring water into the city from the Edisto River. Although presented primarily as a device for fire fighting, it did not convince a legislature which had previously required a building code as a means to prevent further disaster in Charleston. In any case, without the backing of the city council it had no chance. So it was that in 1848, ten years after the fire and in a city where epidemics were commonplace, 10 percent of the houses lacked any water supply at all and the rest relied largely on cisterns and shallow wells for a liquid which was "for the most part undrinkable, and hardly fit for washing or culinary purposes."[22]

How much Charleston's scarce resources were attributable to the fire, as opposed to the depression which followed it, is difficult to determine. Mayor Pinckney claimed a severe immediate impact in the sudden interruption of the city's "industry and enterprize" by which "[l]abor [was] deprived of its employment, industry of its reward,—and the capital that sustained them, . . . utterly perished." Assuredly, trade came momentarily to a halt. Surely, too, the destruction of whole blocks of stores along King Street and of the new commercial development on Pearl stifled commercial revival. Nonetheless, within weeks, local merchants, fearful lest their trade go elsewhere, were advertising as far away as Macon, Augusta, Columbus, and Milledgeville in Georgia, assuring old customers that they were still in business. Charleston papers were full of ads for construction materials as demand for them soared. And property owners whose buildings had escaped the fire profited from an acute housing shortage, "taking advantage of the *necessity of the times*" by rent gouging.[23]

Long range, however, the most demonstrable fire-induced business change was the collapse of two of the city's three insurance companies. Caught with fire claims they were unable to pay fully, they closed their doors and settled as best they could. When a similar phenomenon had occurred in New York after its great 1835 fire and all but three local companies had failed, new corporations were quickly formed to replace the old. But Charleston experienced no such rebound. As a result, those needing insurance were saddled with excessively high costs, because South Carolina taxed premiums paid to out-of-state companies. Even more damaging was the consequent outflow of the funds which local insurance companies would have invested in Charleston banks, where they would add to the reserves against which businessmen could borrow. And the situation only worsened when the one company which survived the fire reduced its capital by half in 1843 and left yet more business to the strangers who had opened offices in Charleston since 1838.[24]

Merchants, irritated at the bind in which they found themselves, tried in 1842 to form a mutual insurance company of the sort common in Boston—but that venture too died aborning. Neither the burden of high rates nor the opportunity "to keep the profits of insurance business amongst us, and to increase our permanent wealth" could garner the initial capital needed to start the company. It was not that there was no money to be invested, but that Charlestonians doubted that any new venture would work in their city. We are fearful and reserved, one of them lamented. "And besides we must bear in mind that in *some* of our *projects* we have been *rather* unfortunate."[25] And they could not all be blamed on the fire.

• • •

While Charleston was nearly broken on the wheel of adversity, Boston was only stretched. By comparison with the southern city, her calamities seemed minor. Early in 1839, fire swept through the North End, destroying homes and shops of mechanics up to the value of $80,000. The following winter a severe storm damaged many vessels in the harbor, and only weeks later the Boston-New York steam packet *Lexington* burned and sank off Long Island, with the loss of nearly all aboard. That same winter a smallpox epidemic claimed 175 lives.[26] Hideous though they were to their sufferers, these catastrophes were spread out over two years and had no cumulative or lasting impact on the city.

For both fire and epidemic, Boston was as well prepared as any American city. But like its contemporaries, the city contained large areas densely packed with wooden buildings. In such a North End enclave, fire hit on a bitter cold January night. High winds spread the flames. Below-zero temperatures froze the brakes on the hand-propelled engines and iced the hoses so heavily that at times only a small trickle of water could be coaxed from them. Then a sudden drop in the wind and the simultaneous positioning of the fire's forward edge on a street wide enough to be an effective firebreak ended the menace to the rest of the city.[27]

But fortuitous circumstance was not the city's only insurance. By 1839 its fire department was all under the discipline of a city engineer, its fire companies controlled by officers chosen in elections approved by city hall. No dedication to "voluntary or gratuitous" service had impeded the changes deemed necessary for the "security of the community." No fireman in any company was under twenty-one, albeit two-thirds were between twenty-one and thirty. Comprised largely of mechanics in the construction trades, the companies remained closely knit socioeconomic groups.[28] But the old competition among them had been ended by centralizing direction of fire fighting and requiring that the men link their engines and hoses to play the maximum stream.

Shocked though it was a year later by a smallpox epidemic in the age of vaccination, Boston's medical establishment also was sufficiently in place to require only a single special smallpox hospital to supplement extant facilities. Those who died and the kin who mourned them suffered as much as did the individuals similarly afflicted by Charleston's scarlet and yellow fever epidemics. But proportionately they were a smaller part of the city's total population. Like the five hundred men thrown out of work by the North End fire, their losses made little impact on the total economy.

The *Lexington* affair, however, was more like a Charleston disaster. As soon as the news trickled into the city one "could hardly get to the post office there was such a mob. . . ." The vessel, carrying at least seventy-five passengers, was also heavily laden with freight, its decks piled high with bales of raw cotton destined for Massachusetts mills. But despite its highly combustible cargo, the *Lexington* forced its boilers—designed for wood but stoked with coal—for the speediest run from New York to Providence, where Boston-bound passengers connected with the Boston and Providence Rail Road. Although it was a sound vessel, the *Lexington* was overworked to meet the demanding schedule its owners set to attract business from competing lines. No thought had been given to safety. When sparks set fire to the cotton, pandemonium ensued. Crew and officers failed at their posts. Lifeboats were launched before they were filled, and then badly launched. Few survived.[29]

Even though the loss of Boston citizens was not so great as Charleston's in the *Home* and the *Pulaski* disasters, the city was shocked. Activities were organized to raise funds for the needy families of victims. As in Charleston, a public meeting was called. Assembling in Faneuil Hall, it demanded federal legislation to insure steamboat safety. But with a temper different from Charleston's, the Boston meeting also sought to make expiation, to acknowledge a community as well as a corporate guilt. It probed those feelings "which connect the past with the present, the living with the dead." It pondered the cultural values which lay behind such disasters. Lawyer and orator George Hillard stressed his own and his auditor's responsibility for the *Lexington*'s fate. "We are," he said, "proverbially an impatient race. . . . Delay is intolerable to us, and the swiftest form of conveyance finds the most favor in our eyes. We are also proverbially a thrifty people, and we want to travel cheaply as well as rapidly." These were the traits to which the People's New Line had appealed in its advertisements "FARE REDUCED. NO MONOPOLY" on fast service.[30] And these were the traits which Bostonians were no more likely to change than were Charlestonians to surrender honor and volunteerism. In the end, then, catastrophes served less to change the cities than to demonstrate the values which shaped the less dramatic periods of their citizens' lives.

14

The Uses of Adversity

It was in meeting panic and depression after a euphoric boom that Boston most fully displayed her economic resilience, pragmatic diversity, and entrepreneurial drive. Although some of her citizens failed, and others experienced severe losses, and others were revealed in all their corruption, the city emerged from hard times largely unscathed. Indeed, by 1843 Boston was notably stronger than she had been when the 1837 panic struck. She lost none of her regional dominance. Her banks still controlled New England's credit and currency. Her Massachusetts hinterland remained the country's most industrialized state. Her radial railroad system tied her docks to inland mills. And, reflecting these strengths, Boston was not just a participant; she was a shaping force in the national economy.

Yet the very centrality of her position had made her more sensitive than Charleston to early premonitions of panic. By the spring of 1836 money was already short. Interest rates soared to 18 percent and ice merchant Frederic Tudor suspected that local banks "[had spread] too much sail to the breeze." Actuary Nathaniel Bowditch feared that even demands for as little as $4,000 in specie would "break more than one Bank." By November interest rates on short-term loans had shot up to 45 to 50 percent, at a time when money could still be had in Charleston for a mere 6 percent. The economy had been overstimulated by "enterprize in every direction[, u]ndertaking to do more work than there [were] hands to do it." So vastly inflated were prices, lamented woolens manufacturer Samuel Appleton, that "all the necessaries and Luxurys of Life [were] excessively high." His uncle William, who predicted in December 1836 that high prices would soon force a "reckoning day," saw his prediction fulfilled in March, when prices started to slip. And his forecast that a "man worth

The Uses of Adversity

One Hundred thousand dollars and [who] owes three will be fortunate if he pays his debts" took only a little longer in coming. Indeed, on May 2 the *Post* actually rejoiced that no business had failed the day before.[1]

Two weeks later the picture was still bleaker. "The violent pecuniary revulsion that has been anticipated for more than a year," merchant Amos Lawrence noted, "has at length overtaken this country, and is more severe than our worst fears." On May 11, following New York's lead, Boston banks, with but two exceptions, suspended specie payments. Their joint decision was sanctioned by a "large meeting of citizens," while the banks agreed among themselves to open their books for mutual inspection and thus check further emission of bank notes. While the bank actions resembled Charleston's, the mercantile response was far more extreme. For a while, so Harrison Gray Otis feared, even the "bone & gristle" of Boston's commerce—the Lymans, Lawrences, and Appletons—were in real danger.[2]

Suspension also engendered an anger considerably more vocal than anything in Charleston. Radical Locofoco Democrats met to protest the effects of suspension on workingmen. Filling a room in the old Supreme Court building with "yells and shouts," they protested the likelihood that wages would soon be paid in worthless paper money. Merchants and traders were no less indignant with federal requirements that postage and customs duties be paid in specie at a time when none was available. At various meetings, their fears icy cold and their tempers hot, they threatened to renege on their outstanding customs bonds and to seize their mail from the post office by force. "The mercantile community, and in fact the whole people, here," Boston's port collector warned President Van Buren, "are in a very excited state[.]"[3]

Overt violence was avoided by a partial federal retreat. Postmaster Nathaniel Greene decided to extend credit rather than demand specie or accept bank notes. District Attorney John Mills prolonged the time allowed merchants to redeem their customs bonds. Meanwhile Boston's traditional devices for maintaining a stable currency worked almost as well as they did in the best of times. Bank notes circulated at face value as the old Suffolk system was supplemented by the Association of Boston Banks, which had been organized to police the emission of paper during suspension. By fall, just as in Charleston, the crisis seemed to be over. In January 1838 Mayor Samuel A. Eliot congratulated his city on having escaped the "general distress" with which the panic had "convulsed" the rest of the nation.[4]

• • •

Nonetheless the panic exerted pressures that eroded trust and revealed practices which contemporaries took as evidence of widespread corruption.

Commenting on the municipal court's grand jury docket in the winter of 1841–1842, when one-seventh of the cases before it involved business fraud, conservative judge Peter Thacher came down hard on the "officers of banks and other monied corporations" who had been tempted. It was bad enough that a broker had embezzled from his clients and that a lawyer had defrauded his. But neither gained the public attention lavished on the teller who had embezzled $23,500 or the conspiracy between two bank clerks and two brokers to cheat and defraud two city banks of $72,000.[5]

Even those cases paled by comparison with the operation of the banks which failed through the malfeasance of their directors and officers. The doubtful practice of the Franklin and Lafayette banks was not confined to their steady emission of unbacked bank notes. Their managers had rifled the tills for private speculations. Within a three-year period Franklin's entire capital had been thus squandered, while it had acquired obligations for twice that amount. In so doing, "scarcely a provision of the charter" had not been "deliberately and repeatedly violated." When its president, Josiah Dunham, was questioned about these practices, he pleaded that his illiteracy had kept him in ignorance. If the father thereby escaped the toils of the law, the son did not. Josiah Jr., who was cashier of the Lafayette Bank (organized in 1836 in a move to manipulate the Franklin out of its troubles), was eventually convicted of perjury for the brash inaccuracy of his cashiers' reports to state officials.[6]

The failure of the Dunhams and their two small South Boston banks, however tawdry, had only a minor effect on the city. But the shock when the Commonwealth Bank closed its doors resembled an earthquake. It had been Boston's major depository for federal funds after President Jackson had ordered their removal from the Bank of the United States. (The Franklin had been a federal depository too.) It was directed so entirely by Democratic party stalwarts that the response to its failure was political as well as financial. Hall H. How, commissioner for building the new custom house; District Attorney John Mills; John Henshaw, a brother of the port collector; Samuel Lewis, the collector's brother-in-law and a United States debt commissioner; and Adams Bailey, deputy collector of customs, had all served on its board. Its president until his death in a carriage accident only weeks before the failure was John K. Simpson, the federal pension agent.[7]

Even so, the questions raised about the Commonwealth's management demanded a judgment on whether it had engaged in illegalities or had only been rather cavalierly dedicated to the interests of those who made its policy. There was no doubt that individual directors had been allowed unlimited overdrafts as well as generous loans. At his death president

Simpson owed his institution nearly $260,000. Altogether its directors owed the bank for loans equal to twice its half-million-dollar capital. The bank had also been generous in lending to the Warren Associates, whose land speculations in South Boston were risky at best and which had been allowed to borrow $250,000 without security. Moreover, the bank's accounts were so entangled with those of other institutions that knowledgeable men charged the Commonwealth with dragging down half a dozen other institutions in its wake.[8]

Democrats as well as Whigs politicized the aftermath. It would seem that 1838 could have been a Democratic year in Boston, since the Whigs were so divided over the fifteen-gallon law and the temperance issue that they ran two competing tickets. But the Democrats were also split. The city organization, long dominated by David Henshaw, represented an enthusiastically entrepreneurial group whose Jacksonianism had rested on the encouragement which opposition to old monopolies gave new men on the make. Tainted by the Commonwealth's failure, Henshaw was replaced as collector of the port by George Bancroft, paladin of rural and workingmen Democrats. On the one hand this was a move which Van Buren had been contemplating as part of building his Locofoco faction nationally; on the other, it opened the way for the rare Massachusetts election of a Democratic governor in 1839 and 1842. Although it did nothing to alter Whig dominance in Boston, it also did nothing to assuage Whigs, who viewed both the old Democratic leadership and the Commonwealth's directors as "cormorants and paupers, . . . mendicant adventurers who storm the political fortresses for the sake of plunder. . . ."[9]

Viewed more positively, the collapse of weak banks did strengthen the position of the survivors. Soon after the Commonwealth went down, merchant-politician Nathan Appleton concluded that city banks collectively had more specie on hand than they had had at any time since 1821 and that paper currency was so contracted that Boston banks could at once safely resume specie payments, expand currency, and extend credit. The pressure for resumption, however, was not so great as in Charleston—partly because the Suffolk Bank had put small notes into circulation to meet consumers' demands for a currency to carry on daily transactions. Boston could afford to wait for New York and Philadelphia to resume in order to insure that local banks' specie gains would not be siphoned southward.[10]

Some four or five banks, one of them a federal depository, did, however, break ranks and began paying out specie in April 1838, with no particular ill effects. Nonetheless, those tied to the Suffolk system waited until August, even though, in the spring, they expanded commercial loans to feed business recovery. By January 1839 there seemed no reason to challenge Mayor Samuel A. Eliot's inaugural observation that the city had weathered the "low point of depression" and was on the road back to prosperity.[11]

* * *

Then, on October 10, 1839, hardware dealer William Brooks wrote in his diary that the "whole commercial & business community have been thrown into excitement . . . by the failure of the U.S. Bank at Philadelphia & the suspension of Specie payments at that place." Thus did depression descend with full force. Yet Boston did not plummet into an abyss like that which swallowed Charleston's hopes for economic growth. Indeed, her power within the national economy expanded, as Nathan and William Appleton managed efforts to lend Philadelphia banks the funds needed to pay specie and, by extension, restore banking throughout the country. Nonetheless, banking per se was less central to the hard times of the early 1840s than it had been in the panic years. Now the whole economy was in trouble. Imports fell, manufactures were down, construction slowed, and business confidence was hard to restore. After short periods of seeming improvement, poorer months followed. Nothing was predictable. Entrepreneurs grasped at the ups and sighed with the downs in rents, international trade, real estate, and textile dividends. Yet collectively they were dealt no blow as severe as that which the collapse of the cotton market inflicted on Charleston. Nor, despite their chorus of jeremiads, did they fall into the unalleviated gloom which afflicted the southern city.[12]

Business leaders assessed their opportunities as well as their losses and hoped that driving prices down would help their trade and manufactures regain their erstwhile competitive advantage. It was with satisfaction that they watched food prices, thought to be very high in 1837, fall until in 1843 they were "cheap enough." Stockholders campaigned to extend the advantage which low cotton prices offered by driving down both operatives' wages and managers' salaries so that Massachusetts textile mills would be restored to their former profitability. By 1843 they had effected their "reform." That same year Abbott Lawrence, in business for over three decades, was cheered by prices as low as they had ever been. William Appleton agreed that it was so. The result, from their perspectives, was that things were "far better [in Boston] than [in] any other part of the Country. . . ."[13]

Less privileged citizens, however, questioned whether times were improving as wages were cut. The limited trade-union activity which remained late in the 1830s and into the 1840s was directed not at reducing hours but at reversing pay cuts. The first such activity was the May 1837 meeting of the journeymen caulkers and carpenters of Charlestown and

Boston, who denounced wage reductions made in response to the panic. In 1841 forty or more dockworkers rioted against using a horse-powered pulley system to replace manpower in unloading cargo; four stevedores were tried and convicted for their role in what had started as a quasi-Luddite demonstration but degenerated into "Cork" men fighting "North of Ireland" men. Significant of a more lasting organization were the Journeymen Bootmakers, whose association, formed in 1835, had tried to impose a union shop on shoemaking establishments. Brought into Judge Thacher's court in 1840 by an irate fellow worker claiming he had been denied employment as a result, six association members were convicted of conspiracy for attempting to gain a minimum wage through collective action.[14] Overall, however, labor protest was minimal. Workers accepted cuts rather than risk losing their jobs. In the long run, the deflation to which they thus contributed probably did improve Boston's commercial advantage. Unquestionably, in the short run continued production at reduced wages rather than massive and persistent unemployment characterized their lot.

Nonetheless, unemployment did increase markedly, and those who had been discharged were little cheered by any propitious omens their plight might generate. Concerned for survival, many of them were reduced to seeking charity. As usual, women and children received most attention. The Children's Aid Society made special exertions to provide clothing for offspring of the "necessitous poor." The Widows' Society, its annual budget increased by special donations from Theodore Lyman until he died in 1839, helped more than one hundred women in 1837 and 1838. Attending to a broader clientele, the Massachusetts Congregational Charitable Society, the Young Men's Benevolent Society, and the Roman Catholic Mutual Relief Society all increased aid to the destitute. But many agencies found their efforts curtailed rather than expanded as charitable contributions declined. The Children's Aid Society saw subscriptions of life members diminish by 50 percent in 1837. The same year the Seaman's Aid Society experienced a shattering 90 percent cut in revenues. In 1841 the Howard Benevolent Association, precursor to the Red Cross, also suffered a major cut.[15]

Some philanthropists' assumptions were challenged by the surge in joblessness. Charles Barnard, city missionary of the Warren Street Chapel, questioned the conventional wisdom that the unemployed were the authors of their own misery. Their poverty stemmed, he believed, from lacking the physical resources "to pass unharmed through a period of pecuniary inaction and distress." The rise in young men's lawlessness and older citizens' pauperism was but "proof . . . that certain classes of our fellow citizens are not prepared for the changes to which a community like this will long be exposed. Neither their circumstances nor their principles warrant the expectation, that they will pass through seasons of vicissitude and trial with unimpaired innocence or increased virtue. . . ."[16]

Yet what was to be done with them? It was not until 1842 that physician Walter Channing pressed formation of the Boston Employment Society. And even that group was less concerned with finding jobs for the unemployed than keeping out-of-town job-seekers from inundating the city and adding to its jobless. So the society urged most of its registrants to return to the farms and villages whence they came. During the very worst of the depression, in the winter of 1842–1843, the society found employment for but 222 of its more than 1,200 applicants, while it convinced 343 to go "home."[17] The rest probably were left to the newly organized Soup and Bread Society, which for that one winter fed the poor with no questions asked.

Nor was the city's government notably more responsive. Even in the worst years of the depression, during the early 1840s, the House of Industry received no greater proportion of the city budget than it had during the slump of 1828–1831. Indeed, when the panic first broke in 1837, Mayor Eliot set the city's official attitude: "[T]hough, doubtless, many of the laboring classes are abridged of their comforts, in consequence of the want of constant employment, yet it is satisfactory to observe that the necessity of entire support, at the public expense, is not greatly extended." The city, however, was obliged to support 13 percent more paupers in 1843 than it had when Mayor Eliot made his observation—though it was done with little increase in costs.[18]

• • •

Panic and depression did, of course, have political repercussions, as taxpayers pressed to reduce the costs of city government. Yet their results were far more limited than the governmental change which depression induced in Charleston. On the one hand, the public purse had played a much smaller role in assisting private economic development. And on the other, Boston's resources were sufficiently ample to limit cuts to paring down projected improvements rather than curtailing the powers and responsibilities of city government. Thus although the city council debated eliminating the tax on personalty and equalizing real property assessments, it ended up increasing the tax rate to keep total revenues stable, going up from a rate of fifty cents on $100 assessed valuation in 1837 to sixty-two cents in 1843.[19]

The two major alterations which a new budget consciousness imposed were a systematic program for amortizing the city's long-term debt and the surrender of grandiose plans for a new city hall. When, in the 1820s,

Mayor Quincy had undertaken to modernize Boston, the city began acquiring a permanent and highly visible debt. Reduced somewhat in the early 1830s, it increased again as prosperity fed the public's willingness to build schools, improve streets, and add to city institutions. It was only after the onset of depression that the council finally mended the slipshod budgetary practices which increased the debt first by regularly using short-term loans to eke out cost overruns and other deficiencies in the annual budget and then by extending them indefinitely. By adopting new appropriation procedures and funding the entire debt through city bonds, the council committed itself in 1840 to a systematic reduction of the debt by regular annual repayments. Within five years the debt was cut 30 percent. Yet even in 1841 Boston's per capita debt burden had been light, a mere $19 compared to New York's $31, Charleston's $39, and Baltimore's $46.[20]

Much more visible than the new budgeting devices was the decision not to build a new city hall. Yet mayor and council did not remain in their crowded meeting rooms and offices in the Old State House and Faneuil Hall, nor did the city's administrative offices remain scattered, almost at random, in surrounding buildings. While the realities of 1840 demanded that constructing the long-planned new city hall at a cost of $300,000 be abandoned, they did not preclude remodeling the old Court House for $20,000. However much the council's decision to do so may have cut off future aspirations for a more suitable structure, it did garner a "convenient" headquarters from which to carry on the city's business. And with the exception of delaying the water works still longer, it left the rest of the city's regular building program much as it had been. A new municipal hospital for the insane was opened in 1839; the next year work began on a general city hospital.[21] In addition, one or two new school buildings opened each year. Prudent trimming rather than drastic surgery was the sum of hard times' impact on city government.

If governmental changes were minimal, so were political ones. Although Democrat Marcus Morton carried the state in 1839, in 1840 the governorship and control of the state house returned to the Whigs as the national election swept the Jacksonians out of the White House. Bostonians formed a Harrison Club, most improbably built a log cabin on Charles Street, dispensed hard cider to a party which the previous year had been split over temperance, and staged vast parades and rallies that attracted as many as 50,000 marchers. For a while election violence threatened, as Whig attacks on Democratic parades and mutual vandalism of opposing clubhouses led to threats of retaliatory riots. Common sense, however, prevailed, and the vote went off calmly, though not without the largest Boston turnout for a national election since the old Federalist-Jeffersonian contests. So solidly Whig did Boston go that in December their men won back three of the five wards the Democrats had carried the year before. Well-connected William Brooks congratulated himself that "10 of the 12 wards in the city are [now] Whig." "[T]his is," he added, "all as it should be."[22]

Democrats had failed to make the most of labor's discontents and an endorsement by the virtually extinct Workingmen's party. Whigs had played hard on Jacksonian responsibility for panic and depression. Yet the November election results were also shaped by the fact that, although 80 percent of Boston's eligible voters went to the polls, that 80 percent was but 45 percent of all Boston males over twenty-one.[23] But no less important in understanding the election was the fact that Boston's politics were defined once again in national terms—that it had been a contest between two unified parties, the Whigs and the Democrats. Moreover, the members of each were part of a national political network, as few Charlestonians were.

Democrats, it was true, triumphed in national elections more frequently than did Whigs, and Boston's political strength lay in being the Whig bastion of a predominantly Whig state. Even the 1840 reapportionment of legislative seats, which reduced the city's representation in the general court from fifty-six to thirty-five, did not threaten that political strength, for on critical issues economic power lay behind and reinforced it.[24] Additionally, Boston's city government remained in the hands of men who shared a commercial as well as a Whiggish point of view. After the panic as before, a majority of each chamber of the city council engaged in trade. Significant numbers wielded economic power, though they were fewer than in the boom years. Between 1837 and 1843 one-half of the mayors and aldermen and one-quarter of the common councilmen sat on boards of corporate directors. So although after 1837 common councilmen were somewhat less likely to be wealthy or upper class, somewhat more likely to be mechanics, and somewhat less likely to be professional men, they retained a consensus which rested on commercial interests and values.[25]

• • •

While it would be tempting to attribute councilmen's decline in wealth to a decline in Boston's collective or per capita wealth, it would also be misleading. Yet it was true that from 1837 onward, "ruin & Bankruptcy stare[d] merchants in the face in all directions." Small traders went down quietly, and even wholesalers might fail almost unnoticed. In the first month of the 1837 panic, at least fifty or sixty Bostonians failed. But the issue was not publicly dramatized until May, when Israel Thorndike, Jr.'s, world collapsed around him. Though he believed himself to be worth over a million dollars, he simply could not pay his debts. Without the protection of a comprehensive bankruptcy law, whose enactment Boston merchants had sought unsuccessfully for years, he lost everything except the income from a paltry $20,000 provided in his father's will for any of his children who might succumb to indigence. But thereafter and until the Commonwealth Bank collapsed, failures declined. Then, in January 1838, merchant George Pratt introduced a new and more extensive run of bankruptcies when he lost his entire fortune of about $1.3 million in the city's largest failure. Other wealthy men avoided his "terrible mortification" only by cutting back to the bone. Merchant Henry Lee's family was so hard pressed in 1837 that Henry, Jr., had to give up his militia company activity, and the family remained with its back to the wall until Henry, Sr., turned over his business to Henry, Jr., in 1841. Patrick Tracy Jackson, leading textile and railroad entrepreneur, was stripped of so much of his fortune that he had to sell his Boston mansion for $30,000 and move out of town.[26]

While the decline and fall of titans got the limelight, petitions filed under the bankruptcy law Massachusetts passed in 1839 laid bare the pervasive and widespread pattern of smaller failures. Of the more than 250 who went through proceedings in 1841 and 1842, one half were engaged in commerce of some kind, and one-seventh were self-proclaimed merchants. Only one-quarter of the bankrupts were mechanics, and a mere 2 percent professionals. Then in 1842, when the new federal bankruptcy law went into effect, the numbers soared. One hundred petitions were filed in Boston federal district court the day after the law took effect, and a thousand poured in during the first month.[27] Although many were doubtless not Bostonians, many were; and local newspaper readers could not ignore the failure stories any more than businessmen could overlook the number of commercial men who had been struck down. And even if no Boston banks failed after 1840, the ten which had closed their doors in the previous three years boded ill when fraud and embezzlement proceedings raised questions about how other banks were being run. When Bradlees and Lowells were tainted by "disgraceful" expositions of wrongdoing, it is little wonder that anxiety made many possessors of small capital unsure of their future.[28]

Yet for all that, most Bostonians of property—be it small or large—fared well or, at the least, did not decline in the depression years. Overall property assessments increased by 23 percent (or 4 percent per annum) during those years, after having increased at 6 percent per year in the early 1830s. The rate at which individuals' property increased slowed down, but it was still more likely to increase or stay the same than to decrease. Even merchants were about as likely to increase as to decrease their total worth in five panic and depression years as they had been in the previous six boom years, although probably very few were as shrewd as Amos

Lawrence in advising his son of the uses of adversity: "If any considerable fall should produce failures, *then* is the time for new beginners to start with safety, as the *fashion* would be to *look sharp,* before they leap." Doubtless even fewer did as well as Amory Appleton, who realized an estate of $116,000 from "his own earnings" after only six years in business.[29]

There is thus little in Boston's experience to justify the contention that the panic and depression momentarily reversed the national movement toward economic inequality. On the other hand, the evidence is not convincing either that it was the depression and panic which entrenched the wealthy or that initial wealth was the most powerful determinant of increasing riches in those same years. Of the forty richest Bostonians in 1837—all of whom had over $100,000 assessed property at some time between 1833 and 1842—only 48 percent increased their wealth between 1838 and 1843, while 33 percent declined and 18 percent moved, died, or dropped completely from the ranks of the propertied. The picture thus presented is not especially remarkable, for at every level of initial wealth Bostonians were more likely to increase than decrease their property holdings. It is true that the rich were less likely to have disappeared altogether from published tax records than their less affluent neighbors. But beyond that, they shared the insecurities and the opportunities of hard times in much the same proportions as other propertied Bostonians.[30] The traumas of Thorndike, Jackson, and Pratt were as real as, if less representative than, Peter Chardon Brooks's virtual oblivion to the panic. Boston's very rich did not, it is true, live like her humbler citizens, but they did live in the same economic world. They were set apart more by how much they possessed than by the direction in which that wealth moved. That they were more likely to prosper than decline—even in hard times—was a trait they shared with other propertied Bostonians in about equal portions.

• • •

Behind individual prosperity lay Boston's economic resources, not least of which was the transportation system which tied it to national and international trade. The railroads built before the panic carried increasingly heavy traffic and reaped satisfying profits. In 1839 the Boston and Lowell's annual dividend rose to 8 percent, where it stayed throughout the 1840s. Boston and Worcester dividends never fell below 6 percent, and the company could sell new stock at or above par even in the worst depression years. Although it declined somewhat from its peak, the Boston and Providence also maintained a steady 6 percent in the early 1840s. So reliable did railroad profits seem that in 1838 Massachusetts, for the first time, allowed insurance companies to put their capital in railroad stock. Thereafter the companies invested $54,000 in 1838, doubled that amount by 1840, and quadrupled it two years later.[31]

Under such propitious circumstances, the depression saw a steady extension of New England's transportation network. The Boston and Worcester completed its double tracking in 1843. The Eastern, which had reached only to Salem in 1838, connected with Portsmouth, New Hampshire, two years later. Also stretching northeast, the Boston and Portland connected Lowell with the Maine border in 1841 and, joining its fate then and there with the financially troubled Boston and Maine, began pressing still farther into northern New England.[32]

Boston's second round of railroad building, however, resembled Charleston's ventures more than had the first. Only a Massachusetts state loan steadied the Boston and Maine. The Western Rail Road's goal of connecting New England with the Ohio and Mississippi valleys resembled the Louisville, Cincinnati, and Charleston project—as did the argument that by reaching the Hudson River it would drain New York's commerce by diverting cargoes from cheap water to costly land transportation. Nonetheless, its immediate goal of crossing the Berkshire and Taconic ranges to link Boston and Albany was accomplished—though with state aid more extensive than any other Massachusetts railroad had received.

But that recourse to the public purse was not solely a reaction to panic and depression. At an 1835 public meeting in Faneuil Hall, called to forward the Western line, merchant-politician Abbott Lawrence had argued that the road would "double and quadruple the whole business of the city" by connecting Boston with the Mississippi. Originally fixing its capital at $2 million, the legislature within a year increased its capitalization by 50 percent and committed the state to buy $1 million of its stock. But the willingness to depart from previous state policy—so reminiscent of the South Carolina experience—sprang rather from Springfield's insistence on having a railroad than from Boston's desire to compete with New York. For similar reasons, Massachusetts continued to subsidize the railroad's construction throughout the depression years. In 1837 the general court voted it a state-backed loan of more than $2 million, with Baring Brothers floating state bonds to fund the loan at the same time that these English bankers were peddling South Carolina bonds to fund the Cincinnati and Charleston project. Two years later the Western was back at the State House for another loan of $1.2 million, which it soon supplemented by the additional $1 million it borrowed from Albany. Only after still another Massachusetts loan for $700,000 in 1841 was the Western finally completed, at a cost of $9 million, two-thirds of which public funds had furnished.[33]

In the enthusiasm of completing so massive an internal improvement, the limited stimulus it would bring to Boston's commercial growth was obscured. On an acre and a quarter in South Cove the company was already building a huge merchandise depot, allegedly the "largest building in the world under one roof, without pillars or partition walls"—if one excepted a single Russian building. Also in 1841, the year the line was completed, a delegation, including Mayor Jonathan Chapman, Western Rail Road treasurer Josiah Quincy, Jr., and editor Nathan Hale, traveled to Albany to celebrate the event. Sanguine of the road's future, Mayor Chapman toasted its anticipated results: "This union of interests and enterprise is destined to accomplish far more for the prosperity of both cities than any of us can now anticipate."[34]

But it was rather the reverse—at least for Boston. No amount of oratory could veil the reality that the road could not both make profits and set rates low enough for Boston to compete with New York. Yankees insisted that privately incorporated railroads be judged by their ability to make profits for their investors. Most of the Bostonians who had made sizable initial investments in the Western had long since sold out their holdings, convinced that its enormous debt made it a poor investment. Springfield men, whose interests were realized by securing a direct connection to Boston on which to ship their own products and who comprised a near majority on the board of directors, were unwilling to set rail rates low enough to compete with cheap Hudson River shipping rates. And only that would have given Boston her sought-after advantage over New York in attracting the western trade which flowed across the Erie Canal and down the river. In short, geographical realities limited Boston's commerce as they did Charleston's. But they were also far less constricting.

So it was that although Boston's trade did not overtake New York City's, it did improve. Fed not only by radial railroads but by a steadily developing coastal trade in which she surpassed Philadelphia to become America's second port, Boston maintained a fleet of locally built and owned vessels which dominated coastal shipping. Almost equally healthy was her foreign commerce. Though her exports had peaked in 1832 and her imports in 1836, her export trade at least remained steady through 1843 at notably higher levels than it had been prior to 1832, and her import trade held its own.[36]

But the coup which made Boston the envy of New York was attracting Mr. Cunard's steam packets. With assistance from the city council and encouragement from local merchants, the East Boston Company undertook to "provide suitable conveniences for the accommodation" of the new line, which was subsidized by the British government. By a rare and successful packaging of private and public incentives, the Cunard line was lured to a brand new and rent-free 1,200-foot pier and adjacent freight docks on the harbor side of Noddles Island. Not surprisingly, when the first packet, the *Unicorn,* arrived in June 1840, the city tendered a "most elegant dinner" to 450 guests. There merchants joined politicians in lauding Boston's achievement of Charleston's dream, realizing "the last link in the chain that is to unite the head waters of the Missouri with the remotest Marts of the ancient world."[37]

It was, however, less the joining of "the new line of steam packets" with "the great western railroad" than the fast access to European commercial news which advantaged Boston. The Cunard's biweekly service tied Boston to England and the continent more closely even than New York was linked. Building on that base, Boston by 1842 had overnight mail and express service to New York and a twenty-four hour connection to Philadelphia, while Washington could be reached in less than two days. The carriers and agencies of William Harnden's express service, both foreign and domestic, so expedited communication that Boston merchants could write orders in their shops on June 1 for goods from the English Midlands and have them on sale exactly two months later—the time it would normally take an order from Charleston just to reach the Midlands.[38]

With so many advantages, Boston showed signs of economic recovery long before Charleston. Despite the vicissitudes of various real estate ventures after 1837, sales were greater in 1842 than they had been even at the 1836 high point of speculation. Insurance companies had grown steadily since 1838, with only three of the nineteen companies doing business in both years showing fewer resources in 1842 than in 1838. Thomas Perkins estimated that the city's twenty-four insurance companies in 1841 had an aggregate capital of $6 or $7 million. Another analyst believed that in 1842 their capital provided $3.5 million to Massachusetts banks, $200,000 to railroads, $1 million for mortgages, and another $1 million for other kinds of loans.[39]

Although insurance companies had invested only $50,000 in manufacturing by 1842, Boston's artisanal production held its own between 1837 and 1845. Not all ventures, of course, grew. Some, like brass and copper founding, chain making, silversmithing, and typecasting appeared to decline. On the other hand, tinsmithing, machinery fabrication, and flint glass production showed solid growth. And in piano making Boston could "safely defy the whole world." Jonas Chickering alone built 853 more instruments in 1845 than he had in 1837, an 83 percent increase. Thus, though still primarily a commercial city, Boston had already risen to third place nationally in per capita manufacturing—well behind Philadelphia but only slightly behind New York. Moreover, her commerce was stoked by the steadily increasing textile factories in her hinterland, whose finished products Boston sold at prices low enough to compete with British goods.[40]

Well might Boston celebrate her economic recovery in 1843. Physically the city was growing again. "[H]undreds of houses, were built last year and as many will go up this year." The new stock exchange on State Street would soon modernize stock trading. Specie was again plentiful, and a man could easily borrow whatever he needed for a reasonable 4 or 5 percent. "Our Imports [are] quite great,—large enough.—Manufactories [are] flourishing." "Railways . . . are before the wind." "We seem to be doing well," Peter Chardon Brooks reflected in his seventy-sixth year. "Boston is in good heart."[41]

PART VI · CONCLUSION

15

The Web Spun

As a Yankee visitor, having descended St. Michael's tower and completed his tour of Charleston, might, in 1828, have sat on his host's south-facing piazza to discuss the city's future while they both enjoyed a late afternoon breeze; so a southern guest, warmed by a hearth fire in Harrison Gray Otis's small study, might have mulled over with his host the portents for Boston's future. Either conversation would likely have touched on the forces which shaped urban life, making some cities flourish, dooming others.

The most obvious determinants were those of place—a city's physical resources and liabilities. The depth and size of her harbor, her proximity to winds and ocean currents as well as to other ports were all vital to trade. Climate, the fertility of her region's soil, and, more recently, her access to water power determined her products. Nature, not men, set these bounds and provided these opportunities for commerce as it did for the agriculture and manufacture on which that commerce depended.

But cities were not inert pawns of place; their courses were also shaped by the "times"—the regional, national, even international dynamics of economics and politics. The new technology of steam power, a force to revolutionize both transportation and manufacturing, gave to urban America of the 1830s a vigorous forward thrust. So, too, Jacksonian politics reshaped the uses to which government, partisan organizations, and private corporations might be put.

Finally, cultural factors—some as pervasive as the times, others as distinctive as place—mediated how two unique places would respond to the times both shared, how their peoples would mold their own futures. The skills, the education, the attitudes, the past experiences, the values which each city's inhabitants shared not only defined their community as it was but set the boundaries for what that community might become. Rooted in the past, some cultural factors had within them the potential for change. Others precluded it. Yet no matter whether cities attempted to fend off new pressures, or to adapt to them, or to take hold of them and drive ahead, each had to retain enough of the old to provide continuity and community cohesion.

The interaction of the resources of place, the dynamic of the times, and the rigidity or flexibility of cultural prescriptions set the bounds and opened the vistas of each city's future. How each dreamed her dreams and framed her goals, developed her resources and responded to external pressures, chose who would make the choices and who would be served by them determined the style—and the future—of each city.

Had the same guests and hosts resumed their conversations in 1843 they would have seen the two cities' different urban styles more clearly. By then both Boston and Charleston had experienced the dynamics of the 1830s in the economics of boom and bust and the politics of bank and tariff. They had both responded positively to the transportation revolution in order to retain and enlarge their roles as port cities. But the suitability of Carolina's climate and soil for cotton culture in an era of soaring demand for raw cotton shaped a resistance to manufacturing, which New England's hardscrabble soil made it readier to embrace. And if the unchangeable endowments of Massachusetts included long, harsh winters, they also provided Boston a deeper and larger harbor than Charleston's shallow channel and small basin. In addition, however hazardous Massachusetts Bay's hidden reefs and fog-shrouded islets, large vessels could navigate them more readily than they could cross the growing, shifting sandbar in Charleston harbor.

Yet it was their pasts, their economic heritages, their social systems, their patterns for acceptable behavior which finally defined how each city met internal obstacles and responded to external challenge, how each framed and achieved her goals. Prevailing practice determined how rapidly urban institutions and individual attitudes could be changed without endangering the cultural values on which the survival of the city was thought to depend.

• • •

Boston's chief economic resource in 1843, as it had been in 1828 or 1780, was her people—their skills, their talents, their commitment to work. But a slave labor force and its attendant culture denied Charleston the same

The Web Spun

rich endowment. In the southern city differing priorities restricted social investment in developing the skills of all workers. There, a different system of financial rewards and a different measure of social status fostered attitudes at odds with the work ethic. There, men on the make found fewer incentives to invest their lives in urban pursuits, whether mechanic or mercantile. There the work force grew but slowly, if it grew at all, in the 1830s.

Boston not only was more given to work, she attracted more people to do it. That a great many people moved out of Boston as well as in did not much matter, for between 1830 and 1840 her population grew by at least 38 percent, while Charleston's increased by a bare 2 percent.[1] Moreover, the population which Boston retained stimulated her economy. Her businessmen, her professionals, and her master mechanics were more likely to stay put than were Charleston's, although they were no more tied to the city by church or club affiliation or participation in civic affairs than were their southern counterparts.[2]

If it was the opportunity to work and to thrive economically which held Bostonians in town, Charleston apparently offered less opportunity. She lost residents as fast as she gained them. And the work force she retained was used less productively than Boston's. Forty-four percent of the city's labor force and one-quarter of her working males were engaged in domestic labor—an activity which employed only 15 percent of all Boston workers and only 2 percent of male workers. Moreover, it was only in the commercial preparation of food and the making and selling of clothing that Charleston employed roughly the same proportion of workers as did Boston. In construction, in the furniture business, in machine fabrication, Boston employed proportionately from two to seven times as many artisans and salesmen as did the southern city. Such statistics were but grist for Boston's famed census taker Lemuel Shattuck, who summed up their meaning for both city and hinterland. Boston in 1845 was "the central point" because there "great plans [had] been devised for bringing into profitable use, within their own territory, the industry and skill . . . of the New-England people."[3]

Given the nation's growing population, it is less Boston's growth than Charleston's stasis which demands explanation. Center of a declining agricultural region, Charleston was throttled by her hinterland. Not only did she fail to attract a mobile rural population into the city—she could not keep her own people from joining the Carolina migration to the rich new cotton land of Georgia and Alabama. It was not because European immigrants rejected Charleston that her population lagged, for Charleston's foreign-born population was proportionately as great as Boston's in the late 1840s. Rather it was her failure to attract and hold rural-born Americans, a group only half as large a part of Charleston's population as Boston's was of hers.[4]

Effective in utilizing her labor force, Boston was also wonderfully adept in using her capital, both within the city and in the hinterland, to develop the industry and railroads which increased her own prosperity. Here too the northern and the southern cities differed markedly. While there is no conclusive evidence that slavery directly impeded southern investment in manufacturing and railroads, there is much to demonstrate that it was slave labor which made planting the preferred investment even when soil wore out and prices dropped. Nonetheless, some contemporaries did prod Charlestonians to invest and Carolinians to employ their state's excess labor and up-country water power in operating the textile mills which would maximize returns on their most abundant raw material and stem the outpouring of population.[5]

William Gregg puzzled the matter throughout the 1840s as he tried to convince his fellow Charlestonians to establish steam-powered mills in the city and country folk to build mills along the fall line.[6] But neither his articles nor the example of his Graniteville mill altered their reluctance. Planting, even when it meant migration, was preferable to all other occupations. Persistent popular suspicion of corporations was reinforced by the railroads, which produced small irregular dividends, divided planter-shippers from urban investors, and stimulated Charleston's staples trade only minimally. Not that Carolinians disdained economic gain; but their experience of the 1830s cotton boom reinforced their traditional preference for agricultural ventures and their long-term loyalty to agrarian values. Even the entrepreneurial vanguard was ambivalent. James Hamilton and Robert Hayne both had heavy commitments in plantations remote from Charleston's orbit.

There was little such ambivalence in Boston, in part because neither agrarian values nor agricultural profits competed with urban commercial success for respectability or returns. Ambitious Yankees had since the eighteenth century honed the managerial skills suited to the early needs of the industrial revolution. Therefore, when new opportunities offered they had both the liquid capital and the ability to dovetail investments and integrate production which together produced safe and steady returns from railroads and manufacturing. Early success reinforced the process championed by the likes of William Appleton, who in 1841 alone was involved in a railroad company, a wharf company, and at least ten textile companies while he also traded actively in Manila, Calcutta, and Canton goods and played a critical role in stabilizing banking and currency nationwide.[7]

Both her diverse experience in using human and capital resources and her ability to respond to and amend tradition appropriately to changing times gave Boston her distinct advantage in the 1830s. Although she never caught up with New York—the port city against which all others measured themselves—in trade or population, she did recoup her losses of the 1820s as Charleston did not. And although in the 1850s she lost much of her textile trade as well as the Cunard packet line to New York and invested enough capital in western railroads to curtail development at home, she nevertheless made the innovations in the 1830s which shaped much of subsequent American industrialization and railroading.

Just as for a while each Boston achievement seemed to enhance her assets, each Charleston failure seemed to multiply her handicaps. Even building the longest railroad in the world produced little effect. If the thin 136-mile ribbon of single track was in 1834 the subject of local pride, it did not become a model for imitation. In freights, passengers, and profits it compared poorly with the network of short lines which made Boston a hub. "What then must be the fate of the thousand schemes that have no . . . support," asked a disheartened Charlestonian as he viewed "roads which . . . [ran] into uninhabited wilderness in the absurd and chimerical expectation that they would create commerce and build New Yorks in a day?"[8]

* * *

Behind all the calculations and statistics, the counting of bales and the totaling of horsepower, the assessment of resources and the evaluation of experience lay critical differences in values. Share the same plans for urban growth they might. But the business ethic which shaped Boston's dedication to achieving that growth was central to her entire culture, while it was only peripheral in Charleston. Yet if Southrons disdained Yankees' shrewd, sharp proclivity to calculate closely, they also rued their own fantasts' chimeras which came to naught, like that "magnificent dream" of a Louisville, Cincinnati, and Charleston railroad, which ended as a "pinewoods avenue from Branchville to Columbia."[9]

The business ethic was not necessarily crass—a subject for embarrassment, a commitment to something less than honorable. Indeed, among its Yankee practitioners it was a matter of pride. When young Unitarian minister Ezra Stiles Gannett questioned its inherent Christianity, merchant-congressman Nathan Appleton upheld that ethic as the very hallmark of progress. "That every individual shall be entitled to the benefit of his own acquisitions[,] the fruit of his own labour is the fundamental principle of civilization and of course of morals. [T]ake this away & you reduce man to the savage state." It was not that business gain was justified only as an instrument for supporting "objects of public utility, of charity and even of religion." It was that there was "no purer morality" than that of "the counting room."[10]

If the planters' code of honor dominated the value system of a society in which relatively few were planters, so the business ethic merged with the work ethic as the central precept taught Boston youth. Experienced fathers in private letters exhorted their sons to prudence and persistent exertion; success manuals gave the same message to aspiring but less privileged youth. Preachers broadcast similar advice from the pulpit, as did lecturers from the podium. Schoolbooks, teachers, and school awards put it at the core of public education. The difference was not that Charlestonians ignored the need for business probity, any more than that they questioned economic gain. Rather it lay in their disinclination to discuss the positive aspects of either at any length and their inherent suspicion that business practices ignored gentlemanly honor more than they should. Sermons inveighed against mercantile preoccupation with profits and the "device[s] of accumulation," going so far as to chastise those who abandoned useful businesses only because they were unprofitable. Letters among family and friends advised tempering the collection of just debts with consideration for its potentially "ruinous" consequences on the debtors and their kin.[11] City ordinances setting the price of bread reflected local commitment to fair value over market value. In Boston a merchant was assumed to be a gentleman unless there was evidence to the contrary. In Charleston the press exhorted businessmen to act like gentlemen, while private discourse talked of gentlemen who engaged in business. That was why the Middletons, gentlemen and planters somewhat engaged in business, found James Adger's attempts to buy the family wharf so trying. Adger, a canny Scots-Irish merchant, made his bid in the depression year of 1842. The family, eager for cash but indignant at being haggled with, refused Adger's bid, and Ralph Izard wrote his brother Nathaniel that he even "despise[d] talking to the fellow," whom he considered "a regular sneak."[12]

How very different were the values of Mayor Theodore Lyman, whose social rank as a wealthy member of a distinguished Boston family was no less than the Middletons' in Charleston. Yet this gentleman of property and standing praised his city for its "habits of remarkable enterprise and industry" and its people, who were "as much distinguished for the love of occupation as for success in their undertakings." Younger and less established, Charles Paine bore disgruntled testimony to the pervasiveness of Lyman's standards. "[I]t is easily sketched—the romance, the chivalry, the sentiment of our times—& they may be described as follows, to wit, early rising, prudence, economy, perseverance, diligence, good business habits, & the like. . . ."[13]

Paine resented the sentiments which "doomed" him to the "beaten dusty, turnpike road" of business—but gave in to them from necessity. Nor could wealth free Nathan Appleton's son Thomas from the constraints of his hometown values. He could not live as a "painter or poet" in Boston, where artists were scorned and "mercantile success" venerated.[14] Yet Charleston's conscious cultivation of gentlemanly leisure encouraged bank president John Cogdell's dedication to sculpting and lawyer Charles Fraser's to painting. Business there was instrumental, a means to something else, whether it was planting or the talented amateurism which adorned Charleston's intellectual life.

On the other hand, neither Charlestonians' instrumental understanding of business nor their dedication to a different honor furthered entrepreneurial ventures. Tristram Tupper, local businessman and former railroad president, warned against their proclivity to subordinate all other economic activity to agriculture. A company could not thrive, he warned, if it sacrificed profits to agrarian values. Specifically, railroads could not place low-cost service to planters ahead of shareholders' dividends and expect to flourish. What was commonplace in Boston would be a "radical change" in Charleston—or so Tupper described it in his 1843 assertion that directors' first responsibility was to "render [their corporations] profitable."[15]

Contrasting values also molded different relationships between government and business, politics and economics. After twenty years of ministering to Charleston's Unitarian congregation, Boston-born Samuel Gilman was still uneasy with parishioners who made politics "the scale of merit and excellence" which snared the community's most "talented and promising young men" from "the other prizes and functions of life." It was this exaltation of public service above all else which made political involvement in every community activity appropriate. Accordingly, government not only assisted economic development through private corporations as it did not in Boston; it subjected the process to "vehement, eager, passionate, and absorbing" politics.[16]

It is true that Otises, Lawrences, and Appletons had once toyed with the idea of state-owned railroads and contemplated public investment in private transportation companies. It is also true that Massachusetts lent its resources to lines otherwise unable to complete construction in the panic and depression years. Nonetheless, Boston's politics remained subservient to economics—in railroads as in tariffs and banks. Although she valued public service, supported philanthropy, sponsored cultural institutions, maintained churches, and cherished family, the City on a Hill judged her public successes and failures in terms economic.

. . .

If the age of Jackson was exciting, it was also frightening. To planter-postmaster Alfred Huger, abolitionism threatened nothing less than the loosing of servile insurrection. To Judge Peter Thacher, trade unionism, ethnic riot, and the unrestrained behavior of the lower classes were no less ominous. Those with property, power, or position at stake eyed disregard for established authority uneasily, whether it came from rebellious children, undisciplined immigrants, roistering sailors, or defiant blacks. And much as they revered their revolutionary heritage, they feared social upheaval. Yet Boston displayed flexibility in rationalizing her institutions to meet new challenges. The city was able to rein in the anarchy of volunteer fire companies, the mutiny of militia units, the nativism which used arson and violence, and the politics of protest. There the traditional community network of personalized relationships was modernized within an increasingly institutional system in which citizens were paid to perform public service, in which efficient completion of a municipal task counted for more than the human satisfaction in performing it.

Underlying that flexibility, that ability to rationalize and institutionalize, was a social contract premised on a widely shared belief that mobility up the ladder of the middling ranks was not just possible but likely. Believing that, as individuals, they could improve their lot by their own efforts, middle-interest Bostonians were optimistic about change. The many who had come to the city from the country had consciously linked their own future to that of the metropolis. Change which promised security or prosperity for the one was perceived as progress for the other. And the public schools, which instilled this faith and prepared the young for their economic and political roles, were controlled by elected neighborhood officials and endorsed by workingmen's organizations. If it was a device by those in power to co-opt, it was also a mechanism of those who were willing—even eager—to be co-opted.

Less easily and readily, however, could Charleston address her unease, for the dynamic change implicit in the times menaced the stablility of a society evenly divided between slave and free, a society held together by an intricate network of personal and political bonds. In Charleston community commitment to individual mobility through hard work or individual effort could only erode the barrier between slavery and freedom. There the need to perpetuate the prevailing social and institutional arrangements was paramount. It was this tension, this "want of repose" which Harriet

The Web Spun

Martineau believed made Charleston distinctive. A city alternately "restlessly gay or restlessly sorrowful, . . . angry or exulting, . . . hopeful or apprehensive," it was never calm, content, or satisfied. It was, in short, a "society . . . composed of two classes, which entertain[ed] a mortal dread of each other."[17]

Seldom discussed openly by Charlestonians, this anxiety was mulled over privately by close friends, "men who [had] eaten . . . many bad dinners together" and were "confident in each other." Postmaster Alfred Huger confessed to a fellow Democrat and fellow Carolinian, Secretary of War Joel Poinsett, that national issues dimmed to triviality in the face of threats to their society, their security as planters. "[T]he Bank, & the 'Metallic basis' & the 'paper currency,' are all debatable questions, but the *'Black Currency[']* is *not."* "What signifies to *me,* all the jargon about Whigs & Conservatives &c &c," he agonized, "if the abolitionists stand between me & the White Gate at Longwood?"[18]

That specter created Charlestonians' ambivalence about change, their distrust of what Northerners and Europeans increasingly called progress. Proclaiming their dedication to programs for economic development, their commitment to efficient government and a disciplined fire department, they nonetheless pulled back whenever the social fabric showed rents or even signs of stress. In oblique references to the Vesey affair, in demands for ever stronger policing of black behavior, in vigilante action against any challenge to the laws of slavery, Charlestonians defined the narrow social limits within which change could occur. Nothing must disrupt the social web which knit the city's white population together.

• • •

Yankee visitor and southern guest might each assure his host that Boston and Charleston had much in common: their long histories as port cities, their colonial and revolutionary pasts, the philanthropy in which their citizens engaged, the clubs in which they socialized, the churches where they worshipped, and the circles in which they discussed the art, literature, and politics of the day. In 1843 as in 1828, both cities still believed their future, like their past, lay in commerce.

But just as clear were the differences which separated them. Boston had in the intervening years extended her role in national and even international affairs. Both her politics and her economics linked her to the rest of the country. She had spun a complex institutional web—commercial, transportational, and financial—of which she was the center; she had extended that web to interlock with similar networks elsewhere. Declining even in regional importance during those same years, however, Charleston had watched cotton culture move west and the new cotton trade flow through New Orleans and Mobile. She remained on the periphery of national and international trade, shipping most of her exports and imports through New York. Neither an entrepreneurial-financial center nor a transportation hub, she lacked the power to develop her hinterland in ways to serve her trade. And, isolated first by nullification and then by an extremist response to antislavery, her politics became ever more provincial—meaningless outside state boundaries. Charleston's web remained spun of personal ties; Boston's was one increasingly of institutional linkages. The one was the promise of permanence, the other the pledge of progress.

Appendix A

THE QUANTIFICATION OF BIOGRAPHICAL DATA

We compiled biographical data on the residents of each city from a variety of sources. Their residences, their business names and locations, as well as their or their spouses' occupations came primarily from city directories (for Boston: 1829, 1834, 1835, 1836, and 1841; for Charleston: 1828, 1830, 1835, and 1841). The assessments for Boston property holding were derived from printed lists of those paying more than $25 annual taxes in 1829, 1836, and 1841. The assessments were supplemented by inventories in the Suffolk County Probate Records, 1828–1835. Charleston's property holding was impossible to measure systematically because the only source so registering property was the Charleston County Probate Records, 1828–1843. Therefore urban and rural slaveholding was garnered from the microfilmed federal manuscript censuses of 1830 and 1840 for the whole Charleston District. Real property ownership was determined through deeds recording land purchases made at any time from 1820 to 1843 in the Charleston County Registry of Mesne Conveyance. All other data came from indexing a variety of sources, primarily daily newspapers and municipal, church, club, philanthropic, and corporate records—both manuscript and published.

Although Boston's greater size led us to sample and to select among biographical sources more than we did with Charleston data, and although the kinds and extent of the records available differed in the two cities, we have maintained comparability as far as we could.

SELECTION PROCESS FOR CANDIDATES FOR THE ELITE

We gave most intensive and extensive attention to a group whom we labeled "candidates for the elite," those who by occupation, political post, corporate directorship, significant wealth, or holding of office in churches or clubs were likely to have wielded power, prestige, or influence.

A. OCCUPATIONS
1. Planters (Charleston only)
2. Merchants
    a. In Charleston: Factors, wholesale merchants, commission merchants. Auctioneers and brokers were entered as candidates for the elite but removed from consideration as high-prestige occupations when we created occupational categories for analysis (see below).
    b. In Boston: Wholesale merchants who were generally identified by their business locations on Kilby and State streets and along the wharves or by their owning business property assessed at $15,000 or more. Those who called themselves commission merchants did not qualify automatically, since small traders used this term as they did not in Charleston.
    c. In both cities retail merchants were excluded unless they qualified by having some other source of power, influence, or prestige.
3. Corporation officers: Presidents, treasurers (occurred only in Boston), bank cashiers. When the occupational categories were created for analysis, these occupations were included among high-prestige mercantile occupations.
4. Professions:
    a. Lawyers and judges
    b. Physicians (except Thomsonians, herbalists, and dentists)
    c. Clergymen of all denominations unless they were lay preachers
    d. College presidents and professors, but not other teachers
    e. Editors and published authors
    f. Engineers and architects (in Charleston only). These occupations, however, were excluded from the category of high-prestige occupations, as were editors in both cities (for analysis of Occupational categories, see below).

B. POLITICAL POSTS
1. Federal offices: Senator, representative, collector of the port, customhouse naval officer, postmaster, judge, cabinet member

The Quantification of Biographical Data 227

    2. State offices: Representative, senator, governor, treasurer

    3. Boston city government: Mayor, alderman, councilman, warden (principal ward officer), land commissioner, auditor, treasurer, marshal, assessor, judge, overseer of the poor, board of consulting physicians, school committee, primary school committee

    4. Charleston city government: Intendent, mayor, warden, alderman; commissioners of the orphan house, Marine Hospital, workhouse, poorhouse, free schools, health, markets, streets and lamps, pilotage, Shirras Dispensary, firemaster, port warden, assessor, attorney, guard captain, harbor master

    5. Charleston Neck government: Commissioner for cross roads, commissioner of the poor

C. CORPORATE DIRECTORSHIPS

    All were included

D. WEALTH

    1. Boston: Those whose total taxable property was valued at at least $20,000 in 1829, 1836, or 1841. The city set assessments at 50 percent of actual worth. When the analytical category of "rich" was created, $15,000 assessment or $30,000 of taxable property was the minimum measure. In the absence of assessment information, probate inventories for any year of the 1830s of $20,000 or more were substituted.

    2. Charleston: Those whose probate inventories, which systematically excluded land values, were $10,000 or more; those listed in the 1830 or 1840 federal manuscript census as having twenty or more slaves resident in the city, on a plantation somewhere in the Charleston District, or both; those whom the Charleston County Registry of Mesne Conveyance records list as having acquired either five city lots or one plantation or two lots of country land suitable for planting at some time between 1820 and 1843; and those otherwise known to have a plantation. (The record of deeds is quite full for the entire Charleston District. Where twenty or more rural slaves were listed in the manuscript census under a person's name, it was assumed that he or she owned a plantation. The census lists slaves living on the property, not the number of slaves owned by the head of house. Thus the number of resident slaves is only a surrogate for slave ownership.)

E. SOCIAL POSITION

    1. Officers in any club, philanthropic organization, or specialized professional-occupational association except militia and fire companies. In Charleston, membership on the Charleston Library Society Book Committee and the Chamber of Commerce Appeals Committee was

treated as officeholding. Otherwise committee service was treated simply as evidence of membership.
2. Church lay officers: Titles vary by denomination but include vestrymen, wardens, elders, deacons, moderators, presidents, and treasurers.

This selection process generated 2,308 candidates for the Charleston elite and 4,403 candidates for the Boston elite. In both groups women were sparsely represented: the 131 in Charleston and 413 in Boston qualified almost exclusively by wealth or social position. Given Boston's larger size, with a population twice that of Charleston's in 1830 and three times as large in 1840, it is evident that we did cast our selection net somewhat more widely in Charleston in collecting candidates for the elite.

SAMPLING SELECTION PROCESSES

To insure that we could analyze groups which included those who were clearly nonelite, we drew samples from groups whose actions showed they were actively part of city life but included those in no way qualified as candidates for the elite. These samples probably exclude most of those who were very short-term residents, but constitute a reasonable pool of those free white males resident in either city (Table A-1). Charleston's free blacks were analyzed as a separate group.

Because we had already compiled records for all those Charlestonians who voted in the October 1830 state election and for all who served on juries for the Court of General Sessions between 1828 and 1841, we pulled random samples from those who did not qualify for elite candidacy: five out of every eight nonelite jurors ($N = 658$) who could be identified as coming from Charleston or Charleston Neck (but not from elsewhere in the Charleston District) and five out of every twelve nonelite voters ($N = 1,054$). We intended to pull a sample of firemen, but because the number of nonelite fire fighters amounted only to 246, we used the total population. When jurors or voters were analyzed as a whole, i.e., both the elite candidates and the distinctly nonelite within the group, the nonelite cases were weighted up (by the inverse of their sampling fraction, that is to say, 1.6 for nonelite jurors and 2.4 for nonelite voters) so that the nonelites represented their correct proportions of each of the groups. When these samples were used to analyze the nonelite, the actual unweighted numbers in the sample were used.

Because we had no similar voter list for Boston, we drew instead 10 percent random samples by a computer-generated list of random numbers

The Quantification of Biographical Data

from an 1834 anti-Jackson, pro–Bank of the United States petition, which yielded 490 nonelite petitioners and identified 202 of our elite candidates as signers. A similar procedure with an anti-Bank, pro-Jackson petition yielded 283 nonelite petitioners and identified thirty elite candidates as signers. The total number of petitioners (about 10,120), both pro-Bank and anti-Bank, was somewhat larger than the number of votes cast in the 1834 gubernatorial election in Boston (7,585), but their distribution resembled the tallies of Whig (73 percent) and Democratic (27 percent) ballots counted for the governorship that year. Somewhat less systematic, because of the state of the records for Boston's municipal court, were the lists of jurors we compiled from searching all the case record packets we could find for the period from 1828 to 1841. Of the 2,218 names on the grand and traverse jury panels, we took a sample of every third name to generate the 428 nonelite and 280 elite candidate juror sample. Finally, the fireman sample was drawn from four lists of the Boston fire companies published from 1839–1842, selecting three from every seven names for a total sample of 606, only 41 of whom were elite candidates.

DATA ENTRY

The data record format was identical for the elite candidates and the nonelite within a city, although far more information was available and recorded for the elites. In addition, the categories for both cities were nearly identical. After each individual was assigned an identification number reflecting elite, nonelite, and sample status, the following information was coded for him or her:

Card 1: Full name, gender, marital status, occupation (Charleston, for periods 1828–1832, 1833–1838, 1839–1843; Boston, for the years for which directories were consulted—1829, 1836, 1841; except for petitioners: 1829, 1834, 1841), spouse's occupation, residence (with same dates as occupation), business location (same dates as occupation in Boston; 1826–1835 and 1836–1843 in Charleston), birth year, death year, jury service (by times served in Charleston, by type of jury service in Boston); birthplace, first nationality, or ethnic identification; the number of slaves resident in his/her city establishments in 1830 and 1840 (Charleston only); pro- or anti-Bank petitioner (Boston only); value of estate at probate (Boston only).

Card 2: Political affiliation (in Charleston, four options by date: nullifier-Unionist, 1828–1833; other 1828–1832, 1833–1838, 1839–1843; and whether an 1830 voter; in Boston five options by date: 1831, 1832, 1834–

1837, 1838–1839, 1840); denominational and church affiliation and offices held; fire company affiliations and offices held; militia company affiliations and highest rank held; club, philanthropic, and associational activity coded to distinguish members from officers and divided 1828–1835, 1836–1843; number of real properties owned in the city (Charleston only); presence in fire sample (Boston only).

Card 3 (for Charleston cases): Number of slaves resident in the country in 1830 and 1840, number of real properties owned in the country, locations of country properties, value of estate at probate, corporations in which stock was owned, corporations served as director or officer (1828–1832, 1833–1838, 1839–1843), school of bachelor's degree or lower, graduate school or evidence of professional training.

Card 3 (for Boston cases): Real and personal property assessments for individuals and businesses in 1829, 1836, and 1841; kinds of businesses in which stock was owned; corporations served as director or officer (1828–1836, 1837–1843); school of bachelor's degree or lower; graduate school or evidence of professional training.

Card 4: City, state, and federal elective and appointive offices held.

All these data were keypunched, verified, and put on disk by the Social Science Research Institute of the University of Maine at Orono. Garrett Bozylinsky, Assistant Director for Computing, analyzed the data using the Statistical Analysis System (SAS) procedures and its custom programming capabilities for constructing additional variables. Over 50,000 lines of SAS code were generated. Data, full documentation, and programs are now archived on tape and are available from the Inter-university Consortium for Political and Social Research, Ann Arbor, Michigan.

ANALYSIS

It is not feasible to review the entire analytical process, which has filled our bookcases and closets with computer printouts ranging in utility from trivial to central. It is, however, essential to define how various categories and measurements were constructed.

OCCUPATIONAL CATEGORIES

Although we started by modifying and using the categories defined in Theodore Hershberg et al., "Occupation and Ethnicity in Five Nineteenth Century Cities: A Collaborative Inquiry," *Historical Methods Newsletter,* VII (June 1974), 187–89, we found those rankings too blunt an instru-

The Quantification of Biographical Data

ment for our purposes, just as we found that using specific occupations impeded analysis by their very multiplicity. Thus we evolved the system which together addressed the questions of prestige rankings and division of occupation by economic sector. We divided agricultural, professional, and mercantile occupations into high-, middle-, and low-prestige groups. High prestige was largely defined by the selection criteria noted above for determining candidates for the elite. Low prestige was largely defined by low salaries or wages, transciency, and working for an employer. The middle rank fell in between. Government employment we did not categorize by prestige, since major officeholders turn up in the analyses for political power. Mechanics' ranking shows up predominantly in wealth and property assessments because city directories and other sources of occupational identification make no distinction between master and journeyman. The economic sector in which mechanics worked, however, was vitally important in assessing human resources. We therefore divided them by product: food, metal and machinery, clothing, footware and other leather goods, construction and building trades, shipbuilding, printing and publishing, tallow products, home furnishing, fine metals and instruments, and a category for unspecified products and another for miscellaneous classifications. For similar reasons we divided service occupations into personal, lodging and food, transportation, entertainment, and other. Then we thrust gentlemen, the retired, students, and paupers into a rather meaningless residual category just to give them a place where they would not turn up as missing data.

INDICES OF ECONOMIC AND POLITICAL POWER, WEALTH, AND SOCIAL STATUS

Even more than the occupational categories, these indices reflect judgments we have made based on long exposure to the full panoply of records and documents about how the two cities operated in the 1830s. The numerical weights assigned to various indicators only symbolize those judgments. They made it possible for us to utilize data too numerous to be handled in any other way. But to the extent that there is any objective justification for the weights assigned beyond the traditional standards and practices which all historians use, it is that numerical symbols permitted us to employ categorical indicators in a systematic manner—by counting them. Sometimes we disagreed with the conclusions toward which the mindless computer directed us because they did not comport with the literary evidence. Then, if we did not discover a programming or other technical error, we reassessed the findings against all other evidence until they made sense.

Appendix A

INDEX OF ECONOMIC POWER IN BOSTON

Each person's index is set at 0 and then increased by 1 for the presence of each one of the following indicators: having more than $30,000 of business property in 1829, 1836, 1841; serving on board of the Provident Institute for Savings 1828–1835, 1836–1843. Each person's index is increased by 2 for service on each corporate board of directors, 1828–1836, 1837–1843. Two to nine indicators signal modest economic power, ten or more indicate great economic power.

INDEX OF ECONOMIC POWER IN CHARLESTON

Each person's index is set at 0 and then increased by 1 for the presence of each one of the following indicators: having 100 or more plantation slaves in 1830, 1840; serving on each corporate board of directors, 1828–1832, 1833–1838, 1839–1843; holding office in the Bar Association, the Chamber of Commerce, or the Medical Society, 1828–1835, 1836–1843. One to four indicators betoken modest economic power, five or more equal great economic power.

INDEX OF POLITICAL POWER IN BOSTON

Each person's index is set at 0 and then increased by 1 for the presence of each one of the following indicators: each term served as mayor, alderman, councilman, overseer of the poor, school committeeman; city judge, assessor, auditor, attorney; state representative, senator, judge, major appointive official; federal congressman, senator, major court official. One to five indicators signal modest power, six or more denote great political power. (N.B.: State legislators and all city officials except judges were elected or appointed annually.)

INDEX OF POLITICAL POWER IN CHARLESTON

Each person's index is set at 0 and then increased 1 for the presence of each one of the following indicators: each term served as intendent, mayor, warden, alderman; service on major city commissions, 1828–1832, 1833–1838, 1839–1843; each term served as state legislator, senator; each appointment as state judge or major administrative official. One to three indicators suggest modest political power, four or more betoken great political power. (N.B.: Although elected city officials were chosen annually, state legislators were elected to two-year terms, senators to four-year terms. Service on city commissions is grouped so that a single indicator may record up to five years of service.)

MEASURE OF WEALTH IN BOSTON

Use of actual assessment figures eliminated the need for indicators. Nonetheless the vagaries of the assessment process must be noted, as well as the fact that, by city rule, assessments represented only half the market value of the property assessed. Because assessments had to be coded to the nearest $1,000 and because the published assessment had to be doubled to determine the full assessment, variations of less than $2,000 are hidden. Those with $30,000 or more assessed property (after doubling the published assessment) in 1829, 1836, or 1841 form the category "rich," comprising both the modestly and the very wealthy. Those with $80,000 or more real or total property assessment (after doubling the published assessment) or with $50,000 of assessed personality (after doubling the published assessment) in 1829, 1836, or 1841 are understood to have great wealth.

INDEX OF WEALTH IN CHARLESTON

Each person's index is set at 0 and then increased by 1 for the presence of each one of the following indicators: having twenty or more urban slaves, 1830, 1840; having fifty or more rural slaves, 1830, 1840; acquiring ten or more urban properties, 1820–1843; acquiring three or more rural properties, 1820–1843; owning stock in five or more companies at any time 1828–1843; leaving an estate valued, exclusive of land, at $20,000 or more. One or two indicators signify modest wealth; three or more, great wealth.

INDEX OF STATUS IN BOSTON

Each person's index is set at 0 and then increased by 1 for the presence of each one of the following indicators: high-prestige occupation, 1829, 1836, 1841; an undergraduate degree; a graduate degree; membership in a club with upper-class membership generally (Harvard undergraduate clubs, the Athenaeum, Massachusetts Historical Society, Pilgrim Society, "The Club," Saturday Fish Club, Saturday Night Club, Wednesday Evening Club); holding office in a social or philanthropic organization which generally elected its officers from the upper class (Harvard Corporation and Overseers, Boston Dispensary, Lying-In Hospital, Massachusetts General Hospital, Mount Auburn Cemetery, Provident Institution for Savings, Massachusetts Infirmary for Lung Diseases, Massachusetts Eye and Ear Infirmary, Social Law Library); holding major lay office in an Episcopal, Unitarian, or Congregational church. Two to five indicators signify modest status; six or more betoken high status.

Appendix A

INDEX OF STATUS IN CHARLESTON

Each person's index is set at 0 and then increased by 1 for the presence of each one of the following indicators: high-prestige occupation, 1828–1832, 1833–1838, 1839–1843; an undergraduate degree, a graduate degree, membership in a club with upper-class membership generally (Academy of Fine Arts, Jockey Club, Literary and Philosophical Society, St. Cecilia Society, Strawberry Club, South Carolina Agricultural Society); holding office in a social organization which generally elected its officers from the upper class (Charleston Library Society, Hibernian Society, South Carolina Society); holding major lay office in an Episcopal church; plantation ownership. Two to three indicators signify modestly high status, four or more denote very high status.

Specific application of these analytical tools is made in the text and footnotes. Because it has been our purpose not to write a text addressing statistical tables and charts, we have treated the quantified evidence like all other evidence. The tables which follow, however, have been included to demonstrate and clarify the interaction of the various indices.

TABLE A-1. How representative of Boston's and Charleston's free adult male residents are the 1834 Boston pro- and anti-Bank petition sample and the 1830 Charleston voter list?

Occupations	Peter Knights's sample of Boston household heads from the U.S. 1830 census[1] ($N = 385$)	Sample of 1834 Boston petitioners ($N = 1,012$)	All voters in Charleston 1830 state and federal election[2] ($N = 2,562$)
Planters	—	—	6.8%
Professionals	3.6%	2.0%	10.2%
Semiprofessionals	1.8%	2.8%	
Proprietors, managers, and officials	14.5%	10.0%	11.9%
Petty proprietors, clerical, and sales	19.1%	24.8%	17.4%
Unskilled, menial semi-skilled, and unskilled	39.4%	40.7%	21.7%
Miscellaneous (includes government employees in Pease data) and unknown	21.3%	19.4%	31.9%
TOTAL	99.7%	99.7%	99.9%

[1] Peter R. Knights, *The Plain People of Boston, 1830–1860: A Study in City Growth* (New York: Oxford University Press, 1971), 107.
[2] Jane H. Pease and William H. Pease, "The Economics and Politics of Charleston's Nullification Crisis," *Journal of Southern History*, XLVIII (August 1981), 338.

The Quantification of Biographical Data

TABLE A-2. The distribution of elite candidates among occupational categories

Occupational category	Boston Those of known occupation in 1829 (N = 1,988)	1841 (N = 2,341)	Charleston Those of known occupation in 1828–1832 (N = 1,349)	1839–1843 (N = 1,121)
Planting	—	—	17.9%	9.5%
High professional	17.8%	20.7%	18.0%	18.2%
High mercantile	30.0%	33.0%	24.0%	33.5%
Farming	—	—	.1%	.4%
Middle professional	2.1%	2.1%	2.0%	2.9%
Middle mercantile	17.5%	15.7%	8.8%	11.3%
Low professional	2.6%	2.7%	1.6%	2.6%
Low mercantile	8.8%	6.7%	8.6%	4.2%
Government	2.9%	4.1%	4.5%	6.0%
Mechanic	14.8%	12.9%	11.0%	9.3%
Service	1.6%	1.8%	2.9%	1.7%
Other	2.0%	.1%	.4%	.3%
TOTAL	100.1%	99.8%	99.8%	99.9%

TABLE A-3. The distribution of elite candidates in the indices or measures of power, influence, prestige, and wealth

	Percentage of elite candidate Bostonians in each category (N = 4,403)		Percentage of elite candidate Charlestonians in each category (N = 2,308)
Economic power		Economic power	
none (0–1)	77%	none (0)	82%
modest (2–9)	20%	modest (1–4)	16%
great (10–24)	3%	great (5–13)	3%
Political power		Political power	
none (0)	82%	none (0)	91%
modest (1–5)	16%	modest (1–3)	7%
great (6–17)	2%	great (4–12)	2%
Status		Status	
minimal (0–1)	82%	minimal (0–1)	77%
modest (2–5)	16%	modest (2–3)	18%
high (6–12)	2%	high (4–9)	5%
Rich ($30,000 or more)		Wealth	
no	91%	none (0)	79%
yes	9%	modest (1–2)	20%
		great (3–5)	2%

TABLE A-4. Cross-tabulations of power, prestige, influence and wealth

Boston's	Economic power	Political power	Status	Rich/ Wealth	Influence on education
Economically powerful ($N = 1,000$)	100%	17.7%	28.4%	34.9%	20.5%
Politically powerful ($N = 782$)	35.4%	100%	31.9%	23.1%	32.2%
Modest or high status ($N = 763$)	39.6%	31.1%	100%	32.4%	49.7%
Rich ($N = 763$)	45.8%	23.8%	24.3%	100%	19.7%

Charleston's	Economic power	Political power	Status	Wealth
Economically powerful ($N = 424$)	100%	24.1%	48.1%	43.9%
Politically powerful ($N = 208$)	49.1%	100%	49.5%	40.9%
Modest or high status ($N = 539$)	37.9%	19.1%	100%	17.8%
Wealthy ($N = 486$)	38.3%	17.5%	55.1%	100%

TABLE A-5. Religious affiliation of the powerful, influential, prestigious, and wealthy[1]

Religious affiliation	Boston				Charleston			
	Economically powerful (N = 453)	Politically powerful (N = 365)	Modest/high status (N = 412)	Rich (N = 349)	Economically powerful (N = 268)	Politically powerful (N = 143)	Modest/high status (N = 350)	Wealthy (N = 281)
Baptist	5.0%	9.3%	3.4%	4.6%	2.2%	4.9%	.6%	.7%
Catholic	—	.3%	1.0%	.9%	2.6%	1.4%	2.0%	2.8%
Congregational	15.5%	17.3%	12.1%	9.5%	8.2%	9.8%	8.0%	10.7%
Episcopal	22.5%	18.1%	36.2%	32.7%	53.0%	51.7%	66.6%	53.4%
Jewish	—	—	—	—	3.0%	2.1%	1.4%	4.3%
Lutheran	—	—	—	—	4.1%	10.5%	4.6%	7.8%
Methodist	.2%	.8%	.2%	.9%	1.9%	.7%	.9%	1.8%
Presbyterian	—	—	—	—	19.0%	13.3%	10.9%	14.9%
Unitarian	54.3%	50.1%	44.9%	49.3%	5.2%	4.9%	4.3%	3.2%
Other	2.5%	4.1%	2.2%	2.4%	.7%	.7%	.7%	.4%
TOTAL	100.0%	100.0%	100.0%	100.3%	99.9%	100.0%	100.0%	100.0%

[1] Those of modest or great economic or political power, modest or high status, rich or of modest or great wealth whose religious affiliation is known.

Appendix B

PROPERTY DISTRIBUTION AND CHANGES IN PROPERTY OWNERSHIP

Determining the actual extent of wealth and measuring changes in property holdings over time are knotty problems because systematic evidence about wealth is both sparse and inaccurate. Even quantifiable evidence, like impressionistic verbal descriptions, was significantly distorted by the manner in which it was compiled by contemporaries.

Boston published annual lists of the assessments on taxable real property and personal property—but only if it was located in the city and if the owner paid taxes of $25 or more (which included a $2 poll tax). Because the actual tax rate varied from 39½ mills in 1829 to 47½ in 1836 to 60 in 1841, the minimum real value of printed assessments also shifted from a high of $5,800 in 1829 to $4,800 in 1836 to $3,800 in 1841. Moreover, taxpayer protests that assessments did not respond to declining prices after 1837 suggests that short-term variations in price were not reflected in assessments. In addition, city residents' investments in land or business outside Boston—including manufacturing and transportation stock—were excluded from Boston taxes. And, finally, the basis for assessing real property admittedly differed from ward to ward and, with few exceptions, taxable personal property, which included primarily commercial and manufacturing supplies and equipment, ships, and investments in Boston corporations, was assessed more by guesswork than solid evidence. Property owners were allowed to file statements of worth but seldom did so.

Nonetheless, property assessments provide the most systematic basis for establishing total wealth and changes in property ownership over time in Boston. The tax assessment lists for 1829, 1836, and 1841 were chosen to chart that change from the late 1820s doldrums to Boston's peak boom year to the depression's depth. Within these constraints, 1829 and 1841 were chosen specifically to coincide as closely as possible with the decennial census years from which Charleston property changes had to be derived.

If using Boston assessments is fraught with risks and reservations, determining changes in Charleston property on the basis of slaves reported in the decennial censuses of Charleston and Charleston Neck for 1830 and 1840 demands even more extensive qualification. In the first place, the urban slaves reported in the manuscript census were those resident in each household—not necessarily those owned by the head of house. Some might be slaves hired to work in the house; others might belong to household members unnamed in the census. Moreover the household head might well own slaves resident elsewhere in the city.

Trickier still was rural slave ownership, which was derived from the manuscript censuses of the low-country north of Beaufort and south of Georgetown: the parishes of St. John's Colleton, St. Paul's Colleton, St. James's Goose Creek, St. Andrew's, St. John's Berkeley, St. Stephen's, St. Thomas's and St. Denis's, Christ Church, and St. James Santee. Thus the rural slave ownership measure excludes slaves on Charleston-owned plantations elsewhere. Moreover, while it is highly probable that rural slaves resident on a plantation belonged to the person listed as household head, it is not certain. Nonresident planters might not be listed and the resident managers or overseers might be given as household heads. Wills and inventories also suggest that sizable numbers of field slaves might belong to several family members but be worked on a single plantation. Finally, the very form of the 1840 census raises doubts about its accuracy. Large sections list household heads alphabetically and total slave holdings in numbers evenly divisible by five or ten.

Most problematic of all is that slaves were but one type of property—even though they were the most widely held form of property. It is true that Lee Soltow does report that, for all Southerners both rural and urban, the 1860 census data display a close and consistent direct correlation between the number of slaves owned and the size of a person's total estate.[1] Nonetheless, we used slave data as a surrogate for all wealth reluctantly and only because data for other types of property are unavailable. Although the Charleston city council voted several times in the late 1830s to publish tax lists, none was reported published, and we doubt that any was before 1859. Judging changes in wealth by the value of real property is

1. Lee Soltow, *Men and Wealth in the United States, 1850–1870* (New Haven: Yale University Press, 1975), 135, 139.

hazardous, for it was often bought, sold, and transferred with no indication of its price or value. Consequently, in the interest of examining sources more likely to produce usable data, we decided not to double the time we spent examining deeds to trace the disposition as well as the acquisition of property for more than three thousand people over a twenty-five-year period. Finally, the only available list of Charleston shareholders was for stock held in the South Carolina Canal and Rail Road Company in a single year. Thus neither real property nor corporate stock offered a feasible alternative or supplement to using slave holdings to judge changes in property over time.

BOSTON

Peter Knights's sample[2] of male heads of house in Boston in 1830 and 1840 makes clear that more than 73 percent in 1830 and 67 percent in 1840 fell completely outside the ranks of the "propertied" as we have defined them: those who paid taxes of $25 or more and whose assessments were published by the city. We used the lists for 1829, 1836, and 1841,[3] which include, with variations caused by changing tax rates, only those with property assessments of $1,900 to $2,900 or more. Because property was assessed at half its value, the minimum property for inclusion in the printed lists was actually $3,800 to $5,800. The tables which follow include only those whose property was assessed at high enough levels to pay $25 or more in taxes for two or three of the years 1829, 1836, 1841. Those whose property met that level once but only once before 1841 are counted in the tallies of those who disappeared from published assessment lists in subsequent years. All others are excluded altogether.

Yet it would be incorrect to assume that all the rest were poor or even totally unpropertied. Because probate inventories and private observations indicate that modest houses sold for between $400 and $800 in the 1830s, it is safer to assume that the totally unpropertied were those with less than $400 wealth and not subject to any Boston tax except the poll tax. Men paying only the poll tax made up 50 percent of Knights's sample in 1830 and 42 percent in 1840. Yet they too may have been better off than those figures imply, for then as now, wages and salaries were a better indicator of economic well-being, at least for artisans and clerical employees, than

2. Peter R. Knights, *The Plain People of Boston, 1830–1860: A Study in City Growth* (New York: Oxford University Press, 1971), 92.
3. Boston Assessing Department, *List of Persons, Copartnerships and Corporations Who Were Taxed $25 and Upwards in the City of Boston for 1829, 1836, and 1841* (Boston: City Printer, 1830, 1837, and 1842).

either personalty or, beyond the price of a house, real estate. Moreover, as Lee Soltow[4] has demonstrated for mid-nineteenth-century America, property ownership was at least partially a function of a man's age, with men in their twenties the least likely to own property at the level of Boston taxables listed in published assessments. Knights's observations on the median ages of those with various levels of property argue that this was a factor in Boston of the 1830s. The median age of those with less than $400 property remained constant at 36.9; for those with $401 to $2,000, the median age rose from 36.3 in 1830 to 37.1 in 1840; for those with property from $2,001 to $20,000, the median age dropped from 41.3 to 39.8 respectively, while for those worth more than $20,000 the median age remained steady at 50.

All these qualifications should be kept in mind in judging the tables which follow. All tables, it should be noted, double the printed assessment to reflect the assessors' real judgment rather than the official convention of assessing at half the real value. Additionally, it should be remembered that just as the poor are excluded altogether, those assessed for $20,000 or more were automatically included in the elite pool, for which they may have no other qualification.

The tables address the following pools:

1. All those of the 4,403 elite candidates (see Appendix A for definition) who paid taxes of $25 or more in 1829, 1836, and/or 1841. For any one elapsed time period between two tax years this comprised at most 23 percent of the pool of elite candidates.

2. All those of the juror sample (which included 280 elite candidates in its pool of 708) who paid taxes of more than $25 in at least two years. For any one time period this comprised at most 22 percent of the sample.

3. All the pro- and anti-Bank petitioners who paid more than $25 taxes in two years. The pro-Bank petitioners (202 elite candidates and 490 nonelite) and the anti-Bank petitioners (30 elite candidates and 283 nonelite) are treated as a single group whenever possible to approximate as closely as this study can the Boston electorate. Significantly, for any one time period, those paying $25 taxes in two tax years comprised at most 10 percent of the joint petitioner samples.

COMMENTS ON TABLE B-1

Table B-1 addresses the proportions of Bostonians whose property increased, decreased, or remained static. One reads it, as one does all the

4. Soltow, *Men and Wealth*, 27–31.

other tables, in the light of one's own definition of what comprised economic success or failure, what measures satisfactory economic accomplishment. If one assumes that barely holding one's own in good years is a token of failure in a competitive society but that doing so in bad times more nearly approaches success, one finds that the proportions of economic success and failure among those who continued to live in Boston remained almost constant over time.

Category	Timespan	Success	Failure
Elite candidates	1829–1836	69%	32%
	1836–1841	72%	28%
Juror samples	1829–1836	70%	29%
	1836–1841	78%	22%
Petitioner samples	1829–1836	62%	38%
	1836–1841	78%	22%

COMMENTS ON TABLES B-2, B-3, AND B-4

These tables all address the degree to which the amount of property one held at the beginning of a period influenced whether one's property changed at all and whether it increased or decreased. They qualify the premise that the more property one had, the more likely that property was to increase and the less likely to decrease. In the panic and depression years those of great wealth were, on the whole, both less likely to increase their property and more likely to decrease it. The greater apparent stability of assessments among the less propertied may reflect only that changes of less than $2,000 are invisible (see Appendix A, "Measure of Wealth in Boston").

COMMENTS ON TABLES B-5, B-6, AND B-7

These tables address the size of changes, gains, and losses. There is little question that gains were greater both in dollars and in the percentage of increase over previous assessments in good times than they were in bad. But even in bad years the gains were substantial. Losses did not vary as much by good times and bad as did gains.

COMMENTS ON TABLES B-8 AND B-9

These tables address the question of the relation of occupation to property accumulation. Table B-8 shows that the proportions of various occupational groups among increasers, decreasers, and the static are largely the same. Table B-9, however, shows notable variations among the proportions of given occupational groups increasing and decreasing their property, and also considerable variation within occupational groups by good times and bad. It suggests that those in high-prestige occupations in any economic sector and in mercantile occupations of any rank were those most likely to increase their property in good times. One may argue that that reflects a business prudence or experience less marked among other occupations. In any case, the high proportion of mercantile occupations among all groups, their strong performance in good times, and their ability to hold their own in bad is characteristic of Boston's commercial economy.

CHARLESTON

Although no study has been made of Charleston's property holdings in the 1830s, Michael P. Johnson[5] has addressed wealth distribution in 1860. The city's wealth as the total of what free citizens reported as their individual worth to the census takers that year amounted to $38,336,150, of which 52 percent was in real estate. But William H. Gibbes, census marshal, believed that the city assessors' books more accurately recorded total wealth as $54,597,879, of which 46 percent was in real estate. Johnson reports that 70 percent of the 1860 free households had less than $2,000 of property (cf. Knights's 1830 Boston sample of 73 percent); 20 percent with property ranging in worth from $2,000 to $18,000 (cf. Boston's 19 percent between $2,001 and $20,000 in 1830); and 10 percent with property over $18,000 (cf. Boston's 7 percent over $20,000 in 1830). Johnson also noted that nonslave wealth was concentrated most heavily among the wealthiest 1860 Charlestonians, and thus implies that slaves were the most widely distributed property.

Because urban slave holdings, no matter how small, are used to measure Charlestonians' wealth, the following tables necessarily include levels of wealth much lower than those included in the Boston tables. Fifty-five percent of Charleston's elite candidates were urban slave owners in both 1830 and 1840; 46 percent of Charleston jurors (606 elite candidates and 442 nonelite equivalents), and 39 percent of the 1830 voters (898 elite candidates and 1,285 nonelite equivalents) also owned urban slaves in both census years. The jurors include all elite candidates who were jurors 1830–1840 and a sample of five-eighths of other jurors not known definitely to live outside Charleston and Charleston Neck. The sample has

5. Michael P. Johnson, "Wealth and Class in Charleston in 1860" (Paper presented at the Citadel Conference on the South, April 19–21, 1979), 1–6.

been multiplied by 1.6 to produce equivalents which can be added to the population of elite candidate jurors. The 1830 voters include all elite candidates who voted in the 1830 Charleston and Charleston Neck election of state legislators and five-twelfths of others who voted in that election. The sample has been multiplied by 2.4 and added to the population of elite candidate voters.

The tables which follow, like the Boston ones, are subject to various interpretations according to the reader's expectations. They differ from the Boston ones in that they cannot differentiate good years from bad. They are also confined to white slave owners because blacks could not be voters, jurors, or elite candidates and because a large part of free black slaveholding was likely to involve quite different relationships between owners and slaves. But it should be noted that, so far as is known, none of the Boston elite candidates or petitioner or juror samples include blacks.

COMMENT ON TABLE C-1

This table is most usefully read in comparison with table B-1 showing Boston's increasers, decreasers, and the static, 1829–1841. Bostonians

Category	Property increased	Property decreased	Property remained static
Elite Candidates			
Charleston 1830–1840	40%	29%	22%
Boston 1829–1841	69%	27%	5%
Jurors			
Charleston 1830–1840	49%	31%	20%
Boston 1829–1841	70%	20%	10%
1830 Charleston voters 1830–1840	47%	36%	17%
1834–Boston petitioners 1829–1841	62%	31%	7%

were more likely to increase their property and less likely to have the same amount than were Charlestonians. But Charlestonians were about equally likely to decrease their wealth by decade's end as were Bostonians.

COMMENTS ON TABLE C-2

This table reflects far less correlation between the amount of property with which Charlestonians started the decade and the amount they possessed at decade's end than did Boston's changes in assessments.

COMMENTS ON TABLES C-3, C-4, C-5, AND C-6

These tables suggest somewhat larger proportional increases and decreases in urban slave holdings than the increases and decreases in Boston's assessments for the entire decade. Rural slaveholding changes resemble the Boston assessment pattern more closely.

COMMENTS ON TABLE C-7

This table implies the improbability that Charlestonians who decreased their urban slave holdings did so to shift capital to other investments. Those whose urban slave holdings increased have almost identical investment patterns as those whose urban slave holdings decreased. Both, however, differ markedly from the static, who uniformly were apparently less likely to chance investment in anything.

COMMENTS ON TABLES C-8 AND C-9

More than anything else, these tables suggest that occupation was somewhat less a factor in property accumulation in Charleston than it was in Boston. While it is also clear that those of mercantile occupations comprised a smaller proportion of Charleston slave owners than they did of Bostonians taxed $25 or more, this may be explained by the nature of the different kinds of property involved and the fact that all slave ownership was analyzed, while Boston property worth less than $3,800 in 1841 or $4,800 in 1836 or $5,800 in 1829 was not.

TABLE B-1. Changes in property assessment among Bostonians assessed on taxable property over $5,800 in 1829 and $4,800 in 1836.

Categories of taxpayers	Time span	Number with assessments known in both years	Those whose assessments			TOTAL
			Increased	Decreased	Remained static	
Elite candidates	1829–1836	693	69%	25%	7%	101%
	1836–1841	1,000	53%	28%	19%	100%
	1829–1841	610	69%	27%	5%	101%
Juror sample	1829–1836	98	70%	16%	13%	99%
	1836–1841	156	52%	22%	26%	100%
	1829–1841	99	70%	20%	10%	100%
1834 petitioner sample—pro- and anti-Bank	1829–1836	71	62%	32%	6%	100%
	1836–1841	116	55%	22%	23%	100%
	1829–1841	61	62%	31%	7%	100%

TABLE B-2. Did the amount of assessed property Bostonians had in 1829 influence the amount they had in 1836?

Those whose 1829 assessments exceeded $5,800 (by the amount of that 1829 assessment):	Number	Those whose assessments		Changed less than $2,000	Those who disappeared from published assessments in 1836	TOTAL
		Increased	Decreased			
Elite candidates[1]	937					
$5,800–$30,000	616	49%	16%	6%	28%	99%
$31,000–$100,000	261	53%	21%	3%	23%	100%
$101,000+	60	57%	27%	0%	17%	101%
Jurors	136					
$5,800–$30,000	109	45%	9%	12%	35%	101%
$31,000–$100,000	24	71%	25%	0%	4%	100%
$101,000+	3	100%	0%	0%	0%	100%
1834 petitioners	86					
$5,800–$30,000	64	45%	33%	6%	16%	100%
$31,000–$100,000	18	78%	17%	0%	6%	101%
$101,000+	4	25%	75%	0%	0%	100%

[1] Correlation (Pearsonian) between elite candidates' 1829 and 1836 assessed property values is .697.

Property Distribution and Changes in Property Ownership

TABLE B-3. Did the amount of assessed property Bostonians had in 1836 influence the amount they had in 1841?

Those whose 1836 assessments exceeded $4,800 (by the amount of that 1836 assessment):	Number	Those whose assessments		Changed less than $2,000	Those who disappeared from published assessments in 1841	TOTAL
		In-creased	De-creased			
Elite candidates[1]	1,257					
$4,800–$30,000	822	43%	15%	19%	23%	100%
$31,000–$100,000	359	40%	36%	9%	14%	99%
$101,000+	76	46%	33%	4%	17%	100%
Jurors	195					
$4,800–$30,000	150	36%	14%	26%	24%	100%
$31,000–$100,000	34	56%	32%	6%	6%	100%
$101,000+	11	73%	18%	0%	9%	100%
1834 petitioners	147					
$4,800–$30,000	112	42%	17%	17%	24%	100%
$31,000–$100,000	27	52%	37%	7%	4%	100%
$101,000+	8	38%	25%	0%	38%	101%

[1] Correlation (Pearsonian) between elite candidates' 1836 and 1841 assessed property values is .897.

TABLE B-4. Did the amount of assessed property Bostonians had in 1829 influence the amount they had in 1841?

Those whose 1829 assessments exceeded $5,800 (by the amount of that 1829 assessment):	Number	Those whose assessments		Changed less than $2,000	Those who disappeared from published assessments in 1841	TOTAL
		In-creased	De-creased			
Elite candidates[1]	937					
$5,800–$30,000	616	45%	14%	4%	36%	99%
$31,000–$100,000	261	44%	23%	1%	32%	100%
$101,000+	60	38%	28%	0%	33%	99%
Jurors	136					
$5,800–$30,000	109	47%	12%	9%	31%	99%
$31,000–$100,000	24	58%	25%	0%	17%	100%
$101,000+	3	67%	33%	0%	0%	100%
1834 petitioners	86					
$5,800–$30,000	64	44%	19%	6%	31%	100%
$31,000–$100,000	18	50%	28%	0%	22%	100%
$101,000+	4	50%	25%	0%	25%	100%

[1] Correlation (Pearsonian) between elite candidates' 1829 and 1841 assessed property values is .640.

TABLE B-5. How great was the change in property assessments for Bostonians who paid taxes of $25 or more?

Category of those whose assessments changed	Number of changers	Change (in $1,000s)		Change as percentage of previous assessment	
		Mean	Median	Mean	Median
Elite candidates					
1829–1836	693	11.3	6	58%	25%
1836–1841	610	16.4	8	77%	39%
1829–1841	1000	3.6	2	31%	8%
Elite jurors					
1829–1836	78	14.2	6	53%	25%
1836–1841	119	7.0	4	39%	16%
1829–1841	81	21.0	14	94%	53%
Nonelite jurors					
1829–1836	20	3.3	3	46%	29%
1836–1841	37	0.5	0	2%	0%
1829–1841	18	2.1	0	31%	0%
Elite pro-Bank petitioners					
1829–1836	56	9.3	4	47%	18%
1836–1841	89	4.8	2	59%	12%
1829–1841	49	10.8	6	53%	38%
Nonelite pro-Bank petitioners					
1829–1836	8	0.3	1	17%	13%
1836–1841	14	1.7	0	26%	0%
1829–1841	5	2.0	0	35%	0%

TABLE B-6. How great was the gain for those Bostonians whose property assessments increased?

Category of those whose assessments increased	Number of increasers	Increase (in $1,000s)		Increase as percentage of previous assessment	
		Mean	Median	Mean	Median
Elite candidates					
1829–1836	476	24.0	12	98%	90%
1836–1841	530	17.3	10	78%	44%
1829–1841	418	33.3	16	131%	74%
Elite jurors					
1829–1836	55	23.4	14	84%	50%
1836–1841	72	18.3	12	76%	43%
1829–1841	61	31.0	18	134%	100%
Nonelite jurors					
1829–1836	14	5.1	4	70%	53%
1836–1841	9	3.5	4	48%	29%
1829–1841	8	6.5	7	88%	73%
Elite pro-Bank petitioners					
1829–1836	37	21.3	8	87%	50%
1836–1841	53	19.0	10	115%	67%
1829–1841	32	24.6	13	102%	60%
Nonelite pro-Bank petitioners					
1829–1836	2	8.0	8	133%	133%
1836–1841	5	5.2	6	76%	75%
1829–1841	2	7.0	7	108%	108%

NOTE: Anti-Bank petitioners with known assessments are too few to give numbers of any meaning. They are therefore excluded from this table.

TABLE B-7. How great was the loss for those Bostonians whose property assessments decreased?

Category of those whose assessments decreased	Number of decreasers	Decrease (in $1,000s)		Decrease as percentage of previous assessment	
		Mean	Median	Mean	Median
Elite candidates					
1829–1836	171	20.8	8	39%	33%
1836–1841	277	19.8	10	39%	33%
1829–1841	162	23.8	12	47%	22%
Elite jurors					
1829–1836	14	12.6	5	36%	27%
1836–1841	25	19.4	8	35%	25%
1829–1841	14	15.0	8	40%	35%
Nonelite jurors					
1829–1836	2	3.0	3	25%	25%
1836–1841	9	5.5	4	38%	38%
1829–1841	6	2.3	2	23%	25%
Elite pro-Bank petitioners					
1829–1836	18	14.9	7	32%	27%
1836–1841	20	29.0	7	42%	23%
1829–1841	16	16.1	9	44%	32%
Nonelite pro-Bank petitioners					
1829–1836	4	3.5	3	33%	29%
1836–1841	1	2.0	2	11%	11%
1829–1841	1	4.0	4	40%	40%

NOTE: Anti-Bank petitioners with known assessments are too few to give numbers with any meaning. They are therefore excluded from this table.

TABLE B-8. Did those whose assessments increased differ from those whose assessments decreased or stayed the same according to whether or not they engaged in high prestige occupations? Did they differ according to the economic sector in which they worked?

Category	Time span	Number whose occupation was known in initial year of time span	High-prestige occupation in any economic sector	Economic sector				
				Professional	Mercantile	Mechanic	Other	Total
Elite candidates								
	increased 1829–1836	339	53%	14%	67%	15%	3%	99%
	increased 1836–1841	396	47%	16%	61%	18%	5%	100%
	decreased 1829–1836	127	50%	23%	57%	14%	6%	100%
	decreased 1836–1841	182	56%	18%	64%	11%	7%	100%
	static[1] 1829–1836	39	28%	13%	49%	31%	8%	101%
	static[1] 1836–1841	114	55%	18%	65%	11%	6%	100%
Jurors								
	increased 1829–1836	59	41%	2%	76%	22%	0%	100%
	increased 1836–1841	66	44%	6%	70%	21%	3%	100%
	decreased 1829–1836	15	40%	13%	80%	7%	0%	100%
	decreased 1836–1841	22	36%	0%	77%	9%	14%	100%
	static[1] 1829–1836	9	33%	11%	56%	22%	11%	100%
	static[1] 1836–1841	33	21%	3%	67%	24%	6%	100%
1834 petitioners								
	increased 1829–1836	39	49%	10%	77%	13%	0%	100%
	increased 1836–1841	63	40%	16%	59%	17%	8%	100%
	decreased 1829–1836	21	43%	24%	43%	19%	15%	100%
	decreased 1836–1841	24	44%	4%	75%	13%	8%	100%
	static[1] 1829–1836	2	0%	0%	100%	0%	0%	100%
	static[1] 1836–1841	26	38%	12%	62%	27%	0%	101%

[1] Those whose assessment changed less than $2,000.

TABLE B-9. Did increases, decreases, or stasis in property assessments depend on the occupations in which taxables were engaged?

Category	Percentage of each occupational group whose assessments 1829–1836				Percentage of each occupational group whose assessments 1836–1841			
	Increased	Decreased	Changed less than $2,000	Total	Increased	Decreased	Changed less than $2,000	Total
Elite candidates								
High-prestige occupations	70%	25%	4%	99%	53%	29%	18%	100%
Professional	58%	35%	6%	99%	55%	27%	18%	100%
Mercantile	72%	23%	6%	101%	56%	27%	17%	99%
Mechanic	63%	23%	15%	101%	69%	19%	12%	100%
Other	52%	35%	13%	100%	49%	33%	18%	100%
Jurors								
High-prestige occupations	75%	19%	6%	100%	66%	18%	16%	100%
Professional	25%	50%	25%	100%	80%	0%	20%	100%
Mercantile	68%	20%	12%	100%	54%	20%	26%	100%
Mechanic	76%	6%	18%	100%	58%	8%	33%	99%
Other	50%	0%	50%	100%	29%	43%	29%	101%
1834 petitioners								
High-prestige occupations	68%	32%	0%	100%	54%	24%	22%	100%
Professional	44%	56%	0%	100%	71%	7%	21%	99%
Mercantile	75%	23%	3%	101%	52%	25%	23%	100%
Mechanic	56%	44%	0%	100%	52%	14%	33%	99%
Other	0%	75%	25%	100%	71%	29%	0%	100%

Property Distribution and Changes in Property Ownership

TABLE C-1. Changes in urban slaveholding, 1830–1840, among Charlestonians resident in both years

Categories of residents whose slaveholding is known	Number known to be resident in both years	Those whose slave holdings			
		Increased	Decreased	Remained unchanged	TOTAL
Elite candidates	1,268	49%	29%	22%	100%
Jurors[1]	609	49%	31%	20%	100%
1830 voters[2]	849	47%	36%	17%	100%

NOTE: In this and in all the tables which follow:

[1] Jurors include all elite candidates who were jurors 1829–1841 and a sample of 5/8 of other jurors not known definitely to live outside Charleston and Charleston Neck. The sample has been multiplied by 1.6 and added to the population of elite candidate jurors.

[2] Voters include all elite candidates who voted in the 1830 Charleston and Charleston Neck election of state legislators and 5/12 of others who voted in that election. The sample has been multiplied by 2.4 and added to the population of elite candidate voters.

The total slave population of both city and neck was 21,268 in 1830 and 21,900 in 1840.

TABLE C-2. Did the number of urban slaves which Charlestonians owned in 1830 influence the number which they owned in 1840?

Category (by the number of slaves owned in 1830)	Number of owners	Those 1830 urban slave owners whose urban slave holdings			1830 urban slave owners missing in 1840[1]	TOTAL
		Increased	Decreased	Remained unchanged		
Elite candidates[2]	1,268					
0	539	32%	—	25%	43%	100%
1–10	493	37%	28%	8%	27%	100%
11–20	154	31%	40%	8%	21%	100%
21+	82	9%	55%	0%	37%	101%
Jurors	881					
0	304	39%	—	24%	37%	100%
1–10	470	33%	30%	14%	24%	101%
11–20	78	29%	39%	10%	22%	100%
21+	29	14%	69%	0%	17%	100%
1830 voters	1,517					
0	581	26%	—	16%	58%	100%
1–10	741	28%	28%	7%	37%	100%
11–20	150	24%	45%	7%	24%	100%
21+	45	11%	67%	0%	22%	100%

[1] Includes those listed in 1830 census as household heads but not so listed in 1840.
[2] Correlation (Pearsonian) between elite candidates' 1830 and 1840 urban slave holdings is .378. For those who owned rural slaves in 1830 and 1840 the correlation between their rural slave holdings in 1830 and 1840 is .201.

TABLE C-3. How great was the change in Charlestonians' urban slave holdings between 1830 and 1840?

Category of those with urban slave holdings	Number of cases	Change in number of urban slaves owned (includes those whose holdings did not change)		1830–1840 change as percentage of 1830 urban slave holdings (excludes those whose holdings did not change)	
		Mean	Median	Mean	Median
Elite candidates	840	2	0	37%	0%
Elite jurors	397	2	1	45%	0%
Nonelite jurors	131	0	0	25%	14%
Elite 1830 voters	578	2	1	39%	0%
Nonelite 1830 voters	116	0	0	17%	−37%

TABLE C-4. How great was the gain for those Charlestonians whose urban slave holdings increased from 1830 to 1840?

Category of those whose urban slave holdings increased	Number of increasers	Increase in number of urban slaves owned		1830–1840 increase as percentage of 1830 urban slave holdings	
		Mean	Median	Mean	Median
Elite candidates	409	8	6	148%	80%
Elite jurors	206	7	5	150%	86%
Nonelite jurors	94	4	3	183%	100%
Elite 1830 voters	293	8	5	146%	80%
Nonelite 1830 voters	108	4	3	192%	150%

TABLE C-5. How great was the loss for those Charlestonians whose urban slave holdings decreased from 1830 to 1840?

Category of those whose urban slave holdings decreased	Number of decreasers	Decrease in number of urban slaves owned		1830–1840 decrease as percentage of 1830 urban slave holdings	
		Mean	Median	Mean	Median
Elite candidates	247	7	5	62%	59%
Elite jurors	121	6	4	59%	50%
Nonelite jurors	68	4	4	86%	100%
Elite 1830 voters	187	6	5	59%	75%
Nonelite 1830 voters	118	4	4	75%	89%

TABLE C-6. By how much did the rural slaveholding of elite candidate Charlestonians change from 1830 to 1840?

Category	Number of rural slaveholders	Change in number of rural slaves owned		1830–1840 change as percentage of 1830 rural slave holdings	
		Mean	Median	Mean	Median
Those whose rural slaveholding increased	41	60	32	145%	67%
Those whose rural slaveholding decreased	26	−19	−12	−27%	−21%
All those with rural slaves in both 1830 and 1840[1]	69	29	8	76%	17%

[1] Correlation (Pearsonian) between elite candidates' 1830 and 1840 rural slave holdings is .201.

TABLE C-7. What capital investments other than urban slaves did elite candidate urban slaveholders in Charleston have?

Those whose urban slave holdings	Investment in plantation slaves					Investment in land			Corporate investment
	Owned 20 or more plantation slaves in 1830	Owned 20 or more plantation slaves in 1840	Owned 50 or more plantation slaves in 1830	Owned 50 or more plantation slaves in 1840	Owned 100 or more plantation slaves in 1830	Owned 100 or more plantation slaves in 1840	Owned rural land sometime between 1820 and 1843	Owned 1-5 urban lots sometime between 1820 and 1843	Owned 6 or more urban lots sometime between 1820 and 1843	Owned corporate stock or government bonds sometime between 1828 and 1843
Increased (N = 409)	8%	11%	5%	8%	2%	5%	24%	57%	12%	34%
Decreased (N = 247)	9%	12%	5%	9%	1%	4%	30%	55%	14%	35%
Remained static (N = 184)	6%	3%	1%	7%	6%	2%	16%	45%	3%	24%

TABLE C-8. Did those whose urban slave holdings increased differ from those whose slave holdings decreased or stayed the same according to whether or not they engaged in high-prestige occupations? Did they differ according to the economic sector in which they worked?

1830 urban slaveholders also holding slaves in 1840	Number whose occupation is known for 1828–1832	High-prestige occupation in any economic sector	Economic sector					
			Agricultural	Professional	Mercantile	Mechanic	Other	TOTAL
Elite candidates								
Increasers	364	55%	16%	21%	44%	14%	5%	100%
Decreasers	217	55%	15%	23%	41%	13%	8%	100%
Remained the same	150	57%	10%	18%	53%	13%	7%	101%
Jurors								
Increasers	286	31%	10%	3%	55%	25%	6%	99%
Decreasers	173	32%	11%	2%	54%	25%	7%	99%
Remained the same	112	28%	4%	3%	65%	22%	6%	100%
1830 Voters								
Increasers	358	41%	12%	17%	44%	21%	6%	100%
Decreasers	265	34%	9%	18%	39%	26%	8%	100%
Remained the same	130	37%	6%	17%	48%	25%	4%	100%

TABLE C-9. Did increases, decreases, and stasis in urban slaveholding depend on the occupations in which the slaveholders were engaged?

Category and occupation, 1828–1832	Number of 1830 urban slaveholders of known occupation	Percentage of each occupational group whose urban slaveholding, 1830–1840			
		Increased	Decreased	Remained the same	TOTAL
Elite candidates					
High-prestige occupations	404	49%	30%	21%	100%
Agricultural	107	55%	31%	14%	100%
Professional	153	50%	32%	18%	100%
Mercantile	327	49%	27%	24%	100%
Mechanic	99	52%	29%	19%	100%
Other	45	38%	40%	22%	100%
Jurors					
High-prestige occupations	175	50%	32%	18%	100%
Agricultural	55	53%	39%	9%	101%
Professional	18	66%	17%	17%	100%
Mercantile	381	48%	29%	23%	100%
Mechanic	182	50%	30%	20%	100%
Other	50	52%	34%	14%	100%
1830 Voters					
High-prestige occupations	285	51%	32%	17%	100%
Agricultural	75	56%	33%	11%	100%
Professional	151	40%	41%	19%	100%
Mercantile	449	48%	33%	19%	100%
Mechanic	307	40%	42%	18%	100%
Other	69	50%	37%	13%	100%

Note on Sources

Because of the hundreds of items it would necessarily contain, we have decided against a formal bibliography. The most important items are cited in the notes. Nonetheless, a few observations are in order.

Although we have used a good many repositories, the vast bulk of primary material for both cities is concentrated in relatively few.

MANUSCRIPTS

Boston:
  Massachusetts Historical Society
  Baker Library, Harvard Business School
Charleston:
  South Carolina Historical Society
  Caroliniana Library, University of South Carolina
  Southern Historical Collection, University of North Carolina
  Historical Society of Pennsylvania
Both cities:
  Library of Congress

PRINTED MATERIAL

Boston:
  Boston Public Library
  Massachusetts Historical Society
  Baker Library, Harvard Business School

Charleston:
   Charleston Library Society
   South Carolina Historical Society
   Caroliniana Library, University of South Carolina
Both cities:
   Widener Library, Harvard University

The Documents of the City of Boston 1834 et seq. (cited in many notes) refers to the microfilm of printed Boston city documents filmed by Graphic Microfilm of New England for the Boston Public Library. Reels one through five cover the years 1834–1843. Other documents, both manuscript and printed, are housed in the Massachusetts State Archives, the South Carolina State Archives, and the National Archives.

Finally, special mention should be made of the Genealogical Society of Utah, which houses a vast collection of probate data and church records collected primarily for genealogists. These materials, filmed in a project sponsored by the Church of Jesus Christ of Latter-day Saints, can be used in Salt Lake City considerably more conveniently than in their original condition and diverse locations.

Abbreviations

AAL-MHS	Amos A. Lawrence Papers, Massachusetts Historical Society
AB-LC	Alexander Brown & Sons Papers, Library of Congress
Ad-MHS	Adams Papers, Massachusetts Historical Society
AJ-LC	Andrew Jackson Papers, Library of Congress
AL-MHS	Amos Lawrence Papers, Massachusetts Historical Society
Am-MHS	Amory Family Papers, Massachusetts Historical Society
Ap-MHS	Appleton Family Papers, Massachusetts Historical Society
APH-SCHS	Allston Pringle Hill Papers, South Carolina Historical Society
AV-SCHS	Arnoldus Vanderhorst Collection, South Carolina Historical Society
B-MHS	Brooks Family Papers, Massachusetts Historical Society
B&LRR-BL	Boston & Lowell Collection, Baker Library, Harvard Business School
BFP-USC	Benjamin Franklin Perry Papers, Caroliniana Library, University of South Carolina
BH-SCHS	Bacot-Huger Collection, South Carolina Historical Society
BL	Baker Library, Harvard Business School, Boston, Massachusetts
BPL	Boston Public Library, Boston, Massachusetts
CC	College of Charleston, Charleston, South Carolina
CC-USC	Christopher Cotes Papers, Caroliniana Library, University of South Carolina
D-HSP	Drayton Collection, Col. William Drayton Papers, Historical Society of Pennsylvania

DU	Perkins Library, Duke University, Durham, North Carolina
EE-MHS	Edward Everett Papers, Massachusetts Historical Society
EF-LC	Edward Frost Papers, Library of Congress
EG-SHC	Elliott-Gonzales Papers, Southern Historical Collection, University of North Carolina
EN-MHS	Everett-Noble Diaries, Massachusetts Historical Society
EPS-USC	Elihu Penquite Smith Papers, Caroliniana Library, University of South Carolina
FF-MHS	Forbes Family Papers, Massachusetts Historical Society
FHE-LC	Franklin Harper Elmore Papers, Library of Congress
GEE-MHS	George Edward Ellis Papers, Massachusetts Historical Society
HC-LC	Henry Clay Papers, Library of Congress
HGO-MHS	Harrison Gray Otis Papers, Massachusetts Historical Society
HH	Houghton Library, Harvard University, Cambridge, Massachusetts
HHR-DU	Harriott Horry Rutledge Letters, Duke University
HL-BL	Henry Lee Collection, Baker Library, Harvard Business School
HM-MHS	Horace Mann Papers, Massachusetts Historical Society
HSL-USC	Hugh Swinton Legaré Papers, Caroliniana Library, University of South Carolina
HSP	Historical Society of Pennsylvania, Philadelphia, Pennsylvania
HWST-USC	Howland, Ward, Spring and Taft Co. Papers, Caroliniana Library, University of South Carolina
JCC-USC	John Caldwell Calhoun Papers, Caroliniana Library, University of South Carolina
JEC-USC	James Edward Calhoun Papers, Caroliniana Library, University of South Carolina
JG-USC	James Gadsden Papers, Caroliniana Library, University of South Carolina
JH-USC	James Hamilton Papers, Caroliniana Library, University of South Carolina
JHH-LC	James H. Hammond Papers, Library of Congress
JHH-USC	James H. Hammond Papers, Caroliniana Library, University of South Carolina
JJA-HH	John James Audubon Papers, Houghton Library, Harvard University
JLP-LC	James L. Petigru Papers, Library of Congress

Abbreviations 263

JLP-USC	James Louis Petigru Papers, Caroliniana Library, University of South Carolina
JMG-SHC	James M. Gage Papers, Southern Historical Collection, University of North Carolina
JP-HSP	Joel Poinsett Papers, Historical Society of Pennsylvania
JWM-SCHS	John W. Mitchell Correspondence, South Carolina Historical Society
KA-USC	Kincaid-Anderson Family Papers, Caroliniana Library, University of South Carolina
L-MHS	Lamb Family Papers, Massachusetts Historical Society
LC	Library of Congress, Washington, D.C.
LC-SCHS	Langdon Cheves Collection, South Carolina Historical Society
Le-MHS	Lee Family Papers, Massachusetts Historical Society
LM-DU	Louis Manigault Papers, Duke University
LPLSC-SCA	Legislative Papers, Legislative System, City of Charleston, South Carolina Archives
LS-MHS	Lemuel Shaw Papers, Massachusetts Historical Society
LW-LC	Levi Woodbury Papers, Library of Congress
M-SCHS	Manigault Papers, South Carolina Historical Society
M-SHC	Milligan Papers, Southern Historical Collection, University of North Carolina
MA	Massachusetts Archives, State House, Boston, Massachusetts
MF-USC	Manly Family Papers, Caroliniana Library, University of South Carolina
MHL-BL	Massachusetts Hospital Life Insurance Company Collection, Baker Library, Harvard Business School
MHS	Massachusetts Historical Society, Boston, Massachusetts
MK-SHC	Mitchell King Papers, Southern Historical Collection, University of North Carolina
MK-USC	Mitchell King Manuscripts, Caroliniana Library, University of South Carolina
MM-USC	Miscellaneous Manuscripts, Caroliniana Library, University of South Carolina
MMIC-BL	Mercantile Marine Insurance Company Collection, Baker Library, Harvard Business School
MV-LC	Martin Van Buren Papers, Library of Congress
NA	National Archives, Washington, D.C.
NB-LC	Nicholas Biddle Papers, Library of Congress
NEHGS	New England Historical and Genealogical Society, Boston, Massachusetts

NRM-SHC	Nathaniel Russell Middleton Papers, Southern Historical Collection, University of North Carolina
R-USC	Rutledge Family Papers, Caroliniana Library, University of South Carolina
RYH-USC	Robert Young Hayne Papers, Caroliniana Library, University of South Carolina
S-SHC	Singleton Papers, Southern Historical Collection, University of North Carolina
SAM-DU	Samuel Arell Marsteller Papers, Duke University
SB-BL	Suffolk Bank Collection, Baker Library, Harvard Business School
SCA	South Carolina Archives, Columbia, South Carolina
SCH-SCHS	Shirley Carter Hughson Collection ("Letters of the Period of Nullification"), South Carolina Historical Society
SCHS	South Carolina Historical Society, Charleston, South Carolina
SHC	Southern Historical Collection, University of North Carolina, Chapel Hill, North Carolina
STA-MHS	Samuel Turell Armstrong Papers, Massachusetts Historical Society
STM-MHS	Samuel Torrey Morse Papers, Massachusetts Historical Society
T-BL	Tudor Family–Ice Company Collection, Baker Library, Harvard Business School
TBW-BL	Wharves and Docks Collection; Thomas B. Wales & Co., Central Wharf, Baker Library, Harvard Business School
TD-NA	Treasury Department Records, National Archives
THP-MHS	Thomas Handasyd Perkins Papers, Massachusetts Historical Society
TJ-USC	Timothy W. Johnson Manuscripts, Caroliniana Library, University of South Carolina
USC	Caroliniana Library, University of South Carolina, Columbia, South Carolina
W-MHS	Winthrop Papers, Massachusetts Historical Society
WA-BL	William Appleton & Co. Collection, Baker Library, Harvard Business School
WC-MHS	Warren-Clarke Family Papers, Massachusetts Historical Society
WCM-USC	Williams-Chesnut-Manning Collection, Caroliniana Library, University of South Carolina
WD-USC	William Christopher Dukes Manuscripts, Caroliniana Library, University of South Carolina

Abbreviations

WHL	Waring Historical Library, Medical University of South Carolina, Charleston, South Carolina
WJ-MHS	William Jenks Papers, Massachusetts Historical Society
WL-DU	William Law Papers, Duke University
WMP-USC	William Mazyck Porcher Manuscripts, Caroliniana Library, University of South Carolina
WO-USC	William Ogilby Papers, Caroliniana Library, University of South Carolina
WP-MHS	Walcott-Pickman Family Papers, Massachusetts Historical Society
WPM-SHC	William Porcher Miles Papers, Southern Historical Collection, University of North Carolina
YS-USC	Yates Snowden Collection, Caroliniana Library, University of South Carolina

Notes

1: The Places and Their People

1. Anne Royall, *Mrs Royall's Southern Tour; or, Second Series of the Black Book* (Washington: n.p., 1831), II, 3; Samuel Cram Jackson, Diary, Oct. 18, 1832, Southern Historical Collection, University of North Carolina, Chapel Hill (hereafter SHC).
2. Medical Society of South Carolina, Minute Book, Dec. 2, 1829, typed copy, Waring Historical Library, Medical University of South Carolina (hereafter WHL).
3. George Townsend Fox, Journal, Sept. 16, 1831, British Records in Relation to America in Microform, Series B; Enoch Cobb Wines, *A Trip to Boston, in a Series of Letters to the Editor of the United States Gazette* . . . (Boston: C. C. Little & James Brown, 1838), 60, 25–26.
4. In 1829, a third of Boston's most powerful and wealthy men lived on just seven streets: Beacon, Chestnut, Mount Vernon, Summer, Washington, and Tremont streets and Franklin Place. (See Appendix A for source and derivation of quantified biographical information.) See also Edward Pessen, "The Lifestyle of the Antebellum Urban Elite," *Mid-America*, LV (July 1973), 180–81.
5. John Morrill Bryon, "Boston's Granite Architecture c. 1810–1860" (Ph.D. dissertation, Boston University, 1972), 59–60.
6. Charlotte Brooks Everett to Edward Everett, Dec. 23, 1829, Nov. 29, 1833, Edward Everett Papers, Massachusetts Historical Society (hereafter EE-MHS).
7. Robert Howard Lord et al., *History of the Archdiocese of Boston in Various Stages of its Development, 1604 to 1943* (New York: Sheed & Ward, 1944), II, 126, estimates the Catholic population at 7,040 in 1829; Lemuel Shattuck, *Report to the Committee of the City Council Appointed to Obtain the Census of Boston for the Year 1845* . . . (Boston: John H. Eastburn, 1846), 43, reports 1,875 Negroes in 1830.
8. Quotations from Boston Society for the Religious and Moral Instruction

of the Poor, *Annual Report* ([Boston]: n.p., annual): 1826, 25; 1827, 14; 1834, 6–7. Boston City Council, *Report of the Committee to Whom was Referred the Consideration of . . . Improving that Part of the Common Lying West of Charles Street* (Boston: n.p., 1829), 11. The latter reports on the physical conditions as well.

9. Harrison Gray Otis to George Harrison, June 10, 1832, Harrison Gray Otis Papers, MHS (hereafter HGO-MHS); Allen Jason Share, "British Travellers and American Cities, 1830–1860: Images and Realities" (Ph.D. dissertation, University of Toledo, 1973), 139–40; John J. Audubon to Robert Howell, August 13, 1832, J. J. Audubon Papers, Houghton Library, Harvard University (hereafter JJA-HH).

10. Charleston *Courier,* Oct. 27, 1830, put 55% in the western wards.

11. Quotations from Harriet Martineau, *Retrospect of Western Travel* (London: Saunders & Otley, 1838), I, 228; Silas Pinckney Holbrook, "South Carolina," *New England Magazine,* I (1831), 246; Royall, *Southern Tour,* 8.

12. United States Fifth Decennial Census, *Statistics of the United States of America as Collected and Returned by the Marshals . . .* (Washington: Blair & Rives, 1831), 95, gives the city's population as 12,838 whites, 15,349 slaves, and 2,102 free blacks, while the Neck had 3,016 whites, 5,919 slaves, and 1,119 free blacks; Julian J. Petty, *The Growth and Distribution of Population in South Carolina* (Spartanburg, S.C.: The Reprint Company, c. 1943, 1975), 73.

13. Of 228 known planters, 56% lived in the two northern wards and the Neck, 1828–1832, as did 33% of the 297 known merchants and 44% of the 227 known professionals. Of all those who wielded any power or influence, 60% lived and worked in the same section of the city. And, if nonelite jurors are representative of all other Charlestonians with no such claim, 94% of them lived and worked in the same section. Of all Charleston's 1830 mechanic voters without power or wealth, 57% lived north of Queen Street, and 42% of its shopkeepers lived on King Street or in the third ward of which the commercial reaches of King Street were part.

14. Ernest M. Lander, Jr., "Charleston: Manufacturing Center of the Old South," *Journal of Southern History,* XXVI (August 1960), 345; idem, *The Textile Industry in Antebellum South Carolina* (Baton Rouge: Louisiana State University Press, 1969), 7–28.

15. J. L. Dawson and H. W. DeSaussure, *Census of the City of Charleston, South Carolina, for the year 1848 . . . Prepared under the Authority of the City Council* (Charleston: J. B. Nixon, 1849), 92; Petty, *Population in South Carolina,* 70.

16. George C. Rogers, Jr., *Charleston in the Age of the Pinckneys* (Norman: University of Oklahoma Press, 1969), 52; idem, "The Transition to the Nineteenth Century Economy," in Ernest M. Lander, Jr., and Robert K. Ackerman, *Perspectives in South Carolina History, the First 300 Years* (Columbia: University of South Carolina Press, 1973), 87–89.

17. Doddridge Crocker & Co. to Thomas Lamb, April 10, 1828, Lamb Family Papers, MHS (hereafter L-MHS); Charleston Chamber of Commerce, *Report of a Special Committee . . . to Inquire into the Cost, Revenue, and Advantages of a Rail Road . . .* (Charleston: A. E. Miller, 1828), 22; *Southern Agriculturist and Register of Rural Affairs,* II (May 1829), 204–5.

18. Samuel Eliot Morison, *The Maritime History of Massachusetts, 1783–1860* (Boston: Sentry Books, c. 1921, 1961), 216; Francis Xavier Blouin, Jr., "The Boston Region 1810–1850: A Study of Urbanization on a Regional Scale" (Ph.D. dissertation, University of Minnesota, 1978), 279, Appendix II; Boston *Daily Advertiser,* Jan. 11, 1828; United States Department of State, *Report of the Secretary . . . of Such Articles Manufactured in the United States . . .* (Washington: Gales & Seaton, 1824), 18, 24–25.
19. From 43,928 to 61,392.
20. Boston *Morning Post,* August 3, 1830; Morison, *Maritime History,* 232–34, 261, 273–76.
21. Abbott Lawrence to Edward Everett, Feb. 25, 1826, EE-MHS. Quotation from Charles Francis Adams to John Quincy Adams, April 29, 1828, Adams Papers, MHS (hereafter Ad-MHS).
22. Samuel Appleton, draft document, 1828, Appleton Family Papers, MHS (hereafter Ap-MHS); Peter C. Brooks to Edward Everett, Feb. 2, 1829, EE-MHS.

2: The Economic Heritage

1. Amos Lawrence to Amos A. Lawrence, July 26, 1835, Amos A. Lawrence Papers, MHS (hereafter AAL-MHS).
2. The family connection has been elaborated especially in Peter D. Hall, "Family Structure and Class Consolidation among Boston Brahmins" (Ph.D. dissertation, State University of New York at Stony Brook, 1973), 154, and Kenneth W. Porter, *The Jacksons and the Lees: Two Generations of Massachusetts Merchants, 1765–1884* (Cambridge: Harvard University Press, 1937), I, 89–94. The practice of admitting outsiders is clearly revealed in Samuel D. Warren's correspondence, 1831 ff., Warren-Clarke Family Papers, MHS (hereafter WC-MHS); and correspondence of Captains David Low and James W. Low with Thomas Lamb, 1825–1831, L-MHS.
3. John McCardell, *The Idea of a Southern Nation: Southern Nationalists and Southern Nationalism, 1830–1860* (New York: W. W. Norton & Co., 1979), 73; Bertram Wyatt-Brown, *Southern Honor: Ethics and Behavior in the Old South* (New York: Oxford University Press, 1982), 182–83. Of 324 known merchants and factors, 1828–1832, 53 (17%) held deeds to plantation land recorded in the Charleston, South Carolina, Registry of Mesne Conveyance (hereafter RMC) between 1820 and 1843. All or most land transactions made in Charleston were recorded, regardless of where the land was located, but the deeds are most complete for the low-country north of Beaufort and south of Georgetown.
4. Rosser H. Taylor, "The Gentry of Ante-Bellum South Carolina," *North Carolina Historical Review,* XVII (April 1940), 117; William Ogilby, Consular Report on Charleston Trade, 1833, William Ogilby Papers, Caroliniana Library, University of South Carolina (hereafter WO-USC).
5. Gregory Allen Greb, "Charleston, South Carolina, Merchants 1815–1860: Urban Leadership in the Antebellum South" (Ph.D. dissertation, University of California at San Diego, 1978), 151–52; Edwin J. Perkins, *Financing Anglo-American Trade: The House of Brown, 1800–1860* (Cambridge: Harvard University Press, 1975), 110; David Low to Thomas Lamb, May 7 and July 13, 1825, L-MHS; D. Crocker & Co. to Thomas Lamb, March

5, 1828, L-MHS; Alexander Brown & Sons to Adger & Black, Sept. 30, 1828, Alexander Brown & Sons Papers, Library of Congress (hereafter AB-LC).
6. Charleston Chamber of Commerce, *Rules for the Government . . .* (Charleston: W. Riley, 1828, 1836); idem, Awards Records, South Carolina Historical Society (hereafter SCHS).
7. William Sullivan, *A Discourse Delivered before the Boston Mechanic Association . . . February 7, 1832* (Boston: Carter and Hendee, 1832), 5–7; Boston *Daily Advertiser and Patriot,* Jan. 11 and 20, 1836; William T. Davis, *Professional and Industrial History of Suffolk County, Massachusetts* (Boston: Boston History Co., 1894), II, 130–31.
8. Boston *Morning Post,* Aug. 20, 1835; Amos Lawrence to Amos A. Lawrence, Dec. 5, 1836, AAL-MHS.
9. Charleston *Courier,* Sept. 22, 1834; Elias Horry, Will, Aug. 16, 1833, Charleston Country Probate Records, vol. H, 40–51.
10. James Jackson Putnam, *A Memoir of Dr. James Jackson . . . and his Brothers* (Boston: Houghton Mifflin, 1905), 131–53.
11. Oscar Handlin and Mary Fludd Handlin, *Commonwealth: A Study of the Role of Government in the American Economy: Massachusetts, 1774–1861,* rev. ed. (Cambridge: Belknap Press, 1969), 99–121, 161–63.
12. Edwin M. Dodd, *American Business Corporations until 1860 with Special Reference to Massachusetts* (Cambridge: Harvard University Pres, 1954), 233, 212–13; Massachusetts, *Laws Passed . . . Beginning May 1828 and Ending March 1831* (Boston: Dutton and Wentworth, 1831), 323–33.
13. Silas P. Holbrook, "South Carolina," *New England Magazine,* I (1831), 249; South Carolina, *Statutes at Large,* David McCord, ed., (Columbia: A. S. Johnson, 1840), VIII, vi–vii; Carl Siracusa, *A Mechanical People: Perceptions of the Industrial Order in Massachusetts* (Middletown, Conn.: Wesleyan University Press, 1979), 19; Robert F. Dalzell, Jr., "The Rise of the Waltham-Lowell System and Some Thoughts on the Political Economy of Modernization in Ante-Bellum Massachusetts," *Perspectives in American History,* IX (1975), 236–38; Robert V. Spalding, "The Boston Mercantile Community and the Promotion of the Textile Industry in New England, 1813–1860" (Ph.D. dissertation, Yale University, 1963), 35–37. An insight into the differences in the two cities' ability to attract and consolidate capital through incorporation is given by the numbers and diversity of stock commonly traded in each. In 1829, reports on Charleston's securities trade listed shares in 4 local banks, the Bank of the United States, and 2 insurance companies. Boston in the same year listed 17 local banks, 16 insurance companies, 5 manufacturing companies, and 2 other corporations. In 1843 Charleston listed 5 local banks, 5 out-of-town banks, 1 insurance company, 1 canal, and 1 railroad. By 1843 Boston was trading shares in 24 local banks, 18 insurance companies, 23 manufacturing companies, 14 railroads, and 6 other corporations. Charleston *Courier,* Jan. 5, 1829, and April 14, 1843. Joseph G. Martin, *Seventy-three Years' History of the Boston Stock Market . . . 1798 to 1871 . . .* (Boston: The Author, 1871), 42 ff.
14. In both the South Carolina Canal and Rail Road Company and the Charleston and Liverpool Line Packet Company holders of more than 40 shares could cast only one vote for each ten additional shares; in the Bank of Charleston, holders of more than 25 shares had a single vote for each addi-

tional ten shares and, if they held more than 75 shares, they needed 20 shares for each additional vote.
15. Gavin Wright, *The Political Economy of the Cotton South: Households, Markets, and Wealth in the Nineteenth Century* (New York: W. W. Norton & Co., 1978), 114, emphasizes the rational, profit-oriented reasons for investing in land and slaves. Nineteen percent of the 324 known merchants and factors in 1828–1832 and 17% of the 318 in 1833–1838 either owned plantation land at some time between 1820 and 1843 or owned plantation slaves in 1830 or 1840. Twenty-nine percent of 243 known high-prestige professionals in 1828–1832 and 25% of the 245 in 1833–1838 shared in at least one of these indicators of planting.
16. Charleston *Courier*, March 8, 1833; Aug. 20, 1835; Daniel Cannon Webb, Journal, II, 1829, SCHS; Anthony Barbot to Thomas Lamb, April 10, 1833, L-MHS; James L. Petigru to Jane P. North, Dec. 24, 1835, in James L. Petigru, *Life, Letters and Speeches*, James P. Carson, ed. (Washington: W. H. Lowdermilk & Co., 1920), 180; James R. Pringle to Louis McLane, Jan. 28, 1833, "United States Treasury: Correspondence of the Secretary . . . with Collectors of Customs, 1789–1833," Record Group 56, M178, roll 32, National Archives.
17. Of 206 known bank shareholders, 63 owned rural land while 170 owned city land. At any one time no more than 19 listed themselves as planters. Of 330 railroad investors, 108 owned rural land while 260 owned city land. The maximum number listed at any one time as planters was 27. Of a list of about 360 original shareholders in South Carolina Canal and Rail Road Company, *Bylaws* . . . (Charleston: J. S. Burges, [1834]), about 90% of them could be found in Charleston directories.
18. In Boston the percentage of bank stock holders who were merchants ranged, in any one time, from 47% to 55%. In Charleston the range was from 54% to 74%. The percentage of bank shareholders engaged in any kind of commercial activity ranged from 67% to 82% in Charleston but held constant at 79% in Boston.
19. Of Boston share owners, 44% invested in different kinds of corporate ventures; of Charleston's stockholders only 24% invested in even one other corporation.
20. Adam Tunno, Inventory, 1833, Charleston, S.C., Probate Records, vol. G, 554–59; Israel Thorndike, Inventory, July 30, 1833, Suffolk County, Mass., Probate Court, Record Book 130, pt. 2, 60–66. John D. Forbes, *Israel Thorndike, Federalist Financier* (New York: Exposition Press, 1953), 134–40, chronicles Thorndike's investments.
21. Dalzell, "The Rise of the Waltham-Lowell System," 260, 263; Amos Lawrence to George C. Shattuck, July 2, 1833, quoted in Spalding, "The Boston Mercantile Community and the Promotion of the Textile Industry," 53. For expectations of profits from planting see John Berkley Grimball Diary, June 3, 1832, SHC; and Archie V. Huff, *Langdon Cheves of South Carolina* (Columbia: University of South Carolina Press, 1977), 155–56, 196–202. Nicholas Biddle to N. Silsbee, December 17, 1829, and [Statement of Shareholding in BUS], December 26, 1829, Nicholas Biddle Papers, LC (hereafter NB-LC). Fred Bateman and Thomas Weiss's *A Deplorable Scarcity: The Failure of Industrialization in the Slave Economy* (Chapel Hill: University of North Carolina Press, 1981), 141, discusses planters' failure to diversify.

22. Harrison Gray Otis, *Speech to the Citizens of Boston* . . . (Boston: J. H. Eastburn, 1830), 18; Catherine LaCroix, Will, Sept. 13, 1831; Louisa Elizabeth Cabeuil, Will, April 19, 1833; and Sarah C. Wing, Will, Feb. 12, 1834; all in Charleston, S.C., Probate Records, vol. G, 517–18, 690, 736–40.
23. Hall, "Family Structure and Class Consolidation," 238–40; Gerald T. White, *A History of the Massachusetts Hospital Life Insurance Company* (Cambridge: Harvard University Press, 1955), 50–51.
24. White, *Massachusetts Hospital Life*, 1–50, quotation at 37; Hall, "Family Structure and Class Consolidation," 399.
25. James G. Smith, *The Development of Trust Companies in the United States* (New York: H. Holt and Co., 1928), 245; Hall, "Family Structure and Class Consolidation," 389; Boston *Daily Advertiser*, July 21, 1829, and Jan. 21, 1834.
26. Oriental Bank, Correct List of Stockholders, Oct. 1, 1832, Oriental Bank Collection, Baker Library, Harvard Business School (hereafter BL); Norman S. B. Gras, *The Massachusetts First National Bank of Boston, 1784–1934* (Cambridge: Harvard University Press, 1937), 550.
27. Hall, "Family Structure and Class Consolidation," 398. For Charleston eleemosynary institutions' investments see, for example, Society for the Relief of Orphans and Widows of the Clergy of the Protestant Episcopal Church in South Carolina, Treasurers Book, 1830, SCHS; German Friendly Society, Minutes, Jan. 16, 1833, typescript, College of Charleston; New England Society, Minute Book, Dec. 22, 1836, SCHS. John B. Grimball Diary, June 8, 1832, SHC.

3: Boston's Boom Years

1. Gardiner Greene to Nicholas Biddle, Nov. 22, 1828, NB-LC; Frederic Tudor, Diary, June 21, 1828, and June 3, 1829, Tudor Family–Ice Company Collection, BL (hereafter T-BL).
2. Robert V. Spalding, "The Boston Mercantile Community and the Promotion of the Textile Industry in New England, 1813–1860" (Ph.D. dissertation, Yale University, 1963), 48; *Great Rail Road Meeting* (Boston: Massachusetts Journal, 1830), broadside; Charleston *City Gazette*, Aug. 7, 1829.
3. Joseph Tuckerman, *Second Semiannual Report, 1829* (Boston: Bowles & Dearborn, 1829), 3–6; idem, *Prize Essay on the Wages Paid to Females for their Labour* (Philadelphia: Carey & Hart, 1830), 12–15; Boston *Daily Advertiser*, Dec. 1, 1829.
4. Boston *Courier*, July 17, 1830, quoted in Stephen Salsbury, *The State, the Investor and the Railroad: The Boston & Albany, 1825–1867* (Cambridge: Harvard University Press, 1967), 76; William R. Lawrence, ed., *Extracts from the Diary and Correspondence of the Late Amos Lawrence* . . . (Boston: Gould and Lincoln, 1855), 103; Lemuel Shattuck, *Report of the Committee of the City Council Appointed to Obtain the Census of Boston for the Year 1845* . . . (Boston: John H. Dearborn, 1846), Appendix, 53.
5. *Spirit of the Age and Journal of Humanity*, I (August 1833), 33; Boston *Daily Advertiser*, Jan.–Feb. 1829 and Feb. 9, 1830; Petition of Samuel L. Lewis and others for a Bank in Boston, Feb. 9, 1833, MS Massachusetts Senate Document #9378, Massachusetts Archives (hereafter MA); Mill Pond Wharf Corporation, Memorandum of Purchase, March 21, 1833,

Mill Pond Wharf Corporation Collection, BL; Lewis Wharf Company, *Report of the Board of Directors . . . at Annual Meeting, held April 6, 1840* (Boston: Beals & Greene, 1840), 3–13; Samuel E. Morison, *Maritime History of Massachusetts, 1783–1860* (Boston: Sentry Books, c. 1921, 1961), 225n.
6. Morison, *Maritime History,* 274–76, 290; Shattuck, *Census of Boston . . . 1845,* Appendix, 53; Robert G. Albion, *Square Riggers On Schedule: The New York Sailing Packets to England, France, and Cotton Ports* (Hamden, Conn.: Archon Books, c. 1938, 1965), 50, notes New York's similarly triangular trade.
7. Harrison Gray Otis, *Speech to the Citizens of Boston . . .* (Boston: J. H. Eastburn, 1830), 13–15; Boston *Daily Advertiser,* Sept. 1, 1831; Central Wharf and Wet Dock Corporation, Trustees Minute Book, July 31, 1839, Central Wharf and Wet Dock Corporation Collection, BL.
8. Of 137 known investors in wharves and docks, 76 were known to hold stock in Boston banks, 67 in local insurance companies, 44 in railroads, 31 in textile manufacture, and 26 in city land companies.
9. Of 30 known directors, 21 had more than $30,000 taxable property at sometime during the decade; 20 served on at least one other corporate board.
10. Boston *Daily Advertiser,* Jan. 4, 1831, Jan. 6, 1836.
11. Amos Lawrence to Amos A. Lawrence, Nov. 15, 1836, AAL-MHS.
12. John A. Lowell to Nathan Appleton, Jan. 15, 1833, Ap-MHS. Of the 68 known investors whose occupations were known in 1829, 77% were in commerce; of the 71 known in 1836, 67%; of the 57 in 1841, 74%. Of the 69 whose tax assessments for 1829 were listed in printed assessors' rolls, 40% were assessed at over $50,000; of the 86 in 1836, 48%; of the 89 in 1841, 51%. Those worth more than $150,000 increased from 4 in 1829 to 17 in 1836 and then decreased to 13 in 1841. Of the 105 known textile investors, 53% were known to have held bank stocks, 48% insurance stock, 33% railroad stock, and 30% wharf stock.
13. Paul F. McGouldrick, *New England Textiles in the Nineteenth Century: Profits and Investments* (Cambridge: Harvard University Press, 1968), 81.
14. Amos A. Lawrence, Draft article [1836], AAL-MHS; Boston *Daily Advertiser,* Oct. 26, 1836.
15. Frederic Tudor, Diary, Oct. 2, 1831, T-BL; William Appleton, Diary, inserted fragment, vol. 167, Dec. 31, 1831, William Appleton & Company Collection, BL (hereafter WA-BL); James W. Paige to Nathan Appleton, Dec. 20, 1831, Ap-MHS; Harrison Gray Otis to George Harrison, Sept. 27, 1833, HGO-MHS.
16. William Sullivan to William Appleton, May 5, 1832, WA-BL; Boston *Morning Post,* May 1, 1833; Frederic Tudor, Diary, May 22, 1833, T-BL.
17. United States Treasury Department, *Documents Relative to the Manufactures in the United States Collected and Transmitted to the House of Representatives . . .* (Washington: Duff Green, 1833), I, 433–69.
18. Josiah Quincy, *A Municipal History of the Town and City of Boston during Two Centuries* (Boston: C. C. Little and J. Brown, 1852), 252; Boston *Daily Advertiser,* Aug. 19, 1831.
19. A special committee of the Massachusetts Charitable Mechanics Association attempted to define the distinction only then emerging between mechanic and manufacturer in April 1837: "A mechanic is one who operates

in his trade by the use of implements applied by the hand—one who uses his appropriate tools with appropriate skill. This is sometimes called 'handicraft.' The manufacturer is one who by skilful use of machinery produces from the raw material articles which usually pass through the hands of the mechanic before they are applied to the purposes of life." Massachusetts Charitable Mechanics Association, *Annals,* Joseph Buckingham, comp. (Boston: Crocker & Brewster, 1853), 284. Gary J. Kornblith, "From Artisans to Businessmen: Master Mechanics in New England, 1789–1850" (Paper delivered at the Organization of American Historians annual meeting, April 1978), 3, argues that the shift came in the 1830s, when mechanics ceased their early celebration of the "new machine technology." Boston *Morning Post,* Sept. 20, 1832; James L. Homer, *An Address Delivered before the Massachusetts Charitable Mechanic Association* (Boston: The Association, 1836), 25.

20. Willard Badger et al., Broadside, Nov. 1, 1832, and Boston Steam Factory, [Broadside] *Statement of the Object and Design . . . Made before the Committee, to Whom Was Referred the Petition for an Act of Incorporation,* March 11, 1833, MHS. The Boston Water Power Company had rented out rooms and power to independent mechanics in 1827–1829. [Rent and Memorandum Book], vol. HF-1, Boston Water Power Company Collection, BL; Allan R. Pred, *The Spatial Dynamics of U.S. Urban-Industrial Growth, 1800–1914* (Cambridge: MIT Press, 1966), 159; U.S. Treasury Department, *Documents Relative to the Manufactures,* I, 432–69; *The Young Mechanic . . . ,* I (May 1832), 74–75.

21. P. P. F. DeGrand to John Quincy Adams, Jan. 29, 1834, and Public Meeting of Merchants, Traders, Mechanics and Others, [Printed Notice, Jan. 11, 1834], both Ad-MHS.

22. Boston *Daily Advertiser,* Jan. 13 and July 24, 1834; Harrison Gray Otis to George Harrison, Jan. 13, 1834, HGO-MHS; Charles Francis Adams to John Quincy Adams, Feb. 17, 1834, and Abbott Lawrence to John Quincy Adams, Jan. 28, 1834, Ad-MHS.

23. Boston *Morning Post,* May 2, 1834.

24. Joseph G. Martin, *Seventy-three Years' History of the Boston Stock Market . . . 1798–1871 . . .* (Boston: The Author, 1871), 42–43; Massachusetts, *Laws Passed . . . Beginning May, 1828, and Ending March 1831* (Boston: Dutton and Wentworth, 1831), 577–81; [Nathan Appleton], *An Examination of the Banking System of Massachusetts in Reference to the Renewal of Bank Charters* (Boston: Stimpson & Clapp, 1831), 36.

25. Francis X. Blouin, "The Boston Region, 1810–1850: A Study of Urbanization on a Regional Scale" (Ph.D. dissertation, University of Minnesota, 1978), 184–225, especially 190–92.

26. Ebenezer T. Andrews to Samuel T. Armstrong, Nov. 24, 1836, Samuel T. Armstrong Papers, MHS (hereafter STA-MHS).

27. Of 579 directorships in area banks held by Boston men, 1828–1836, 351 were held by men who directed at least one other corporation, and 168 served on three or more boards.

28. David R. Whitney, *The Suffolk Bank* (Cambridge: Riverside Press, 1878), 7–20; Peter Temin, *The Jacksonian Economy* (New York: W. W. Norton Co., 1969), 51, 75; Martin, *Seventy-three Years of the Boston Stock Market,* 43–46.

29. Nicholas Biddle to Thomas H. Perkins, June 7, 1831, Letterbook, and

P. P. F. DeGrand to Biddle, Feb. 2, 1834, NB-LC. Charlotte Everett to Edward Everett, Feb. 21, 1834, EE-MHS.

30. Boston Citizens, *An Exposition of Facts and Arguments in Support of a Memorial to the Legislature of Massachusetts, . . . in Favor of a Bank of Ten Millions* (Boston: Dutton and Wentworth, 1836), 5–35, quotation at 25.

31. Boston Merchants, *A Petition . . . in 1834, to the Legislature of Massachusetts, for a Repeal of the Usury Laws and a Joint Report on the Subject* (Boston: Eastburns, 1850), 3–8; Boston *Daily Advertiser,* March 28 and Oct. 31, 1836; Amos W. Stetson, *State National Bank. Eighty Years. An Historical Sketch . . .* (Boston: The Directors, [1891]), 51–58; Frederic Tudor, Diary, Feb. 3, 1837, T-BL.

32. Federal census counted 61,392 in 1830; city census, 78,603 in 1835. In 1830 there were 3,448 aliens; in 1835, 7,684. The proportion of the population age 15 to 60 went from 64.96% in 1830 to 64.66% in 1840. (The city census employed an incomparable age distribution.) In 1830 there were 111.43 females per 100 males; in 1835 the ratio was 103.58 females to 100 males. Boston *Daily Advertiser,* Aug. 30, 1830; Boston *Morning Post,* Dec. 16, 1835; Shattuck, *Census of Boston . . . 1845,* 45, 50. Peter R. Knights, *The Plain People of Boston, 1830–1860* (New York: Oxford, 1971), 107, finds 39.4% of his 1830 population sample engaged in manual labor. In addition, a substantial number of the 21.3% in miscellaneous and unknown occupations were probably engaged in manual labor occupations unlisted in city directories. His 1840 sample was 38.7% manual labor and 15.8% unknown and miscellaneous.

33. Diane Lindstrom, *Economic Development in the Philadelphia Region, 1810–1850* (New York: Columbia University Press, 1978), 11; Suffolk Bank, Directors Records, Minutes, vol. 5, Suffolk Bank Collection, BL; U.S. Treasury Department, *Documents Relative to Manufactures,* 433–69; William Appleton, Diary, Dec. 1836, vol. 167, WA-BL.

34. Carl Siracusa, *A Mechanical People: Perceptions of the Industrial Order in Massachusetts* (Middletown, Conn.: Wesleyan University Press, 1979), 155–59; Boston *Morning Post,* March 12 and 27, May 23, July 23, and Sept. 10, 1832; Charleston *Courier,* May 30, 1832.

35. *Circular to the Mechanics of the City of Boston and Vicinity . . . February 11, 1834* (Boston: Artisan Office, 1834), broadside; Frederick Robinson, *An Oration Delivered before the Trades Union of Boston and Vicinity* (Boston: C. Douglas, 1834), 31–32, 26–28.

36. Boston *Morning Post,* Dec. 6, 1832; Robinson, *Oration . . . before the Trades Union,* 13–14.

37. Boston *Morning Post,* April 11, Oct. 6, and June 26, 1835; Boston Journeymen Bootmakers Society, *Constitution . . . Adopted October 12, 1835* (Boston: Mudge and Dexter, 1837), 2; Amos A. Lawrence to Amos Lawrence, May 17, 1836, Amos Lawrence Papers, MHS (hereafter AL-MHS).

38. Josiah Quincy, *An Address to the Board of Aldermen and Members of City Council . . . January 1, 1828* (Boston: N. Hale, 1828), 14; Homer, *Address,* 19; Boston *Morning Post,* Dec. 22, 1835; Joseph Tuckerman, *First Semiannual Report,* 1830 (Boston: Bowles & Dearborn, 1830), 5.

39. William Appleton, Diary, Jan. 1835 and Jan. 1, 1836, vol. 167, WA-BL; Central Wharf and Wet Dock Corporation, Dividend Book, Central Wharf

and Wet Dock Corporation, Collection, vol. A-5, BL; Shattuck, *Census of Boston . . . 1845,* Appendix, 57; Martin, *Seventy-three Years of the Boston Stock Market,* 66; Boston *Daily Advertiser,* Jan. 27 and Oct. 3, 1836.
40. Edward Everett, Diary, April 17 and 18, 1835, EE-MHS; Frederic Tudor, Diary, May 15, 1836, T-BL; *Southern Rose,* V (March 4, 1837), 108; Robert C. Winthrop to J. Temple Bowdoin, March 27, 1837, Winthrop Papers, MHS (hereafter W-MHS); *Spirit of the Age and Journal of Humanity,* June 13, 1833. Of the 44 mechanics in 1836 who were assessed for property of $30,000 or more, 17 were in the building trades.
41. Walter Firey, *Land Use in Central Boston* (Cambridge: Harvard University Press, 1946), 58; Fatherless and Widows' Society, *Twentieth Annual Report* (Boston: Perkins & Marvin, 1837), 8–9.
42. Of 209 stockholders whose property assessments are known, 118 were assessed for less than $10,000 in 1836, and only 30 for $30,000 or more of taxable property.
43. Winnisimmet Company, Annual Reports, 1836, 1838, 1839, and Minutes of Directors Meetings, 1833–1853, BPL. Boston *Morning Post,* July 19 and Aug. 14, 1832; Boston *Daily Advertiser,* Nov. 2, 1836.
44. William H. Sumner, *A History of East Boston . . .* (Boston: J. E. Tilton, 1858), 426–53; East Boston Wharf Company Minute Book, 1833–1866, 1–16, East Boston Wharf Company Collection, BL; East Boston Company, *Description of East Boston, and a Statement of the Property of the East Boston Company* (Boston: n.p., 1836), 5–11; *A Sketch of Improvements at East Boston* (Boston: J. T. Buckingham, 1836); Frederic Tudor to Robert H. Gardiner, June 2, 1836, T-BL.
45. South Cove Corporation, *First Annual Report of the Board of Directors . . . to the Stockholders* (Boston: Perkins, Marvin & Co., 1834), 5–15, 19–23; idem, *Seventh Annual Report . . .* (Boston: Crocker & Brewster, 1840), 5–8; idem, *Third Annual Report . . .* (Boston: Crocker & Brewster, 1836), 12; idem, *Fourth Annual Report . . .* (Boston: Crocker & Brewster, 1837), 15.
46. Boston *Daily Advertiser,* Sept. 17, 1831; Boston *Morning Post,* March 24, 1835; Massachusetts, *Laws of the Commonwealth . . . Passed . . . May 1831 and Ending March 1833* (Boston: Dutton and Wentworth, 1833), 820; Boston Wharf Company, *First Annual Report* (Boston: n.p., 1837), 5–8.
47. Of the 1,000 men who held corporate directorships throughout the decade, only 349 were assessed on $30,000 or more of property and only 284 enjoyed moderately high or great social status. Of the 524 whose assessments were published for 1836, 45 were assessed for more than $100,000; 297 at $30,000 or less.

4: Charleston's Dream of Prosperity

1. J. L. Dawson and H. W. DeSaussure, *Census of the City of Charleston, South Carolina, for the Year 1848 . . .* (Charleston: J. B. Nixon, 1849), 101, 132, 135.
2. George McDuffie, *Speech . . . at a Public Dinner Given to Him by the Citizens of Charleston, May 19, 1831 . . .* (Charleston: A. E. Miller, 1831), 29; Anne Royall, *Mrs. Royall's Southern Tour; or, Second Series of the Black Book* (Washington: n.p., 1831), II, 23.

3. Charleston *Mercury,* Dec. 8, 1832; Charleston *Courier,* Jan. 17, 1833, Oct. 29, 1832, March 30, Jan. 11, and Feb. 11, 1833. Mitchell King to William Drayton, Jan. 15, 1833, Drayton Collection, Col. William Drayton Papers, Historical Society of Pennsylvania (hereafter D-HSP), notes the earlier failure of the sugar refinery.
4. Charleston *City Gazette,* July 24, 1829, and Jan. 11, 1833; Charleston *Courier,* Aug. 5, 1829, Aug. 26, 1834, Jan. 16, 1830; Pitray & Viel & Co. to Thomas Lamb, Dec. 2, 1832, L-MHS; [Alexander Brown & Sons] to James Adger, Jan. 11, 1833, AB-LC.
5. Carl N. Degler, *Place over Time: The Continuity of Southern Distinctiveness* (Baton Rouge: Louisiana State University Press, 1977), 54–55; Gavin Wright, *The Political Economy of the Cotton South: Households, Markets, and Wealth in the Nineteenth Century* (New York: W. W. Norton, 1978), 112–13; Archie V. Huff, Jr., *Langdon Cheves of South Carolina* (Columbia: University of South Carolina Press, 1977), 155–56; James L. Petigru to Hugh Swinton Legaré, September 16, 1834, James L. Petigru Papers, USC (hereafter JLP-USC); Petigru to Jane P. North, Dec. 24, 1835, in James L. Petigru, *Life, Letters and Speeches* . . . , James P. Carson, ed. (Washington: W. H. Lowdermilk, 1920), 180; Ernest M. Lander, Jr., *The Textile Industry in Antebellum South Carolina* (Baton Rouge: Louisiana State University Press, 1969), 80, 45–49; while Lander reports significant textile manufacturing growth between 1828 and 1838, he concludes that South Carolina textiles failed because northern mills were not only larger and more profitable but produced cheaper and better-quality goods. Fred Bateman and Thomas Weiss, *A Deplorable Scarcity: The Failure of Industrialization in the Slave Economy* (Chapel Hill: University of North Carolina Press, 1981), 120, 125, argue that unwillingness to transfer capital from agriculture to industry and the noneconomic rewards of planting deterred industrialization.
6. Ernest M. Lander, Jr., "Charleston: Manufacturing Center of the Old South," *Journal of Southern History,* XXVI (August 1960), 342–43. In January 1830, 29% of the rice brought into the city had been cleaned. Of the remainder chronicled daily in the Charleston *Courier*'s shipping news, the Lucas Mills cleaned 45%. The output of Bennett's extensive Cannonsboro Mills, with 36 pestles, cannot be quantified because the milled rice was not reshipped to city wharves but was, apparently, shipped out to other ports directly from the mills.
7. Charleston, *Ordinances* . . . *from the 5th February, 1833 to the 9th May, 1837* . . . (Charleston: A. E. Miller, 1837), 57; Charleston *Courier,* June 22 and 25, 1832. The proportion of total rice exports shipped out uncleaned rose from 3% in 1823–1824 and 7% in 1829–1830 to 15% in 1835–1836. Dawson and DeSaussure, *Census of Charleston, 1848,* 102. Jacob F. Schirmer, Diary, Oct. 15, 1833, SCHS, reports a shipment of rough rice to a newly built rice mill in Boston.
8. Lander, "Charleston: Manufacturing Center," 330–351. Charleston *Courier,* July 27, 1832, Nov. 12, 1833, Feb. 10, 1834, May 12 and July 3, 1835.
9. U.S. 23rd Congress, 1st Session, House of Representatives, *Report of the Committee on Naval Affairs on Navy Yard, Charleston, S.C.* . . . *June 24, 1834* ([Washington]: Gales & Seaton, [1834]), 19. U.S. Fifth Census, MS, National Archives Microfilm, M19, Roll 170.

10. Charleston *Courier*, Aug. 2, 1831; Hibernian Society, Secretary's Book No. 3, 1827–1847, typed copy, 83, USC; Nathan Appleton, *Speech . . . in Reply to Mr. McDuffie of South Carolina, on the Tariff . . . 30th of May, 1832* (Washington: Gales & Seaton, 1832), 18; Arthur H. Cole, *Wholesale Commodity Prices in the United States, 1700–1861* (New York: Johnson Reprint, c. 1938, 1969), 106; U.S. 23rd Congress, *Report . . . on the Navy Yard, Charleston, S.C.*, 19; Schirmer, Diary, May 11, June 17, July 7, and Aug. 27, 1835, SCHS.
11. Charleston *Mercury*, Aug. 17, 1831, and Edward R. Laurens, *An Address Delivered in Charleston, before the Agricultural Society of South Carolina, on September 18, 1832* (Charleston: The Society, 1832), 9–14, both lament the exodus of white mechanics. Charleston *Courier*, May 18, 1835, reports the decline of the taxable slave population from 14,705 in 1828 to 13,939 in 1834. Free black population in the city declined from 2,107 in 1830 to 1,558 in 1840; see Dawson and DeSaussure, *Census of Charleston, 1848*, 5–6. The year 1832 saw peak free black interest in emigration to Liberia. "Opinions of a Free Man of Colour by a South Carolinian," *African Repository*, VIII (October 1832), 239–43; Samuel C. Jackson, Diary, Nov. 17, 1832, SHC.
12. George T. Fox, Journal, Nov. 5, 1834, British Records in Relation to America in Microform, Series B; Charleston *Courier*, Nov. 3, 1830, July 29, 1831, Aug. 2, 1834. Charleston, *A Collection of the Ordinances of the City Council . . . from the 10th Day of October 1826 to the 13th Day of March, 1832 . . .* (Charleston: A. E. Miller, 1832), 41–42. Ordinance of Feb. 1, 1830, permitted mechanics to hire out slaves of their trade without paying the tax which all other owners of slaves hired out were required to pay.
13. Charleston *Courier*, Nov. 11, 1833; Richard Yeadon, Jr., to William Drayton, Nov. 12, 1833, D-HSP; John Kirkpatrick & Company to William Law, Feb. 22, 1834, William Law Papers, Duke University (hereafter WL-DU).
14. Charles Fraser to Robert C. Winthrop, April 29, 1834, W-MHS; Howland, Ward & Taft to Samuel Dana, May 21, 1834, Howland, Ward, Spring & Taft Company Papers, USC (hereafter HWST-USC); Charleston *Courier*, May 19, 1834.
15. Charleston *Courier*, Nov. 8, 1834; South Carolina Comptroller General, Reports to the Legislature, 1834–1838, in South Carolina, *Acts and Resolutions* (Columbia: State Printer, 1834–1838). Samuel H. Dickson, *Address Delivered at the Opening of the New Edifice of the Charleston Apprentices' Library Society . . . 13th January, 1841* (Charleston: W. Riley, 1841), 29; J. R. J. Gage to James M. Gage, April 3, 1836, JMG-SHC.
16. J. Mauldin Lesesne, *The Bank of the State of South Carolina: A General and Political History* (Columbia: University of South Carolina Press, 1970), 6–11; Dawson and DeSaussure, *Census of Charleston, 1848*, 160.
17. Lesesne, *The Bank of the State of South Carolina*, 18.
18. Robert Y. Hayne to Nicholas Biddle, Dec. 18, 1834, NB-LC.
19. James L. Petigru to Hugh S. Legaré, May 31, 1835, Hugh Swinton Legaré Papers, USC (hereafter HSL-USC); Bank of the State of South Carolina, *A Compilation of All Acts, Reports and other Documents . . . Affording Full Information Concerning that Institution* (Columbia: A. S. Johnson &

A. G. Sumner, 1848), 201; Joseph Johnson to Nicholas Biddle, June 3, 1835, NB-LC.
20. Charleston *Courier,* June 6, 1835; Peter Bacot to Nicholas Biddle, June 3, 1835, NB-LC.
21. James Hamilton to Nicholas Biddle, Feb. 12, 1836, NB-LC; Bank of Charleston, Bonds and Mortgage Ledger, SCHS; James Hamilton to Levi Woodbury, July 10, 1836, and letterpress copy of Woodbury to Hamilton, July 20, 1836, Levi Woodbury Papers, LC (hereafter LW-LC).
22. Of its first 15 directors (1836–1838) 40% were modestly wealthy and 13% were very wealthy. Even more significant, 67% wielded great economic power in the city.
23. Quotations in Charleston *Courier,* May 11 and 30, 1833; see also Dec. 12, 1833, and May 15–30, 1834. States Rights Party, *Proceedings and the Resolutions and Address Adopted . . . in Charleston . . . 9th September, 1830* (Charleston: A. E. Miller, n.d.), 6–8.
24. [Alexander Brown & Sons] to James Adger, July 2, 1830, AB-LC; Ogilby, Consular Report, 1833, WO-USC.
25. Dawson and DeSaussure, *Census of Charleston, 1848,* 135, 81. David M. Williams, "The Shipping of the North American Cotton Trade in the Mid-Nineteenth Century" (Paper given at St. Johns, Newfoundland, Maritime Conference, May 1979), 1–23, comes to similar conclusions for the entire American cotton trade.
26. Dawson and DeSaussure, *Census of Charleston, 1848,* 133, 101. Wright, *The Political Economy of the Cotton South,* 96, notes that the mid-1830s saw a confluence of high cotton prices and rising productivity. Cotton prices in Charleston reached their 1830s peak in 1836, at 17 to 20 cents per pound. Earlier peaks had occurred in 1816–1818, when prices had ranged from 19 to 34 cents, and in 1825, when they ranged from 24 to 32 cents. Lander, *Textile Industry,* 31.
27. Samuel G. Stoney, *The Story of South Carolina's Senior Bank: The Bank of Charleston, Mother of the South Carolina National Bank of Charleston* (Charleston: The Bank, 1955), 5, 14.
28. Charleston *City Gazette,* Dec. 3, 1830; Charleston *Courier,* May 22 and 27, 1834.
29. Charleston *Courier,* May 27, 1834; Samuel C. Jackson, Diary, Oct. 19, 1832, SHC; Carl Arfwedson, *The United States and Canada, in 1832, 1833 and 1834* (New York: Johnson Reprint, c. 1834, 1969), I, 378; Benjamin Elliott, *Reports of the Historical Committee of the Charleston Library Society* (Charleston: A. E. Miller, 1835), 7; Charleston *Courier,* June 8, 1835.
30. Charleston *Mercury,* June 11, 1835; Schirmer, Diary, Sept. 1, 1835, SCHS.
31. Richard [Bacot] to Dewar Bacot, Sept. 7, 1836, Bacot-Huger Collection, SCHS (hereafter BH-SCHS); Schirmer, Diary, April 29, 1836, July 15, 1834, June 10 and 24, 1835, Jan. 26, 1836, SCHS; Charleston *Mercury,* April 16, 1836.
32. Samuel Eastman, "A Yankee in the South," Caroline S. Davies, ed., *New England Quarterly,* X (March–June 1937), 74; Fox, Journal, Oct. 1834; Charleston *Courier,* Oct. 5, 1835; Hibernian Society, Secretary's Book, No. 3, July 15, 1833, Dec. 1, 1835, typed copy, USC.
33. Charleston *Mercury,* April 29, May 20, and June 3, 1836.
34. Of the 337 men who wielded any economic power and whose occupations

are known between 1828 and 1832, 41% were merchants or factors, 14% engaged in other commerce, 19% were planters, and 17% were professionals. Of the 297 whose occupations were known from 1833 to 1838, 45% were merchants or factors, 9% were engaged in other commerce, 20% were planters, and 18% were professionals. Of 424 who at any time between 1838 and 1843 held any economic power, only 52% lacked status attributes of the upper class and 15% were in the highest reaches. Twenty-four percent held political office of some sort.

5: Hub and Hinge

1. Charleston *Mercury,* March 15, 1831; John Perrier to Thomas Lamb, [June] 1, 1833, L-MHS; J. L. Dawson and H. W. DeSaussure, *Census of the City of Charleston, South Carolina, for the Year 1848* . . . (Charleston: J. B. Nixon, 1849), 74, 78–79, 81.
2. H. A. S. Dearborn to Henry Clay, Jan. 22, 1832, Henry Clay Papers, Library of Congress (hereafter HC-LC); Alan F. January, "The First Nullification: The Negro Seamen Acts Controversy in South Carolina, 1822–1860" (Ph.D. dissertation, University of Iowa, 1976), 228–67; Charleston *Courier,* July 27, 1831, March 1, 1835, July 22, 1843; U.S. 19th Congress, 1st Session, Senate, *Report of the Secretary of the Navy, with the Report of the Officer Appointed to Examine the Harbors of Charleston and St. Mary's . . . January 23, 1826* (Washington: Gales and Seaton, 1826), 16–17.
3. Charleston *Courier,* May 31, 1833, Sept. 2, 1834; Gregory Allen Greb, "Charleston, South Carolina, Merchants, 1815–1860: Urban Leadership in the Antebellum South" (Ph.D. dissertation, University of California at San Diego, 1978), 200, 177; South Carolina, *The Statutes at Large . . . ,* David J. McCord, ed. (Columbia: A. J. Johnston, 1839), VIII, 386–88, 429–31, 418–21.
4. Quotation from Charleston *Mercury,* April 13, 1831. Charleston *Courier,* Nov. 15, 1833, July 12, 30, Aug. 9, 23, Nov. 19, 1834, all report moves throughout the state for branch lines. South Carolina Canal and Rail Road Company, *Semi-Annual Report of the Directors to the Stockholders, November 1833* (Charleston: A. E. Miller, 1833), 5, carries the decision not to build branch lines.
5. Patrick S. Brady, "Political and Civil Life in South Carolina, 1787–1833" (Ph.D. dissertation, University of California at Santa Barbara, 1971), 148–49; George C. Rogers, Jr., *The History of Georgetown County, South Carolina* (Columbia: University of South Carolina Press, 1970), 230. Of the Santee Canal Company's 14 directors from 1828 to 1832, 64% were wealthy, 15% were planters, and 46% were merchants or factors.
6. South Carolina Canal and Rail Road Company, *First Semi-Annual Report to the President and Directors* . . . (Charleston: A. E. Miller, 1828), 23; Elias Horry, *An Address Respecting the Charleston and Hamburg Rail Road . . . the 2d October 1833* . . . (Charleston: A. E. Miller, 1833), 4–7; Samuel M. Derrick, *Centennial History of the South Carolina Railroad* (Spartanburg, S.C.: Reprint Company, c. 1930, 1975), 76: South Carolina Canal and Rail Road Company, *Annual Report . . . May 7, 1832* (Charleston: William S. Blain, 1832), 5; Charleston *Courier,* Aug. 19, 1833.
7. "Survey of railroad route from Charleston to Hamburg," in B. J. Howland,

comp., "[Annotated collection of printed matter on] South Carolina Canal and Rail Road Company," SCHS; Derrick, *Centennial History of the South Carolina Railroad*, 73–75; Charleston *Courier*, Feb. 24, 1829, Jan. 26, 1830.

8. Greb, "Charleston Merchants," 118; Charleston *Courier*, Jan. 7, 1830; South Carolina Canal and Rail Road Company, *Annual Report . . . 1832*, 5; idem, *By-Laws . . . Adopted by the Stockholders, 12th Jan. 1835* (Charleston: J. S. Burges, 1835), 18–19; South Carolina, *Statutes at Large*, VIII, 354–63, 380, 384–85.

9. Shareholders are listed in South Carolina Canal and Rail Road Company, *By-Laws*, 6–7; idem, *Semi-Annual Statement to 31st October 1833* [n.p., n.d.].

10. Horatio Allen, *Reports . . . to the Board of Directors of the South Carolina Canal and Rail Road Company, 1830–1831, 1832* (Charleston: J. S. Burges, 1831, 1832), and Alexander Black, *Report Exhibiting the Present State of the Work . . . on the Charleston and Hamburg Rail Road . . . October 18, 1831* (Charleston: William S. Blain, 1831), give the details of the building process. Charleston *Courier*, Nov. 22, 1833; Randall Hunt, "Journal of a Traveller from Charleston, So. Car., to New Haven, Conn. 1832," 7–8, SCHS.

11. Hunt, "Journal of a Traveller," 7–8; Derrick, *Centennial History of the South Carolina Rail Road*, 97, 104.

12. Charleston *Courier*, May 7, 1833, and Sept. 2, 1833–May 21, 1834. The proportion of cotton brought in by rail is approximate. Ulrich B. Phillips, *A History of Transportation in the Eastern Cotton Belt to 1860* (New York: Octagon Press, c. 1908, 1968), 160, reports rail freight by the calendar year, and Dawson and DeSaussure, *Census of Charleston . . . 1848*, 101, reports total cotton receipts by the crop year.

13. Charleston *Courier*, June 22, Nov. 4 and 28, 1833, July 19, 1834; Horatio Allen to J. & J. Townsend, April 2, 1834, Miscellaneous Manuscripts, USC (hereafter MM-USC); South Carolina Canal and Rail Road Company, *Report . . . June 10, 1833* (Charleston: James S. Burges, 1833), 3–7; idem, *Semi-Annual Report . . . October 31, 1834* (Charleston: James S. Burges, 1835), 3–4; idem, *Reports, December 31, 1835, and January 1836* (Charleston: A. E. Miller, 1836), 5–6.

14. Charleston *Courier*, March 31, 1843; South Carolina Canal and Rail Road Company, *Semi-Annual Report . . . January 7, 1837* (Charleston: A. E. Miller, 1837), 3–4, 6; Robert Gilchrist to John Townsend, February 4, 1836, MM-USC.

15. South Carolina Canal and Rail Road Company, *Semi-Annual Report . . . January 1843* (Charleston: Miller & Browne, 1843), 23. Dawson and DeSaussure, *Census of Charleston . . . 1848*, 101. While Charleston's average annual sales of upland cotton increased 20% in the five years after the railroad was in operation, only three of the five years above the median sales for the ten crop years 1828–1838 came after the railroad was built. How much was attributable to the railroad per se is thus difficult to judge. But annual national sales of upland went up 45% for those same five years, suggesting the likelihood that at least part of Charleston's gains came simply from increased crops.

16. South Carolina, *Statutes at Large*, VIII, 380; Charleston *City Gazette*,

Jan. 25, 1831; Charleston *Courier,* Jan. 27, 1831; South Carolina Canal and Rail Road Company, *Annual Report . . . May 7, 1832* (Charleston: William S. Blain, 1832), 5–6.
17. Charleston *Courier,* Dec. 3, 1832, Aug. 19, 1833; South Carolina, *Statutes at Large,* VIII, 380.
18. Charleston *Courier* and *Mercury,* Aug. 1833. Quotation from *Mercury,* Aug. 17, 1833.
19. Charleston *Mercury,* Aug. 21, 1833; Charleston *Courier,* Aug. 31 and Sept. 2, 1833.
20. South Carolina Canal and Rail Road Company, *Semi-Annual Report . . . November 4, 1833* (Charleston: A. E. Miller, 1833), 4; Charleston *Courier,* Sept. 3, 1833 and quotation, June 11, 1834; Matthews & Bonneau, Statement of Calhoun Cotton Sales, July 24, 1834, June 24, 1835, July 9, 1836, John C. Calhoun Papers, USC (hereafter JCC-USC).
21. Of the 257 investors whose occupation is known, 1833–1838, 18% were in professional and 58% in mercantile occupations. Of all known railroad investors, 79% at some time between 1820 and 1843 acquired real property in St. Philip's and St. Michael's parishes, and 32% acquired rural property in the same period.
22. Samuel E. Morison, *The Maritime History of Massachusetts* (Boston: Sentry Books, c. 1921, 1961), 265–94; Robert G. Albion, *The Rise of New York Port* (New York: Scribners, 1939), 402.
23. Francis X. Blouin, Jr., "The Boston Region, 1810–1850: A Study in Urbanization on a Regional Scale" (Ph.D. dissertation, University of Minnesota, 1978), 286–93.
24. Blouin, "The Boston Region," 220; Boston *Daily Advertiser,* Jan. 5, June 13, and Nov. 26, 1828; Harrison Gray Otis, *An Address to the Board of Aldermen and Members of the Common Council, . . . January 5, 1829* (Boston: John H. Eastburn, 1829), 10–11; Stephen Salsbury, *The State, the Investor, and the Railroad: The Boston and Albany, 1825–1867* (Cambridge: Harvard University Press, 1967), 68; [Petition of the City of Boston to the State Legislature], Feb. 12, 1829, MS Senate Document 8717.1, MA.
25. Boston *Daily Advertiser,* Jan. 29 and Feb. 26, 1829; Salsbury, *The State, the Investor, and the Railroad,* 72–75.
26. Otis, *Address . . . January 5, 1829,* 11; Great Rail Road Meeting, July 12, 1830, Broadside; Salsbury, *The State, the Investor, and the Railroad,* 76–77; "Memorial of Sundry Inhabitants or Holders of Real Estate in Boston . . . ," MS House Document, Jan. 20, 1831, 11371, MA; Boston *Daily Advertiser,* March 14, 1831; quotation from Frederic Tudor diary, March 13, 1831, T-BL.
27. Boston and Lowell Railroad, *Annual Report of Board of Directors, 1831* (n.p.: 1831), 3–4; Robert V. Spalding, "The Boston Mercantile Community and the Promotion of the Textile Industry in New England, 1813–1860" (Ph.D. dissertation, Yale University, 1963), 59–60.
28. Arthur M. Johnson and Barry E. Supple, *Boston Capitalists and Western Railroads: A Study in Nineteenth Century Investment Process* (Cambridge: Harvard University Press, 1967), 35.
29. Typed notes, 1830, from the Record Book of the Proprietors of the Locks and Canal Company on the Merrimack River, Boston and Lowell Collec-

tion, BL (hereafter B&LRR-BL); Boston and Lowell Rail Road, "Circular Letter . . . to the Proprietors in the Manufactories at Lowell," Feb. 10, 1831, Miscellaneous Manuscripts, MHS; A[bbott] L[awrence] to H. G. Otis, Feb. 23, 1831, HGO-MHS; Frederic Tudor, Diary, April 1, 1831, T-BL.

30. Patrick T. Jackson to Kirk Boott, Jan. 18, 1830, typed copy, B&LRR-BL; James J. Putnam, *A Memoir of Dr. James Jackson . . . with Sketches of His Brothers* (Boston: Houghton, Mifflin, and Co., 1905), 148–50; Mill Pond Wharf Corporation, "Schedule of Estates Owned by the Proprietors . . . October 14, 1831," Mill Pond Wharf Corporation Collection, BL.
31. Boston and Lowell Rail Road Company, *Annual Reports, 1836* (n.p.: 1836), and *1837* (n.p.: 1837); Joseph G. Martin, *Seventy-Three Years of the Boston Stock Market* . . . (Boston: The Author, 1871), 77.
32. Massachusetts, *The Act to Establish the Boston and Worcester Rail Road Corporation, Together with Two Additional Acts* . . . (Boston: J. E. Hinckley & Co., 1833), 4, 7–8, 15–20.
33. George Morey to Harrison Gray Otis, June 11, 1832, HGO-MHS.
34. Frederic Tudor, Diary, April 8, 1834, T-BL; Alexander H. Everett, Journal, April 5 and 8, 1834, MHS; [Third Annual Report of the Boston and Worcester Rail Road Corporation], Feb. 2, 1835, MS Senate Document 9565, MA; Boston and Worcester Rail Road, *First Annual Report . . . to the Stockholders* (n.p.: 1832), 4–7.
35. Boston and Worcester Rail Road, *Report of the Directors . . . at a Special Meeting of the Stockholders on the Eighteenth of January 1833* (Boston: Stimpson & Clapp, 1833); Salsbury, *The State, the Investor, and the Railroad*, 119–22, 128; Boston *Daily Advertiser*, Jan. 6, 1836. South Carolina Canal and Rail Road Company, *Reports . . . 1836, 1837, 1839, 1840;* Boston and Worcester Rail Road, *Report of a Committee of Directors . . . on a Proposition of the Directors of the Western Rail Road to Reduce Rates* . . . (n.p.: 1840), 29; Martin, *Seventy-Three Years of the Boston Stock Market* . . . , 77.
36. Walter M. Whitehill, *Boston: A Topographical History*, 2d ed. (Cambridge: Belknap Press, 1968), 103–4.
37. Boston and Providence Rail Road, *Report of the Board of Directors to the Stockholders* . . . (Boston: J. E. Hinckley & Co., 1832), 79–82; George Morey to Harrison Gray Otis, June 11, 1832, HGO-MHS; Martin, *Seventy-Three Years of the Boston Stock Market*, 77; Whitehill, *Boston*, 102.
38. Johnson and Supple, *Boston Capitalists and Western Railroads*, 37; Boston *Daily Advertiser*, Jan. 13, March 10, and April 2, 1830, and Jan. 20, 1831; Boston *Morning Post*, Aug. 3, 1835.
39. [Report of a Joint Legislative Committee on a Petition to Construct a Railroad from Boston to Salem], March 15, 1833, MS House Document 12252, MA; Boston *Daily Advertiser*, July 23, 1836; Johnson and Supple, *Boston Capitalists and Western Railroads*, 44–45. Average annual dividends for the Eastern to 1844 were 5.3%; Boston and Lowell, 6.4%; Boston and Worcester, 5.9%; Boston and Providence, 6.3%. Martin, *Seventy-Three Years of the Boston Stock Market*, 77.
40. Harrison Gray Otis quoted in Salsbury, *The State, the Investor, and the Railroad*, 78.
41. South Cove Corporation, *Third Annual Report of the Directors . . . to the Stockholders* . . . (Boston: Crocker & Brewster, 1836), 10.

6: Pragmatic Politics and the Politics of Passion

1. Boston *Daily Advertiser,* March 18, 1834.
2. *Memorial of a Committee of the Citizens of Charleston, South Carolina, against the Proposed Increase of the Tariff. February 9, 1824* . . . (U.S. 18th Congress, 1st session, House of Representatives, Document Number 64 [Washington: Gales & Seaton, 1824]), 3. Charleston *Courier,* July 7, 1830.
3. James Hamilton, Jr., to Martin Van Buren, July 16, 1829, Martin Van Buren Papers, LC (hereafter MV-LC); Robert Y. Hayne, *An Oration Delivered in the Independent or Congregational Church, before the State Rights and Free Trade Party . . . on the 4th of July, 1831* . . . (Charleston: A. E. Miller, 1831), 7.
4. Hayne, *Oration . . . 4th of July, 1831,* 7; Harriott Pinckney Rutledge Holbrook to Edward Rutledge, [ca. Oct. 13, 1832], Rutledge Family Papers, USC (hereafter R-USC); Daniel E. Huger to William Drayton, Jan. 28, 1831, D-HSP.
5. Charleston *Courier,* Dec. 7 and 14, and Oct. 28, 1829.
6. A letter to the editor, Charleston *Courier,* Oct. 29, 1829, dates the tax change as 1786, but it should probably refer to the legislation of 1784; see Jerome Nadelhaft, *The Disorders of War: The Revolution in South Carolina* (Orono: University of Maine at Orono Press, 1981), 126. Charleston *City Gazette,* July 25, 1829.
7. Resolution of a nullification meeting, Sept. 21, 1830, in Charleston *Courier,* Sept. 23, 1830; Charleston *Mercury,* Sept. 1, 1832.
8. Alicia H. Middleton to N. R. Middleton, Sept. 9, [1830], N. R. Middleton Papers, SHC (hereafter NRM-SHC).
9. The analysis of the election and of political composition which follows is from Jane H. Pease and William H. Pease, "The Economics and Politics of Charleston's Nullification Crisis," *Journal of Southern History,* XLVII (August 1981), 335–62, especially 338–52.
10. Charleston *Mercury,* Oct. 15 and Dec. 8, 1830; Charleston *Courier,* Dec. 9 and 16, 1830.
11. James L. Petigru to William Elliott, Sept. 7, 1831, in James Louis Petigru, *Life, Letters and Speeches of James Louis Petigru, the Union Man of South Carolina,* James Petigru Carson, ed. (Washington: W. H. Lowdermilk & Co., 1920), 85; J. S. Colburn to Nathan Appleton, Feb. 7, 1832, Ap-MHS.
12. Hayne, *An Oration, Delivered in the Independent or Congregational Church . . . 4th of July, 1831,* passim; William C. Dukes, Journal and Diary, July 4, 1831, William Christopher Dukes Manuscripts, USC (hereafter WD-USC).
13. Charleston *Courier,* July 28 and 29, 1831, quotation from the former; Charleston *Mercury,* Aug. 11, 1831, July 6 and 7, 1832.
14. J. C. Schultz to Maria Schultz, Feb. 24, 1832, MM-USC; John B. Grimball, Diary, Oct. 8, 1832, John Berkley Grimball Diary, SHC.
15. M. D. Richardson to W. Gilmore Simms, Oct. 25, [1831], in Charleston *City Gazette,* Nov. 19, 1831.
16. James Hamilton to Waddy Thompson, Aug. 31, 1832, James Hamilton Papers, USC (hereafter JH-USC); Jacob F. Schirmer, Diary, Sept. 2, 1832, SCHS; Charleston *Courier,* Sept. 3, 1832.

17. James L. Petigru to William Elliott, Sept. 4, 1832, Petigru, *Life, Letters, and Speeches,* 90–91. Pinckney received 1,112 votes out of a total 2,062; see city returns in Charleston *Courier,* Sept. 5, 1832. *Courier,* Sept. 11, 1832; Schirmer Diary, Sept. 8 and 14, 1832, SCHS; quotation from James H. Smith to William Elliott, Sept. 26, 1832, Elliott-Gonzales Papers, SHC (hereafter EG-SHC).
18. Harriet Martineau, *Retrospect of Western Travel* (London: Saunders & Otley, 1838), I, 232–33; Mitchell King to Hugh S. Legaré, Sept. 14, 1833, Mitchell King Papers, USC (hereafter MK-USC); John Lide Wilson, "A Pasquinade of the Thirties: Charleston, S.C." (Undated broadside, Duke University Library); Charleston *City Gazette,* Sept. 15, 1832.
19. Samuel C. Jackson, Diary, Oct. 20, 1832, SHC; Mrs R. M. R[utledge] to Edward Rutledge, Oct. 10, 1832, R-USC; James L. Petigru to Hugh S. Legaré, Oct. 29, 1832, Yates Snowden Collection, USC (hereafter YS-USC).
20. Charleston *Courier,* Oct. 11, 1832.
21. Schirmer Diary, Nov. 11–12, 1832, SCHS; Charleston *Courier,* Nov. 15, 1832; Charleston *Mercury,* Nov. 29, 1832.
22. Charleston *Mercury,* 1831–1832, passim; Joel R. Poinsett to Andrew Jackson, Oct. 16, 1832, Andrew Jackson Papers, Library of Congress (hereafter AJ-LC); Andrew Jackson to Levi Woodbury, Sept. 11, 1832, Levi Woodbury Papers, Library of Congress (hereafter LW-LC); Charleston *Courier,* Nov. 13, 1832; Joel R. Poinsett to Andrew Jackson, Nov. 16, 1832, AJ-LC; James R. Pringle to Louis McLane, Dec. 4, 1832, U.S., Treasury Department, Record Group 56, Microcopy 178, Roll 32, National Archives (hereafter TD-NA); Andrew Jackson to Joel R. Poinsett, Nov. 7, 1832, Joel Poinsett Papers, Historical Society of Pennsylvania (hereafter JP-HSP).
23. [Louis McLane] to James R. Pringle, Nov. 6, 1832, TD-NA.
24. Young Men's Free Trade and State Rights Association, "Preamble and Resolutions Passed at a Meeting of the . . . Association. December 17th, 1832," MS, photostat, USC, from the John Adolphus Bernard Dahlgren Papers, LC; Robert Y. Hayne to Sir, Dec. 26, 1832 [printed orders to Hayne's aides-de-camp], James H. Hammond Papers, LC; Joel R. Poinsett to Andrew Jackson, Feb. 22, 1833, AJ-LC; William G. Simms to James Lawson, Nov. 25, [1832], in William Gilmore Simms, *The Letters of William Gilmore Simms,* Mary S. Simms Oliphant et al., eds., 5 vols. (Columbia: University of South Carolina Press, 1952–1956), I, 47; Mitchell King to Hugh S. Legaré, May 5, 1833, in Shirley Carter Hughson, ed., "Letters of the Period of Nullification" (transcribed excerpts from Huger Family letters), South Carolina Historical Society (hereafter SCH-SCHS).
25. H. A. DeSaussure to William Drayton, Jan. 10, 1833, D-HSP; J. R. Pringle to Louis McLane, Jan. 20 and Feb. 2, 5, and 7, 1833, Record Group 56, MC 178, Roll 32, TD-NA; Joel R. Poinsett to Andrew Jackson, Feb. 9, 1833, AJ-LC; Petigru, *Life, Letters, and Speeches,* 118; Virginia Louise Glenn, "James Hamilton, Jr., of South Carolina: A Biography" (Ph.D. dissertation, University of North Carolina, 1964), quotation on 190.
26. Joel R. Poinsett to Andrew Jackson, Jan. 28, 1833, AJ-LC; Joel R. Poinsett to William Drayton, Jan. 8, 15, and 16, 1833, D-HSP; the quotations are from Joel R. Poinsett to Andrew Jackson, Jan. 16, 1833, AJ-LC.

27. William G. Simms to James Lawson, January 22, [1833], in Simms, *Letters*, I, 51–52; Mitchell King to [Hugh S.] Legaré, March 5, 1833, MK-USC; Charleston *Mercury*, March 5, 1833.
28. Mitchell King to Hugh Swinton Legaré, May 5, 1833, MK-USC.
29. James L. Petigru to Hugh S. Legaré, July 15, 1833, Petigru, *Life, Letters, and Speeches*, 125; Mitchell King to Hugh S. Legaré, Sept. 14, 1833, MK-USC; William H. Pease and Jane H. Pease, "Walker's *Appeal* Comes to Charleston: A Note and Documents," *Journal of Negro History*, LIX (July 1974), 287–92.
30. Charleston *Mercury*, July 27 and 31, 1833; Charleston *Courier*, Aug. 23, 1833.
31. Alfred Huger to Hugh S. Legaré, Sept. 1, 1834, SCH-SCHS; Charleston *Mercury*, Aug. 16, 1833; Charleston *Courier*, Aug. 17, 1833.
32. Charleston *Courier*, Sept. 4, 1833. The militia oath and reorganization dispute can be followed in Charleston *Courier*, Jan. 11, Feb. 14 and 26, March 1 and 19, and April 5, 1834; and in Washington Light Infantry, Minute Books (typescript), Minute for Feb. 7, 1834, CC. For the court test of the oath see Charleston *Courier*, June 7, 10, and 24, 1834; and Thomas S. Grimké, *Argument . . . Delivered in the Court of Appeals of the State of South-Carolina . . . on the 2d and 3d April, 1834; in the Case of the State, ex relatione Edward M'Crady, against Col. B. F. Hunt; on the Constitutionality of the Oath in the Act for the Military Organization of this State . . .* (Charleston: J. S. Burges, 1834), passim.
33. Savannah *Georgian*, copied in the Boston *Daily Advertiser*, Oct. 24, 1834; James L. Petigru to Hugh S. Legaré, Oct. 26, 1834, Petigru, *Life, Letters, and Speeches*, 162–63. The quotation is from Grimball, Diary, Oct. 14, 1834, SHC.
34. Charleston *Courier*, Oct. 16, 1834, for the election returns; James L. Petigru to Hugh S. Legaré, Dec. 15, 1834, Petigru, *Life, Letters, and Speeches*, 166–71.
35. Charleston *Courier*, Dec. 8, 1834. The oath is printed in South Carolina, *The Statutes at Large . . .* , David J. McCord, ed. (Columbia: A. S. Johnston, 1839), VI, 438.
36. Of 208 individuals identified as being politically powerful, 36% exerted modest economic power and another 13% wielded great power. Of the same group 34% enjoyed modest wealth, 7% great wealth. Finally, 34% enjoyed modestly high status, and 16% very high status.
37. James L. Petigru to J. Chesnut, Dec. 9, 1834, Williams-Chesnut-Manning Collection, USC (hereafter WCM-USC); Robert Y. Hayne to Patrick Noble, Sept. 21, 1835, Robert Young Hayne Papers, USC (hereafter RYH-USC); James Hamilton, Jr., to James H. Hammond, Feb. 10, 1836, JHH-LC; Charleston *Mercury*, March 23, 29, and 31, 1836.
38. William Appleton, Diary (fragment), Oct. 12, 1830, WA-BL; Boston *Daily Advertiser*, Nov. 2, 1830, gives the election returns; Otis, *Speech to the Citizens of Boston . . .* , 4; Nathan Appleton, *Speech . . . in Reply to Mr. McDuffie of South Carolina, on the Tariff . . . 30th of May, 1832* (Washington: Gales & Seaton, 1832), 16–17; Boston *Morning Post*, Jan. 30, 1833.
39. Amos Lawrence to Nathan Appleton, Jan. 31, 1832, Ap-MHS; Nathan Appleton, *Speech . . . in Reply to Mr. McDuffie . . .* , 18; William

Appleton, Diary, Jan. 1, 1833, WA-BL; Charles F. Adams to John Q. Adams, Jan. 21, 1832, Ad-MHS; Harrison Gray Otis to George Harrison, March 11, 1833, HGO-MHS.

40. Charleston *Courier,* Dec. 9, 1830; "List of Loans to Members of Congress, Editors of Newspapers, and Officers of the Government, at the Bank of the United States & its Branches," [1821–1832], NB-LC; John Potter to Nicholas Biddle, Sept. 21, 1830, and J. Cowperthwait to Nicholas Biddle, Nov. 5, 1831, both in NB-LC.

41. Jean A. Wilburn, *Biddle's Bank: The Crucial Years* (New York: Columbia University Press, 1967), 77. Boston *Morning Post,* Dec. 21, 1832. The dissension in the Boston branch of the BUS is touched on in D[aniel Webster] to Nicholas Biddle, Sept. 24, 1832, and in an unsigned enclosure marked "Private" in Daniel Webster to Nicholas Biddle, Nov. 19, 1832, NB-LC.

42. Peter Temin, *The Jacksonian Economy* (New York: W. W. Norton Co., 1969), 64–67.

43. Charles F. Adams to John Q. Adams, Feb. 7, 1834, Ad-MHS. Appleton's battle with Biddle is detailed in William Appleton, Diary, Jan. 1834; Henry Lee et al. to William Appleton, Feb. 3, 1834 (forwarded to Biddle the same day); William Appleton to Nicholas Biddle, Feb. 4, 1834, and two more letters, same to same, Feb. 9 and 14, 1834, all in WA-BL. Nicholas Biddle to William Appleton, Feb. 19, 1834, NB-LC.

44. Abbott Lawrence to Nicholas Biddle, Feb. 24 and March 10, 1834, NB-LC; William Appleton, Diary, March 18, 1834, WA-BL; Boston Committee of Citizens, *Report of the Boston Committee Appointed . . . on the sixth of March [1834], to Take Charge of the Protest of the Citizens of Boston Against the Usurpations of the Executive Government of the United States . . .* (Boston: J. E. Hinckley and Co., 1834), 1; U.S., 23rd Congress, 1st Session, House of Representatives, Document 175, *Memorial of the Citizens of Boston, Massachusetts, in Relation to the Currency,* March 17, 1834.

45. Of the sample of 699 probank petitioners examined, 309 (44%) engaged in commerce and 242 (35%) were mechanics, while only 113 (16%) represented occupations of high prestige. A total of 634 (91%) wielded no economic power in the city, and of the remainder only 12 (2%) had extensive economic power. Only 4% possessed $30,000 or more of assessable property. The 65 petitioners who, between 1828 and 1836, exercised some economic power held a total of 84 corporate directorships, of which 37 were seats on bank boards.

46. William Appleton, Diary, March 1828, WA-BL.

47. The vote reported by the Boston *Daily Advertiser,* Nov. 6, 1828, was 3,121 to 845; Charles F. Adams to John Q. Adams, Dec. 3, 1828, Ad-MHS. The National Republican program is suggested in the *Daily Advertiser,* Oct. 22, 1830, reporting a party rally in Faneuil Hall.

48. John D. Williams et al. to Harrison Gray Otis, Sept. 9, 1830, HGO-MHS; Arthur B. Darling, "Jacksonian Democracy in Massachusetts, 1824–1848," *American Historical Review,* XXIX (Jan. 1924), 279; Harrison Gray Otis to George Harrison, May 20, 1831, HGO-MHS; Alexander H. Everett, Journals, Diary No. 6, July 13, 1833, Everett-Noble Diaries, MHS (here-

after EN-MHS); [Anti-Masonic Convention, Resolution concerning nomination for Lt.-Governor, undated, but probably 1831, signed John Baily and Benjamin F. Hallett], STA-MHS; William Foster to Silas Wright, Jan. 3, 1835, MV-LC.

49. Charles F. Adams to John Q. Adams, Jan. 19, 1834. For concerns of the Workingmen see Boston *Mirror,* Oct. 25, 1833; also Frederick Robinson, *An Oration Delivered before the Trades Union of Boston and Vicinity* . . . (Boston: C. Douglas, 1834), 18–24, 28–29. John K. Simpson to Martin Van Buren, Nov. 19, 1835, MV-LC. Edward Pessen, "Did Labor Support Jackson?: The Boston Story," *Political Science Quarterly,* LXIV (June 1949), 263, argues that the presence of many Whigs within Workingmen's party ranks suggests that the party was merely a "front organization" for the Whigs. Horace Mann to Mary Peabody, July 4, 1834, Horace Mann Papers, MHS (hereafter HM-MHS).

50. John Barton Derby, *Political Reminiscences, Including a Sketch of the Origin and History of the "Statesman Party"* (Boston: The Author, 1835), 12–15; Charles G. Greene to Levi Woodbury, Nov. 13, 1834, LW-LC; Boston *Daily Advertiser,* April 25 and July 8, 1836; Charles G. Greene to Levi Woodbury, July 2, 1836, and John M. Fiske to Levi Woodbury, July 5, 1836, both in LW-LC.

51. Edward Everett, Diary, Aug. 9, 1828, EE-MHS; Charles F. Adams to Louisa C. Adams, Jan. 31, 1829, Ad-MHS; Boston *Morning Post,* April 4, 1833; Pessen, "Did Labor Support Jackson?" 265–69; Robert T. Bower, "Did Labor Support Jackson?: The Boston Story. Reply," *Political Science Quarterly,* LXV (Sept. 1950), 441–44. Ronald P. Formisano, *The Transformation of Political Culture: Massachusetts Parties, 1790s–1840s* (New York: Oxford University Press, 1983), 247–49, 272–73.

52. In the gubernatorial contests of 1834, 1835, and 1836 Bostonians cast 5,590 (73%), 4,127 (62%), and 4,772 (62%) votes for Whig candidates; 1,995, 2,491, and 2,894 for the Democratic candidates: Boston *Daily Advertiser,* Nov. 13, 1834, and Nov. 15, 1836. Of the total sample of 313 of the antibank petitioners only 8 (3%) wielded any economic power, and only 1 (a mere .3%) possessed wealth of $30,000 or more. Of the 164 whose occupations could be identified, 97 (59%) were mechanics, and 41 (25%) engaged in commerce. It is likely that many of the 149 unidentified were laborers and mechanics. The antibank petitioners were not identified by occupation in the petition, as the probank signers were.

53. Of a total sample of all pro- and antibank petitioners in Boston, 1,013 individuals, 35% were engaged in mercantile pursuits. Among 2,562 Charleston voters in 1830, 29% were engaged in commerce. Mechanics, laborers, and those whose occupations are unknown numbered 50% of all Boston petitioners, 44% of Charleston voters. But in Boston professionals comprised but 5%, while in Charleston they were 10% of the voters. And if one combines planters and professionals, they cast 17% of Charleston's ballots in 1830.

54. Between 1828 and 1833 Charleston returned 34 different men to the South Carolina legislature. Of them 29% were planters, 38% professionals, 12% men of commerce, 8% mechanics, and 12% one-time government employees. Of the 194 men Boston returned to Massachusetts's legislature,

1828–1835, 29% to 30% were professionals, 49% to 52% were engaged in commerce; 13% to 17% were mechanics; and fewer than 2% to 5% were paid government employees.

7: Policing the City and Providing Welfare

1. Thomas Wetmore and Edward G. Prescott, eds., *The Charter and Ordinances of the City of Boston, together with the Acts of the Legislature Relating to the City* (Boston: J. H. Eastburn, 1834), 10–11.
2. Josiah Quincy, *Address to the Board of Aldermen, of the City of Boston, Jan. 3, 1829 . . . on Taking Final Leave of the Office of Mayor* (Boston: Crocker & Brewster, 1829), 22–24, puts the figure of the funded debt at just over $637,000. Lemuel Shattuck, *Report to the Committee of the City Council Appointed to Obtain the Census of Boston for the Year 1845 . . .* (Boston: John H. Eastburn, 1846), 96, sets the total 1828 city debt in excess of $949,000, while an ardently anti-Quincy broadside, "Look to Your Interest," dated Dec. 8, [1828], BPL, sets the city's debt at $1,193,779.98. Josiah Quincy II, *A Municipal History of the Town and City of Boston during two Centuries: From September 17, 1630 to September 17, 1830* (Boston: C. C. Little and J. Brown, 1852), 183–84, 59 ff. Quincy, *Address . . . Jan. 3, 1829*, 8–11.
3. Quincy, *Address . . . Jan. 3, 1829*, 12–21.
4. Broadside, "Worse and Worse!!" [Dec. 15, 1828], BPL; Boston *Daily Advertiser,* Dec. 13, 15, 16, and 17, 1828; Charles F. Adams to John Q. Adams, Dec. 17, 1828, Ad-MHS; [Harrison Gray Otis] to William Sullivan, Dec. 16, [1828], draft, HGO-MHS; *Daily Advertiser,* Dec. 23, 1828.
5. Harrison Gray Otis, *An Address to the Board of Aldermen and Members of the Common Council of Boston on the Organization of City Government, January 5, 1829* (Boston: John H. Eastburn, 1829), 5–7, 10–11.
6. Of the 32 mayors and aldermen who served at some time between 1828 and 1836, the occupations of 17 were given in the 1829 directory and 18 in the 1836 directory. Of those, between 47% and 61% were in mercantile occupations. Of the entire 32, 59% were rich; 34% enjoyed significant social standing. Of the 57 who served at any time between 1828 and 1843, 65% also served in the legislature during the same period. Of the 211 councilmen between 1828 and 1836 of known occupation in 1829 or 1836, 22% to 26% were merchants, 18% storekeepers and middle-rank commercial men, and 13% to 14% were grocers or commercial employees. Of the entire 211, 18% were rich, and 23% enjoyed modest or high social status. Of the 348 who served on the council at any time between 1828 and 1843, only 26% also served as state legislators in the same period. Only 2 mechanics served as aldermen. At least 43 served in the council and regularly occupied 19% to 24% of its seats. Only 2 or 3 Democrats served as mayor or alderman; at least 30 served on the Council. While none of Boston's seven mayors between 1828 and 1843 served more than three years, three did serve three years, and two served two years. Thirty-two (64%) of the 50 aldermen served more than one year but only 16 (32%) served more than two. Of the 348 councilmen, 156 (45%) served only one year and only 94 (27%) served for more than two years.
7. Charles P. Huse, *The Financial History of Boston, from May 1, 1822 to*

January 31, 1902 (Cambridge: Harvard University Press, 1916), 49–61; Shattuck, *Census of Boston . . . 1845*, Appendix, 59.
8. Huse, *Financial History*, 36–42; City of Boston, *The Ordinances of the City of Boston, Passed since the Year 1834* . . . (Boston: John H. Eastburn, 1843), 68–71.
9. Huse, *Financial History*, 38–39; Josiah Quincy, *An Address to the Board of Aldermen and Members of the Common Council on the Organization of City Government, January 1, 1828* (Boston: N. Hale, 1828), 12–15.
10. Quincy, *Municipal History*, 148–49; Boston *Daily Advertiser*, Feb. 6, 1828, December 15, 1830, and September 10, 1828.
11. Boston Board of Commissioners of Health, Records [1832], June 20, 1832, MS, Boston Public Library (hereafter BPL); Frederic Tudor, Diary, June 25, 1832, T-BL.
12. Boston Board of Commissioners of Health, *Report of the Medical Deputation Appointed to Visit New York, for the Purpose of Making Observations Relative to the Disease now Prevailing in That Place* ([Boston, 1832]); Boston Board of Commissioners of Health, Records [1832], June 20, 21, 1832, BPL; Boston *Morning Post*, Aug. 1, 1832; Nathaniel I. Bowditch to Henry Bowditch, July 25, 1832, Forbes Family Papers, Massachusetts Historical Society (hereafter FF-MHS); *Morning Post*, July 23, 1832; Nathaniel I. Bowditch to Henry Bowditch, July 9, 1832, FF-MHS; *Morning Post*, July 24, 1832; Shattuck, *Census of Boston . . . 1845*, Appendix, 77; Boston City Marshal, *Report, December 29, 1834*, passim, included in Documents of the City of Boston, 1834 et seq. (Microfilm for Boston Public Library by Graphic Microfilm of New England).
13. Roger Lane, *Policing the City, 1822–1885* (Cambridge: Harvard University Press, 1967), 17; Wetmore and Prescott, *Charter and Ordinances of Boston*, 227.
14. Quincy, *Address . . . Jan. 3, 1829*, 21–22; Boston *Daily Advertiser*, March 14, 1829; Boston *Morning Post*, June 29, 1833; Huse, *Financial History*, 15–18; Lane, *Policing the City*, 37; Shattuck, *Census of Boston . . . 1845*, 177; and Lane, *Policing the City*, 59, 61.
15. Boston Aqueduct Corporation, Records, 1795–[1851], MS; and President and Directors' Records, 1806–1851, MS, both in BPL, provide a skeletal outline of the vicissitudes of the company.
16. Daniel Treadwell, *Report Made to the Mayor and Aldermen of the City of Boston, on the Subject of Supplying the Inhabitants of That City with Water* (Boston: True & Greene, 1825), 3–14; Josiah Quincy, *An Address to the Board of Aldermen, and Members of the Common Council, of Boston, on the Organization of the City Government, January 2, 1826* (Boston: True and Greene, 1826), reprinted in *The Inaugural Addresses of the Mayors of Boston* (Boston: Rockwell & Churchill, 1894), 54; Loammi Baldwin, *Report on the Subject of Introducing Pure Water into the City of Boston* (Boston: J. H. Eastburn, 1834), 40–46, 54–55; [Theodore Lyman, Jr.], *Communication to the City Council on the Subject of Introducing Water into the City* (Boston: J. H. Eastburn, 1834), 25–29; Boston Aqueduct Corporation, Records, Sept. 25, 1835, and President and Directors' Records, Feb. 26, 1835, BPL; Thomas A. Dexter to Samuel T. Armstrong, Feb. 18, 1836, STA-MHS; R. H. Eddy, *Report on the Introduction of Soft*

Water into the City of Boston (Boston: J. H. Eastburn, 1836), 36–40; Boston *Daily Advertiser,* July 2, 1836.

17. Boston *Daily Advertiser,* Aug. 18, 23, and Nov. 30, 1836; Boston *Morning Post,* Jan. 25, Feb. 25, and March 1, 1837; Boston Common Council, *Report of the Committee . . . on the Expenditures to be Incurred by the Introduction of Pure Water and for the Liquidation of the City Debt . . . May 18, 1837,* Document Number 9, in Documents of the City of Boston, 1834, et seq.

18. The petitions are printed in Boston Common Council, Document Number 9, . . . *Papers Relating to the Introduction of Pure Water* (Boston: J. H. Eastburn, 1838); Boston *Morning Post,* March 31, April 3 and 7, 1838; Boston Common Council, Document Number 25, *Report of the [Standing] Committee on the Introduction of Soft Water into the City, September 1839* ([Boston: J. H. Eastburn, 1839]), 9–11, 1–6; Massachusetts General Court, *An Act to Incorporate the Spot Pond Aqueduct Company* (n.p., n.d.).

19. Boston Aqueduct Corporation, President and Directors' Records, Feb. 14, 1840, and Corporation Records, March 13, 1840, BPL; Boston Common Council, Document Number 25, *Report of the Joint Special Committee to Whom was Referred the Subject of Introducing a Supply of "Pure Soft Water"* . . . ([Boston, 1844]), 3; Robert A. McCaughey, *Josiah Quincy, 1772–1864: The Last Federalist* (Cambridge: Harvard University Press, 1974), 201.

20. Wetmore and Prescott, *Charter and Ordinances of Boston,* 20; Quincy, *Municipal History,* 140–42, 144; Boston Common Council, *Report of the Committee of the City Council with the Opinion of Messrs Prescott, Jackson and Webster on the Powers and Duties of the Overseers of the Poor* (Boston: True and Greene, 1825), 12.

21. Shattuck, *Census of Boston . . . 1845,* 108, 113; Boston House of Industry, *Twelfth Annual Report* [1835], 3, Common Council Document Number 13, in Documents of the City of Boston, 1834 et seq.; Boston *Daily Advertiser,* Jan. 13, 1830; Boston Overseers of the Poor, *Report [Jan. 1 to Dec. 31, 1833],* 1–4, in Documents of the City of Boston, 1834 et seq.; *Daily Advertiser,* Jan. 6, 1836.

22. Boston Common Council, Document Number 7, *Report of the Standing Committee on the Houses of Industry, Correction and Reformation . . .* [March 1835], in Documents of the City of Boston, 1834 et seq.; Boston Board of Aldermen, Document Number 13 [*Report of the Committee on the Jail, and the Houses of Industry, Correction and Reformation . . . Dec. 15, 1834*] ([no title page, Boston, 1834]), 15; Boston Common Council, *Report of the Standing Committee on Houses of Industry . . . [on] the Number of Persons That Have Been Sentenced to the House of Industry by the Justices of the Police Court* [1835], 2; Boston House of Industry, *Fourteenth Annual Report . . . April 1837,* 4; Boston Common Council, Document Number 6, *Report of the Communication of the Mayor Relating to his Interview with the Overseers of the Poor* [1837], 2–4; and Document Number 5, *Report from the Joint Committee on the Auditor's Report and Estimates* [1837], 2–4, the four preceding all in Documents of the City of Boston, 1834 et seq.

23. Only 2% of Charleston's 49 wardens and intendents serving 1828–1835 belonged to no social groups, and 53% of them belonged to ten or more

clubs. Of the 35 whose church affiliations are known, 12 worshipped at St. Philip's, 5 at other Episcopal churches, 5 at St. John's Lutheran church, 5 at the Scots Presbyterian (First) Church, 3 at the Circular (Congregational) Church; and 2 each at the Unitarian and Second Presbyterian churches. One worshipped at the First Baptist Church.

24. Among the 91 Boston councilmen 1828–1836 whose church affiliation is known, more than half were Unitarian, but only 11 worshipped at Second Church (Unitarian), 8 at King's Chapel, and 8 at New South. St. Paul's (Episcopal) claimed 9. Twelve of the 19 mayors and aldermen for the same period were Unitarian, of whom four attended King's Chapel and four New South. Of the Episcopalians, three attended Trinity and two, St. Paul's. Clubbing patterns show that of all 211 councilmen, 1828–1836, 30% are not known to have belonged to any club whatsoever; of all 32 aldermen and mayors only 19% were similarly asocial. The distribution for lower and upper chambers in the various categories of clubs during those same years suggests a very modest likelihood of councilmen and aldermen having extensive social contacts. For example, while 50% of the aldermen belonged to philanthropic groups, only 30% of the councilmen did; similar proportional differences occur among upper-class clubs, 31% and 17%; and reform groups, 31% and 18%. The comparison of shared economic interests among Boston's councilmen rests on the 54% of them who were in mercantile occupations in 1829 and the 57% of them who were in such occupations in 1836, and its aldermen, for whom the comparable proportions are 53% and 78%. In Charleston, 85% of city council members had slaves resident in their homes or businesses in 1830; 48%, ten or more slaves.

25. Of the 134 commissioners 1828–1843, only 24 (18%) possessed even moderate wealth, and although 45% of the 33 men serving 1828–1832 enjoyed modest or high social standing, only 21% of the 59 serving 1839–1843 did so. Most notably, the proportion of men in high-prestige occupations declined from 78% in 1828–1832 to 51% in 1839–1843, while the proportion of mechanics increased from none to 17% in the same period. Of the total 134 commissioners 1828–1843, 121 belonged to one or more clubs or organizations. While philanthropic organizations drew 39% of the commissioners, 53% belonged to an ethnic group society, and 51% belonged to clubs with no other purpose than sociability. Of the 80 whose religious affiliation we know, 36% were Episcopalian, 19% were Presbyterian, 11% Lutheran, 10% Jewish; smaller proportions were Baptist, Catholic, Congregational, Unitarian, and Swedenborgian. The absence of Methodists from our tally may reflect both very limited remaining church rolls and the fact that Methodists concerned with the care of the sick acted through their own Benevolent Association.

26. Charleston Department of Health, *Digest of Acts of Assembly of South Carolina, and Ordinances of the City of Charleston, Relative to Health Department. Compiled by Order of Board of Health from 1763 to 1869* . . . (Charleston: Daily Republican Office, 1870), 3ff; Charleston *Mercury,* June 4, 1836; Charleston, *Ordinances of the City of Charleston: From the 5th February, 1833 to the 9th May, 1837* . . . (Charleston: A. E. Miller, 1837), 30–32; M. Foster Farley, *An Account of the History of Stranger's Fever in Charleston, 1699–1876* (Washington, D.C.: Univer-

sity Press of America, 1978), 88–89; Joseph I. Waring, *A History of Medicine in South Carolina, 1825–1900* (Charleston: South Carolina Medical Association, 1967), 40; Charleston *Courier,* May 18, 1830, and April 16, 1831; J. L. Dawson and H. W. DeSaussure, *Census of the City of Charleston, South Carolina, for the Year 1848* . . . (Charleston: J. B. Nixon, 1849), 239–47.

27. Charleston *Courier,* June 26, 28, and Aug. 10, 1832.
28. Charleston *Courier,* Nov. 3, 1832; William C. Dukes, Journal and Diary, [Nov. 2, 1832], vol. IX, USC.
29. Charleston *City Gazette,* Nov. 8 and 10, 1832.
30. Charleston *City Gazette,* Nov. 8, 1832; Charleston *Mercury,* July 9, 1833; Charleston *Courier,* July 2, 1834; *Mercury,* Sept. 18, 1835 and June 2, 1836; *Courier,* Dec. 7, 1833.
31. Daily reports of new cholera cases and deaths were issued in the public press between the end of August and the beginning of November: see Charleston *Courier* and *Mercury,* passim. A summary of deaths appeared in the *Mercury,* Nov. 4, 1836. For special city provisions to deal with the epidemic see *Mercury,* Sept. 13 and Oct. 11, 1836. John Bachman to John J. Audubon, Sept. 3, 1836, in Catherine L. Bachman, *John Bachman . . . The Pastor of St. John's Lutheran Church, Charleston* (Charleston: Walker, Evans & Cogswell, 1888), 141–42, and William M. Porcher to Robert M. Deveux, Sept. 15, [1836], William Mazyck Porcher Papers, USC (hereafter WMP-USC) discuss cholera as a class phenomenon.
32. Henry L. Pinckney, *A Report; Containing a Review of the Proceedings of the City Authorities, from the 4th September, 1837, to the 1st August, 1838* . . . (Charleston: Thomas J. Eccles, 1838), 41–42; Charleston Alms House [Poor House], Records, MS, 35 vols. (1801–1916), Oct. 8, 1835, SCHS.
33. Richard Shryock, *Medicine and Society in America* (New York: New York University Press, 1960), 106; Charleston *Courier,* July 22, 1831; for the building of the new marine hospital in Charleston, Resolution of the Charleston City Council, Nov. 29, 1830, and S. D. Ingraham to James Jervey, April 19, 1831, both in U.S. Treasury Department, Record Group 56, MC 178, Roll 32, National Archives; *Courier,* July 22, 1831; and U.S. General Accounting Office, Miscellaneous Treasury Accounts of the General Accounting Office, 1790–1894 [Expenditures for the Charleston Marine Hospital], MC 235, Roll 825, Number 66-442, National Archives.
34. Charleston, *A Collection of the Ordinances of the City Council of Charleston from the 10th Day of October 1826 to 13th Day of March, 1832* . . . (Charleston: A. E. Miller, 1832), 53; Robert Mills, *Statistics of South Carolina* . . . (Spartanburg, S.C.: Reprint Company, c. 1826, 1972), 396; Edward P. Cantwell, "A History of the Charleston Police Force," in *Year Book, 1908, City of Charleston, So. Ca.* (Charleston: Daggett Printing Co., 1909), Appendix, 3–19; Jack K. Williams, *Vogues in Villainy: Crime and Retribution in Ante-Bellum South Carolina* (Columbia: University of South Carolina Press, 1959), 72–73; Charleston *Courier,* Aug. 30, 1834. The annual account of city finances was published each year at the end of August in the city press of Charleston. For 1832–1833 the city guard accounted for 13.5% of all expenditures (Charleston *Courier,* Aug. 31,

1833); for 1833–1834, 13.5% (*Courier*, Aug. 30, 1834),; 1836–1837, 9.5% (Charleston *Mercury*, Sept. 1, 1837). For 1835–1836, when total city expenses ran well above normal, the proportion dropped to 4% (*Mercury*, Sept. 2, 1836).

35. Charleston *Courier*, Dec. 4, 1833, and July 23, 1835; Benjamin Elliott and Martin Stroebel, *The Militia System of South Carolina, Being a Digest of the Acts of Congress Concerning the Militia, Likewise of the Militia Laws of this State . . . Also the Patrol and Quarantine Laws . . .* (Charleston: A. E. Miller, 1835), xxxix–xl.

36. South Carolina, *Statutes at Large . . .* , David J. McCord, ed. (Columbia: A. S. Johnston, 1840), VII, 319–20; Michael S. Hindus, *Prison and Plantation: Crime, Justice, and Authority in Massachusetts and South Carolina, 1767–1878* (Chapel Hill: University of North Carolina Press, 1980), 138–52. Charleston Poor House Commissioners, *Report of the Free Colored Poor* (Charleston: Burges and James, 1842), 7–8; [Printed table of Work House fees, 1830], BH-SCHS.

37. Charleston Board of Fire Masters, Record Book, 1819–1836, MS, December 23, 1834, SHC.

38. Charleston Board of Fire Masters, Record Book, Feb. 1, 1828, SHC; Charleston, *Ordinances . . . 1826–1832*, 18–21; the quotation is from the Charleston *Courier*, March 1, 1830. For reports of the various fires see Charleston *City Gazette*, Feb. 19, 1833; *Courier*, Feb. 16, 1835; Charleston *Mercury*, Feb. 16, 1835; *Courier*, June 8, 1835; and *Mercury*, June 9, 1835. General Hamilton's public notice is in *Courier*, June 11, 1835.

39. Charleston Alms House [Poor House], Records, Jan. 29, 1829, SCHS. For the three periods 1828–1832, 1833–1838, 1839–1843 the commission was comprised respectively of 58%, 56%, and 44% professional men and 21%, 22%, and 44% of men with mercantile occupations. Of the 36 men who served as commissioners, only one was a planter by occupation, and none was a mechanic. Of the 36, 42% were of modest or great status; and 50% enjoyed either modest or significant political power, either from long service to the Poor House or from other posts.

40. Dawson & DeSaussure, *Census of Charleston . . . 1848*, 49–50. In 1830–1831, for example, of 350 inmates in the Poor House only 17% were Charlestonians, while 20% were Irish; and of the 236 getting outdoor relief 54% were from the city, whereas only 7% were Irish. Charleston Alms House [Poor House], Records, Jan. 29, 1829, July 15, 1830, and October 20, 1831, SCHS; also Charleston *Courier*, Sept. 2, 1831.

41. Of the 51 commissioners of the Orphan House who served 1828–1843, 16 had attended undergraduate college, 2 had M.D.'s, 18 had either studied law or been admitted to the bar, and 1 held an LL.D. Forty-three percent of these commissioners were moderately wealthy and 10% were men of substantial wealth. Fully 73% of them were of modest or high status.

42. Dawson & DeSaussure, *Census of Charleston . . . 1848*, 43–45; Charleston *Mercury*, Aug. 6, 1840.

43. Charleston *Courier*, Aug. 10 and 19, 1835, and for the quotation, Aug. 21, 1835. The proposal for an intendent's salary was turned down by a vote of 429 to 266; Charleston *Mercury*, July 29, 1836. Charleston, *Ordinances . . . 1833–1837*, 73–77.

44. Charleston *Mercury,* May 17 and June 17, 1836.
45. Charleston *Mercury,* June 17, 25, and 29, 1836; Charleston, *Ordinances* . . . *1833–1837,* 80; *Mercury,* July 4 and Aug. 6, 1836.
46. Charleston *Mercury,* Aug. 10, 1836; Charleston, *Ordinances* . . . *1833–1837,* 87–92; *Mercury,* Sept. 5, 1836.
47. "Petition of the City Council [of Charleston] Praying a Change in the City Guard," [1836], MS, South Carolina, Legislative Papers, 1830–1859, Legislative System, City of Charleston, South Carolina Archives (hereafter LPLSC-SCA); Robert Y. Hayne, *Address to the City Council of Charleston, Delivered on Eighth November, 1836* (Charleston: A. E. Miller, 1836), 5; Robert Y. Hayne, *Report of the Proceedings of the City Authorities of Charleston, During the Past Year, Ending September 1st, 1837* . . . (Charleston: A. E. Miller, 1837), 10, 13.
48. Hayne, *Address to the City Council . . . Eighth November, 1836,* 6–10; ["Memorial from Charleston City Council, November 8, 1836, to Modify Certain Streets"], LPLSC-SCA; Charleston *Mercury,* Feb. 1, 7, and 18, 1837; Charleston, *Ordinances . . . 1833–1837,* 139–40, 157–63; and Hayne, *Report of the Proceedings of the City Authorities . . . September 1st, 1837,* 15–17, 19–31.
49. "Memorial of the City Council Regarding the Regulation of Fires, etc.," [1836?], LPLSC-SCA; "An Act for the Better Regulation of the Fire Department in the City of Charleston," Charleston, *Digest of Ordinances . . . from the Year 1783 to . . . 1844,* 353–54; Charleston, *Ordinances . . . 1833–1837,* 164–69; ["Memorial of the City of Charleston to the House and Senate of South Carolina, November 22, 1836, Relating to Wharves"], LPLSC-SCA; "Petition of the City Council that the Charter . . . be Amended so as to Change the Titles of Intendent and Warden . . . ," [1836], LPLSC-SCA.
50. Charleston, *Ordinances . . . 1833–1837,* 115–17; Hayne, *Address to the City Council . . . Eighth November, 1836,* 17–18; Charleston, *Ordinances . . . 1833–1837,* 141–56; Hayne, *Report of the Proceedings of the City Authorities . . . September 1st, 1837,* 7n.
51. Charleston, *Ordinances . . . 1833–1837,* 169–70; Charleston *Mercury,* April 19, 1837.
52. Charleston *Mercury,* May 15, 1837; Hayne, *Report of the Proceedings of City Authorities . . . September 1st, 1837,* 3.
53. Charleston *Mercury,* Sept. 6, 1837.
54. Charleston *Mercury,* Nov. 24, 1836; Hayne, *Report of the Proceedings of the City Authorities . . . September 1st, 1837,* 12.

8: Education, Work, and Cultural Values

1. Boston school expenditures are given in Lemuel Shattuck, *Report to the Committee of the City Council Appointed to Obtain the Census of Boston for the Year 1845* . . . (Boston: J. H. Eastburn, 1846), Appendix, 32. Data on the number of schools and on school enrollment are from Boston School Committee, *Report . . . on the State of the Schools in the City of Boston, Nov. 29, 1829* ([Boston]: S. N. Dickinscn, [1829]), passim; Jonathan Chapman, *Address . . . to the City Council . . . January 2, 1843* (Boston: J. H. Eastburn, 1843), 12; and Carl F. Kaestle and Maris A. Vinovskis, *Education and Social Change in Nineteenth-Century Massachusetts* (Cambridge,

Eng.: Cambridge University Press, 1980), 21, 259–62. Charleston data are from J. L. Dawson and H. W. DeSaussure, *Census of the City of Charleston, South Carolina, for the Year 1848* . . . (Charleston: J. B. Nixon, 1849), 54–55; Charleston *Mercury,* Dec. 5, 1839; and Commissioners of Free Schools, "Reports of the Commissioners of Free Schools," (1828–1842), MSS, LPLSC-SCA. United States, *Sixth Census or Enumeration of the Inhabitants of the United States* (Washington: Blair and Rives, 1841), 8–9, 11, 44–45, 47.
2. The number and variety of proprietary schools were derived from advertisements in the Charleston *Mercury* and *Courier,* 1828–1843.
3. Morris Goldsmith, *Directory and Stranger's Guide, for the City of Charleston and Its Vicinity* . . . (Charleston: Office of the Irishman, 1831), 129; Fellowship Society, Records, 1762–1947, MS (microfilm copy), Minute, March 14, 1832, USC; Joshua W. Toomer, *Oration . . . at . . . first Centennial Anniversary of the South Carolina Society, in Charleston, . . . Twenty-eighth March . . . 1837* (Charleston: A. E. Miller, 1837), 26; Charleston *Courier,* Dec. 8, 1829; German Friendly Society, Minutes, 1828–1833, typescript, Minute, Nov. 5, 1828, Oct. 27, 1830, CC; Peter K. Guilday, *The Life and Times of John England, First Bishop of Charleston* . . . , 2 vols. (New York: America Press, 1927), I, 56–57, 549; II, 170–71; *Gospel Messenger,* XIII (March 1835), 69.
4. Jane H. Pease and William H. Pease, "Social Structure and the Potential for Urban Change: Boston and Charleston in the 1830s," *Journal of Urban History,* VIII (February 1982), 171–95, especially 185–87; idem, "Intellectual Life in the 1830s: The Institutional Framework and the Charleston Style," in Michael O'Brien and David Moltke-Hansen, eds., *Intellectual Life in Antebellum Charleston* (Knoxville: University of Tennessee Press, 1985).
5. Elias Vanderhorst to Elias and Lewis Vanderhorst, Jan. 28, 1839, Arnoldus Vanderhorst Collection, SCHS (hereafter AV-SCHS); Elias Horry, Will (Nov. 16. 1829), in Edward Frost Papers, LC (hereafter EF-LC); Samuel H. Dickson, *Address Delivered at the Opening of the New Edifice of the Charleston Apprentices' Library Society . . . 13th January, 1841* (Charleston: W. Riley, 1841), 12.
6. Charleston *Courier,* Feb. 4, 1841, April 10 and 12, 1843.
7. For the full College of Charleston story see Pease and Pease, "Intellectual Life and the Charleston Style."
8. College of Charleston, Board of Trustees, Minutes, Nov. 3, 1835, typescript copy, CC.
9. Charleston *Mercury,* July 21, 1837.
10. Charleston *Mercury,* Aug. 9, 1837.
11. Charleston, *Ordinances of the City of Charleston, from the 24th May, 1837 to the 18th March, 1840* . . . (Charleston: B. R. Getsinger, 1840), 146–52; Charleston *Mercury,* July 18, 1839, and Aug. 5, 1840, for the quotation.
12. Harrison Gray Otis, *Speech to the Citizens of Boston, on the Evening Preceding the Late Election* . . . (Boston: J. H. Eastburn, 1830), 13; Thomas H. Perkins, Journals, 1789–1854, Sept. 12, 1835, MHS; Amos Lawrence to Amos A. Lawrence, March 16, 1840, AAL-MHS; Edward Everett, *A Memoir of Mr. John Lowell, Jun.* . . . (Boston: Charles C. Little and

James Brown, 1840), 4; Boston *Morning Post,* Sept. 18, 1838, excerpts from Boston Lyceum, Ninth Annual Report; William Elliott to wife, Aug. 25, 1836, EG-SHC.

13. Josiah Quincy, *An Address to the Board of Aldermen and Members of the Common Council on the Organization of City Government, January 1, 1828* (Boston: N. Hale, 1828), 10–11; and *Address to the Board of Aldermen, of the City of Boston, Jan. 3, 1829 . . . on Taking Final Leave of the Office of Mayor* (Boston: Crocker & Brewster, 1829), 17.
14. Boston School Committee, *Report of the Committee on the Distribution of Medals, December 11, 1838,* Document Number 30, 4–5, and Samuel A. Eliot, *Mayor's Address to the School Committee* [January 1839], Document Number 3, passim, in Documents of the City of Boston, 1834 et seq.
15. Shattuck, *Census of Boston . . . 1845,* 72; William H. Pease and Jane H. Pease, "Paternal Dilemmas: Education, Property, and Patrician Persistence in Jacksonian Boston," *New England Quarterly,* LIII (June 1980), 154–59.
16. Shattuck, *Census of Boston . . . 1845,* 65, 67; Boston Primary School Committee, *Report of the Primary School Committee on Improvements* (Boston: J. H. Eastburn, 1833), 8–16; Joseph M. Wightman, comp., *Annals of the Boston Primary School Committee, from its first Establishment in 1818 to its Dissolution in 1855* (Boston: G. C. Rand, 1860), 149; Joseph W. Ingraham to Samuel A. Eliot, Dec. 4, 1838, in "Ten Documents in Regard to the Primary Schools of Boston," MSS, BPL; Wightman, *Annals,* 161, 133, 153.
17. Boston School Committee, [*Report of a Sub-committee of the School Committee*] *to Take into Consideration the Present System of Instruction Prescribed for the English Grammar and Writing Schools . . .* ([Boston, 1830]), 6–19; Wightman, *Annals,* 177–78; Boston School Committee, *Regulations . . . Adopted May 1838,* Document Number 15, and Boston School Committee, *Report of the Subcommittee Appointed to Inquire into the Origins of the Primary School Committee* [1839], Document Number 7, both in Documents of the City of Boston, 1834 et seq.
18. Boston City Council, *Report of the Joint Committee Appointed to Consider the Expediency of Applying to the Legislature for an Alteration of the City Charter in Relation to . . . the School Committee* (Boston: [J. H. Eastburn], 1834), Document Number 6, Documents of the City of Boston, 1834 et seq.; Massachusetts, *Laws Passed . . . beginning January 1834 and ending April 1836* ([Boston: Dutton and Wentworth, 1837]), 220–21; Boston *Daily Advertiser,* May 22, 1834; Boston, *The Ordinances of the City of Boston, Passed Since the Year 1834 . . .* (Boston: John H. Eastburn, 1843), 58–59. Boston School Committee, *Report of the Distribution of the Pupils in the Grammar Schools of the City of Boston* (Boston: John H. Eastburn, 1837); Boston School Committee, *To the Citizens of Boston* [Report on changes in the school system] ([Boston, 1836]), 8–12; and *Report on Changes in the Distribution of Scholars in the Public Schools,* Document Number 3, 1–15, all in Documents of the City of Boston, 1834 et seq.
19. Carl Siracusa, *A Mechanical People: Perceptions of the Industrial Order in Massachusetts* (Middletown: Wesleyan University Press, 1979), 84, quoting Horace Mann's speech, Lancaster, [Mass.], May 19, 1851; Benevolent Societies of Boston, Association of Delegates, *First Annual Report* (Boston:

I. R. Butts, 1835), 13; William Ellery Channing, *Lectures on the Elevation of the Laboring Portions of the Community* (Boston: William D. Ticknor, 1840), Lecture I, 6; William Hague, *True Charity a Check to Pauperism* . . . (Boston: Gould, Kendall and Lincoln, 1841), 12–13; Boston *Morning Post,* Dec. 29, 1835; William Jenks, Diary, Nov. 26, 1835, in William Jenks Papers, MHS (hereafter WJ-MHS).
20. Joseph T. Buckingham, *An Address Delivered before the Massachusetts Charitable Mechanic Association* . . . *October 7, 1830,* 16–17; *Hints to Young Tradesmen, and Maxims for Merchants* (Boston: Perkins and Marvin, 1838), 80–84; Choate quoted in Siracusa, *Mechanical People,* 84; Grattan quoted in Burton J. Bledstein, *The Culture of Professionalism: The Middle Class and the Development of Higher Education in America* (New York: W. W. Norton and Co., 1976), 249.
21. Thomas H. Perkins to J.P.C., copy, Sept. 18, 1826, Thomas Handasyd Perkins Papers, MHS (hereafter THP-MHS); Abbott Lawrence to Amos Lawrence, July 21, 1831, AL-MHS; Amos Lawrence to A. A. Lawrence, Oct. 5, 1827, and Jan. 31, 1829, AAL-MHS.
22. Anon., *An Appeal to the Good Sense of a Great People* (Charleston: Dan J. Dowling, 1835), 10; Harriet Martineau, *Retrospect of Western Travel,* 2 vols. (London: Saunders and Otley, 1838), I, 234; Samuel H. Dickson, *Address Delivered at the New Edifice of the Charleston Apprentices' Library Society* . . . *13th January, 1841* (Charleston: W. Riley, 1841), 19.
23. Bishop John England to John H. Howard, July 25, 1840, copied in Boston *Morning Post,* Sept. 9, 1840; Anne C. Loveland, *Southern Evangelicals and the Social Order, 1800–1860* (Baton Rouge: Louisiana State University Press, 1980), 104–6; *Morning Post,* July 25, 1842.
24. *American Annals of Education and Instruction,* IV (December 1834), 554; Shattuck, *Census of Boston* . . . *1845,* 74. If one assumes that all 39 of the College of Charleston students in 1834 were local boys and that the white population of the city and Neck was about 20,000, then roughly 1 : 500 attended college; the ratio for Boston college youths to the total population of that city was, according to Shattuck, 1 : 929 in 1833. According to the *American Annals* Charleston enrolled 150 medical students in 1834, Harvard only 82.
25. James J. Putnam, *A Memoir of Dr. James Jackson* . . . (Boston: Houghton, Mifflin & Co., 1905), 244–45, 256; Boston Medical Association, *Boston Medical Police: Rules and Regulations of the Boston Medical Association* (Boston: J. H. Eastburn, 1830), [5]–12; Massachusetts Medical Society, "Annual Meeting of the Fellows of the Massachusetts Medical Society," *Medical Communications of the Massachusetts Medical Society* (1836), Appendix, items of June 2, June 1, 1831, and May 25, 1836; Boston *Morning Post,* April 3, 1839; Gerard W. Gewalt, "Massachusetts Lawyers: A Historical Analysis of the Process of Professionalization, 1760–1840" (Ph.D. dissertation, Clark University, 1969), 118.
26. Pease and Pease, "Intellectual Life and the Charleston Style"; South Carolina, *Statutes at Large* . . . , David J. McCord, ed. (Columbia: A. S. Johnston, 1839), VII, 497; Medical Society of South Carolina, Minutes, Sept.–Oct. 1835, and especially Oct. 12, 1835, and Feb. 1, 1840, typescript, WHL; Samuel H. Dickson, *Annual Report to the President and Board of*

Trustees of the Medical College of the State of South Carolina . . . (Charleston: Burges and James, 1841), 8.

27. Boston School Committee, *Subcommittee Report on Removing the High School to the Adams School House* . . . [1837]; Boston Common Council, *Report of the Standing Committee on Public Instruction on Petition of Samuel Prince* . . . *[relating to the] High School for Girls*, [1836], Document Number 1, 9–11, 6–10, both in Documents of the City of Boston, 1834, et seq.
28. Receipted bill, A. W. Talvande to William Kincaid, May 1831, Kincaid-Anderson Family Papers, USC (hereafter KA-USC); German Friendly Society, Minute, May 1, 1833, CC; Charleston *Courier*, January 4, 1843; James L. Petigru to Jane Petigru North, August 4, 1835, James L. Petigru Letters (copies), LC (hereafter JLP-LC); Harriott Horry Rutledge to Mrs. Edward C. Rutledge, Sept. 17, [1841], and same to same, June 18, 1841, Harriott Horry Rutledge Letters, DU (hereafter HHR-DU).
29. Charleston *Courier*, Aug. 11 and 19, 1841.

9: Class, Family, and Church

1. Lee Soltow, *Men and Wealth in the United States, 1850–1870* (New Haven: Yale University Press, 1975), passim. In recent historical writing the stasis of the rich has been emphasized, but virtually every table in Edward Pessen, *Riches, Class, and Power Before the Civil War* (Lexington, Mass.: D. C. Heath & Co., 1973), testifies also to the existence of some mobility.
2. Of the 111 upper-class Charlestonians (those having four or more status indicators, one of which could be occupation as planter and another ownership of a plantation employing twenty or more slaves), 86% were not men of great wealth, but 85% owned a plantation. Of the twenty-six with great wealth (those with three or more wealth indicators, one of which could be owning a large plantation with fifty or more slaves), 58% were upper class. George T. Fox, Journal, Nov. 5, 1834 (British Records in Relation to America, Series B), found Charleston the last bastion of aristocracy in America and identified it solely with planters. See also John P. Radford, "Culture, Economy, and Urban Structure in Charleston, South Carolina, 1860–1880" (Ph.D. dissertation, Clark University, 1974), 53; Carl N. Degler, *Place Over Time: The Continuity of Southern Distinctiveness* (Baton Rouge: Louisiana State University Press, 1977), 56.
3. Boston's social theory was overt and most persistently addressed by and to mechanics. Joseph T. Buckingham, *An Address Delivered to the Massachusetts Charitable Mechanics Association* . . . *October 7, 1830* (Boston: The Association, 1830), 1–11, 19; James T. Austin, *An Address Delivered to the Massachusetts Charitable Mechanics Association* . . . *October 3, 1839* (Boston: The Association, 1839), 25–26; George Lunt, *An Address Delivered Before the Massachusetts Charitable Mechanics Association, September 26, 1844* . . . (Boston: The Association, 1844), passim. But see also Edward Everett, *An Address Delivered Before the Mercantile Library Association* . . . *September 13, 1838* (Boston: William D. Ticknor, 1838), passim. Of Boston's upper-class persons (those with six or more status indicators), 33% enjoyed great wealth. Of the 189 very wealthy (those with property worth $80,000 or more) only 19% were upper-class.
4. Ralph W. Emerson, "Ode Inscribed to W. H. Channing," in Frederic I.

Carpenter, ed., *Ralph Waldo Emerson* . . . (New York: American Book Company, 1934), 392; Edward Everett to [unknown], June 11, 1831, EE-MHS; Amos Lawrence to Amos A. Lawrence, July 30, 1831 and April 9, 1838, AAL-MHS; Joshua Prescott, *A Digest of the Probate Laws of Massachusetts* . . . (Boston: John Weston, 1824), 75–84; Alice Hansen Jones, "American Probate Inventories: A Source to Estimate Wealth in 1774 . . . ," in Ad Van Der Woude and Anton Schuurman, eds., *Probate Inventories: A New Source for the Historical Study of Wealth, Material Culture and Agricultural Development* . . . (Wageningen: Afdeling Agrarische Geschiedenis Landbouwhogeschool, 1980), 239.

5. Suffolk County, Mass., Probate Record Books, 123–42. Specific wills cited include Ann Amory McLean Lee, Oct. 13, 1834, vol. 132, pt. 2, 225–44; William Phillips, June 18, 1827, vol. 125, 525–29; Rufus L. Barrus, June 15, 1840, vol. 138, pt. 1, 305–7; John Whitney, February 27, 1837, vol. 135, pt. 1, 113–14. Elaborate trust provisions may be found in the wills of Israel Thorndike, July 30, 1833, vol. 130, pt. 2, 60–66; and Joseph Head, Feb. 20, 1837, vol. 135, pt. 1, 91–93.
6. Charleston County, S.C., Probate Records, 1825–1845 (volumes cited only by date are from LDS Genealogical Society microfilm; those with volumes from MS copies are in SCA); Peter Gaillard, Feb. 5, 1833, 18KS No. 28, MS copy, SCA, could leave plantations to three daughters because he had provided his five sons with "Lands and Negroes" during his lifetime. For specific wills cited: John Parker, Jan. 22, 1833, 656–62, 665; Harriott Maxwell, April 16, 1844, 359–64; Elias Horry, Sept. 23, 1834, 40–51. South Carolina, Secretary of State, Marriage Settlements 1824–1842, vols. 9–16, SCA.
7. Charleston County, S.C., Probate Records, Wills of John McKee, Oct. 6, 1831, 527–29; Anna Carpenter, July 10, 1829, 329–31; Arthur Middleton, Jan. 31, 1837, 269–70; and John Julius Pringle, March 20, 1843, 284–88, allocated plantation slaves among children; Paul Weston, March 31, 1837, 279–81; Moses Andrews, July 18, 1826, 41–44; Lavinia Benson, Dec. 3, 1831, 555–56.
8. Charleston County, S.C., Probate Records, Addition to the will of Adam Tunno, Jan. 8, 1833, 651–55. Among the wills which provided maximum freedom to slaves were those of Robert Little, March 13, 1843, 227–81, providing that Mary Kirk be free to leave South Carolina taking her children with her; Jacob A. Lange, Jan. 27, 1832, 575–76, who ordered that Nancy and her son John be emancipated when state law permitted; Molly Neyle, Oct. 12, 1831, a free woman of color, who provided for Barbara, whose emancipation papers, signed years earlier, had never been recorded; and Thomas Inglis, Aug. 31, 1835, 145–46, who required that David pay his heirs $4 a month for the privilege of hiring his own time and retaining his own wages; James Bean, Feb. 6, 1837, 231.
9. John Pierce, Memoirs, September 28, 1833, VI, 86–87, MHS; Boston *Morning Post,* July 1, 1835; Marjorie Drake Ross, *The Book of Boston Federal Period 1775–1837* (New York: Hastings House, 1961), 98, 102, 104.
10. Robert A. McCaughey, *Josiah Quincy, 1772–1864: The Last Federalist* (Cambridge: Harvard University Press, 1974), 1–10; Frederic Tudor, Diary, passim, T-BL; Amos Lawrence and Amos A. Lawrence Papers, 1832–1843, MHS.
11. Large Charleston houses described in real estate advertisements, Charleston

Mercury, Jan. 23, 1838, Jan. 12 and Feb. 6, 1839; Charleston *Courier,* Sept. 1 and 17 and Nov. 21, 1842; Pierce, Memoirs, Sept. 28, 1833, VI, 86, MHS; Harrison Gray Otis to Eliza Otis, June 30, 1840, HGO-MHS; Lee Family Papers, 1830–1834, passim, MHS (hereafter Le-MHS); Charlotte Brooks Everett to Edward Everett, Nov. 29, 1833, EE-MHS.

12. Suffolk County, Mass., Probate Records, Inventories of William Taylor, Sept. 10, 1832, vol. 130, pt. 2, 158; Thomas D. Moore, Oct. 28, 1833, vol. 131, pt. 2, 383–84; George Berry, Nov. 10, 1834, vol. 132, pt. 2, 305.
13. Suffolk County Probate Records, Samuel H. Boyden inventory, Aug. 20, 1832, vol. 130, pt. 2, 120; Ellis Cook, Executor's Account [1831], vol. 130, pt. 1, 383; Stephen Dix inventory, Sept. 24, 1832, vol. 130, pt. 2, 219–24; John Amory inventory, Oct. 29, 1832, vol. 130, pt. 2, 317–22, and will, Sept. 10, 1832, vol. 130, pt. 2, 191–94.
14. Edward Everett Hale, *A New England Boyhood* (Boston: Little, Brown, c. 1893, 1964), 4; William Elliott to [Mrs. William Elliott], Aug. 25, 1836, EG-SHC. For Boston dinner parties in general see William Appleton, Diary, Jan.–May 1841, WA-BL; Peter C. Brooks, Diary, Nov.–Dec. 1837, MHS; Richard Henry Dana, *The Journal* . . . , Robert F. Lucid, ed. (Cambridge: Harvard University Press, 1968), I, 52–131; Alexander H. Everett, Journal, March 28 and Oct. 20, 1832, 1833–1834, passim; John Pierce, Memoirs, VIII, 518–19, MHS.
15. James Stuart, *Three Years in North America,* 2nd ed. (Edinburgh: Robert Cadell, 1833), II, 135–36; John B. Grimball, Diary, May 9–Nov. 7, 1832, SHC.
16. Ann McLean Lee, Will, Oct. 13, 1834, vol. 132, pt. 2, 225–44; Rebecca Tolman, Inventory, Aug. 27, 1832, vol. 130, pt. 2, 138, in Suffolk County Probate Records. Louisa Elizabeth Cabeuil, Inventory, April 23, 1833, 564–65; Sarah Clement, Inventory, Feb. 9, 1832, 509; and Harriet Hockley Bampfield, Will, Sept. 10, 1830, 433–35, in Charleston County Probate Records.
17. Buckingham, *An Address* . . . *October 7, 1830,* 12.
18. Verse quoted in Bertram Wyatt-Brown, *Southern Honor: Ethics and Behavior in the Old South* (New York: Oxford University Press, 1982), 190. Edward Pessen, "The Lifestyle of the Antebellum Urban Elite," *Mid-America,* IV (July 1973), 166–67, deals with the general pattern; William H. Pease and Jane H. Pease, "Paternal Dilemmas: Education, Property, and Patrician Persistence in Jacksonian Boston," *New England Quarterly,* LIII (June 1980), 148, 164–65, deals with marriages in Boston.
19. Edward Brooks, *An Answer to the Pamphlet of Mr. John A. Lowell* . . . (Boston: Eastburn's, 1851), 464–65, and Benjamin Pickman, Memorandum, June 1, 1829, Walcott-Pickman Family Papers, MHS (hereafter WP-MHS) both treat the furniture gift. H. G. Otis to George Harrison, Aug. 20, 1836, HGO-MHS; Henry Jenks to Harriet Jenks, Aug. 14, 1837, and Elizabeth Jenks to same, Sept. 5, 1837, WJ-MHS, display family efforts to block mesalliances in Boston; Harriott Kinloch Middleton to Francis Kinloch, Feb. 24, 1839, Langdon Cheves Collection, SCHS (hereafter LC-SCHS), and James L. Petigru to Adelle P. Allston, Oct. 18, 1836, Allston Pringle Papers, SCHS (hereafter APH-SCHS), record similar events in Charleston. South Carolina Secretary of State, Marriage Settlements, 1824–1845, SCA.

20. Caroline Gilman, *Recollections of a Southern Matron* (New York: Harper & Brothers, 1838), 271–72, describes marriage forms; Charleston Second Presbyterian Church, Records of Session, April 16, 1825, typed copy, USC, describes church modification of the marriage tie.
21. South Carolina Marriage Settlements, IX, 392–94, and XI, 51–55, SCA. Charleston County, S.C., Probate Records, Charles Mathews, Will, Dec. 21, 1831, 119–20, illuminates the dynamics of a free black buying up his slave child and grandchildren. John Fable, Will, July 6, 1831, 860–61, as a white father bequeaths funds to his slave children; Grocer Peter Borch, Will, Oct. 11, 1833, 704, and sailor Henry Kirk, Will, July 25, 1832, 609, make bequests to their free black children; Elias Lynch Horry, Codicil, July 8, 1831, 862, and Thomas Hanscome, Will, Jan. 3, 1832, 960–71, contain bequests from wealthy upper-class men which the probate court honored at the request of the executors.
22. Of the 414 Boston rich whose religion is known, 49% were Unitarian, 33% Episcopalian, and 9% Congregationalist. Of the 547 of known religion who were economically powerful, 54% were Unitarian while 23% were Episcopalian and 15% were Congregationalist. Lemuel Shattuck, *Report to the Committee of the City Council Appointed to Obtain the Census of Boston for the Year 1845* . . . (Boston: John H. Eastburn, 1846), 125, reports Boston church membership in 1845 as: 3,833 Baptists, 1,631 Episcopalians, 2,331 Methodists, 4,830 Congregationalists, 2,810 Unitarians, and 1,428 Universalists. There is no similar summary for Charleston.
23. G. D. Bernheim, *History of the German Settlements and of the Lutheran Church in North and South Carolina* . . . (Spartanburg, S.C.: Reprint Company, c. 1872, 1974), 421–23; St. Matthews Evangelical Lutheran Church, *100 Years of Christian Life and Service* . . . (Charleston: The Church, 1940), [3–5].
24. Barnett A. Elzas, *The Jews of South Carolina* . . . (Spartanburg, S.C.: Reprint Company, c. 1905, 1972), 155–58, 208–9; Kaal Kadosh Bet Elohim, Minutes of the Board of Trustees, July 4, 1840, Beth Elohim Archives.
25. Peter K. Guilday, *The Life and Times of John England* . . . (New York: America Press, 1927), I, 334–37; St. Mary's Roman Catholic Church, Charleston, Vestry Book, MS, Oct. 8, 1837, in Church Archives, St. Mary's Rectory; John England, "Letter in Behalf of the Catholic Congregations . . . May 28, 1838," in Sebastian G. Messmer, ed., *Works* . . . (Cleveland: Arthur H. Clark, 1908), VI, 385.
26. The story is told in detail in the Boston *Morning Post,* Feb. 21–April 25, 1842, passim; Robert H. Lord et al., *History of the Archdiocese of Boston* . . . , 3 vols. (New York: Sheed and Ward, 1944), II, 301–19. In the end, neither side won. O'Bierne was sent to Portland; O'Flaharty was posted to Salem.
27. *The Gospel Messenger and Southern Episcopal Register,* VII (March 1830), 65, and IX (March 1832), 67–68.
28. Henry M. Bruns to Joseph Milligan, April 7, 1835, Milligan Papers, SHC (hereafter M-SHC); Albert D. Betts, *History of South Carolina Methodism* (Columbia: The Advocate Press, 1952), 201; William Capers et al., *Exposition of the Causes and Character of the Difficulties in the Church in Charleston in the Year 1833* . . . (n.p.: n.p., [1833]), 16.

29. Capers, *Exposition of the Causes* . . . , 3–17; *A Rejoinder to "An Exposition of the Late Schism in the Methodist Episcopal Church in Charleston"* (Charleston: W. Riley, 1834), 6–7; Charleston *Courier,* Oct. 14, 1834; Charleston *Mercury,* May 10, 1837.
30. John Honour, Chairman of Methodist Protestant Church, claimed a "huge number of coloured persons" in Congregational Church Records, May 1, 1838, vol. 12, 208; Capers is quoted in Betts, *History of . . . Methodism,* 178. Robert F. Durden, "The Establishment of Calvary Protestant Episcopal Church for Negroes in Charleston," *South Carolina Historical Magazine,* LXV (April 1964), 65, asserts that Charleston churches could accommodate only one-fourth of the city's slave population in 1840. For testimony of crowding and special services see St. Michael's Protestant Episcopal Church, Vestry Book, 1824–1869, Vestry and Wardens Minutes, typed copy, Sept. 29, 1833 (USC); St. Philip's Protestant Episcopal Church, Journal, 1823–1831, typed copy, Oct. 21, 1827, and Aug. 24, 1828 (USC); St. John's German Lutheran Church, Minutes, 1830–1845, typed copy, July 15, 1831, and May 5, 1837; Second Presbyterian Church, Records of Sessions, 1809–1852, Genealogical Society of Utah microfilm, July 11, 1834; Gilman, *Recollections of a Southern Matron,* 269–70, describes class system; Charleston *Mercury,* Feb. 18, May 12, 25, and 26, 1837, describes the city council action.
31. Jacob Schirmer, Diary, Aug. 31, 1837, Oct. 27, 1840, SCHS; Charleston *Mercury,* April 6 and Nov. 14, 1840.
32. Pauline Holmes, *One Hundred Years of Mount Vernon Church* (Boston: The Church, 1942), 2, n. 3; Boston *Morning Post,* Jan. 18, 22, 24, and 28, 1842.
33. Boston *Morning Post,* Dec. 13 and 17, 1842, Jan. 3 and Feb. 22, 1843.
34. David Henshaw, *Letters on the Internal Improvements and Commerce of the West* (Boston: Dutton and Wentworth, 1839), 19–20.
35. There were 204 Boston elite candidates who belonged to two churches. Of the 15 who joined Baptist churches as their second affiliation, 12 had left Baptist churches to do so. Of the 70 who joined a Congregational church as their second affiliation, 61 had previously been Congregationalists. But of the 57 who joined an Episcopal church as a second church, only 39 had previously been so affiliated, and only 30 of the 56 whose second church was Unitarian had come from Unitarian ranks. There is less evidence of church mobility in Charleston, but there 25 of the 29 who had an Episcopal church as a second affiliation were initially Episcopalians. Methodist church membership lists are missing for both cities, as are Baptist ones for Charleston. Of the 25 with a Presbyterian or Congregational second affiliation, 17 had had a similar first affiliation.
36. Of the 268 of 424 Charlestonians with economic power whose religious affiliation is known, 53% were Episcopalians, 8% Congregationalists, 19% Presbyterians, and 5% Unitarians. Of the 281 of 486 wealthy whose affiliation is known, 53% were Episcopalians, 11% Congregationalists, 15% Presbyterians, and 3% Unitarians. Of the 390 high-status Bostonians whose church affiliation is known, 17% attended St. Paul's, 14% Trinity, and 15% King's Chapel. Of the 337 rich Bostonians of known church affiliation, 14% attended St. Paul's, 17% Trinity, and 18% King's Chapel. But

of the 353 politically powerful, the respective percentages were 9%, 4%, and 9%; and for the 444 economically powerful, 11%, 8%, and 13%.

37. Thirty-one percent of Charleston's 225 economically powerful, 34% of her 117 politically powerful, 37% of her 281 high status, and 29% of her 231 wealthy whose church membership was known belonged either to St. Philip's or St. Michael's.
38. St. Philip's Protestant Episcopal Church, Minutes of the Vestry and Congregation, 1832–1868, typed copy, May 15, 1835, USC; Charleston Board of Commissioners for Opening and Widening Streets . . . , Minutes, 1818–1866, June 6, 1835, 62–66, SCHS; Charleston *Mercury,* June 12 and 16, 1835.
39. From 1839 to 1844 Boston's Congregational church membership was between 68% and 71% female; Boston City Missionary Society, *Fourth Annual Report . . . 1844* (Boston: The Society, 1845), 7. Paul Trapier, "Notices of Ancestors and Relatives . . . ," 90, SCHS, reported that Charleston's St. Michael's had but 23 male and over 200 female communicants in 1840. St. Philip's in 1824 had 29 white male and 263 white female communicants. Albert S. Thomas, *An Historical Account of the Protestant Episcopal Church in South Carolina, 1820–1957* (Columbia: R. L. Bryan Co., 1957), 255.
40. Trapier, "Notices of Ancestors," 76–85, 89, SCHS; Trinity Protestant Episcopal Church, Vestry Book, V, March 30, 1834–Jan. 14, 1838, New England Historical and Genealogical Society (hereafter NEHGS); Congregational Circular Church Records, XII, July 2–11, 1831, Jan. 14, 1833, June 8 and 25, 1834, SCHS; S. K. Lothrop, ed., *Proceedings of an Ecclesiastical Council in the Case of the Proprietors of Hollis Street Meeting House and Rev. John Pierpont* (Boston: W. W. Clapp & Son, 1841), passim.

10: Play and Philanthropy

1. Much of the information in this chapter is drawn from a wide variety of sources including newspapers, association reports, letters, diaries, and journals. Because of the scattered and diverse nature of the sources, no effort has been made to cite each specific datum except for quotations and statistical observations.
2. Boston Society for the Religious and Moral Instruction of the Poor, *Annual Report for 1827* ([Boston]: n.p., [1828]), 14.
3. Jacob Rhett Mott, *Charleston Goes to Harvard: The Diary of A Harvard Student of 1831,* ed. Arthur H. Cole (Cambridge: Harvard University Press, 1940), 52.
4. Louis Manigault, "Journal of a Trip to Saratoga, Quebec, Boston, &c. . . . ," [ca. Aug. 24–Sept. 5, 1825], Louis Manigault Papers, Duke University (hereafter LM-DU); Samuel Cram Jackson, Diary, Nov. 8, 1832, SHC.
5. Charleston *Courier,* Feb. 23, 1835. Nancy L. Struna, "The North-South Races: American Thoroughbred Racing in Transition, 1823–1850," *Journal of Sport History,* VIII (September 1981), 40–41.
6. Charleston *Courier,* April 23, 1831.
7. Record of Pianos Sold and Hired, 1828–1848, Siegling Music House Collection, SCHS.

8. *The Southern Rose*, VII (1839), 248, explicitly addressed the musical comparison between Charleston and Boston. *Boston Musical Gazette*, I (May 2, 1838).
9. *American Annals of Education and Instruction*, n.s., III (August 1833), 377. *Boston Musical Gazette*, I (May 2, 1838).
10. Boston Academy of Music, *Third Annual Report* (Boston: Perkins and Marvin, 1835), 4; *First Annual Report* (Boston: Perkins and Marvin, 1833), 4.
11. Charles Francis Adams to Louisa C. Adams, Aug. 2, 1828, Ad-MHS; Carl Arfwedson, *The United States and Canada, in 1832, 1833, and 1834*, 2 vols. (New York: Johnson Reprint, c. 1834, 1969), I, 135; *Boston Musical Gazette*, II (April 17, 1839).
12. Charleston *Courier*, March 9, 1832; Charlotte Everett to Edward Everett, March 21, 1830, EE-MHS.
13. Much of the material in the section which follows is derived from Jane H. Pease and William H. Pease, "Social Structure and the Potential for Urban Change: Boston and Charleston in the 1830s," *Journal of Urban History*, VIII (February 1982), 171–95.
14. Hibernian Society, *Constitution and Rules . . . Adopted . . . 1827, Revised . . . 1838* (Charleston: The Society, 1838), 7–18; Hibernian Society, Secretary's Book No. 3, 1827–1847 (typescript), 20–31, 115, 89, 14–105, USC; Charleston *Mercury*, Oct.–Dec. 1838.
15. Derived from memberships published in Hibernian Society, *Constitution and Rules*, 21–30; George C. Congaware, *The History of the German Friendly Society of Charleston, South Carolina, 1766–1916* (Richmond: Garrett and Massie, 1935), 206–17; Societé Française of Charleston, *Constitution and By-Laws . . .* (Charleston: John J. Furlong & Son, 1934), 11–15; Joshua W. Toomer, *Oration . . . at the . . . First Centennial Celebration of the South Carolina Society . . . 1837* (Charleston: A. E. Miller, 1837), 90–97.
16. British Charitable Society, *Report of the British Charitable Society . . .* (Boston: Eastburn's, 1832), 6; German Charitable Society, *Constitution . . .* (Cambridge: Charles Folsom, 1835); Boston Irish Protestant Association, *Circular Letter . . .* , 2d ed. (Boston: The Association, 1837), 6; Società Italiana di Benevolenza, *Costituzione della Società Italiana di Benevolenza . . .* (Boston: I. R. Butts, 1842); Boston Roman Catholic Mutual Relief Society, *Constitution . . . Revised and Adopted . . . 1837* (Boston: Samuel N. Dickinson, 1837), 2; Harrison Club of Boston, *The Constitution and By-Laws . . .* (Boston: n.p., 1840), 3–7; Massachusetts Historical Society, *Proceedings*, I (1791–1835), xli–xliv; Boston Athenaeum, *Chronological List of the Proprietors . . . from its Foundation to . . . 1882 . . .* ([Boston: n.p., 1882]), 1–7; Boston Society of Natural History, *Act of Incorporation . . .* (Boston: Eastburn, 1832).
17. Of the 423 elite candidates who were members of Boston's mercantile associations at any time between 1828 and 1843 whose occupations are known, 85% were in a mercantile occupation in 1829, 87% in 1836, and 87% in 1841. Of the 230 similarly defined members of its mechanic associations, 60%, 60%, and 69% were active mechanics in those years.
18. Of the 290 elite candidates who were members of Charleston's mercantile associations at any time from 1828 to 1843, 72% were in a mer-

cantile occupation in 1830, 73% in 1835, and 79% in 1840. Of the 321 similarly defined members of mechanics' associations, 29%, 25%, and 21% were active members in those years. The New England Society was 70%, 69%, and 79% mercantile.

19. Henry Laurens Pinckney, *Address Delivered before the Methodist Benevolent Society . . . July, 1835* (Charleston: E. J. Van Brunt, 1835), 17.
20. J. L. Dawson and H. W. DeSaussure, *Census of the City of Charleston . . . 1848* (Charleston: J. B. Nixon, 1849), 41. The estimate is for 1848, but is probably not far off for the 1830s.
21. Charleston *City Gazette,* Feb. 4, 1831.
22. Richard S. Fay, *An Oration Delivered before the Citizens of Boston on the Fifty-Eighth Anniversary of American Independence* (Boston: J. H. Eastburn, 1834), 18.
23. [Samuel A. Eliot], "Public and Private Charities in Boston," *North American Review,* LXI (July 1845), 134–49, especially 141, 143–47.
24. William Appleton, Diary, Jan. 1835, vol. 167, WA-BL.
25. William Appleton, Diary, Jan. 1, 1841, WA-BL.
26. William Appleton, Diary, Dec. 31, 1843, WA-BL; William R. Lawrence, ed., *Extracts from the Diary and Correspondence of the Late Amos Lawrence . . .* (Boston: Gould and Lincoln, 1855), Diary, Dec. 17, 1837, at 141–42.
27. The total number of patients served by the dispensary in 1832–1833 was 2,049; in 1835–1836, 1,640; in 1841–1842, 1,957; see "Abstract of the Returns of the Ten Visiting Physicians of the Dispensary," Circular [1833], MHS; Boston *Daily Advertiser,* Nov. 21, 1836; "Abstract from the Reports of the Visiting Physicians of the Dispensary for the Year Ending Sept. 30, 1842," Circular [1842], MHS. Of 242 elite candidates who are known to have contributed to the Boston Dispensary 1828–1843, 68% were rich, 64% were of high status.
28. Boston *Morning Post,* March 10, 1842; Boston *Daily Advertiser,* July 30, 1828. Ronald Story, *The Forging of an Aristocracy: Harvard and the Boston Upper Class, 1800–1870* (Middletown, Conn.: Wesleyan University Press, 1980), 8, cities gifts of $1 million to Massachusetts General Hospital (1800–1860), $80,000 to the Boston Dispensary, and $40,000 to the Lying-In Hospital.
29. Boston Lying-In Hospital, *Act of Incorporation . . .* (Boston: J. E. Hinckley & Co., Sept. 1832), 8, 18. Boston also boasted the privately funded McLean Hospital for the mentally sick (part of Massachusetts General Hospital), the Eye and Ear Infirmary, and the Perkins Institute for the Blind.
30. Ladies' Benevolent Society, Journal II, 1824–1871 (typescript copy), USC, passim.
31. Boston *Daily Advertiser,* April 24, 1828; Boston Asylum and Farm School for Indigent Boys, Appendix, in *Annual Report* (Boston: Samuel N. Dickinson & Co., 1845), 33.
32. William Russell, *Address on Infant Schools; Delivered at the Request of the Managers of the Infant School Society* (Boston: Hiram Tupper, 1829), 3.
33. Henry C. Wright, Journal, Feb. 1, 1835, BPL. The division between orthodox and liberal is noticed in *Ladies Magazine,* II (January 1829), 42. The

similar split in Charleston is noted in "Veritas" to the editor, Charleston *Mercury,* Nov. 17, 1831.
34. Henry C. Wright, Journal, Jan. 28, 1835, BPL.
35. Toast to "Women," offered at the St. Patrick's Day celebration of the St. Patrick's Benevolent Society and the Irish Volunteers, Charleston *Mercury,* March 20, 1837.
36. *Gospel Messenger,* XII (Sept. 1835), 257–58. The clergyman is unidentified but was very likely Daniel Cobia.
37. *Gospel Messenger,* XIII (Jan. 1837), 349; Charleston *Mercury,* Jan. 5, 1837; and quotation, *Mercury,* May 3, 1838.
38. Fatherless and Widows' Society, *Constitution and Report for 1827* (Boston: W. L. Lewis, 1827), 2.
39. Boston Female Moral Reform Society, *Second Annual Report . . . October 17, 1837* (Boston: Isaac Knapp, 1837), 7–9.
40. Joseph Tuckerman, *Prize Essay: On the Wages Paid to Females for their Labour* (Philadelphia: Carey & Hart, 1830); Joseph Tuckerman, *Second Quarterly Report Addressed to the American Unitarian Association* (Boston: Bowles & Dearborn, 1827), 5.
41. House of Industry, *Annual Report for 1834,* Document No. 11, 19, Documents of the City of Boston, 1834 et seq; Seaman's Aid Society of the City of Boston, *First Annual Report* (Boston: David H. Ela, 1834), 11.
42. Charleston *City Gazette,* February 4, 1831. Benevolent Society of Boston, Association of Delegates, *Report of the Committee of Delegates from the Benevolent Societies of Boston* (Boston: Tuttle & Weeks, 1834), 20.
43. Horace Mann to Mary Peabody, Oct. 4, 1836, HM-MHS; Boston *Morning Post,* Jan. 30, 1843. From early February to mid-April 1843 the Soup and Bread Society dispensed, in Wards 1, 2, and 3, over 3,500 gallons of soup, in excess of 35,000 loaves of bread, and more than 500 gallons of milk to 1,558 persons and 391 families at a total expenditure of over $1,000; *Morning Post,* April 20, 1843.
44. Robert Mills, *Statistics of South Carolina . . .* (Spartanburg: Reprint Company, c. 1826, 1972), 327; Ladies' Benevolent Society, Journal II, 1824–1871 (typescript copy), 117–18, USC; German Friendly Society, Minutes of the German Friendly Society, Aug. 6, 1828–Sept. 25, 1833 (typescript copy), minute for Jan. 25, 1832, CC; Pickney, *Address . . . Before the Methodist Benevolent Society,* 14–15; Ladies' Benevolent Society, Journal II, 82.

11: Disorder, Violence, and Community Control

1. Boston *Morning Post,* June 15, 1838, April 23, 1839; Charles Jackson et al., *Report on the Establishment of a Farm School* ([Boston: n.p., 1832]), 3–7; Charleston *Courier,* April 23 and July 2, 1832.
2. Port Society of the City of Boston, *An Account of the Port Society . . . and of the Proceedings at its Third Anniversary Meeting . . .* (Boston: S. N. Dickinson, 1832), 2; Boston Seaman's Friend Society, *Address of the Directors . . . to the Christian Public* ([Boston: n.p., 1828]), passim; Boston Seaman's Friend Society, *Annual Report . . . 1831* (Boston: T. R. Marvin, 1831), 8–9; Boston *Morning Post,* May 24, 1833; Charleston Bethel Union, Annual Report (1827) ([Charleston]: n.p., [1828]), 3–24.
3. Warren Dutton to N[athan] Appleton, Aug. 15, 1834, Ap-MHS.

4. Comittee to Investigate the Destruction of the Ursuline Convent, *Report of the Committee, Relating to the Destruction of the Ursuline Convent, August 11, 1834* (Boston: J. H. Eastburn, 1834), passim; Michael S. Hindus, "A City of Mobocrats and Tyrants: Mob Violence in Boston, 1747–1863," *Issues in Criminology*, VI (Summer 1971), 69; Boston *Daily Advertiser*, Aug. 12 and 13, 1834.

5. Roger Lane, *Policing the City: Boston, 1822–1885* (Cambridge: Harvard University Press, 1967), 30; Boston *Daily Advertiser*, Aug. 14 and 13, 1834; *Report of the Committee, Relating to the Destruction of the Ursuline Convent*, 2.

6. Boston *Daily Advertiser*, Aug. 15, 1834; Theodore Lyman, Jr., *Address Made to the City Council of Boston, January 5, 1835* (Boston: Eastburn, 1835), 31; *Daily Advertiser*, Aug. 22, 1834; *Report of the Committee, Relating to the Destruction of the Ursuline Convent*, 14; Robert Howard Lord et al., *History of the Archdiocese of Boston . . .*, 3 vols. (New York: Sheed and Ward, 1944), II, 237–38.

7. Lyman, *Address Made to the City Council . . . January 5, 1835*, 17–23; Massachusetts, *Laws . . . Passed by the General Court in the Years 1837 and 1838* (Boston: Dutton and Wentworth, 1839), 270–71.

8. Boston *Morning Post*, June 12–15, 1837. The official report of the city-appointed Joint Committee of Investigation appeared in the *Morning Post*, June 26, 1837.

9. Frederic Tudor, Diary, June 11, 1837, T-BL; Horace Mann, Journal, June 11 and 13, 1837, MHS; Boston *Morning Post*, July 6 and 15, and June 15, 1837.

10. For the quotations from the council's report see *Report of Committee . . . to Inquire into the Origin and Circumstances of the Disturbance of the Public Peace . . . [June 11, 1837]*, Common Council Document No. 12, 7–8, Documents of the City of Boston, 1834 et seq. The battle over the reorganization of the fire department can be followed in the Boston *Morning Post*, July 12–27, 1837; quotation, July 12.

11. Boston *Morning Post*, July 22, 1837; *Ordinances of the City of Boston, Passed since the Year 1834 . . .* (Boston: John H. Eastburn, 1843), 16–23.

12. Lord, *History of the Archdiocese of Boston*, II, 251; Edward Everett, Diary, June 27, 1837 (microfilm, reel 36), EE-MHS.

13. Boston *Morning Post*, Sept. 13, 1837; Robert C. Winthrop to John H. Clifford, Sept. 12, 1837, W-MHS; Lord, *History of the Archdiocese of Boston*, II, 255–56.

14. Mayor Samuel A. Eliot's letter to City Council, Sept. 18, 1837, in *Ordinance and Order [on the Police of the City], October 12, 1837*, Common Council Document No. 15, 1–2, Documents of the City of Boston, 1834 et seq.

15. Massachusetts, *Laws . . . Passed by the General Court in the Years 1837 and 1838* (Boston: Dutton and Wentworth, 1839), 411.

16. Boston Municipal Court, "Representation of the Grand Jury, February Term 1833," MS, Suffolk County Court House; Boston, House of Industry, *Annual Report for 1834*, Document No. 11, 17, Documents of the City of Boston, 1834 et seq; Joseph Tuckerman, *Prize Essay: On Wages Paid to Females for Their Labour* (Philadelphia: Carey & Hart, 1830), 21.

17. Jill Siegel Dodd, "The Working Classes and the Temperance Movement in Ante-Bellum Boston," *Labor History,* XIX (Fall 1978), 510–31.
18. The observation was made by Judge Peter Thacher during a trial in Municipal Court for violation of the fifteen-gallon law; see Boston *Morning Post,* May 28, 1839.
19. Dodd, "Working Classes and Temperance," 513; *Memorial of H. G. Otis [et al.] on the Subject of the License Law,* Massachusetts, Senate Document No. 10, Jan. 1839 [Boston: n.p., n.d.]; Richard Hildreth, *My Connection with the Atlas Newspaper; Including a Sketch of the Amory Hall Party of 1838* . . . (Boston: Whipple and Damrell, 1839), 18; Boston *Morning Post,* Nov. 23, 1839.
20. The Boston *Morning Post* covered the fifteen-gallon law issue extensively throughout 1839. See Sept. 13, 1839, for quotation and April 17, 1839, for the Cummings trial; Dodd, "Working Classes and Temperance," 517–18; *Morning Post,* Feb. 6, 1840.
21. Jonathan Chapman, *Address . . . to the City Council of Boston, January 3, 1842* (Boston: Eastburn, 1842), 6; Boston *Morning Post,* July 21, Nov. 11 and 17, Dec. 11, 1841, and Jan. 27, 1842. The common council refused, however, to back the aldermen in an appeal to the state legislature in February 1842 to repeal the existing license law, whereupon the aldermen refused to issue any liquor licenses for 1842–1843; *Morning Post,* Feb. 18 and April 13, 1842.
22. Boston *Morning Post,* Feb. 17, 1842; John M. Williams, *Proceedings in the Municipal Court . . . Occasioned by the Sudden Death of Hon. Peter O. Thacher . . .* (Boston: Eastburn's Press, 1843), 5–6.
23. A comparison between 1,012 Bostonians who petitioned both for and against the Bank of the United States in 1834 and 708 jurors who served 1829–1841 shows that only 9% of the former and 18%–20% of the latter were in the professions and wholesale trade; and that 35% of the petitioners and 51%–53% of the jurors were in trade at any level. The representation of mechanics, however, was about the same: 33% of the petitioners and 34%–36% of the jurors. On the other hand, jurors were not a compact elite. Only 14% wielded any economic power and 14%, political power; only 5% were rich, and 6% were of distinguished social status. Nevertheless, the overall mix biased juries against the lowest ranks of society, a conclusion which comports with that of Michael Katz in his findings for later in the century in Hamilton, Ontario; Michael Katz et al., "Social History Project, First Research Report, October 1975, York University," Mimeograph.
24. Quoted in Boston *Morning Post,* July 15, 1841.
25. Charleston *Courier,* Aug. 28, 1835.
26. Charleston *Courier,* Aug. 28, 1835; Jacob Schirmer, Diary, July 29, 1835, SCHS; [Amos Kendall] to [Alfred Huger], Aug. 4, 1835, in *Courier,* Aug. 14, 1835.
27. Alfred Huger to [New York City Postmaster Samuel L. Gouverneur], Aug. 1, 1835, quoted in Frank Otto Gatell, ed., "Postmaster Huger and the Incendiary Publications," *South Carolina Historical Magazine,* LXIV (Oct. 1963), 195; *Proceedings of the Citizens of Charleston, on the Incendiary Machinations Now in Progress against the Peace and Welfare of the South-*

ern States (Charleston: A. E. Miller, 1835), 10; Charleston *Courier*, Aug. 12, 1835.

28. Charleston *Courier*, Aug. 22 and 24, 1835; Samuel H. Dickson to Joseph Milligan, Aug. 28, 1835, M-SHC.
29. William H. Pease and Jane H. Pease, "Walker's *Appeal* Comes to Charleston: A Note and Documents," *Journal of Negro History*, LIX (July 1974), 287–92.
30. South Carolina, *Statutes at Large* . . . , ed. David J. McCord (Charleston: A. S. Johnston, 1841), VIII, 364; Charleston *Courier*, Nov. 10, 1834.
31. The constantly evolving body of slave and free black regulations can be traced in the published volumes of legislative enactments and in the volumes of city ordinances. Changes in city regulations were regularly noted in the local press as they occurred.
32. For these particular regulations see, on religion, *Ordinances of the City of Charleston: From the 5th February, 1833 to the 9th May, 1837* . . . (Charleston: A. E. Miller, 1837), 113–14; on wakes, Charleston *Mercury*, Oct. 13, 1835; on liquor, *Ordinances, 1833–1837*, 118–31; and on wages, *Mercury*, Feb. 13, 1837.
33. Charleston, *Ordinances, 1833–1837*, 107–8; Henry L. Pinckney, *A Report Containing a Review of the Proceedings of the City Authorities, From the First September 1838, to First August, 1839* (Charleston: W. Riley, 1839), 46–47.
34. E. Horace Fitchett, "The Traditions of the Free Negro in Charleston, South Carolina," *Journal of Negro History*, XXV (April 1940), 148. Of 685 persons registered in the Free Negro Book for 1828, only 44% were listed in the 1833 volume; of the 741 in the 1833 register, only 61% showed up in the 1838 volume; and of the 931 in the 1838 book, 75% were still listed in 1842. Thus the rates of disappearance from the books either by outmigration, death, or clerical error were 56%, 39%, and 25% for 1828–1833, 1833–1838, and 1838–1842 respectively. South Carolina, Records of the Comptroller General, Charleston District, Free Negro Tax Books, 1828–1856, SCA.
35. Charleston *Courier*, June 29, 1829; Charleston *Mercury*, Oct. 17, Aug. 18, and Dec. 4, 1837; *Courier*, Aug. 18, 1843.
36. South Carolina, *Statutes at Large* . . . , VII, 469–70; Charleston *Courier*, July 31 and Aug. 11, 1835; Peter K. Guilday, *The Life and Times of John England, First Bishop of Charleston* . . . , 2 vols. (New York: America Press, 1927), II, 152–53.
37. William Gilmore Simms, *Slavery in America* . . . (Richmond: Thomas W. White, 1838), 19; Thomas Holt, *Black Over White: Negro Political Leadership in South Carolina during Reconstruction* (Urbana: University of Illinois Press, 1977), 52; Francis Asbury Mood, "Autobiography," [1830–1840], typescript copy, 17–18, USC.
38. Charleston *Mercury*, Sept. 16, 1836; Charleston *Courier*, Jan. 20 and 23, 1835; Richard C. Wade, *Slavery in the Cities: The South, 1820–1860* (London: Oxford University Press, 1964), 153–55.
39. Charleston *Courier*, March 19, 1830.
40. Henry L. Pinckney, *A Report; Containing a Review of the Proceedings of the City Authorities, from the 4th September, 1837, to the 1st August,*

1838 . . . (Charleston: Thomas J. Eccles, Printer, 1838), 37; Charleston *Mercury,* Jan. 28, 1839, and Aug. 27, 1840.
41. [Henry L. Pinckney], *The Mayor's Report, Respecting the General Condition of City Affairs; with Suggestions for the Improvement of the Different Branches of the Public Service* (Charleston: n.p., 1839), 9–10; Charleston *Courier,* Dec. 14 and Oct. 8, 1842; Charleston *Mercury,* Oct. 29, 1838; quotations from June 2, 1838.
42. *Ordinances of the City of Charleston, from the 24th May, 1837 to the 18th March, 1840* . . . (Charleston: B. R. Getsinger, 1840), 190–208; Charleston *Mercury,* July 25, 1840; *Ordinances 1837–1840,* 234–55; for Work House returns see Charleston *Courier,* Dec. 1842–Nov. 1843, passim; *Mercury,* Oct. 17, 1840.
43. Pinckney, *Report to the City Council 1838,* 37.
44. Charleston *Mercury,* Sept. 10, Nov. 2, and Sept. 11, 1840; Legislative System, Charleston Neck, "Petition of a Number of Inhabitants of Charleston Neck [November–December 1838]," SCA; Charleston *Courier,* Oct. 6, 1841; *Mercury,* Nov. 12, 1840.
45. Boston City Council, Board of Aldermen, [*Report on the House of Correction, December 15, 1834*], City Council Document No. 13, 13, Documents of the City of Boston, 1834 et seq.; Pinckney, *Annual Report of the Mayor, 1838–1839,* 47–48.
46. Lemuel Shattuck, *Report to the Committee of the City Council Appointed to Obtain the Census of Boston for the Year 1845* . . . (Boston: John H. Eastburn, 1846), 116.
47. Michael S. Hindus, *Prison and Plantation: Crime, Justice, and Authority in Massachusetts and South Carolina, 1767–1878* (Chapel Hill: University of North Carolina Press, 1980), 76; Charleston County, Records of the Court of General Sessions, Subpoenas and Indictments, 1830–1840, SCA.
48. South Carolina, Charleston District, Presentments of the Grand Jury, October Term 1836, SCA.
49. The best treatment of the relationship between dueling, legal process, and the broad sweep of the South's code of honor is found in Bertram Wyatt-Brown, *Southern Honor: Ethics and Behavior in the Old South* (New York: Oxford University Press, 1982), 327–493.
50. Charleston County, Records of the Court of General Sessions, Subpoenas and Indictments, 1830–1840, SCA. For dueling cases: *State* v. *William Grant* (Jan. 29, 1830), *State* v. *Edward Buchanan* (Jan. 3, 1840), and *State* v. *John B. Gibbes* (May 23, 1840); Schirmer, Diary, Feb. 10, Aug. 26, and Oct. 15, 1834, Nov. 19, 1835, May 25, 1839, and May 22, 1840, SCHS; Charleston County, Records of the Court of General Session, Subpoenas and Indictments, *State* v. *Chisolm,* June 1, 1839.
51. Boston *Morning Post,* Nov. 23, 1840; Washington Light Infantry, Minute Books, 1827–1840 (typescript copies), Minute for May 22, 1829, CC; Suffolk County, Mass., Probate Records, Will of Thomas W. Sears, Sept. 1843, vol. 141, pt. 2, 92–93.
52. Harrison G. Otis, "Statement as Umpire between Henry G. Rice, Complainer, and George Parrish," July 1833, Copy, HGO-MHS; Letters between Peter Chardon Brooks, Edward Brooks, and Frederic Tudor, July 8–Aug. 17, 1837, T-BL; Horace Mann to Elizabeth Peabody, Nov. 12, [1833], HM-MHS.

53. Charleston *Mercury,* March 15, 1837.
54. Boston *Morning Post,* May 28, 1835; Theodore Lyman III, *Papers Relating to the Garrison Mob* (Cambridge: Welch, Bigelow & Co., 1870), 16–23. For the Garrisonian version of the affair see Wendell Phillips Garrison and Francis Jackson Garrison, *William Lloyd Garrison, 1805–1879: The Story of His Life Told by His Children,* 4 vols. (New York: The Century Co., 1885), II, 9–30.

12: Charleston in Panic and Depression

1. Peter Temin, *The Jacksonian Economy* (New York: W. W. Norton Co., 1969), 138–54; Charleston *Mercury,* March 14, 1837.
2. Jacob Schirmer, Diary, March 30, 1837, SCHS. Commodity and stock prices are listed weekly in the Charleston *Mercury.* John B. Grimball, Diary, May 15, 1837, typescript copy, CC; John B. O'Neall to J[oel] R. Poinsett, May 3, 1837, JP-HSP; Alexander Robertson to Robert F. W. Allston, May 13, 1837, in J. H. Easterby, ed., *The South Carolina Rice Plantation as Revealed in the Papers of Robert F. W. Allston* (Chicago: University of Chicago Press, 1945), 389–90; Schirmer, Diary, June 30, 1837.
3. *Observations on the Late Suspensions of Specie Payments by the Banks of Charleston . . .* (Charleston: A. E. Miller, 1840), 5–6; Charleston *Mercury,* May 18, 1837.
4. James R. Pringle to Levi Woodbury, May 19, 1837, United States, Treasury Department, Record Group 56, General Records of the Department of the Treasury, Letters Received by the Secretary of the Treasury from Collectors of Customs, 1833–1869, Series G, Microcopy 174, Roll 14, NA; Charleston *Mercury,* May 26, Oct. 6 and 7, 1837.
5. Charleston *Mercury,* July 8, 1837.
6. Samuel M. Derrick, *Centennial History of South Carolina Railroad* (Columbia: The State Company, 1930), 175–76; Joel R. Poinsett to James B. Campbell, Dec. 9, 1836, in Samuel G. Stoney, ed., "The Poinsett-Campbell Correspondence," *South Carolina Historical and Genealogical Magazine,* XLII (October 1941), 151–53.
7. "Go Ahead" in Charleston *Courier,* May 20, 1834; James Rose to Charles Manigault, March 6, 1835, Manigault Papers, SCHS (hereafter M-SCHS).
8. *Railroad from the Banks of the Ohio River to the Tide Waters of the Carolinas and Georgia* [Report of a public meeting, Aug. 10, 1835] (Cincinnati: James and Gazley, 1835); *Minutes of the Proceedings of a Convention of Merchants and Others, Held at Augusta, Georgia, October 16, 1837 . . .* (Augusta: Benjamin Brantly, 1838); *Minutes of the Proceedings of the Second Convention of Merchants and Others, Held in Augusta, Georgia, April 2d, 1838 . . .* (Augusta: Benjamin Brantly, 1838); *Minutes of the Proceedings of the Third Commercial Convention, Held in Augusta, Georgia, in October 1838 . . .* (Augusta: Benjamin Brantly, 1838); *Proceedings of the Fourth Convention of Merchants and Others, Held in Charleston, S.C. April 15, 1839 . . .* (Charleston: A. E. Miller, 1839).
9. Basil Manly, Diary, Oct. 19, 1836, MF-USC; Charleston *Mercury,* Oct. 12 and 21, 1836.
10. Derrick, *South Carolina Railroad,* 139, 161–64, 179–82; Joel R. Poinsett to James B. Campbell, Dec. 21, 1836, in Stoney, "The Poinsett-Campbell

Correspondence," 154; Frederick A. Porcher, "Memoirs . . . ," Samuel G. Stoney, ed., *South Carolina Historical and Genealogical Magazine*, XLVII (January 1946), 36; F. H. Elmore et al., "South Carolina—Trade and Manufactures in 1836," a tearsheet from the *Family Magazine,* in Franklin Harper Elmore Papers, USC (hereafter FHE-USC).

11. Charleston *Mercury,* Dec. 22, 1838; Louisville, Cincinnati and Charleston Rail Road Company, *Proceedings of the Stockholders . . . 2nd Annual Meeting . . . 16th of October, 1837 . . .* (Charleston: A. E. Miller, 1837), 66–70; Henry L. Pinckney, *A Report; Containing a Review of the Proceedings of the City Authorities, from the 4 September, 1837, to the 1st August 1838* (Charleston: Thomas J. Eccles, 1838), 8, 13–14; Louisville, Cincinnati and Charleston Rail Road Company, *Proceedings . . . 1838* (Charleston: A. E. Miller, 1838), Part II, "Proceedings of the Stockholders . . . September 1838," 32.

12. Louisville, Cincinnati, and Charleston Rail Road Company, *Proceedings . . . October, 1837,* 66–70; South Carolina, *Statutes at Large . . .* , ed. David J. McCord (Columbia: A. S. Johnston, 1839), VI, 571–73; Matthew and Bonneau [Charleston factors] to James E. Calhoun, Nov. 9, 1838, James Edward Calhoun Papers, USC (hereafter JEC-USC).

13. Robert Y. Hayne, *A Call upon the Stockholders of the Louisville, Cincinnati and Charleston Rail Road Company . . .* (Charleston: A. E. Miller, 1838), 29.

14. South Carolina, *Statutes at Large . . .* , ed. David J. McCord (Columbia: A. S. Johnston, 1841), VIII, 96–102; J[ames] Hamilton to Nicholas Biddle, March 2, 1838, NB-LC.

15. South Carolina, *Statutes at Large . . . ,* VIII, 96–102; Charleston *Mercury,* June 25, 1839, and July 1, 1840; Louisville, Cincinnati, and Charleston Rail Road Company, *Proceedings of the Stockholders . . . 22nd, 23rd, 24th, and 25th of November, 1842* (Charleston: A. E. Miller, 1842), 7–8; Ulrich B. Phillips, *A History of Transportation in the Eastern Cotton Belt to 1860* (New York: Octagon, c. 1908, 1968), 220.

16. Louisville, Cincinnati, and Charleston Rail Road Company, *Proceedings . . . 1839* (Charleston: A. E. Miller, 1839), 14; Charleston *Mercury,* Sept. 24, 1839.

17. James Gadsden to James E. Calhoun, Sept. 21, 1839, JEC-USC; same to same, Oct. 10, 1839, James Gadsden Papers, USC (hereafter JG-USC).

18. James Gadsden to James E. Calhoun, Sept. 21, 1839, JEC-USC; same to same, Oct. 9, 1840 and Aug. 22, 1840, both JG-USC; Charleston *Mercury,* Dec. 30, 1839; Louisville, Cincinnati, and Charleston Rail Road Company, *Proceedings . . . 1842,* 12; South Carolina Canal and Rail Road Company, *Semi-Annual Report . . . January 1843* (Charleston: Miller and Browne, 1843), passim; South Carolina, *Statutes at Large . . .* (Columbia: Republican Printing Co., 1873), XI, 235; South Carolina Rail Road Company, *Reports of the President and a Committee of Seven . . .* (Charleston: Walker and Burke, 1846), 3–19, 31–34.

19. J. L. Dawson and H. W. DeSaussure, *Census of the City of Charleston . . . 1848* (Charleston: J. B. Nixon, 1849), 148; Charleston *Courier,* Aug. 7, 1843.

20. Bank of Charleston, Ledger, vol. 1, June 3, 1851, CC; Phillips, *History of Transportation,* 218–19.

21. Charleston *Mercury,* Feb. 7, 1837.

22. The subscription for new stock finally began in January 1839; see Charleston *Mercury*, Nov. 19, 1838; Bank of Charleston, *Proceedings of the Stockholders of the Bank of Charleston . . . the Thirtieth January, 1837 . . .* (Charleston: A. E. Miller, 1837), 15; *Mercury*, Feb. 16 and 24, 1837, for the remarks of "Mercator"; the Miller, Ripley issue is in *Mercury*, April 26, 27, 29, and 30, 1839; Bank of Charleston, Ledger, vol. 2, April 1843, CC.
23. Dawson and DeSaussure, *Census of Charleston, 1848*, 160; Bank of Charleston, *Proceedings of the Stockholders . . . 1839* (Charleston: A. E. Miller, 1839), passim; James Hamilton to Nicholas Biddle, June 4, 1837, NB-LC; Charleston *Mercury*, Dec. 21, 1837.
24. J[ames] Hamilton to Nicholas Biddle, June 4, 1837, NB-LC; Bank of the United States, Pennsylvania, *Report of the Committee of Investigation Appointed at the Meeting of the Stockholders . . . January 4, 1841* (Philadelphia: Crissy and Markley, [1841]), 18–20; J. C. Levy to Nicholas Biddle, Feb. 12, 1839, NB-LC.
25. Patterson & Magwood to Nicholas Biddle, Feb. 3, 1838, and J. C. Levy to Nicholas Biddle, April 17, 1838, both in NB-LC. Fear and dislike of bank control—especially Biddle's—of the cotton market was widespread; see, for example, Charles Hunt to Thomas Lamb, May 6, 1838, and Isaac Sweetser to Thomas Lamb, Nov. 14, 1838, both in L-MHS; J. C. Levy to Nicholas Biddle, May 16 and Dec. 22, 1838, and Feb. 12, 1839, all in NB-LC; Charleston *Mercury*, June 12 and 14, 1839; Robinson & Caldwell, printed letter, Sept. 6, 1839, Singleton Papers, SHC (hereafter S-SHC).
26. Dawson and DeSaussure, *Census of Charleston, 1848*, 95–96; Howland & Taft to Israel Whitney, March 14, 1840, HWST-USC; W. C. Dukes & Co., printed letter, Sept. 7, 1839, S-SHC; Alexander Brown to Elihu P. Smith, Oct. 15, 1839, Elihu Penquite Smith Papers, USC (hereafter EPS-USC).
27. Charleston *Mercury*, Oct. 15, 1839, Oct. 6, 1840, Nov. 13 and 14, 1839; "Truth and Justice," *A Reply to a Pamphlet, Entitled Observations on the Suspensions of Specie Payments by the Bank of Charleston, &c* (Charleston: A. E. Miller, 1840), 3–11.
28. "Truth and Justice," *Reply to a Pamphlet*, 12–13; C. M. Furman to F. H. Elmore, July 29, 1840, Franklin H. Elmore Papers, LC (hereafter FHE-LC); *Reply to a Pamphlet*, 14–15; Charleston *Mercury*, July 20, 1840.
29. For specie holdings see Charleston *Mercury*, Dec. 5, 1839, July 27, 1840, and Dec. 5, 1840; for dividends, Dawson and DeSaussure, *Census of Charleston, 1848*, 160; for stock quotations, *Courier*, 1841–1843; South Carolina, *Statutes at Large . . .* , XI, 110–12; Bank of Charleston, *Proceedings of the Stockholders . . . 1842*, 7, typed copy in possession of the South Carolina National Bank, Charleston, South Carolina.
30. The ins and outs of the political struggles can be followed in the *Courier* and *Mercury*, 1836–1839. See also in particular Henry L. Pinckney, *An Address to the Electors of Charleston District* (Charleston: Burges & Honour, 1836); and Thomas Bennett to J[oel] R. Poinsett, [Aug. 22,] 1838, and Oct. 12, 1838, JP-HSP; Poinsett to James B. Campbell, Aug. 25 and Sept. 10, 1836 in Stoney, "The Poinsett-Campbell Correspondence," 149.
31. *Proceedings of a Meeting of the Democratic Friends of Col. John S. Ashe . . . Charleston, S.C. . . . 15th Sept. 1840 . . .* ([Charleston]: A. E. Miller, 1840), 3–8; Charleston *Mercury*, Sept. 19 and Oct. 6, 1840; Samuel

J. Legaré to William Porcher Miles, Oct. [15?], 1840, William Porcher Miles Papers, SHC (hereafter WPM-SHC); *Mercury,* Dec. 8 and 14, 1840, and Jan. 7, 1841.

32. For the years 1828/9–1832/3, 1833/4–1838/9, and 1839/40–1843/4 respectively, merchants comprised 22%, 52%, and 64% of the city council; mechanics, 12%, 5%, and 0%; and professional men, 51%, 31%, and 20%. The shift in status (those individuals with two or more status indicators) was, in these same periods, from 65% to 49% to 31%; those of notable wealth decreased similarly from 49% to 38% to 31%. But those who had at least some measure of economic power increased their proportion of mayors and aldermen from 54% to 69%, and then dropped to 59%.
33. James M. Walker to Mitchell King, Sept. 7, 1839, MK-SHC.
34. Pinckney, *Report . . . 1837 . . . 1838,* 8, 13–14; Charleston *Mercury,* November 11 and October 27, 1836, and March 7, 1837; *Ordinances of the City of Charleston, from . . . 1837 to . . . 1840* (Charleston: B. R. Getsinger, 1840), 12–16, 48–50; *Proceedings of the City Authorities, from the 4 September, 1837, to the 1st August, 1838 . . .* , 13–14.
35. Charleston *Courier,* Aug. 21, 1835; Charleston Hotel Company, *Treasurer's Accounts Current with the Charleston Hotel Company, 1836, 1837, 1838* ([Charleston]: n.p., 1838); *Courier,* Nov. 25, 1842, June 9, Aug. 3, June 17, and Sept. 19, 1843.
36. Henry L. Pinckney, *A Report Containing a Review of the Proceedings of the City Authorities, from the First September 1838, to First August, 1839* (Charleston: W. Riley, 1839), 27, 36; Charleston *Courier,* June 7, 10, and 13, 1843; Petition of Charleston Citizens to the South Carolina Legislature [1843], South Carolina, Legislature, Legislative System, City of Charleston, SCA.
37. Henry L. Pinckney, *Proceedings of the City Authorities . . . 1838,* 14–16 (quotation) and 20–29; *Proceedings of the City Authorities . . . 1839,* 18–24; Dawson and DeSaussure, *Census of the City of Charleston,* 1848, 48; full statements of city budgets appear annually in the *Mercury* and *Courier.* Returns for commercial inventories and taxable income for St. Philip's and St. Michael's parish are in South Carolina Comptroller-General Reports to the Legislature, in South Carolina, *Acts and Resolutions, 1834–1844* (Columbia: A. H. Pemberton, 1834–1844).
38. *Ordinances of the City of Charleston, from . . . 1837 to 1840,* 57–77; Charleston *Courier,* March 30 and Feb. 22, 1843, Oct. 8, 1842; Charleston *Mercury,* Aug. 27, 1840.
39. Charleston *Courier,* April 13, 1843; *Ordinances of the City of Charleston, From . . . 1833 to . . . 1837* (Charleston: A. E. Miller, 1837), 111–13; Samuel H. Dickson, *Address Delivered at the Opening of the New Edifice of the Charleston Apprentices' Library Society . . .* (Charleston: W. Riley, 1841), 32.
40. Dawson and DeSaussure, *Census of Charleston, 1848,* 12, 31–36; Robert Mills, *Statistics of South Carolina . . .* (Spartanburg: The Reprint Company, c. 1826, 1972), 427; Leonard P. Stavisky, "Industrialism in Antebellum Charleston," *Journal of Negro History,* XXXVI (July 1951), 318–19.
41. For data on declining wage rates see South Carolina Canal and Rail Road Company, *Semi-Annual Report . . . January 1840* (Charleston: A. E. Miller, 1840), 5; and *Semi-Annual Report . . . July 1842* (Charleston:

A. E. Miller, 1842), 5; also Charleston *Courier*, Aug. 26 and Oct. 9, 1841, and Jan. 5, 1842. For general treatment including Charleston see Claudia D. Goldin, *Urban Slavery in the American South, 1820–1860: A Quantitative History* (Chicago: University of Chicago Press, 1976), 51–75.

42. *United States Sixth Census, Compendium of Enumeration of the Inhabitants and Statistics of the United States . . . 1840* (Washington: Blair and Rives, 1840), 102–13, 186–97. Charleston reported $7,323,850 capital invested in commerce in 1840 and $2,157,260 in manufacture within the city; Boston reported $16,293,230 and $5,270,400 respectively. Charleston's capital doubtless included slaves. South Carolina, *Acts and Resolutions, 1834–1844*, 166.

43. *Proceedings of the Fourth Convention of Merchants and Others, Held in Charleston, S.C., April 15, 1839 . . .* , 23–52; William R. Taylor, *Cavalier and Yankee . . .* (Garden City: Anchor Books, Doubleday, 1961, 1963), 156. South Carolina, *Statutes at Large . . .* , VI, 579; Charleston *Mercury*, Dec. 9 and 10, 1840.

44. See Appendix B.

45. Of the 34 failures whose occupations are known for 1833–1838, 47% were merchants or factors and 76% were engaged in commerce of some sort; of the 37 with known occupations between 1839–1843, 54% were merchants or factors and 78% were in some sort of commerce. Twelve percent were planters in the earlier period and only 5% in the latter. Thirty percent of all 46 failures had wielded some economic power. Samuel H. Dickson to Joseph Milligan, Dec. 2, 1838, M-SHC; C. G. Memminger to J. R. Poinsett, May 2, 1837, JP-HSP.

46. Charleston *Courier*, May 17, 1842; South Carolina, *Statutes at Large . . .* , VIII, 430–31; *Courier*, June 2, 1843; Charleston *Mercury*, Sept. 29, 1838; *Courier*, Jan.–May 1843 shows daily packet service from Wilmington, N.C., probably largely confined to passenger travel, since arrivals are not listed in the shipping tallies.

47. Charleston *Courier*, Aug. 17, 1841, and March 18, 1842. The silting problem is noted in Joseph Johnson to J. R. Poinsett, May 3, 1837, JP-HSP, and in correspondence from Charles Hunt and William Prescott, Boston sea captains, Spring and Summer 1838, L-MHS. *Courier*, May 10, 1842.

48. For stock prices see Charleston *Courier* and *Mercury*, 1841–1843. The impact of declining staples prices is noted in Robert Vernon Spalding, "The Boston Mercantile Community and the Promotion of the Textile Industry in New England, 1813–1860" (Ph.D. Dissertation, Yale University, 1963), 152; and in Louisville, Cincinnati, and Charleston Rail Road Company, *Proceedings of the Stockholders . . . 1841* (Charleston: A. E. Miller, 1841), 6. T. C. Marshall to John W. Mitchell, March 15 and May 9, 1842, John W. Mitchell Correspondence, SCHS (hereafter JWM-SCHS); Christopher [Cotes?] to Mrs C. M. Smith, June 9, 1842, EPS-USC; Charleston *Courier*, Sept. 6, 1841; Thomas Bennett to J. R. Poinsett, Oct. 4, 1844, JP-HSP.

13: Meeting Catastrophe

1. Carleton White, *Narrative of the Loss of the Steam Packet Home . . . on a Voyage from New York to Charleston, with Affidavits Disproving the Charges of Misconduct against the Master* (New York: James Armand, 1837), passim.

2. Charleston *Mercury,* Sept. 28, Oct. 20 and 21, 1837, and March 16, 1841; *Proceedings of the Citizens and City Council of Charleston in Relation to the Destruction of the Steamboat Home* (Charleston: Thomas J. Eccles, 1837), 4–5, 6; *Ordinances of the City of Charleston, from the 24th May, 1837 to the 18th March, 1840* . . . (Charleston: B. R. Getsinger, 1840), 38–42.

3. Henry L. Pinckney, *A Report, Containing a Review of the Proceedings of the City Authorities, from the 4th September, 1837, to the 1st August, 1838* . . . (Charleston: Thomas J. Eccles, 1838), 46; Jacob Schirmer, Diary, June 19, 1838, SCHS; Charleston *Mercury,* June 20, 1838; Virginia Louise Glenn, "James Hamilton, Jr., of South Carolina: A Biography" (Ph.D. dissertation, University of North Carolina, 1964), 273; *Mercury,* May 16 and June 23, 1838.

4. W. V. T[hatcher] to George E. Ellis, July 24, 1838, George Edward Ellis Papers, MHS (hereafter GEE-MHS); Charleston *Mercury,* June 23, Aug. 2, Sept. 17 and 20, and Oct. 16, 1838.

5. For the story and impact of these fires on the city see Jane H. Pease and William H. Pease, "The Blood-Thirsty Tiger: Charleston and the Psychology of Fire," *South Carolina Historical Magazine, LXXIX* (October 1978), 281–95.

6. Pinckney, *Report . . . 1837 . . . 1838,* 40–41; Charleston *Mercury,* April 30, 1838; James L. Petigru to Jane P. North, April 30, 1838, in James Petigru Carson, ed., *Life, Letters and Speeches of James Louis Petigru* . . . (Washington: W. H. Lowdermilk & Co., 1920), 196.

7. Thomas Smyth, *Two Discourses on the Occasion of the Great Fire in Charleston, on Friday Night, April 27th, 1838* . . . (Charleston: J. P. Beile, 1838), passim; Charleston *Mercury,* May 16, 1838; James L. Petigru to Jane P. North, April 30, 1838, in Carson, *Life, Letters and Speeches,* 196–97; *Mercury,* Aug. 30, 1838; Smyth, *Two Discourses,* 17–18.

8. Charleston *Mercury,* Oct. 30, 1838; Thomas Y. Simons, *A Report on the History and Causes of the Strangers' or Yellow Fever in Charleston* . . . (Charleston: W. Riley, 1839); Bishop England quoted in Peter K. Guilday, *The Life and Times of John England* . . . (New York: America Press, 1927), II, 160–61; *Mercury,* March 12, 1839; J. L. Dawson and H. W. DeSaussure, *Census of the City of Charleston, 1848* (Charleston: J. B. Nixon, 1849), 236.

9. Guilday, *England,* II, 163–65; Charleston *Mercury,* Aug. 25 and 27, Sept. 17 and 19, 1838; Independent or Congregational Church [Circular Church] Records, vol. 12, 216, SCHS.

10. Charleston *Mercury,* May 1, 5, 9, and 30, 1838. The total amount collected all over the country for Charleston's relief was just over $180,000; *Mercury,* July 7, 1838. Charleston, Records of the Poor House, MS, vol. 1834–1840, 248, SCHS. *Mercury,* May 11 and 2, 1838; Washington Light Infantry, Minutes, MS, 1831–1840, typescript copy, Minute for April 28, 1838, CC.

11. Charleston *Mercury,* Sept. 21, 1838; *Ordinances . . . 1837–1840,* 121–22; Henry L. Pinckney, *A Report, Relative to the Proceedings for the Relief of the Sick Poor, During the Late Epidemic . . . 5th of November, 1838* (Charleston: W. Riley, 1838), 11–12; *Ordinances . . . 1837–1840,* 120; *Mercury,* Nov. 20, 1838, March 18, 1839, and April 30, 1840.

Notes to pages 193–197 317

12. Charleston *Mercury,* May 30 and June 7, 1838; Resolutions of the Citizens of Charleston to the Governor . . . Concerning the Restoration of Charleston, [May 4], 1838, LPLSC-SCA; *Ordinances . . . 1837–1840,* 82–85; *Mercury,* May 15 and 25, 1838; Petition of Charleston Citizens against the Charleston Ordinance Requiring Brick Buildings, [ca. May 24, 1838], LPLSC-SCA.
13. Various petitions from Charleston citizens and from the city council, 1838–1842, all in LPLSC–SCA.
14. See, for example, Petition of Otis J. Chaffe, Nov. 15, 1841, LPLSC-SCA.
15. Pinckney, *Report . . . 1837 . . . 1838,* 43–44; *State v. Keating S. Laurens,* May 2, 1838, Charleston County, Records of the Court of General Sessions, Subpoenas and Indictments, SCA; Schirmer, Diary, June 7, 1838, SCHS; Charleston *Mercury,* June 4, 1838. Dawson and DeSaussure, *Census of the City of Charleston, 1848,* 20 report that in 1848 there were 1,517 wooden and 1,149 brick buildings in the city.
16. Pinckney, *Report . . . 1837 . . . 1838,* 39; the quotation is from "Old Fireman," in Charleston *Mercury,* May 14, 1838.
17. Charleston *Mercury,* June 8, 1838; *Ordinances . . . 1837–1840,* 109–18; Memorial of the City Council of Charleston, Nov. 20, 1838, LPLSC-SCA; *Mercury,* May 21, 1838. Of the 171 firemen whose occupation is known 1833–1838, 43% were mechanics, 20% in middle- and low-prestige commercial occupations, and 5% in similar service occupations.
18. Charleston *Mercury,* March 25, 1839.
19. Charleston *Mercury,* March 28 and April 10, 1839; Charleston, Board of Fire Masters, *A Report . . . and also a Report by the Mayor in Relation to the Ordinance to Reorganize the Fire Department . . .* (Charleston: n.p., 1839), 5–15. Of the 68 firemasters, 1828–1843, 76% owned one or more pieces of urban real estate; 63% owned slaves in 1830 and 57% did so in 1840. Only 22% showed any evidence of wealth. And while 18% of firemasters 1828–1832 exerted great political power, only 6% of 1839–1843 firemasters did.
20. Charleston *Mercury,* May 9, June 7, July 3 and 26, 1839; *Ordinances . . . 1837–1840,* 154–64; Henry L. Pinckney, *A Report Containing a Review of the Proceedings of the City Authorities, from the First September 1838, to First August, 1839* (Charleston: W. Riley, 1839), 66–67.
21. Charleston, City Council, *Memorial and Proceedings . . . on the Subject of Securing the City from Fires* (Charleston: James S. Burges, 1838), 17; William Hume to Henry L. Pinckney, Dec. 18, [1838], in Henry Laurens Pinckney, *Remarks . . . on the Subject of Interments and the Policy of Establishing a Public Cemetery, Beyond the Precincts of the City* (Charleston: W. Riley, 1839), 1–2.
22. Charleston *Mercury,* Aug. 17, 1838; Petition of the Common Council . . . for a Loan [to Establish a Water System], Nov. 28, 1838, LPLSC-SCA; Dawson and DeSaussure, *Census of the City of Charleston, 1848,* 22–24. Of the 10,370 houses in Boston (excluding Noddles Island) in 1845, the year in which the city finally decided to build a municipal water system, 4,324 (42%) had wells producing potable water; 3,210 (31%) were provided aqueduct water. Either as supplement or alternative water supply, 4,445 (43%) had cisterns. Lemuel Shattuck, *Report of the Committee of the City Council Appointed to Obtain the Census of Boston for the Year*

1845 . . . (Boston: John H. Eastburn, 1846), Appendix, 24. Shattuck gives no statistics on how many houses lacked any water supply.
23. Charleston *Mercury,* May 5, 1838, in which Mayor Pinckney describes the scope of the fire to Governor Pierce Butler; *Mercury,* May 2, 1838.
24. The Fire and Marine Insurance Company and the Union Insurance Company both suspended operation; only the Charleston Insurance and Trust Company continued. James C. Mohr, *Radical Republicans and Reform in New York during Reconstruction* (Ithaca: Cornell University Press, 1973), 32; Charleston *Mercury,* April 28 and May 22, 1838; South Carolina, *Acts and Resolutions: 1843* (Columbia: A. H. Pemberton, 1843), 276. A critic of the plan to launch a local mutual insurance company conceded that insurers could save 20% on premiums. Charleston *Courier,* Aug. 30, 1842.
25. Charleston *Courier,* Aug. 24 and Sept. 9, 1842.
26. Boston *Morning Post,* Jan. 25, 1839. Shattuck, *Census of Boston for the Year 1845,* Appendix, 83.
27. Boston *Morning Post,* Jan. 29, 1839.
28. Theodore Lyman, Jr., *Address Made to the City Council of Boston, January 5, 1835* (Boston: Eastburn, 1835), 13; Boston Fire Department, *Sixth Annual Report for 1842,* Document No. 22, Documents of the City of Boston, 1834 et seq.
29. [Rose G. Forbes] to R. Bennett Forbes, Jan. 10, [1840], FF-MHS; Boston *Morning Post,* Jan. 18 and 31, and Feb. 7, 1840.
30. Boston *Morning Post,* Feb. 8, 1840, and March 9, 1839.

14: The Uses of Adversity

1. New South Church, Minutes of the Meetings of the Proprietors, 1803–1850, April 5, 1838, BPL; Frederic Tudor, Diary, June 1, 1836, and Frederic Tudor to Robert H. Gardiner, June 2, 1836, both T-BL; Nathaniel Bowditch to E. Alvord, June 10, 1836, Massachusetts Hospital Life Insurance Company Collection, BL (hereafter MHL-BL); Tudor to Gardiner, Nov. 8 and 19, and June 4, 1836, T-BL; Samuel A. Appleton to Nathan Appleton, Nov. 10, 1836, Ap-MHS; William Appleton, Diary, Dec. 1836, and March 29, 1837, WA-BL; Boston *Morning Post,* May 2, 1837.
2. Amos Lawrence, [Diary], May 13, 1837, in Wiliam Lawrence, ed., *Extracts from the Diary and Correspondence of the Late Amos Lawrence* . . . (Boston: Gould and Lincoln, 1855), 141; Boston *Morning Post,* May 12, 1837; David Henshaw to Levi Woodbury, May 11, 1837, United States Treasury Department, Letters Received by the Secretary of the Treasury from Collectors of Customs, Record Group 56, Microcopy 174, Roll 14, NA; Suffolk Bank Stockholders' Records, Suffolk Bank Collection, vol. 1, Minutes for May 11, 1837, BL (hereafter SB-BL); Harrison Gray Otis to [George Harrison?], fragment, May 16, 1837, HGO-MHS.
3. Boston *Morning Post,* May 13, 1837; David Henshaw to Levi Woodbury, May 15, 1837, Letters Received by the Secretary of the Treasury from Collectors of Customs, RG 56, MC 174, Roll 14, NA; *Morning Post,* May 18, 1837; David Henshaw to Martin Van Buren, May 16, 1837, MV-LC.
4. Boston *Morning Post,* May 26, 1837; David Henshaw to Levi Woodbury, July 10, 1837, Letters Received by the Secretary of the Treasury from Collectors of Customs, RG 56, MC 174, Roll 14, NA; *Morning Post,* May 12,

Notes to pages 202–204

1837; William Appleton, Diary, May 13, 15, 1837, WA-BL; Frederic Tudor, Diary, Sept. 25, 1837, T-BL; Samuel A. Eliot, *Address . . . to City Council of Boston, January 1, 1838* (Boston: Eastburn, 1838), 3.

5. Boston *Morning Post,* March 1, 1842, Dec. 8, 1840, and Jan. 27, 1842. For the teller's case, see the *Morning Post,* Feb. 23, 1842; for the clerks' case, which involved the Eagle and City Banks, see detailed reports in the *Morning Post,* Jan.–April 1842.

6. Boston *Morning Post,* Feb. 3, 1838; *Appeal to the Citizens of Boston to be Read before Voting* (n.p.:n.p., [1838]), 1–10; *Morning Post,* April 13 and 16, 1838.

7. William Appleton, Diary, Jan. 12, 1838, WA-BL; Peter C. Brooks, Diary, Jan. 13, 1838, Brooks Family Papers, MHS (hereafter B-MHS); Boston *Morning Post,* Feb. 17, 1838; Ralph Huntington to Martin Van Buren, Jan. 27, 1838, MV-LC; John B. Derby, *Political Reminiscences . . .* (Boston: The Author, 1835), 155.

8. Massachusetts General Court, *Joint Committee Report on the Commonwealth Bank, 1838,* Senate Document No. 35, 10–11, 21–23, 30–33; the Boston *Morning Post,* Feb. 17, 1838, also carries this report. William Appleton, Diary, Jan. 12, 1838, WA-BL.

9. Harrison Gray Otis to George Harrison, Feb. 15, 1838, HGO-MHS.

10. Nathan Appleton to Samuel Hubbard, Feb. 17, 1838, Ap-MHS; Nathan Appleton to Levi Woodbury, March 14, 1838, United States Treasury Department, Miscellaneous Letters Received, Record Group 56, Series K, NA; for various resolutions of Boston banks concerning the resumption of specie payments see Boston Bank Collection [a single volume of miscellaneous material], BL.

11. Peter P. F. Degrand to Nicholas Biddle, April 5, 1838, NB-LC; Boston *Morning Post,* April 28, 1838; Suffolk Bank Directors' Records, Minutes, Aug. 8, 1838, SB-BL; *Morning Post,* Aug. 11, 1838; Samuel A. Eliot, in *Inaugural Addresses of the Mayors of Boston* (Boston: City Registrar, 1894–1896), I, 231.

12. William G. Brooks, Diary, Oct. 10, 1839, MHS; Frances W. Gregory, "A Tale of Three Cities: The Struggle for Banking Stability in Boston, New York, and Philadelphia, 1839–1841," *New England Quarterly,* LVI (March 1983), 3–38; Nathan Appleton correspondence, March–December 1840, passim, MHS. Having observed "no confidence[,] no Stability" in April 1840, William Brooks continued to be impressed with how "unusually dull" things were a year later. By April 1842 he thought that "confidence [was] returning" (Brooks, Diary, April 24 and 30, 1840, May 23, 1841, and April 30, 1842). Yet in August, Patrick Tracy Jackson announced "perfect stagnation," only to be followed two months later by Harrison Gray Otis's grudging admission that Boston seemed to be "enjoy[ing] a temporary prosperity, or at least an exemption from the severe reverses of other places" (Patrick T. Jackson to N. Appleton, August 14, 1842, Ap-MHS; Harrison G. Otis to George Harrison, Oct. 25, 1842, HGO-MHS).

13. Peter Temin, *The Jacksonian Economy* (New York: W. W. Norton Company, 1969), 48, 157–63; Jeffrey G. Williamson, "American Prices and Urban Inequality Since 1820," *Journal of Economic History,* XXXVI (June 1976), 315; Peter C. Brooks to Edward Everett, May 31, 1843, EE-MHS; Henry Lee, Sr., to Henry Lee, Jr., Feb. 18, 1842, Le-MHS;

same to same, July 18, 1842, in Kenneth W. Porter, *The Jacksons and the Lees: Two Generations of Massachusetts Merchants, 1765–1844*, 2 vols. (Cambridge: Harvard University Press, 1937), I, 125–26; Abbott Lawrence to Robert C. Winthrop, February 15, 1842, W-MHS.

14. Boston *Morning Post*, May 23 and 24, 1837; April 15, 1841; Oct. 9 and 23, 1840. *Law Reporter*, III (Dec. 1840), 304. *Morning Post*, July 19, 1842.

15. Boston Children's Aid Society, *Constitution, as Amended, Oct. 10, 1837* . . . (Boston: Marden and Kimball, 1837), 4; Widows' Society, *Twenty-Second Annual Report* (Boston: William A. Hall, 1839), 3–4; John Pierce, Memoirs, May 25, 1803 to Aug. 19, 1849, VII, 257–59, MHS; Boston *Morning Post*, Dec. 8, 1838; Boston Roman Catholic Mutual Relief Society, *Constitution . . . Revised and Adopted June 5, 1837* . . . (Boston: Samuel N. Dickinson, 1837), 2; Boston Children's Friend Society, *Fourth Annual Report* (Boston: J. Howe, 1837), 10; *Morning Post*, March 1, 1838, and Jan. 23, 1841.

16. Warren Street Chapel, *Proceedings of the Annual Meeting of the Association for the Support of the Warren St. Chapel* . . . (Boston: Tuttle and Dennett and Chisolm, 1838), 17–19.

17. Boston *Morning Post*, July 26, 1842, Jan. 5 and April 18, 1843; Lemuel Shattuck, *Report to the Committee of the City Council Appointed to Obtain the Census of Boston for the Year 1845* . . . (Boston: John H. Eastburn, 1846), 85.

18. Charles P. Huse, *The Financial History of Boston, from May 1, 1822 to January 31, 1902* (Cambridge: Harvard University Press, 1916), 21–22; Samuel A. Eliot, *Address . . . to the City Council of Boston* . . . (Boston: Eastburn, 1838), 9; Massachusetts, Secretary of the Commonwealth, *Abstract of the Returns Relating to the Poor* [1837–1863] (Microfiche, Redgrave Information Resources), passim.

19. Boston, City Council, Committee on Finance, *Reduction of City Debt* (1839), Document No. 12, 7–9, Documents of the City of Boston, 1834 et seq.; Shattuck, *Census of Boston*, Appendix, 59.

20. Shattuck, *Census of Boston*, 96; Boston, City Council, Committee on Finance, *Reduction of City Debt*, 11, 2–6; *The Ordinances of the City of Boston, Passed Since the Year 1834* . . . (Boston: John H. Eastburn, 1843), 12; Boston *Morning Post*, Nov. 24, 1841. In 1840 the city debt was $1,698,232; in 1845, $1,163,266.

21. Boston *Morning Post*, July 2, 1840; Jonathan Chapman, *Address . . . to the City of Boston, January 4, 1841* (Boston: John H. Eastburn, 1841), 11ff., Document No. 16, Documents of the City of Boston, 1834 et seq.; Jonathan Chapman, *Address to the City Council . . . March 18, 1841*, Document No. 9, Documents of the City of Boston, 1834 et seq.; Boston Lunatic Hospital, *Report of the Superintendent, July 1, 1840* (Boston: John H. Eastburn, 1840), Documents of the City of Boston, Document No. 16, 11 ff.; *Morning Post*, October 21, 1840.

22. Harrison Club of Boston, *Constitution and By-Laws* . . . (Boston: n.p., 1840), 3–7; Boston *Morning Post*, May 26, 1840; Philip Hone, *The Diary of Philip Hone, 1828–1851*, ed. Allan Nevins, 2 vols. (New York: Dodd, Mead & Co., 1927), 494–98; *Morning Post*, Oct. 22 and Dec. 15, 1840; William G. Brooks, Diary, Dec. 13, 1840, MHS.

Notes to pages 208–210 321

23. The total number of votes cast was 11,589. See Shattuck, *Census of Boston*, 80, and Appendix, 33, 36, 38. The total number of eligible voters was 14,474.
24. Boston *Morning Post,* Aug. 4, 1837, and Aug. 1, 1840.
25. Of the 17 mayors and aldermen 1837–1843 whose occupation was known in 1841, 59% engaged in commerce; 56% of the 150 councilmen 1837–1843 of known ocupation in 1841 were also in commerce. Of the 28 men who served as mayor or aldermen 1837–1843, 46% were corporate directors in the same period as were 25% of the 180 councilmen. Fifty percent of mayors and aldermen 1828–1836 had assessed property of $30,000 or more, while only 43% of the 1837–1843 mayors and aldermen did. Their social standing was virtually identical in both periods, with 33% and 32% respectively enjoying high status; 23% of 1828–1836 councilmen had been of high status, while only 15% were in the later years. A similar decline occurred in the councilmen assessed for $30,000 or more property from 18% in the early period to only 9% in the later period.
26. Frederic Tudor, Diary, April 10, 1837, T-BL; Oakes Shaw to Lemuel Shaw, April 24, 1837, Lemuel Shaw Papers, MHS (hereafter LS-MHS); William Appleton, Diary, May 9, 1837, WA-BL. For particular activity relating to bankruptcy and imprisonment for debt, see Nathan Appleton to Rufus Davenport, Oct. 25, 1830, Ap-MHS; Boston Merchants Association, *Proceedings of an Association of the Merchants of Boston for the Mutual Benefit of Creditor and Debtor, March 11, 1834* (Boston: J. T. Buckingham, 1834); Boston Chamber of Commerce, *Report and Plan Recommended by the Committee on the Assignment Law* ([Boston: n.p., 1837]). Harrison G. Otis to George Harrison, June 26, 1837, HGO-MHS; Frances Morse Rollins to S. T. Morse, Jan. 20, 1838, Samuel Torrey Morse Papers, MHS (hereafter STM-MHS); Mary Lee to Henry Lee, Jr., Feb. 10, 1839, Le-MHS; Henry Lee business papers, 1837–1847; passim, Henry Lee Collection, BL (hereafter HL-BL); Rose G. Forbes to Bennett Forbes, June 24, [1838], FF-MHS.
27. Lists of insolvents can be found in *Law Reporter,* II (Jan. 1840), 283–85; III (May, Aug., Sept., Oct., Nov., Dec., 1840, and March 1841), 39, 160, 199, 239, 279, 320, and 440; and IV (June, Sept., Nov., and Dec. 1841), 88, 208, 288, and 328; and IV (Jan. and Feb. 1842), 368 and 408. Boston *Morning Post,* March 2 and 31, 1842.
28. Charles H. Parker to Henry Lee, Jr., Jan. 26, 1839, Le-MHS; W. R. Lawrence to A. A. Lawrence, March 17, 1840, AAL-MHS.
29. Shattuck, *Census of Boston,* Appendix, 59; for aggregate individual increases and decreases, see our Appendix B; Amos Lawrence to A. A. Lawrence, Oct. 24, 1836, AAL-MHS; William Appleton, Diary, Jan. 8, 1844, WA-BL.
30. For the argument that the panic and depression momentarily reversed the national trend toward economic inequality see Jeffrey Williamson, "American Prices and Urban Inequality since 1820," *Journal of Economic History,* XXXVI (June 1976), 303–33. For the argument that the panic and depression tended to entrench wealth and that initial wealth was the principal determinant of subsequent greater wealth among the most wealthy, see Edward Pessen, "The Egalitarian Myth and the American Social Reality: Wealth, Mobility, and Equality in the 'Era of the Common Man,' "

American Historical Review, LXXVI (Oct. 1971), 989–1034. Our own analysis of the forty richest Bostonians draws on data Pessen himself presented in "Did Fortunes Rise and Fall Mercurially in Antebellum America? The Tale of Two Cities: Boston and New York," *Journal of Social History,* IV (Summer 1971), 339–57, and on the data described in Appendix B.

31. Joseph Martin, *Seventy-Three Years' History of the Boston Stock Market, 1798–1871* . . . (Boston: The Author, 1871), 75, 77; Stephen Salsbury, *The State, the Investor, and the Railroad* . . . (Cambridge: Harvard University Press, 1967), 215; Mercantile Marine Insurance Company, Schedule of Risks, 1830–1873, Mercantile Marine Insurance Company Collection, BL (hereafter MMIC-BL).
32. Boston and Worcester Railroad Corporation, *Annual Report 1843* (Boston: I. R. Butts, 1843); Boston *Morning Post,* Aug. 29, 1838; William G. Brooks, Diary, Nov. 14, 1840, MHS; Massachusetts, *Acts and Resolves Passed . . . 1839 . . . 1842* (Boston: Dutton and Wentworth, 1842), 360–61.
33. "Western Rail Road. Proceedings of the Meeting at Faneuil Hall, October 7, 1835," Broadside, MHS; Western Rail-Road Corporation, *First Annual Report . . . June 13, 1836* (Boston: Dutton and Wentworth, 1836), 24; also *Third Annual Report . . . 1838* (Boston: S. N. Dickinson, 1838), 17–20; Dorothy Adler, *British Investment in American Railways, 1834–1898,* ed. Muriel E. Hidy (Charlottesville: University Press of Virginia, 1970), 13, n. 55; Salsbury, *State, Investor, and Railroad,* 149–53.
34. Boston *Morning Post,* Dec. 3 and 30, 1841.
35. Western Rail-Road Corporation, *Proceedings of the Annual Meeting . . . Held, by Adjournment, in . . . Boston, March 12, 1840* (Boston: Dutton and Wentworth, 1840), 51; Salsbury, *State, Investor, and Railroad,* 222–28, 155–56, 239–41.
36. Lawrence A. Herbst, "Interregional Commodity Trade from the North to the South and American Economic Development in the Antebellum Period" (Ph.D. dissertation, University of Pennsylvania, 1974), 48, 343; Arthur M. Johnson and Barry E. Supple, *Boston Capitalists and Western Railroads* . . . (Cambridge: Harvard University Press, 1967), 13; Shattuck, *Census of Boston,* Appendix, 53.
37. Boston *Morning Post,* Aug. 8, 1839; William G. Brooks, Diary, Aug. 14, 1839, MHS; *Morning Post,* June 6, 1840; Edward Everett to the Mayor, June 5, 1840, EE-MHS.
38. Boston *Morning Post,* July 22, 1840; Charleston *Courier,* Nov. 4, 1841; *Morning Post,* July 21, 1842, and March 17, 1841; William G. Brooks, Diary, Feb. 4, 1839; *Morning Post,* Jan. 28, 1842; Brooks, Diary, Aug. 1, 1842, MHS.
39. Shattuck, *Census of Boston,* 91; Mercantile Marine Insurance Company, Schedule of Risks, MMIC-BL; Thomas H. Perkins, *Remarks . . . at the Laying of the Corner-stone of the Boston Exchange, August 2, 1841* (Boston: Dickinson, 1841), 11 n. Boston *Morning Post,* March 1, 1842.
40. Mercantile Marine Insurance Company, Schedule of Risks, MMIC-BL; Shattuck, *Census of Boston,* Appendix, 44–49. Shattuck's statistics on manufacturing must be used with caution, for even he distrusts them. Commenting on the tables, Appendix, 44–49, he writes (main text, 86): "It might be inferred from [the aggregate statistics in the Appendix, 44–49] that the manufacturing industry of the city was not as great now [1845] as

in 1837, while the opinion of the best judges on the subject, formed without actual enumeration and investigation, is, that it is nearly twice as great!" We have used the figures just as Shattuck gave them. Boston *Morning Post,* July 30, 1838; Diane Lindstrom, *Economic Development in the Philadelphia Region, 1810–1850* (New York: Columbia University Press, 1978), 49.

41. Peter C. Brooks to Edward Everett, May 31, 1843, EE-MHS; Boston *Morning Post,* Dec. 31, 1842; Brooks to Everett, Feb. 28, March 31, and June 30, 1844, EE-MHS.

15: The Web Spun

1. United States, *Sixth Census or Enumeration of the Inhabitants of the United States,* [*1840*] (Washington: Blair and Rives, 1841); Lemuel Shattuck, *Report to the Committee of the City Council appointed to Obtain the Census of Boston for the Year 1845* . . . (Boston: John H. Eastburn, 1846), 8–13. Boston's total 1840 population as reported by the federal census was 93,383 (*Sixth Census,* 47). A city census taken the preceding month counted 84,401—which Shattuck argues is more nearly correct. The city of Charleston contained 29,261 persons in 1840, the Neck, 11,876 (*Sixth Census,* 226–27).

2. Of those who wielded power, prestige, wealth, or influence and who lived in Boston in 1829, 61% of the 447 professionals, 70% of the 1119 businessmen, and 78% of the 294 master mechanics were still alive and living in Boston in 1841. Only 52% of the 219 professionals living in Charleston sometime from 1828 to 1832, 59% of her 559 businessmen, and 65% of her 149 master mechanics of similar power, prestige, influence or wealth were still alive and living in Charleston at sometime between 1839 and 1843. Of those who persisted over the decade, 44% of Bostonians and 53% of Charlestonians had a known church affiliation, 77% of Bostonians and 84% of Charlestonians belonged to a club of some sort; 6% of Bostonians and 9% of Charlestonians served in a fire company; 3% of Bostonians and 16% of Charlestonians in a militia company.

3. Shattuck, *Census* . . . *1845,* Appendix, 39–43, quotation 33; J. L. Dawson and H. W. DeSaussure, *Census of* . . . *Charleston for the Year 1848* (Charleston: J. B. Nixon, 1849), 29–35.

4. Julian J. Petty, *The Growth and Distribution of Population in South Carolina* (Spartanburg: Reprint Company, c. 1943, 1975), 143; Shattuck, *Census* . . . *1845,* 37; Dawson and DeSaussure, *Census of Charleston, 1848,* 9. Twenty-four percent of Boston's 1845 population and 21% of Charleston's 1848 population were foreign born; 40% of Boston's and only 21% of Charleston's were born in the United States but not in the city.

5. Fred Bateman and Thomas Weiss, *A Deplorable Scarcity: The Failure of Industrialization in the Slave Economy* (Chapel Hill: University of North Carolina Press, 1981), 160; "One of the People," *An Enquiry into the Propriety of Granting Charters of Incorporation for Manufacturing and Other Purposes, in South-Carolina* (Charleston: Walker & Burke, 1845), passim.

6. William Gregg, *Essays on Domestic Industry* . . . (Charleston: Burges & James, 1845).

7. William Appleton, Diary, 1842, vol. 168, WA-BL.

8. Charleston *Mercury,* Aug. 26, 1839.
9. James L. Petigru to H. S. Legaré, Oct. 5, 1839, JLP-USC.
10. Nathan Appleton to E. S. Gannett, Jan. 24, 1828, Ap-MHS.
11. *Gospel Messenger,* XIV (June 1837), 124; Henry D. Cruger to H. A. Middleton, March 2, 1842, LC-SCHS.
12. Ralph Izard Middleton to N. R. Middleton, Sept. 19, 1842, Nathanial R. Middleton Papers, SHC (hereafter NRM-SHC).
13. Theodore Lyman, Jr., *Address Made to the City Council of Boston, January 5, 1835* (Boston: Eastburn, 1835), 16; Charles C. Paine to Henry Lee, Jr., Jan. 31, 1839, Le-MHS.
14. Charles C. Paine to Henry Lee, Jr., Jan. 31, 1839, Le-MHS; Thomas G. Appleton to Nathan Appleton, July 12, 1844, Ap-MHS.
15. Charleston *Courier,* March 31, 1843.
16. Charleston *Courier,* July 31, 1841.
17. Harriet Martineau, *Retrospect of Western Travel,* 2 vols. (London: Saunders & Otley, 1838), I, 238.
18. Alfred Huger to J. R. Poinsett, Sept. 1, 1838, JP-HSP.

Index

Note: Most entries could be sub-divided by Boston and Charleston. To avoid undue clutter, therefore, only where there is a substantial number of entries for one city or the other or where the entry has a character peculiar to the particular city have entries been designated by Boston or Charleston.

Abolitionism, 79-80, 82, 150, 161-62, 164-65, 170, 222-23
Academy of Music, 140
Adams, Charles Francis, 29, 92, 141
Adams, John Quincy, 86
Adger, James, 15, 43, 51, 122, 178, 220
African colonization, 164
Aiken, William, 16
Albany, N.Y., 211-12
Alexander, David, 172
Amelia, 99
American Female Home Education Society, 150
Amory, John, 126-27
Amory, Thomas C., 91
Andrews, Ebenezer T., 30
Andrews, Moses, 125
Anniversary Week, 142
Anti-Imprisonment for Debt Party, 86
Anti-Masonic Party, 86, 144
Appleton, Amory, 210
Appleton, Nathan, 64, 83, 203, 204, 219
Appleton, Samuel, 12, 200
Appleton, Thomas G., 221
Appleton, William, 27, 33, 35, 84-85, 146, 200, 204, 218
Arfwedson, Carl, 50
Armstrong, Samuel Y., 30, 86
Arson, 154-55, 161-62, 192-93
Artisans. *See* Mechanics
Ashe, John S., 181
Association of Benevolent Societies, 114-15, 151

Association of Boston Banks, 201
Athenaeum, 144
Auction system, 28
Audubon, John J., 7, 141
Axson, Jacob, 104

Bailey, Adams, 202
Bamfield, Harriet Hockley, 127-28
Bancroft, George, 203
Bank directors, Boston, 30-31, 202-3
Bank directors, Charleston, 46, 48, 178
Bank of Charleston, 47-48, 171, 177-80, 187
Bank of South Carolina, 46
Bank of Ten Millions, 31-32
Bank of the State of South Carolina, 46, 177, 179, 193
Bank of the United States, 20, 27, 31, 46-47, 84-86
Bank petitioners, Boston, 85, 87-88
Bank war, 27, 29, 31, 45, 84
Banking, Boston, 19-20, 29-32, 84-85, 201-4, 209
Banking, Charleston, 19-20, 46-48, 171-72, 175, 177-80
Bankruptcy, 186, 208-9
Baptists, 133-35
Baptisttown, 7
Barbot, Anthony, 19
Barnard, Charles, 205
Barnwell, William H. W., 132
Barrus, Rufus L., 123

325

Bartol, Cyrus, 116
Battery, 2, 7, 51, 105, 164, 183
Beacon Hill, 2, 35
Bean, James, 125
Bee, Barnard E. (Skilly), 77
Beecher, Lyman, 134
Bennett, Thomas, 43, 44, 47, 187
Benson, Lavinia, 125
Berry, George, 126
Bethel Union, 154
Biddle, Nicholas, 29, 47, 84-85, 178-79
Billings and Holden Society, 141
Bird, William, 44
Black, Alexander, 52, 193
Blacks: legal restrictions on, 163-66; licensing of workers, 106
Blackstone Canal, 68
Blanding, Abraham, 174-75
Board of Aldermen, Boston, 92, 97, 208
Board of Health, Boston, 93
Board of Health, Charleston, 98-99
Boston and Lowell Rail Road, 16-17, 65-66, 210
Boston and Maine Rail Road, 211
Boston and Portland Rail Road, 211
Boston and Providence Rail Road, 68, 210
Boston and Worcester Rail Road, 37, 66, 210-11
Boston Aqueduct Company, 94-95
Boston Associates, 16, 83
Boston Asylum for Indigent Boys, 147
Boston Company, 24
Boston Dispensary, 100, 146-47
Boston Employment Society, 206
Boston English High School, 108
Boston Farm School and Asylum, 147, 153
Boston Female Asylum, 147, 149
Boston Hydraulic Company, 95
Boston Latin School, 108
Boston Lyceum, 112-13
Boston Medical Association, 117
Boston Wharf Company, 26, 38
Botanic medicine, 117
Bowditch, Nathaniel, 21, 200
Bowdoin Square Church, 134
Bowen, Nathaniel, 132
Boyce, Ker, 50, 51, 104, 122, 178, 180-82, 186
Boyden, Samuel, 126
British Charitable Society, 143
Broad Street riot, 155-56
Brodhead, Daniel G., 37, 87
Brooks, Edward, 169

Brooks, Peter C., 4, 12, 169, 210, 214
Brooks, William G., 204, 208
Brotherhood of San Marino, 192
Brunswick, Georgia, Canal Company, 39
Buckingham, Joseph T., 24, 128
Building codes, 193
Business cycles, Boston, 23-25, 27, 29-30, 32, 35, 38, 200-201, 204-6
Business cycles, Charleston, 41-43, 45-46, 48, 171-72, 176-80, 183-88
Business failures, Boston, 29-30, 201, 208-9
Business failures, Charleston, 171, 186
Business fraud, 201-3
Business networks, 13-16
Butler, Pierce, 193

Cabeuil, Louisa E., 20, 127
Calhoun, John C., 173
Cambridge Trotting Park, 139
Capers, William, 133
Capital availability, 14-15, 17-18, 20-22, 173, 185-86, 213, 218
Carolina Archers, 140
Carolina Hotel, 51
Carpenter, Anna, 124
Castle Pinckney Island, 78
Catholics, 131-32, 135, 148, 154-55, 164
Catlin, George, 141
Censorship, 161-62
Central Wharf, 25-26, 35
Centralization in city government, 91, 95-96, 97-98, 101-2, 103-7, 114, 157, 184, 192, 194-96
Chamber of Commerce, 15-16, 144
Channing, Walter, 206
Channing, William Ellery, 115
Chapman, Jonathan, 212
Charity, 144-52, 192, 205-6
Charleston and Liverpool Line Packet Company, 55
Charleston District, 97
Charleston Fuel Society, 149
Charleston Hotel, 52, 183, 191, 193
Charleston Neck, governance of, 97, 106-7, 165-66
Charleston Neck Association, 166
Charlestown, Mass., 131, 154
Chauncey Hall, 113
Chelsea, Mass., 36-37
Cheves, Langdon, 43
Chickering, Jonas, 213
Child care, 103, 147-49
Children's Aid Society, 205

Index

Children's Friend Society, 148
China trade, 25, 84
Chisolm, Octavius, 168
Chisolm's mill, 43
Chisolm's wharf, 51
Choate, Rufus, 115
Cholera epidemic, 93-94, 98-100, 105
Church governance, 131, 136-37
Cincinnati, Order of, 75
Circular Church, 137
Citadel Guard, 101, 105
Citizens' political meetings, Boston, 64, 85, 95, 155-58, 199, 211
Citizens' political meetings, Charleston, 61, 103-4, 161-62, 190
City budget, Boston, 94, 207
City budget, Charleston, 101, 105, 182-84
City council, Boston, 92, 97, 208
City council, Charleston, 97, 181-82
City debt, 91-92, 183-84, 206-7
City Guard, 101, 105, 165
City subsidies for corporations, 58, 64, 95, 173-74, 182-83
City Wharf, 24-25
Class structure, 121-28, 227-28
Class tension, 83, 93, 158-59, 177-78
Classical and Philosophical Seminary, 109
Clement, Sarah, 127
Cobia, Daniel, 109, 132
Cogdell, John S., 105, 221
Cogdell, Richard, 182
Cohen, Mordecai, 122
Colburn, James S., 75
Colcock, Charles, 19
College of Charleston, 108-9, 111-12, 116
Columbia, S.C., 174-76
Commerce, Boston, 3, 11-15, 67, 92
Commerce, Charleston, 7-11, 13-15, 45-46, 49-50, 176-77, 181-82, 197
Common Council, Boston, 92, 97, 208
Commonwealth Bank, 31, 87, 202-3
Congregationalists, 130, 137, 148, 151
Conner, Henry W., 104
Cook, Ellis, 126
Corporate directorships, 38, 52-53, 208, 227. *See also* Bank directors, Boston; Bank directors, Charleston; Economic power
Corporations as business forms, 17-18, 57, 65, 67, 185-86
Cotton trade, 10, 26, 40, 45, 49, 171, 176-79

Country fever. *See* Malaria
Court of General Sessions, 101
Craft's wharf, 51
Craftsmen. *See* Mechanics
Crime, 158, 161, 165-68, 201-3, 205-6
Crocker, Doddridge, 15
Cummings, Gilbert, 160
Cunard Line Packets, 212-13

Data entry, 229-30
Dearborn, Henry A. S., 54
Defiance of law, 79, 159-61, 164-66, 195
DeGrand, Peter P. F., 31
Democratic Party, 87-88, 92, 180-82, 201-3, 207-8
Depression, 172, 179-80, 184-88, 204-10
Dickson, Samuel H., 48, 110, 116, 118, 162, 185, 186
Direct trade, 48-50, 54
Dix, Cecelia, 126
Dix, Stephen, 126
Domingo, Antonio, 36
Drayton, William, 57, 72, 76-77, 84
DuBois, Captain, 190
Duels, 168
Dukes, William C., 75, 179
Dunham, Josiah, 202
Dunham, Josiah, Jr., 202
Dutton, Warren, 154

East Boston, 37
East Boston Company, 37, 69, 212
East Boston Wharf Company, 37
Eastern Rail Road, 69, 211
Eccles, Thomas, 168
Economic power, 38, 52-53, 74, 177-80, 208, 232
Economic values, 14-19, 43, 44, 56, 87, 199, 219-22
Edmonston, Charles, 104
Education Society, 141
Educational values, 110-15, 119
Election bribery, 74-76
Elections, Boston: city, 91-92, 207-8; congressional, 83
Elections, Charleston: city, 73, 75-76, 80; congressional, 180-81; state, 73-74, 76-77, 81, 181
Eliot, Samuel A., 157-58, 201, 204, 206
Elliott, Jesse, 78
Elliott, William, 127
Emancipation, 125, 163
Emerald Isle Society, 143

Emerson, Ralph Waldo, 123
England, John, 109, 116, 131, 164
Entrepreneurial skill, 14-17, 218, 221
Episcopalians, 130, 132, 135-37, 148
Equal Rights Party, 180
Ethnicity, 7-8, 74, 130-32, 143-44. *See also* specific ethnic groups
Evangelicalism, 132-35
Everett, Edward, 86, 157-58
Exclusivity, 142-44, 152
Exports, Boston, 24-25
Exports, Charleston, 40-41, 48-50, 179

Factors. *See* Merchants, Charleston
Family, 13-14, 123-30
Fatherless and Widows' Society, 36, 149
Fay, Richard S., 145
Federalists, 86-87
Fellowship Society, 109
Felonies. *See* Crime
Female Anti-Slavery Society, 150, 170
Female Moral Reform Society, 150
Fenwick, Benedict, 131, 155
Fifteen-gallon law, 159-60
Finney, Charles Grandison, 134
Fire loan, 193
Fire protection, Boston, 91, 95, 157, 198
Fire protection, Charleston, 101-2, 191, 194-96
Firemasters, 195
Fires, 50, 102, 190-94, 198
First Baptist Church, Charleston, 133
Fiske, John M., 87
Flute Club, 141
Force Act (1833), 80
Forrest, Edwin, 141
Forty Thieves, 153
Foster, William, 86
Fox, George T., 2
Fragment Society, 149, 151
Franklin Bank, 30, 202
Franklin medals, 113
Fraser, Charles, 45, 141, 221
Free Bridge Party, 86
Free schools, 108
Free Trade Party, 83
French Benevolent Society, 143
Furman, James, 134

Gadsden, Christopher E., 109
Gadsden, James, 175-77
Gadsden's wharf mill, 43

Galveston Bay and Texas Land Company, 39
Gannett, Ezra Stiles, 219
Garrison, William Lloyd, 79-80, 161, 170
Geography, 1-9, 35-36, 49-50, 69-70, 215
German Friendly Society, 109, 118, 143, 152
Gibbes, James, 15
Gibbes, William H., 243
Gilchrist, Robert, 60
Gilman, Samuel, 221
Gourdin, Henry, 50
Grammar schools, 108, 112-14
Graniteville Manufacturing Company, 185
Grant, Moses, 4
Grattan, Thomas, 115
Gray, Frank, 127
Greene, Charles G., 87
Greene, Gardiner, 23, 84
Greene, Nathaniel, 201
Gregg, William, 184, 218
Gregorian Society, 141
Grimball, John B., 22, 127
Grocers' Party, 86

Hague, William, 115
Hale, Nathan, 63, 212
Hallett, Benjamin F., 159
Hamilton, James, 43, 47, 51, 52, 57, 72, 76, 78, 79, 81, 84, 102, 104, 175, 178-79, 218
Hamilton's wharf, 51
Hancock Bank, 87
Handel and Haydn Society, 140
Harrison Club, 144, 207
Harvard College, 116-17
Harvard Medical School, 117, 147
Hayne, Robert Y., 47, 57, 72, 76-77, 78, 81, 104-7, 173-76, 182, 218
Health care, 93-94, 100, 146-47, 192
Hebrew Harmonic Society, 140
Hebrew Orphan Society, 143
Henry, George, 104
Henry Ewbank, 42
Henshaw, Charles, 87
Henshaw, David, 38, 64, 86, 87, 135, 203
Henshaw, John, 202
Hershberg, Theodore, 230
Hibernian Society, 51-52, 143
High schools, 108, 112, 118
Hillard, George, 199

Index

Hinterland, 55-56, 63, 69-70, 172-73, 185, 216-18
Holbrook, Harriott Pinckney Rutledge, 72
Holbrook, Silas P., 17
Hollis Street Church, 137
Holmes, Isaac E., 47, 48, 51, 52, 181
Home, 189-90
Homer, J. L., 34
Honor, 167-69, 219-22
Horry, Elias, 16-17, 61-62, 110, 124
House of Correction, 90, 91, 96
House of Industry, 96, 147, 151, 158, 206
House of Reformation for Juvenile Offenders, 91, 147, 153
Housing, 36, 50, 126
How, Hall H., 202
Howard Benevolent Association, 205
Huger, Alfred, 80, 161, 222-23
Huger, Daniel E., 72
Hunt, Benjamin F., 196
Hunt, Randall, 58

Imports, Boston, 24-25
Imports, Charleston, 41, 48-50
Inclusivity, 142-44, 152
Independent Republican Party, 180
Indices of economic and political power, wealth, and social status, 231-34
Infant schools, 148
Information flow, 187, 213
Instrumental Association, 140
Insurance companies, 22, 197, 210, 213
Intendents, Charleston. *See* Robert Y. Hayne; Henry L. Pinckney; James R. Pringle
Investment strategies, 14, 18-22
Irish, 4, 131-32, 154-58

Jackson, Patrick Tracy, 16-17, 65, 83, 209
Jackson, Samuel C., 1
Jenks, William, 115
Jews, 130-31
Jockey Club, 139
Johnson, Joseph, 18, 84, 110
Johnson, Michael P., 243
Johnson's Hotel, 51
Journeymen Bootmakers, 205
Judicial process, 166-69
Judicial systems, 90, 101
June, Cornel, 102

Juries, 160
Juvenile Industry Society, 149

Kemble, Frances (Fanny), 141
Kendall, Amos, 161
Kiddell's wharf, 51
King, Mitchell, 78, 79
King's Chapel, 3, 97, 135
Kirk, Edward N., 134
Kirkpatrick, John, 45, 186
Knapp, Jacob, 134
Knights, Peter, 240-241

Labor, Boston, 32-35, 103, 154, 158-59, 201, 204-5, 217-18
Labor, Charleston, 44-45, 58, 103, 184, 191-92, 217-18
Labor organization, 33-34
LaCroix, Catherine, 20
Ladies Benevolent Society, 147, 152
Ladies Garment Society, 149
Ladies Industry Society, 149
Ladies of the Retreat, 109
Lafayette Bank, 202
Lamb, James, 15
Lamb, Thomas, 15
Landfill, 2, 37, 52, 68
Laurens, Keating S., 194
Lawrence, Abbott, 13, 26, 30, 85, 115, 204, 211
Lawrence, Amos, 13, 14, 24, 26, 115, 146, 201, 209-10
Lawrence, Amos A., 112, 126
Lawrence, William R., 126
Lawyers, licensing of, 117-18
Lee, Ann Amory McLean, 123, 127
Lee, Henry, 31, 83, 209
Lee, Henry, Jr., 209
Legaré, Hugh S., 180
Legislative delegations, 88-89, 159, 208
Leisure, 138-42
Levy, Jacob C., 179
Lewis, Samuel, 202
Lewis Wharf, 25
Lexington, 198, 199
Liberator, 79
Libraries, 119
Lifestyles, 125-28, 138-42, 169
Limited liability partnership, 186
Liquor licensing, 160, 163, 165
Locofoco Democrats, 201
Lombard, Ammi, 37
Long Wharf, 3

Louisville, Cincinnati, and Charleston Rail Road, 106, 172-77, 182
Lowell, John, 21
Loyalty oath, 80-81
Lucas, Jonathan II, 43
Lutherans, 130-31, 135
Lying-In Hospital, 103, 147
Lyman, Theodore, 87, 155, 170, 205, 220
Lynch Club, 162

McBee, Vardy, 176
McDuffie, George, 42, 84
McKee, John, 124
Magistrates' and Freeholders' Court, 101, 163
Magwood, Simon, 122
Malaria, 98
Manley, John, 160
Manly, Basil, 134, 173
Mann, Horace, 114, 156, 169
Manufacturing, Boston, 11-12, 26-29, 65-66, 213, 217-19
Manufacturing, Charleston, 8, 10, 43-45, 60, 184-85, 217-19
Marine Hospital, 100, 147
Marriage, 128-30
Marsh, James, 44
Martineau, Harriet, 116, 222-23
Masonic lodges, 144
Massachusetts Congregational Charitable Society, 205
Massachusetts General Hospital, 17, 21, 93, 103, 147
Massachusetts Historical Society, 144
Massachusetts Hospital Life Insurance Company, 20-21
Massachusetts Medical Society, 117
Maxwell, Harriott, 124
Mayors, Boston. *See* Samuel T. Armstrong, Jonathan Chapman, Samuel A. Eliot, Theodore Lyman, Harrison Gray Otis, Josiah Quincy
Mayors, Charleston. *See* Robert Y. Hayne, Jacob S. Mintzing, Henry L. Pinckney, John Schnierle
Mayor's Court, 163-64, 167
Mazyck, Alexander, 104
Mechanics, 103, 272-73, n. 19
Mechanics, Boston, 27-29, 88, 92, 158-59, 198, 209
Mechanics, Charleston, 44-45, 60, 74, 88, 106, 116, 182, 184-85
Medical College of South Carolina, 117

Medical education, 117-18, 146-47
Medical practice, 117
Merchants, Boston, 13-15, 19, 88, 92, 201, 209
Merchants, Charleston, 13-15, 19, 41, 42, 74, 88, 172, 178-79, 182
Merchants Bank, 31
Merrimack Company, 24, 26-27, 35
Methodist Benevolent Society, 144
Methodist Episcopal Church, 132
Methodist Protestant Church, 133
Methodists, 132-33, 135, 164
Mey's wharf, 51
Middleton, Arthur, 13
Middleton, Ralph Izard, 220
Middling Interest Bank, 87
Militia, 75, 78, 80-81, 102, 157-58
Miller, Ripley and Co., 178
Millerites, 134
Milling, 8, 43-44
Mills, John, 201, 202
Mills, Robert, 152
Mintzing, Jacob S., 182, 187
Misdemeanors. *See* Crime
Mob violence, 154-61, 170
Mobility, economic and social, 110-13, 116-17, 121-24, 222
Monopoly, 178-79, 181
Montgomery Guards, 157-58
Moore, Thomas, 126
Morton, Marcus, 207
Mount Washington Association, 38
Municipal Court, 90, 159-60
Music, 140-41
Musical Association, 140

Nahant, 139
National Republican Party, 86-87
Natural History Society, 144
Navigation, 1, 55
New England Association of Farmers, Mechanics and Other Workingmen, 33
New England Asylum for the Blind, 148
New England Mississippi Land Company, 39
New England Society, 144
New England Society of Mechanics and Manufacturers, 28
New York, competition with, 12, 55, 63, 211-12, 219
Nickerson, J. H., 183
Noddles Island, 36, 213
North End, 4

Index

Norton and Carroll's mill, 43
Nullification controversy, 42, 45, 47, 57, 71-82

O'Beirne, Father, 131-32
Occupational categories, 230-31
Occupations, 226
Odd Ladies Mutual Aid Society, 150
O'Flaherty, Thomas, 132
Ogilby, William, 49, 79
Oliver, Francis J., 37
O'Neall, John B., 168, 171
Orphan House, 103, 147
Orphans, 103, 147-49
Otis, Harrison Gray, 2, 29, 64, 67, 83, 86, 92, 112, 125, 159, 169, 201
Overseers of the Poor, 95-96

Paine, Charles, 220
Palmer, Benjamin M., 137
Panic of 1825, 11, 12
Panic of 1837, 105-7, 171, 200-201
Park Street Church, 3, 134
Parker, John, 124
Parkman, George, 93-94
Parrish, George, 169
Patterson and Magwood, 178
Pauperism, 150-52, 158, 161, 206
Pelby, William, 168
Penal system, 167
Penitent Females' Refuge Society, 150
Pennsylvania Bank of the United States, 178, 179
Perkins, Thomas Handasyd, 13, 36, 64, 84, 112, 115, 125, 126
Petigru, James L., 19, 43, 74-77, 79, 81, 104, 119, 122
Phillips, William, 123
Pierce, John, 125
Pierpont, John, 137
Pinckney, Henry L., 61, 73, 76, 82, 99, 106-7, 144, 152, 166, 191-97
Pinckney, Maria H., 79
Pitray and Viel, 15, 42
Plantation ownership, 14, 18-19, 44, 122
Planters and Mechanics Bank, 46, 47
Planters Hotel, 51
Poinsett, Joel R., 78, 79, 80, 84, 181
Police, 94, 100, 105, 158
Police Court, 90, 167
Political economy, 41-42, 48-49, 52-53, 54-58, 63-65, 71-72, 77-78, 111, 172-77, 182-83

Political power, 82, 92, 135-36, 180-82, 208, 226-27, 232
Political styles, 61-62, 71-89, 104
Poorhouse, 102-3, 147
Population, Boston, 7, 12, 32, 216-18
Population, Charleston, 9, 10, 45, 164, 185, 216-18
Port Society, 154
Porter, William D., 110-11
Poverty, 4-7, 93, 95-96, 102-3, 144-52, 205-6
Poyas, James, 44
Pratt, George, 209
Presbyterians, 135
Primary schools, 108, 114-15
Pringle, James R., 19, 73, 84
Prioleau, Samuel, 104
Private schools, 109-10
Privatism, 31-32, 39, 64-70, 94-95
Professionals, Boston, 88, 117-18, 209
Professionals, Charleston, 117-18, 182
Profits, Boston, 16, 18, 19, 31, 38, 65, 66, 210-12
Profits, Charleston, 19, 41, 43, 45, 56, 59, 221
Property, 122-29, 169, 209-10, 222
Proprietors of the Merrimack Locks and Canal, 65
Prostitution, 7, 150, 167
Provident Institution for Savings, 21, 29, 35
Public health, Boston, 91, 93-94
Public health, Charleston, 98-100, 192
Public meetings. *See* Citizens' political meetings
Public safety, Boston, 91, 155-58
Public safety, Charleston, 99-102, 192
Public works, 91, 105-6, 207
Pulaski, 190

Quincy, Josiah, 34, 90-91, 93-95, 113
Quincy, Josiah II, 95, 125, 212

Race tension, 132-33, 170, 194-95
Race week, 139-40
Railroads, 54-70, 139, 172-77, 210-12; costs and dividends of, 59, 65-66, 68, 176-77, 210-11; federal aid for, 57; penetration of, into the city, 60-62, 67-68; state aid for in Massachusetts, 63-64, 65, 211; state aid for in South Carolina, 57-58, 73, 174-75; technology of, 58-59, 66-67

Real estate development, 35-38, 50-52, 66, 183-93
Recession of 1828, 11, 12
Recorder's Court, 101
Recreation, 138-42
Religious affiliation, 130-37
Residential patterns, 2-4, 7-9
Revivalism, 132-35
Rice trade, 10, 41, 49
Robertson, Alexander, 171
Robinson, Frederick, 33-34
Roman Catholic Mutual Relief Society, 205
Rose, James, 13, 173
Royall, Anne, 1, 42
Rural-urban conflict, 72-73
Rutledge, Harriott Horry, 119

Sailors, 54-55, 153-54
St. Andrew's Society, 143
St. Cecelia Society, 140
St. Finbar's Church, 131
St. John's Lutheran Church, 97, 130, 133
St. Mary's Church, Boston, 131-32
St. Mary's Church, Charleston, 131
St. Michael's Church, 133, 135-36
St. Michael's Parish, 97
St. Patrick's Church, 131
St. Patrick's Society, 143
St. Paul's Church, Boston, 135
St. Peter's Church, 109, 132
St. Philip's Church, 97, 133, 135-36
St. Philip's Parish, 97
St. Stephen's Chapel, 132
Samaritan Asylum for Indigent Children, 148
Sampling selection processes, 228-29
Santee Canal, 56
Savannah and Charleston Steam Packet Co., 190
Savells, Asa, 160
Savings Bank for Seamen, 153
Schirmer, Jacob F., 51, 171
Schnierle, John, 182
Scots Charitable Society, 143
Scots Presbyterian Church, 97
Seaman's Aid Society, 149-50, 205
Seaman's Friend Society, 153
Seamstresses, 33, 103, 149-50
Sears, Thomas, 168
Second Presbyterian Church, 133
Second Unitarian Church, 97
'76 Association, 75
Shattuck, Lemuel, 217

Shaw, Lemuel, 64
Shaw, Robert Gould, 37
Shecut, John L. E. W., 10
Shipbuilding, 44
Shipping, Boston, 11-12, 25, 62-63, 212-13
Shipping, Charleston, 40-42, 48-50, 54-55, 187, 189-90
Shirras Dispensary, 100, 146-47
Simms, William Gilmore, 75, 79, 145
Simonds, Artemus, 151
Simpson, John K., 87, 202-3
Sisters of Our Lady of Mercy, 109
Slave insurrection, fear of, 79-80, 100-101, 104, 161-66
Slave ownership, 18, 20, 44-45, 97, 124-25, 127-28, 243-45
Slave trade, 166
Slavery, 115-16, 222-23
Smallpox, 98, 198
Smyth, Thomas, 116
Social control, Boston, 4, 134-35, 140-41, 154-58
Social control, Charleston, 100-101, 105-6, 163-66
Social structure, 144-45, 152
Society for Employing the Female Poor, 149
Society for the Prevention of Pauperism, 115, 148, 151
Soltow, Lee, 239, 241
Soup and Bread Society, 151, 206
South Boston, 36, 38
South Carolina Association, 80, 163, 164
South Carolina Canal and Rail Road, 16, 19, 52, 56-62
South Carolina College, 117
South Carolina Homespun Company, 10
South Carolina Medical College, 117
South Carolina Medical Society, 117
South Carolina Rail Road, 176-77
South Carolina Society, 109, 143
South Cove, 1, 67-68, 212
South Cove Company, 37-38, 67
South Western Rail Road Bank, 175
Southern Steam Packet Company, 187
Specie suspension, 171-72, 179-80, 201, 203-4
Sports, 139-40
Spot Pond Aqueduct Company, 95
Springfield, Mass., 211
State Bank, Boston, 30, 31
State Bank, Charleston, 46
State sovereignty, 71, 75, 80-81

Index

States' Rights and Free Trade Association, 75
Status, 227-28, 233-34
Staunton, Peter, 76
Steam power, 8, 28-29, 43-44, 55-56, 184
Steamboats, 189-90, 198-99
Stewardship of wealth, 146
Stewart, Angus, 51
Stock ownership, Boston, 19-20, 26-27, 36, 65, 67-68
Stock ownership, Charleston, 19-20, 47, 58, 62, 174-78, 182-83
Stocks traded, 269, n. 13.
Stranger's fever. *See* Yellow fever
Strikes, 33-34
Striped pigs, 159
Stuart, James, 127
Success manuals, 115
Suffolk Bank, 31, 203
Suffolk system, 31
Sullivan, William, 27
Sullivan's Island, 139
Sumner, William H., 37
Sunday schools, 148-49

Talvande, Ann M., 118
Tappan, Lewis, 161
Tariff compromise (1833), 79
Tariff issue, Boston, 82-83
Tariff issue, Charleston, 41-43, 71-79
Tax assessment, 92-93, 238-43
Taxation, Boston, 92, 206-7
Taxation, Charleston, 73, 105-7, 163, 166, 184
Taylor, William, 126
Teachers, 114, 118
Temperance, 154, 158-61, 165
Ten-hour day, 33
Textile manufacturing, Boston, 11, 12, 26-27, 65-66
Textile manufacturing, Charleston, 10, 184-85
Thacher, Peter O., 34, 159-60, 168, 202, 205, 222
Theater, 141, 168
Thompson, George, 170
Thomsonian medicine, 117
Thorndike, Israel, 19
Thorndike, Israel, Jr., 208
Time, concept of, 23, 40-41
Tolman, Rebecca, 127
Townsend, Alexander, 64
Trapier, Paul, 136

Trapmann, Lewis, 15
Tremont Bank, 30-31
Trinity Church, Boston, 135, 136
Trinity Methodist Church, 132-33
Trusts, 20-21
Tuckerman, Joseph, 4, 24, 35, 150, 158
Tudor, Frederic, 23, 27, 32, 37, 125, 156, 169
Tunno, Adam, 19, 125
Tupper, Tristram, 221
Turnbull, Robert, 72
Two-party system, 81-82, 86-88

Unemployment, 205-6
Unicorn, 213
Union Bank, 46
Unionists, 46-47, 73-82
Unitarians, 130, 135, 137, 148, 150
United Independents Party, 180
Ursuline Convent, Charlestown, Mass., 131, 134, 154-55
Ursuline Sisters, Charleston, 109, 118

Vacations, 139
Vanderhorst, Elias, 110
Vesey, Denmark, 79-80, 100, 162-63
Vigilantism, 162
Violence, 76-77, 80-81, 167-69. *See also* Mob violence
Voluntary associations, 142-52
Volunteer fire companies, Boston, 91, 154-57, 198
Volunteer fire companies, Charleston, 102, 105, 191, 194-96
Voters, Boston, 88, 208
Voters, Charleston, 73-78, 88

Wages, Boston, 24, 33, 150, 204-5
Wages, Charleston, 44-45, 185
Wainwright, Jonathan, 136
Walker's *Appeal,* 80, 162
Warren Associates, 38, 203
Warren Street Chapel, 205
Washingtonians, 160-61, 165
Water supply, 94-95, 196-97
Wealth, 121-29, 227, 233
Wealth, Boston, 27, 38, 145-46, 208-10
Wealth, Charleston, 52
Webb, Daniel C., 19
Webster, Daniel, 57, 83
Wednesday Evening Club, 142
Welfare, 95-96, 102-3, 192, 206
Western Rail Road, 69-70, 211-12

Western trade, 27
Weston, Paul, 125
Whig Party, 88, 159, 180-81, 203, 207-8
White, Carleton, 189-90
White, Stephen, 37
White Oak Club, 153
White Point Garden, 105, 183
Whitney, John, 124
Widows' Society, 205
Willington, Aaron S., 75
Wills, 123-30
Windward Anchor Society, 154
Wines, Enoch C., 2
Wing, Sarah C., 20
Winnisimmet Company, 36-37, 69
Women, education, 113, 118-19
Women's organizations, 147-52

Women's property, 123-24
Wood, Richard, 162
Work ethic, 96, 113, 114-16, 123, 146, 150-51
Workhouse, 101, 166
Workingmen's movement, 33-34
Workingmen's Party, 86-87, 208
Wragg, Samuel, 13
Wright, Henry C., 148-49

Yeadon, Richard, Jr., 45
Yellow fever, 9, 98, 191-92
Young Men's Benevolent Society, 205
Young Men's Free Trade and States' Rights Association, 78
Young Men's Temperance Society, 165